Imperialism in the Modern World

Sources and Interpretations

EDITED BY

WILLIAM D. BOWMAN
GETTYSBURG COLLEGE

FRANK M. CHITEJI
GETTYSBURG COLLEGE

J. MEGAN GREENE
UNIVERSITY OF KANSAS

PEARSON

Prentice
Hall

Upper Saddle River, New Jersey 07458

Library of Congress Cataloging-in-Publication Data

Imperialism in the modern world / [edited by] William D. Bowman, Frank M.Chiteji, J. Megan Greene.
    p. cm.
    Includes bibliographical references.
    ISBN 0-13-189905-8
    1.   Imperialism—History—19th century—Sources. 2. Imperialism—History—20th century—Sources. 3.
World politics—19th century—Sources. 4. World politics—20th century—Sources. I. Bowman, William
D. (William David). II. Chiteji, Frank M. III. Greene, J. Megan.
    D363.I48 2007
    325'.3209—dc22   2006014755

Editorial Director: Charlyce Jones-Owen
Executive Editor: Charles Cavaliere
Managing Editor: Joanne Riker
Production Liaison: Joanne Hakim
Director of Marketing: Brandy Dawson
Senior Marketing Manager: Emily Cleary
Marketing Assistant: Jennifer Lang
Manufacturing Buyer: Ben Smith
Cover Art Director: Jayne Conte
Cover Design: Bruce Kenselaar
Cover Illustration/Photo: E.McKnight/The National Archives Image Library
Director, Image Resource Center: Melinda Patelli
Manager, Rights and Permissions: Zina Arabia
Manager, Visual Research: Beth Brenzel
Manager, Cover Visual Research & Permissions: Karen Sanatar
Image Permission Coordinator: Annette Linder
Photo Researcher: Beaura Kathy Ringrose
Full-Service Project Management: Bruce Hobart/Pine Tree Composition, Inc
Composition: Laserwords Private Limited
Printer/Binder: R. R. Donnelley

Credits and acknowledgments borrowed from other sources and reproduced, with permission, in this textbook
appear on appropriate page within text.

Pearson Education LTD., London
Pearson Education Singapore, Pte. Ltd
Pearson Education, Canada, Ltd
Pearson Education—Japan
Pearson Education Australia PTY, Limited

Pearson Education North Asia Ltd
Pearson Educación de Mexico, S.A. de C.V.
Pearson Education Malaysia, Pte. Ltd
Pearson Education, Upper Saddle River,
  New Jersey

10 9 8 7 6 5 4 3 2 1
ISBN 0-13-189905-8

Contents

Maps   xvi
Preface   xvii
Introduction   1

Part I
THE IMPERIALISTS   14

Timeline   14

Introduction   15

Jules Ferry, *Le Tonkin et la Mère-Patrie (Tonkin and the Motherland)*   18

Visual Source: Jungles To-Day Are Gold Mines To-Morrow   20

Rudyard Kipling, "The White Man's Burden"   21

Visual Source: "Pears' Soap Advertisement"   23

Herbert Spencer, *Illustrations of Universal Progress*   25

Visual Source: "The Indian Court at the Great Exhibition"   28

Karl Marx, "The British Rule in India"   29

"Emperor Meiji's Letter to President Grant on Iwakura Mission, 1871"   31

Joseph Conrad, "An Outpost of Progress"   33

Visual Source: "British Officer Reclining"   37

Arthur James Balfour, "Problems with Which We Have to Deal in Egypt"   38

"An Ottoman Government Decree Defines the Official Notion
    of the 'Modern' Citizen, June 19, 1870"   41

Visual Source: "Queen Victoria's Golden Jubilee—Victorian Wallpaper"   44

Mary Seacole, *Wonderful Adventures of Mrs. Seacole in Many Lands*   45

FURTHER RESOURCES   47

Part II
THE ANTI-IMPERIALISTS   48

Timeline   48

Introduction   49

Visual Source: "Tippoo's Tiger"   51

M. K. Gandhi, "Civilization"   52

Visual Source: "Gandhi in Western Clothing"   56

Ho Chi Minh, "Equality!"   57

Woodrow Wilson, "Fourteen Points Speech"   59

Godfey N. Uzoigwe, *Britain and the Conquest of Africa*   61

José Martí, "Mother America"   65

Sayyid Jamāl ad-Dīn al-Afghānī, "Lecture on Teaching and Learning"   70

Edward D. Morel, *The Black Man's Burden*   75

Aimé Césaire, *Discourse on Colonialism*   78

José Rizal, *Noli me Tangere (The Social Cancer)*   82

Vladimir Lenin, *Imperialism, the Highest Stage of Capitalism*   87

Visual Source: "Lenin Giving a Speech"   90

Multatuli, *Max Havelaar: Or the Coffee Auctions of the Dutch Trading Company*   91

"Chief Seattle's Oration of the 1850s"   95

FURTHER RESOURCES   **97**

Part III
TOOLS OF EMPIRE   **98**

Timeline   98

Introduction   99

Visual Source: "Perry's Ship"   103

Michael Adas, "Machine as Civilizer"   104

Visual Source: "East African Transport, Old and New Style"   107

Peter Hopkirk, "Spies Along the Silk Road"   109

J. Clinton Cunningham, *Products of the Empire*   112

Daniel Headrick, "Malaria, Quinine, and the Penetration of Africa"   115

Eduardo Galeano, *Open Veins of Latin America: Five Centuries of the Pillage of a Continent* 119

Léopold S. Senghor, "French—Language of Culture"   122

Thomas J. Morgan, "Compulsory Education"   125

Visual Source: "Railroads and Coolies"   128

Theodore Christlieb, *Protestant Foreign Missions: Their Present State*   130

Visual Source: "Belgian Territorial Agent"   133

Kita Ikki, "An Outline Plan for the Reorganization of Japan"   134

Ngugi wa Thiong'o, "Kimathi on Law as a Tool of Oppression"   136

Visual Source: "The Secret of England's Greatness"   138

FURTHER RESOURCES   **139**

Part IV
RECONFIGURATIONS: THE COLONIAL WORLD　　140

Timeline　　140

Introduction　　141

Visual Source: "Meiji Emperor"　　145

Albert Memmi, *The Colonizer and the Colonized*　　146

"Summary of Orders"　　151

"Child Marriage Restraint Act"　　156

Attiya Hanim Saqqaf, "Portrait of the Hard Life of a Woman"　　159

Felix N. Stephen, "Beautiful Maria in the Act of True Love"　　163

Chinua Achebe, "Named for Victoria, Queen of England"　　165

Liang Qichao, "Inaugural Statement for the Eastern Times"　　169

Joyce Cary, *Mister Johnson*　　172

Madelon H. Lulofs, *Rubber*　　175

Visual Source: "Coffee Plantation"　　177

Lady Barker, *Station Life in New Zealand*　　178

Visual Source: "The African and Oriental Bureau and Buying
　　Agency (Advertisement)"　　181

José Carlos Mariátegui, "Outline of the Economic Evolution"　　182

Visual Source: "Advertisement for the Sontag Hotel"　　184

Selections from *The Red Man: An Illustrated Magazine Printed by Indians*　　185

Maps of Cairo in the Mid-Nineteth Century and Singapore　　191

FURTHER RESOURCES　　**192**

Part V
EMPIRE'S TOOLS FOR LIBERATION　　194

Timeline　　194

Introduction　　195

Harry Thuku, "Nairobi"　　197

J. E. Casely Hayford, "Race Emancipation—Particular Considerations:
　　African Nationality"　　201

Orishatuke Faduma, "African Negro Education"　　205

Li Dazhao, "The Victory of Bolshevism"　　208

Martin Buber, "From an Open Letter to Mahatma Gandhi (1939)"　　212

M. K. Gandhi, "Satyagraha in South Africa"   215

Visual Source: "Madras Protest"   218

Claude McKay, "Passive Resistance"   219

Manmohini Zutshi Sahgal, *An Indian Freedom Fighter Recalls Her Life*   220

Visual Source: "Algerian Women Fighters"   225

Truong Nhu Tang, *A Viet Cong Memoir*   226

Brian Loveman and Thomas M. Davies, Jr. (Eds.),
    Che Guevara: Guerilla Warfare   230

Visual Source: "Cuban Protest"   234

Liliuokalani, *Hawaii's Story*   235

Indonesian President Soekarno, "Speech at the Opening
    of the Asian-African Conference"   238

FURTHER RESOURCES   **242**

Part VI
DECOLONIZATION   **244**

Timeline   244

Introduction   245

Ho Chi Minh, "Declaration of Independence of the Democratic
    Republic of Viet-Nam"   247

Visual Source: "Algerian Women Voting"   250

Kushwant Singh, *Train to Pakistan*   251

Kim Il-sung, "The Newly–Emerging Forces Should Unite Under
    the Banner of Independence Against Imperialism"   256

Gamal Abdul Nasser, "The Arab Revolution"   259

An AIM Leader, *Voices from Wounded Knee, 1973*   261

Amílcar Cabral, "National Liberation and Culture"   263

Nelson Mandela, "The South African Freedom Charter"   267

Visual Source: "Namibian Mural"   271

Joe Kane, *Savages*   272

Tsitsi Dangarembga, *Nervous Conditions*   278

Visual Source: "Indonesian Coin"   284

Gustavo Gutiérrez, *A Theology of Liberation: History, Politics, and Salvation* 285

FURTHER RESOURCES   **289**

Part VII
FURTHER RECONFIGURATIONS:
THE POST-COLONIAL WORLD   **290**

Timeline   290

Introduction   291

Mhedi Charef, *Tea in the Harem*   296

Manny "The Revolution That Failed Women"   299

Visual Source: "French Muslim Girl"   304

D. K. Fieldhouse, *Black Africa 1945–80: Economic Decolonization
   and Arrested Development*   305

Jane Kramer, *Unsettling Europe*   311

Henry Yule and A. C. Burnell, Eds., "Definitions from *Hobson-Jobson*"   315

Ian McAuley, *Guide to Ethnic London*   317

Visual Source: "Greenpeace Protest at the Taj Mahal"   321

Edward W. Said, "The Clash of Ignorance"   322

Buchi Emecheta, "The Miracle"   325

Michael Chege, "What's Right with Africa?"   327

"Understanding Climate Change: A Beginner's Guide
   to the United Nations Framework Convention"   332

Visual Source: "WTO Protest"   336

Map: "Western Europe, Muslim Population c. 2005"   337

"AIDS Pandemic"   339

Visual Source: "Masai Herdsmen"   341

FURTHER RESOURCES   **342**

Topical Table of Contents

CULTURE:

Art and Architecture:

"Jungles To-Day Are Gold Mines To-Morrow"   20
"The Indian Court at the Great Exhibition"   28
"Queen Victoria's Golden Jubilee—Victorian Wallpaper"   44
José Rizal   82
"Belgian Territorial Agent"   133
"Advertisement for the Sontag Hotel"   184
Maps of Cairo and Singapore   191

Clothing:

"Gandhi in Western Clothing"   56
"Belgian Territorial Agent"   133
"The Secret of England's Greatness"   138
"Meiji Emperor"   145

Education and Language:

Sayyid Jamāl ad-Dīn Al-Afghānī   70
Léopold S. Senghor   122
Thomas J. Morgan   125
Chinua Achebe   165
Liang Qichao   169
Lady Barker   178
The Red Man   185
J. E. Casely Hayford   201
Orishatuke Faduma   205
Hobson-Jobson   315

Exportation of Civilization:

    Rudyard Kipling   21
    "Pears' Soap Advertisement"   23
    Karl Marx   29
    Joseph Conrad   33
    "British Officer Reclining"   37
    Arthur James Balfour   38
    "An Ottoman Government Decree"   41
    M. K. Gandhi, "Civilization"   52
    José Rizal   82
    Theodore Christlieb   130
    Albert Memmi   146
    Orishatuke Faduma   205
    Amílcar Cabral   263
    Mehdi Charef   296
    Jane Kramer   311
    Buchi Emecheta   325

Promotion of Indigenous Civilizations:

    José Martí   65
    The Red Man   185
    J. E. Casely Hayford   201
    Amílcar Cabral   263
    Joe Kane   272

ECONOMICS:
Agriculture:

    Multatuli   91
    J. Clinton Cunningham   112
    Madelon H. Lulofs   175
    "Coffee Plantation"   177
    Tsitsi Dangarembga   278
    "Masai Herdsmen"   341

Commerce and Trade:

    Jules Ferry   18
    "Jungles To-Day Are Gold Mines To-Morrow"   20
    "Pears' Soap Advertisement"   23
    Joseph Conrad   33

"The African and Oriental Bureau and Buying Agency"   181
"Advertisement for the Sontag Hotel"   184

Industry and Labor:

"The Indian Court at the Great Exhibition"   28
Ho Chi Minh, "Equality!"   57
"East African Transport, Old and New Style"   107
J. Clinton Cunningham   112
"Railroads and Coolies"   128

Imperial and Post-Colonial Economics:

Karl Marx   29
Godfrey N. Uzoigwe   61
José Martí   65
Aimé Césaire   78
Vladimir Lenin   87
Eduardo Galeano   119
José Carlos Mariátegui   182
Che Guevara: Guerilla Warfare   230
Kim Il-sung   256
Joe Kane   272
Gustavo Gutiérrez   285
D.K. Fieldhouse   305
Michael Chege   327
"WTO Protest"   336

ENVIRONMENT AND LANDSCAPE:

"Final Act of Berlin"   10
"Chief Seattle's Oration"   95
J. Clinton Cunningham   112
Madelon H. Lulofs   175
"Coffee Plantation"   177
The Red Man   185
Maps of Cairo and Singapore   191
Joe Kane   272
Ian McAuley   317
"Greenpeace Protest at the Taj Mahal"   321
"Understanding Climate Change"   332
"Masai Herdsmen"   341

MIGRATION:

Mehdi Charef   296
Jane Kramer   311
Ian McAuley   317
Buchi Emecheta   325
"Western Europe, Muslim Population circa 2005"   337

MILITARY:

Edward D. Morel   75
Michael Adas   104
Peter Hopkirk   109
Kita Ikki   134
The Red Man   185
"Algerian Women Fighters"   225
Truong Nhu Tang   226
Che Guevara: Guerilla Warfare   230

POLITICS AND GOVERNMENT:

Political Alliances and Treaties:

"Final Act of Berlin"   10
"Emperor Meiji's Letter to President Grant"   31
Woodrow Wilson   59
Liliuokalani   235
President Soekarno   238
Kim Il-sung   256

Nationalism:

"Emperor Meiji's Letter to President Grant"   31
Kita Ikki   134
"Madras Protest"   218
Ho Chi Minh, "Declaration of Independence"   247
"Indonesian Coin"   284

Political Thought:

Kita Ikki   134
Albert Memmi   146
Li Dazhao   208
Martin Buber   212

M. K. Gandhi, "Satyagraha and Fearlessness"   215
Claude McKay   219
Manmohini Zutshi Sahgal   220
Gamal Abdul Nasser   259
Nelson Mandela   267
Michael Chege   327

Revolution and Protest:

"Tippoo's Tiger"   51
"Lenin Giving a Speech"   90
Harry Thuku   197
"Algerian Women Fighters"   225
Truong Nhu Tang   226
Che Guevara: Guerilla Warfare   230
"Cuban Protest"   234
Voices from Wounded Knee   261
"Greenpeace Protest at the Taj Mahal"   321
"WTO Protest"   336

Political Institutions and the Law:

"Emperor Meiji's Letter to President Grant"   31
Multatuli   91
Ngugi wa Thiong'o   136
"Summary of Orders"   151
"Child Marriage Restraint Act"   156
Harry Thuku   197
Liliuokalani   235
"Algerian Women Voting"   250

RACE AND ETHNICITY:

Rudyard Kipling   21
"Pears' Soap Advertisement"   23
Herbert Spencer   25
Joseph Conrad   33
"British Officer Reclining"   37
Mary Seacole   45
Ho Chi Minh, "Equality!"   57
Edward D. Morel   75
Thomas J. Morgan   125

"Belgian Territorial Agent"   133
Kita Ikki   134
Albert Memmi   146
J. E. Casely Hayford   201
Orishatuke Faduma   205
President Soekarno   238
"Namibian Mural"   271
Joe Kane   272

Religion:

José Rizal   82
Theodore Christlieb   130
"The Secret of England's Greatness"   138
Lady Barker   178
President Soekarno   238
Kushwant Singh   251
Gustavo Gutiérrez   285
Manny   299
"French Muslim Girl"   304
Edward Said   322
"Western Europe, Muslim Population circa 2005"   337

Science and Medicine:

Mary Seacole   45
Sayyid Jamāl ad-Dīn al-Afghānī   70
J. Clinton Cunningham   112
Daniel Headrick   115
Orishatuke Faduma   205
"Understanding Climate Change"   332
"AIDS Pandemic"   339

Social Customs:

"Summary of Orders"   151
"Child Marriage Restraint Act"   156
"Beautiful Maria"   163
Chinua Achebe   165
Joyce Cary   172
Lady Barker   178

"The African and Oriental Bureau and Buying Agency"   181
The Red Man   185
Mehdi Charef   296
Jane Kramer   311
Buchi Emecheta   325

TECHNOLOGY:

"Perry's Ship"   103
Michael Adas   104
"East African Transport Old and New Style"   107
"Railroads and Coolies"   128

WOMEN, GENDER, AND FAMILY:

"Queen Victoria's Golden Jubilee—Victorian Wallpaper"   44
Mary Seacole   45
Theodore Christlieb   130
"Child Marriage Restraint Act"   156
Attiya Hanim Saqqaf   159
"Beautiful Maria"   163
Lady Barker   178
Manmohini Zutshi Sahgal   220
"Algerian Women Fighters"   225
Liliuokalani   235
"Algerian Women Voting"   250
Kushwant Singh   251
"Namibian Mural"   271
Tsitsi Dangarembga   278
Mehdi Charef   296
Manny   299
"French Muslim Girl"   304
Jane Kramer   311
Buchi Emecheta   325

MAPS:

The World, Circa 1850   2–3
The World in 1990   100–01
Foreign Imperialism in East Asia   142
The Scramble for Africa   143
The Modern World   292–3

Preface

This volume originated from our experience teaching world history courses at Gettysburg College. Frustrated by trying to teach all of world history in one or two semesters, we reconstructed our world history offerings by eliminating the long surveys and offering a sequence of thematically-organized classes instead. One such theme was imperialism in the modern world. Imperialism was a truly global topic that could be treated from a variety of different perspectives over a fairly long period of time. Moreover, the political, economic, cultural, and environmental processes connected to imperialism have reconfigured the world in the modern era right up to the present day.

Although the word imperialism certainly connotes a hierarchical relationship in which certain agents act upon other people, we hoped to convey to our students, as we taught different versions of the course, that those people had agency and were actors in their own history. We were challenged, however, by the problem of finding those voices and making them accessible to our students. There were no documentary collections available that centered on this theme and that offered enough of the perspective of the colonized on the problem of imperialism to serve our purposes.

This combination of narrative, documents, and visual sources is the result of our efforts to construct sets of sources for theme-driven world history courses. Accordingly, it offers multiple perspectives on the topics of imperialism, colonization, decolonization, and post-colonialism. It considers the reasons for, reactions to, effects of, resistance to, and enduring legacies of imperialism. As much as we have tried to be geographically and thematically comprehensive, such a task is impossible, and so we have selected readings and images that we think highlight important themes and that offer a broad geographic range. We feel strongly that students should have the opportunity to hear the voices of the people involved, and have therefore used primary sources wherever possible, but in a few instances have chosen secondary sources because they offered a better treatment of a particular theme or topic than we were able to find in a primary source. Further, many years of teaching have shown us that longer pieces that give students a real flavor for authors' positions and arguments work better in the classroom than heavily edited short selections. Thus, we have tried to keep the readings as substantial as possible and have edited them only minimally.

The hallmarks of *Imperialism in the Modern World* are therefore thematic unity, chronological focus, and substantial readings. We believe that this combination of strengths has produced a text particularly well suited for use in a wide variety of world history courses.

We have organized this volume along thematic, rather than strictly chronological lines, although the themes follow a broad chronological order. In the introduction we explore the topic of imperialism and in particular how the imperialism of the late nineteenth and twentieth centuries differed from that of earlier ages. The introduction also includes a document and a demonstration of how that document might be read. The first two parts also help to illuminate the questions of what imperialism is, why it was undertaken during the age of high imperialism, and how it was defended or criticized morally, economically, politically, strategically, socially, or culturally. Part I introduces a series of rationales for imperialism as described by advocates of imperialism. Part II comes at the question of imperialism from the perspective of its opponents. Parts III through VII look at some more concrete dimensions of imperialism. Part III explores the tools with which empires were built. Part IV considers ways in which the newly colonized areas were reshaped or reconfigured by imperialism. Part V examines the appropriation of many tools of empire by colonial peoples in order to liberate themselves. Part VI looks at various dimensions of the decolonization process. And Part VII considers, from the vantage point of the early twenty-first century, some of the many ways in which the age of high imperialism has led to lasting change not only in the colonies and former colonies, but also in Europe and North America.

We have been assisted by many people in the production of this text, and we would like to take this opportunity to thank them. Charles Cavaliere at Prentice Hall has been an exemplary editor. He showed genuine enthusiasm for the project from the beginning and has helped guide it through its various stages. Maria Guarascio, Charles's assistant, has provided timely answers to questions and queries. Bruce Hobart and his team at Pine Tree Composition, especially Carol Lallier, have done much of the hard work of copyediting and producing the final text. Their professionalism and common sense have been reassuring in the end stages of production.

We also owe a debt of gratitude to several individuals who suggested readings or critiqued parts of the text. In particular, the advice of Surendra Bhana, Byron Caminero-Santangelo, Abdin Chande, John Findlay, Sue Greene, Jack Greene, Ousman Kobo, Elizabeth MacGonagle, Tony Melchor, Tony Rosenthal, Tim Shannon, Barbara Sommer, and Kim Warren was extremely helpful in selecting texts for the book. Moreover, several readers engaged by Prentice Hall also made numerous suggestions on ways to improve every aspect of the text, from sharpening our questions to diversifying our readings. It is our pleasure to thank them, both those listed below and those who preferred to remain anonymous: Daniel Headrick, Roosevelt University; Alison Fletcher, Kent State University; Norman G. Raiford, Greenville Technical College; Wayne Ackerson, Salisbury University; Michael F. Pavkovic, Hawaii Pacific University; Heather Streets, Washington State University; and Susan Maneck, Jackson State University. We want to thank Jerry Bentley, whose comments at the 2006 American Historical Association meeting caused us to reconsider some of the language in our introductions.

The library staffs at Gettysburg College, the University of Kansas, and the Library of Congress also aided us by locating particular editions of works or hard-to-find texts. Susan Roach at Gettysburg and Joan Zellers and Sentahun Tiruneh at the Library of Congress were especially helpful in this regard.

Meredith Bartron, Alexandra East, and Lyndsey Rago, three undergraduate students at Gettysburg College, were fundamental to the production of this volume. Meredith and Lyndsey read all of our proposed selections with the students' eye for accessibility and clarity. Their reactions to and recommendations on texts helped us at an early stage in the selection process. Alexandra did heroic work in helping to prepare the manuscript in its final stages, especially during its copyediting phase. Gwendolyn Claassen at the University of Kansas also did extensive work on preparing the manuscript for publication.

We want to thank Carla Pavlick, the History Department Office Administrator at Gettysburg College for all of her assistance over many years of work on this volume. As anyone who has worked in academic institutions knows, support staff are the people who really make them function.

Finally, our deepest expression of gratitude goes to our families, especially our spouses, Magdalena Sánchez, Sheila Chiteji, and Tony Melchor, who have supported us during the many stages of producing *Imperialism in the Modern World.*

William D. Bowman
Frank M. Chiteji
J. Megan Greene

Introduction

If we take imperialism to mean the direct control or extension of control of one people, state, or nation over another, then it is as old as history itself. The tendency to dominate other people is not an African, Asian, Australian, European, Latin American, or North American phenomenon; it is a human one. At all points in the past, we find imperialistic relationships of one type or another. Students of world history, who focus their attention on connected patterns, are aware of this state of affairs. Scholars, too, have spent great time and effort researching and writing on the complicated political, economic, cultural, intellectual, environmental, and social connections and relationships of dependency between peoples, nations, and continents throughout human history. Making connections to the past is critically important to understanding it. Equally important, however, is learning to make proper distinctions. This reader is a compilation of primary and secondary sources, textual and visual documents about global relations primarily in the nineteenth and twentieth centuries. One of its goals is to help students realize that although there are many similarities and continuities between this era and earlier phases of world history, there are also sharp differences. We have kept the thematic, geographical, and chronological focus of the readings relatively compact in order to provide students the opportunity to make connections between the selections and to comprehend some of the ways in which the period of the nineteenth and twentieth centuries represents a new era in global relations.

One important distinction to make in world history is between imperialism and empire. Imperialism may involve a wide variety of informal and formal contacts between peoples and nations. Empires, in the classical definition, are regimes that have consolidated direct political and economic control over territories and subject peoples. Obviously, the two terms are inherently linked, but they should not be used interchangeably. For example, Great Britain in the nineteenth century undoubtedly had imperialistic designs upon China and hoped to exploit it economically and in other ways. Nevertheless, the British never brought much Chinese territory under formal political control as they did the Indian subcontinent. We may choose to speak of the extension of economic and cultural influence around the globe as economic or cultural imperialism, but these activities by themselves do not constitute the formation of an official empire.

At the same time, vast trading networks over routes such as the Silk Road and the sea networks of the Pacific Ocean and the Mediterranean connected peoples and facilitated

The World, Circa 1850

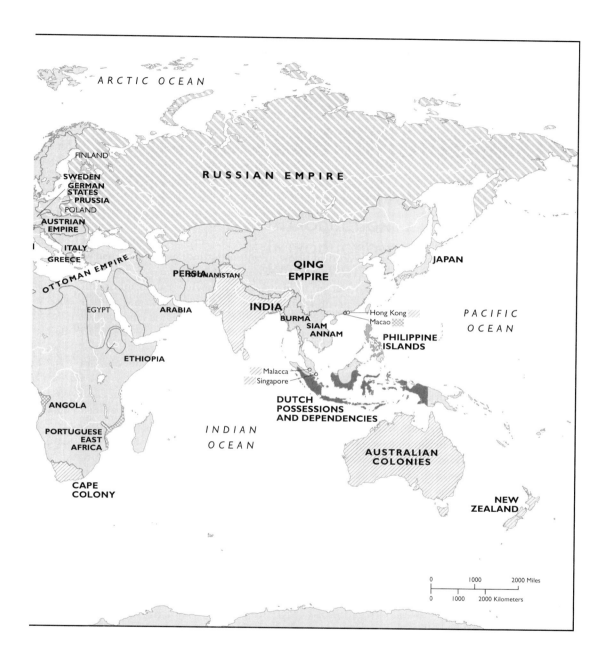

ARCTIC OCEAN

FINLAND

SWEDEN
GERMAN
STATES
PRUSSIA
POLAND

AUSTRIAN
EMPIRE

ITALY

GREECE

OTTOMAN EMPIRE

EGYPT

ARABIA

ETHIOPIA

ANGOLA

PORTUGUESE
EAST
AFRICA

CAPE
COLONY

RUSSIAN EMPIRE

PERSIA

AFGHANISTAN

INDIA

QING
EMPIRE

JAPAN

BURMA

SIAM

ANNAM

Hong Kong
Macao

PHILIPPINE
ISLANDS

PACIFIC
OCEAN

Malacca
Singapore

DUTCH
POSSESSIONS
AND DEPENDENCIES

INDIAN
OCEAN

AUSTRALIAN
COLONIES

NEW
ZEALAND

0	1000	2000 Miles
0	1000	2000 Kilometers

transfers of information, goods, and culture in earlier eras of world history. Through such networks China exerted considerable influence throughout east and southeast Asia for centuries. Chinese goods, technology, and culture were exchanged throughout a region much larger than that over which it had direct political control (its empire). The Indian subcontinent, with its central position between east and west Asia, was often an important center of trade and commerce, not to mention a hub for the spread of religion and language. Arabs were involved in trade, intellectual pursuits, the spread of culture, and many other endeavors in a huge stretch of territory from north Africa to central and eastern regions of Asia. Many Chinese, Indian, and Arab accomplishments and patterns were spread widely across these pathways. These patterns of global interconnectedness demonstrate how extensively polities, economies, and cultures may influence others even in the absence of formal empires.

Throughout much of human history, empires played critical roles around the globe. Han China, Rome, Ghana, Mali, the Aztec Empire, the Incan Empire, Byzantium, the Mongol Empire, and many others have been the subjects of intense study, and much fascinating material about their histories has been written. Most of these empires were land based and involved the use of administrative, military, and political webs of control. Religions, languages, and other cultural practices, as well as diseases and genes, were spread liberally throughout many of these empires, which represented high degrees and diverse dimensions of global interconnectedness. The global centers of political and economic gravity shifted with the changing fortunes of these empires.

Beginning in the fifteenth century, Europe's renewed outward economic orientation, in combination with its improved shipbuilding techniques, caused states like Portugal, Spain, and eventually Holland and Britain to conquer territories to which they were not linked by land and to establish new empires. Following a model more similar to that of Rome with its far-flung and sometimes noncontiguous territories than to any other earlier empire, these overseas empires varied in character, but all of them were rooted first and foremost in the European desire to control new sources of wealth. Portugal and Spain were also heavily invested in transforming the cultures of the territories they brought under control, and sought to spread Catholicism across South and, to a lesser extent, North America, as well as parts of Africa and Asia. The Spanish and Portuguese empires also politically and socially reorganized the indigenous peoples they encountered. The Dutch and British, on the other hand, sometimes used existing political and social structures in their new colonies, in places like India and the Dutch East Indies, to assist in extracting as many resources as possible. Overall, the British approach to North America, Australia, and New Zealand, however, bore a great resemblance to that of the Spanish and Portuguese in the territories they controlled or influenced in that all of them developed settler colonies of one description or another and transformed the territories they acquired.

While these earlier empires are unquestionably important antecedents to the imperialism of the nineteenth century, the imperialism described in this text represented something different. First, the term itself is apparently of nineteenth-century origin. At that time, it described primarily British policies, but we can take it in a broader sense to define a new phase in global relations. Beginning in the mid-eighteenth century, at the latest, empires, especially European-based ones, began to distinguish between commercial trade–based influence and territorial power and the more active and direct extension of political, economic, and cultural control over far-flung lands. This shift was brought about by many developments, not the least of which was the European industrial revolution, which itself built upon earlier patterns of commercial and technological global exchange. By the end of the eighteenth and into the nineteenth century, this shift toward imperialism in the more modern sense of the term intensified and quickened. The industrial revolution, which produced a huge range of technological breakthroughs over several generations, allowed Europeans and North Americans to view the world as their own and to extend their influence worldwide on unprecedented levels. At the same time, the new ideologies of nationalism and political liberalism, created and fostered in part by the American and French revolutions, gave important new impulses and provided rationales for imperialistic expansion in the modern era. Race ideology, also a product of the nineteenth century, provided yet another important ideological element to the rise of modern imperialism. Finally, the consolidation of medical information and practices, won over centuries and coming from different continents, allowed the agents of imperialism to operate in new areas of the world and to think about global relations on new terms.

The nineteenth and twentieth centuries thus represent a new era in global history. The degree of connections between peoples in Africa, Asia, Europe, North America, and South America increased exponentially. In some instances, the movement of populations across the world's oceans became almost the norm, and the historian has to account for why people stayed in place rather than participate in some of the most profound exchanges in human history. Similarly, the trade in goods of all kinds expanded, and global patterns of trade and commerce were more pronounced than they had been in early periods. Moreover, world trade affected to a greater extent the daily lives of people living in both the producer and consumer territories or countries. Disease, always one of the most important features of global exchange, was a central part of the great nineteenth- and twentieth-century global exchanges. Indeed, the efforts to identify, treat, and control diseases intensified in the period and were basic background reasons for the ability of people and goods to move around the globe. By the middle of the nineteenth century, these developments created the conditions for a new era of world history: the age of high imperialism. Although it is wrong to separate wholly this era from previous periods of world history—there were, after all, many important preconditions that set the stage for the age of high imperialism—it is nevertheless true that distinct and dramatic changes occurred in global patterns at this time. People of European ancestry, for example, moved in increasing numbers to South America, North America, and Australia. Other Europeans moved to Africa and Asia to help manage expanding global empires.

To understand something about this new imperialism of the late nineteenth century, we must comprehend its scale and pace. Building on developments in the first half of the century (France had acquired control over Algeria in the 1830s and Indochina in the 1860s, for example), Europeans took formal control of millions of acres of territory, mostly in Africa and Asia, between 1870 and 1900. Through a complicated set of international arrangements, Belgium, and in particular its king, Leopold, became the political overlord of the Congo region in Africa, a territory many times Belgium's size. Great Britain annexed approximately four million square miles of territory and brought sixty-six million new people under its nominal control. Similarly, France's formal overseas empire expanded by approximately three million square miles and twenty-six million people. Germany, a new European state created in 1871, became a colonial power as well in the last decades of the nineteenth century; it took formal possession of about one million square miles with a population of roughly thirteen million people. Most of this territory and these people were in Africa.

Imperial expansion was at the heart of international relations throughout the second half of the nineteenth century and well into the twentieth. Conflicts on the European continent, for example, might be displaced to Africa or Asia. Conversely, territorial rivalries abroad might exaggerate or intensify struggles back in Europe. These sets of reinforcing tensions were true of Anglo-French, Anglo-German, and French-German relations and are an important background cause of the First World War. The buildup of European militaries and commercial naval fleets was also linked to imperial expansion and designs in the period from the 1870s to 1914.

European nations followed different models of expansion overseas. In Africa, where these contrasting patterns can best be seen, Great Britain attempted to establish a commercial empire with trade routes from Egypt to South Africa. The discovery of precious minerals in the latter intensified British interest in the area, of course. In order to secure and extend their economic interests, the British therefore also tended to seek control over territories along a north–south axis of Africa that would link areas over which they already held sway. France, operating largely out of political and economic motives, moved to consolidate its control over western Africa, site of many ancient kingdoms, and by gradually extending its control eastward hoped to thwart Great Britain's imperialist designs. The French were relatively unsuccessful in the latter maneuver, however. Following the lead of its authoritarian prime minister, Otto von Bismarck, Germany took over African coastal lands primarily as political bargaining chips—that is, to be used in the game of European power politics. Thus, Germany took over territories such as Cameroon, German Southwest Africa (Namibia), and German East Africa (Tanzania, Burundi, and Rwanda). The Germans, like their European rivals, also sought out these territories for economic advantage and to extend networks of trade and the supply of raw materials. Pressure from journalists, adventurers, and civilian populations back home was also important in the imperialist project; no country or people wanted to be left behind in the scramble for overseas territories.

Smaller, less politically and economically powerful European states became more active in Africa: Spain in North Africa, Portugal in Angola, and Italy in Libya and Somalia, for example. In these cases, too, earlier patterns of contact allowed for more extensive involvement in African affairs. For example, the Portuguese had already been established in west and east Africa prior to 1870, but their inclination to establish formal colonies in places like Angola and Mozambique gained momentum after the Berlin Conference of 1884–85. So thorough was European colonization of Africa that by the First World War in 1914, only two African states retained formal political independence: Ethiopia, which resisted Italian moves until the 1930s, and Liberia, which was under the protection of the United States.

The role of the United States in world affairs also grew in the nineteenth century. U.S. expansionism began with moves to oust the French and Spanish from the south and west and ended with a dramatic increase in the contiguous territories of the United States over the course of the nineteenth century. The increasing involvement of the United States in global patterns is of course complicated, but highlighting a few red-letter events may help to make it clearer. In 1823, the Monroe Doctrine announced that the U.S. government would seek to be a more active player in the affairs of South America. In 1867, Alaska was acquired for approximately two cents an acre and extended U.S. territory substantially to the west. In the wake of the Spanish-American War (1898), the remnants of the old Spanish empire, including the Philippines, came under American control, and the United States annexed Hawaii. Theodore Roosevelt, President of the United States, sent a U.S. fleet around the world between December 1907 and February 1909 as a demonstration of power and a statement of global interest. Finally, in August 1915 the Panama Canal was opened, which greatly benefited U.S. economic interests and drew the U.S. more directly into Central America. The canal was of course also of profound importance for global economics as such. By the time of the First World War, the United States was already a global player of great consequence, even if the era of its most profound overseas influence was still a few decades away.

As noted previously, the stage was set by the Portuguese, Dutch, and British for European colonial expansion into Asia well before the industrial revolution. Over the course of the nineteenth century, these nascent empires were consolidated, and the old mercantilist systems favored by the Dutch and British were replaced with formal colonial structures in India, Indonesia, and the Philippines. The United States' assertion of its interests in the Pacific in the mid-nineteenth century may have propelled further European extension of its colonial authority into Burma, Malaysia, Vietnam, and even parts of China.

As vast territories in Africa, Asia, and the Pacific were acquired by the new imperialist powers, the societies, polities, and economies of these territories were irreversibly transformed. New colonial governments were constructed that typically employed indigenous people who had been trained in the language and customs of the colonizers. These new political configurations often reshaped social values, and as a consequence, new elite classes of colonial civil servants and others who had absorbed colonial values gradually formed. Not only were social structures and cultural practices changed by the colonial experience but so were landscapes and economies as the imperialists sought ways to fully exploit the land and natural resources of the colonies.

The new imperialist movements of the nineteenth and early twentieth centuries were so profound that they sparked considerable debate, even in the West. Various contemporary views, explanations, and even justifications for new global patterns were offered (most of these views are represented in selections from parts I and II of the reader). Rudyard Kipling, a famous writer and poet and Nobel Prize winner, suggested that European acquisition of overseas colonies and colonials was part of the "The White Man's Burden," the title of his famous poem. Kipling, who had spent time in India and Afghanistan, wrote that European expansion was the duty of "civilized" peoples, who were obligated to send their best and brightest to the new colonies: "we shall be the servants of our captives, who are half-devil, half-childlike." Kipling's was a highly paternalistic view, but he also sought to give a positive, moralistic spin to imperialism, to imbue it with a sense of mission and responsibility.

A far less apologetic view of imperialism was offered by social Darwinists in the last decades of the nineteenth century. Some of them suggested quite plainly that military conquest was the road to global improvement. In this view, European states or the United States acquired territory and political control over peoples because they were fitter and better adapted for the purpose of rule and governing. As Karl Pearson bluntly and brutally claimed, civilization was the result of racial struggle. "The path of progress is strewn with the wreck of nations. . . . Yet these dead peoples are, in very truth, the stepping stones on which mankind has arisen to the higher intellectual and deeper emotional life of today." (Karl Pearson, *National Life from the Standpoint of Science,* p. 64.) Of course, Pearson did not see the global conflicts of the twentieth century, and if he had, he might have been less confident about the relationship between global struggle and progress. Be that as it may, social Darwinism was a very active movement in the last decades of the nineteenth century and provided one way of viewing imperial and colonial relations.

Critics of the new patterns of global relations also emerged, and many of their views are represented in readings from Part II of the text. Economists such as John Hobson, who wrote a study of imperialism in 1902, suggested that on balance overseas colonial adventures were a drain on a country's wealth. Hobson argued that if all the associated costs of maintaining a formal empire were added together, they would represent a net loss to a country like Great Britain. Appearances to the contrary, imperialism was an economic albatross to a country. Why did countries engage in it then? According to Hobson, because even though it was unprofitable for a nation as a whole, it was highly profitable for certain individuals, namely investors who owned trading companies, banks, shipping, and mines, for example. Further, he argued that these individuals, the investing class, had a disproportionate amount of influence in politics. Vladimir Lenin, the famous Russian revolutionary, drew upon Hobson's arguments and combined them with his basic Marxist framework to create a more thorough-going critique of the new imperialism. Lenin claimed that the capitalist system had not yet collapsed because it had found a safety or escape valve in overseas imperialistic adventures. For him, imperialism was the final, highest, or last stage of capitalism. When all of the new markets have been exploited, new labor conflicts and economic tensions, according to Lenin, would lead to the global collapse of capitalism and the new socialist world. In sum, a wide variety of conflicting interpretations of imperialism and colonialism was offered by an equally diverse array of Western authors in the nineteenth and twentieth centuries.

The process of extending colonial influence was complex. Political, military, and economic tools, the subject of Part III, were used to reconfigure the day-to-day patterns of people under European rule. Moreover, cultural patterns were affected in the exchange between colonizer and colonized. Shifts in language, legal standards, gender relations, religious patterns, architecture, and many other areas were all part of the global exchanges brought about by the imperialism of the nineteenth and twentieth centuries. These shifts have had profound and ongoing consequences for our contemporary world. Readers of this volume will find many selections addressing these global reconfigurations in parts IV and VII.

The process by which much of the formal colonial political world was undone was profound and complicated as well. Although decolonization largely occurred between the 1940s and the 1970s, the movements that led up to it began much earlier and were sometimes launched almost simultaneously with European or North American acquisition of territory or influence. People around the world found arguments about European or white superiority unconvincing in the face of sometimes cruel colonial policy. Africans and Asians sometimes used arguments about self-determination, liberation, the political franchise, and individual freedom to argue against colonialism. Latin Americans and Native Americans in North America, who perceived themselves to often be economically and culturally dependent on Europe or the United States, joined in these debates and used similar arguments or molded new ones to fit their particular circumstances. Opponents of imperialism such as Mahatma Gandhi used Indian traditions to fashion a policy of resistance against British political dominance. More radical activists sometimes adopted Marxist ideology or armed conflict to try to undo political and economic regimes, which they found inherently unjust. In addition, the effects of two world wars in changing global relations cannot be underestimated. The conflicts weakened European economies and meant that fewer material and personnel resources were available to manage overseas colonies. The wars, combined with events like the Holocaust, also went a long way toward undermining arguments about European moral superiority. Thus, the political, intellectual, and economic framework for decolonization was already well prepared before the end of the Second World War, even if the formal process occurred after it. The readings from parts V and VI focus on this complicated process and its antecedents.

The age of imperialism, however, has left indelible marks on global patterns. For example, the movement of people from around the world and especially from Asia and Africa to Europe intensified in the late nineteenth century, and the pace of this pattern of migration picked up at various points throughout the twentieth century. The two world wars of the twentieth century brought colonial subjects to Europe both to work in industry and to fight in the conflicts. Some of them would stay. In the 1950s and 1960s, burgeoning European economies meant job opportunities that created a labor demand partially met by overseas workers. The net effect of this global movement of peoples was that European countries and especially their industrial cities were eventually transformed. Centuries of informal and formal imperial relations and contact with societies around the world meant that European urban areas became, over time, global communities.

With decolonization came new configurations of former empires, such as the British Commonwealth, and new alliances between former colonies, such as the Non-Aligned Movement. These nongovernmental structures have facilitated economic, political, and social interactions between states and peoples. The expansion of the British Commonwealth in the era of decolonization to include newly independent states, in particular, has led to a continuing closeness between Britain and many of its former colonies based primarily on common cultural traits and a desire to continue close economic relations. Under the commonwealth system, large numbers of former colonial subjects have immigrated to Britain and have continued to transform its face and landscape. Although France's attempt at constructing a commonwealth was less successful, France nonetheless also maintains close relationships with many of its former colonies and also continues to be reconfigured by the incorporation into French society of many of its former colonial subjects.

In addition, some scholars and commentators have argued that economic conditions and cultural exchanges today reveal signs of a neocolonial world. These individuals look to places like Africa, Asia, and Latin America and discern patterns of dependency upon Europe and the United States in particular. From this perspective, the global resentment of American policies in recent decades becomes clearer. Some people have read the informal extension of American economic might and cultural influence through the lens of the last two centuries. When they do so, they see attempts to "recolonize" their territories through the means of informal imperial control. Other observers, while not denying the importance of the colonial past, contend that people and nations must adjust themselves and reconfigure their politics, economics, and culture to deal with an increasingly globalized world. Such observers are far more optimistic about the influence of western ideas and practices in the modern world. Careful readers of this volume will have noted that this debate has been going on for a long time. The readings in this volume provide the proper historical context for understanding these arguments and global developments. Regardless of where one falls along the spectrum of debate, no one would dispute that from the 1960s onward, global relations have been reconfigured once again. This process of further reconfiguration is addressed in the readings from Part VII.

Each part of the reader contains a number of selections around a central theme in the story of modern imperialism. The selections can be read individually or all together. Each piece has a brief introduction that establishes a general historical context for the reading. At the end of the introduction, teachers and students will find a set of questions intended to promote critical analysis of the piece. Some of the questions will help students relate a reading to other selections in the volume. At the end of each part of the reader are suggestions for further readings and films. The editors have intentionally kept these suggestions brief and have in general preferred accessible and sometimes popular items over scholarly pieces.

*****

As a guide and aid to teachers and students using this text, the editors include in this introduction a discussion of a primary document as an example of how the reader might be used. The document is a selection from the famous Berlin Conference of 1884–85, which was an important meeting to discuss and determine European nations' future relations with Africa. Scholars differ in their assessments of the political and economic background to imperialism in the nineteenth century—some have stressed continuities over a long period of time, and others have seen more abrupt breaks in the pattern of imperialistic adventures. Regardless of one's perspective, the Berlin Conference is widely considered a crucial moment in the history of Europe's relations with Africa and an important step in nineteenth-century imperialism.

The immediate background to the conference was growing European interest in Africa in general and in its interior regions in particular. Several of Africa's major rivers, including the Congo, seemed to provide major trade routes through the continent. Leopold II's (of Belgium) interest in the Congo region was indeed one of the reasons that an international conference on the future of Africa was convened in Berlin beginning in November 1884. Most of the European states, including Great Britain, France, Germany, Russia, Austria-Hungary, Belgium, Portugal, the Netherlands, Spain, and Denmark, were represented. African representatives were not in attendance. In February 1885, the conference members agreed on and signed the General Act of the Conference of Berlin. The following excerpt is taken from that General Act.

> [After a long preamble announcing the nations sending representatives] Wishing, in a spirit of good and mutual accord, to regulate the conditions most favourable to the development of trade and civilization in certain regions of Africa, and to assure to all nations the advantages of free navigation on

the two chief rivers of Africa flowing into the Atlantic Ocean [Congo and Niger]; being desirous, on the other hand, to obviate the misunderstanding and disputes which might in future arise from new acts of occupation ('prises de possession') on the coast of Africa; and concerned, at the same time, as to the means of furthering the moral and material well-being of the native populations, have resolved, on the invitation addressed to them by the Imperial Government of Germany, in agreement with the Government of the French Republic, to meet for those purposes in Conference at Berlin. . . . [Plenipotentiaries, representatives of the various nations, are named].

Who, being provided with full powers, which have been found in good and due form, have successively discussed and adopted:—

1. A Declaration relative to freedom of trade in the basin of the Congo, its embouchures and cir-cumjacent regions, with other provisions connected therewith.
2. A Declaration relative to the slave trade, and the operations by sea or land which furnish slaves to that trade.
3. A Declaration relative to the neutrality of the territories comprised in the Conventional basin of the Congo.
4. An Act of Navigation for the Congo, which, while having regard to local circumstances, extends to this river, its affluents, and the waters in its system ('eaux qui leur sont assimilées'), the general principles enunciated in Articles CVIII and CXVI of the Final Act of the Congress of Vienna, and intended to regulate, as between the Signatory Powers of that Act, the free navigation of the water-ways separating or traversing several States—these said principles having since then been applied by agreement to certain rivers of Europe and America, but especially to the Danube, with the modifications stipulated by the Treaties of Paris (1856), of Berlin (1878), and of London (1871 and 1883).
5. An Act of Navigation for the Niger, which, while likewise having regard to local circumstances, extends to this river and its affluents the same principles as set forth in Articles CVIII and CXVI of the Final Act of the Congress of Vienna.
6. A Declaration introducing into international relations certain uniform rules with reference to future occupations on the coasts of the African Continent.

The Final Act of Berlin then goes on in several chapters and articles to set down precisely how these six general declarations are to be put into action. Article 35 is perhaps the Act's most famous clause:

The Signatory Powers of the present Act recognize the obligation to insure the establishment of authority in regions occupied by them on the coasts of the African Continent sufficient to protect existing rights, and, as the case may be, freedom of trade and of transit under the conditions agreed upon. (Source: Edward Hertslet, *The Map of Africa by Treaty*. Vol. 1: *Abyssinia to Great Britain*. London, 1894. Pp. 20–45.)

At first glance, governmental or diplomatic documents may seem like dry sources for historians. In actuality, they often have a directness and richness that are indispensable for understanding the past. In these short paragraphs from the Final Act of Berlin, for example, we learn much about late nineteenth-century global relations. Teachers and students can read the document to learn about how the regulation of trade of some of Africa's primary rivers was to proceed or why the suppression of the slave trade was included in the discussions and resolutions at Berlin. Article 35, cited above, has usually been interpreted to mean that Europeans established a policy of effective occupation ("sufficient authority" in the language of the act) of African territories as a result of the Berlin Conference. This policy, driven by a wide range of political, economic, and ideological motives, obviously shaped African and European relations for decades to come.

The Final Act also reveals indirectly much about the fundamental relationships of Africans and Europeans in the last decades of the nineteenth century. Perhaps most interesting was that no African representatives were present to negotiate or consult over a document that so clearly bore on their future. Not surprisingly, the participants at the conference drew consistently and heavily on existing European agreements dating back to the Congress of Vienna in 1815 in establishing policies for Africa. Such agreements may not have fit well with African realities or perceptions of trade, commerce, the movement of peoples, or the relationship of competing authorities. A major feature of the Berlin Act, present in these few paragraphs and throughout its many articles, was the combination of economic claims about trade and navigation, on the one hand, with moral arguments and ideological assumptions about the condition of Africans, on the other. This mixing of motives and justifications was a common feature of nineteenth-century imperialism and formed part of the complicated landscape upon which the world's peoples met. We must not underestimate the power and complexity of such intertwined arguments. Nor are the actions that followed from agreements such as the Final Act always easy to unpack.

In the readings from the first two parts of this text, teachers and students will find many selections that describe, analyze, or betray the full range of reasons, justifications, and explanations for the profound global encounters of the nineteenth and twentieth centuries. Many historical factors were often involved simultaneously in the complex exchanges and relations of this age—as seen clearly in the Final Act of the Berlin Conference. We should ask immediately how these many factors and justifications would have been interpreted by different audiences of the day. Many Europeans, for example, would have read the call to suppress the slave trade in Africa as part of their ongoing "civilizing mission" in Africa. Africans, on the other hand, might have found the claim puzzling or distressing given the Europeans' (and others') deep involvement in the slave trade and slaving societies in previous centuries. Pragmatic European politicians, whether they believed in the argument or not, undoubtedly understood that the suppression of the slave trade was an important political justification for the further penetration of Africa's interior, an important goal of the conference.

In the aftermath of the Berlin Conference, many European nations or their representatives acquired more African territory and became more directly involved in the political, economic, social, cultural, and environmental patterns of the continent. In selections from parts III and IV of this reader, students will learn, among many other things, much more about these developments and reactions to them. Further questions will naturally arise and should be kept in mind: To what extent were political settlements like the Berlin Act linked to these profound social, cultural, and economic developments? Are political arrangements merely the background for such developments, or are the two linked in more direct causal relationships?

In sum, the Final Act of the Berlin Conference is a rich document for world history. It can be related to many major global developments of the nineteenth and twentieth centuries. It raises issues and concerns that are also present in many other selections in this reader, and thus students are naturally asked how to weigh and position the relative importance of one source among many others in understanding the world's past. Indeed, this brief reading of the Final Act is a model of how the editors hope this reader should work.

FURTHER RESOURCES

Bukharin, Nikolai Ivanovich. *Imperialism and World Economy.* New York, H. Fertig, 1967.

Gallagher, John, and Ronald Robinson, "The Imperialism of Free Trade." *Economic History Review,* 2d series, vol. 6, no. 1 (August 1953).

Hodgart, Alan. *The Economics of European Imperialism.* New York: Norton, 1978.

Kiernan, V. G. *Marxism and Imperialism: Studies.* New York: St. Martin's Press, 1975.

Low, D. A. *Lion Rampant: Essays in the Study of British Imperialism.* London: Frank Cass, 1973.

McClintock, Anne. *Imperial Leather: Race, Gender, and Sexuality in the Colonial Contest.* New York: Routledge, 1995.

Moon, Parker Thomas. *Imperialism and World Politics.* New York: Macmillan, 1926.

Sandison, Alan. *The Wheel of Empire: A Study of the Imperial Idea in Some Late Nineteenth and Early Twentieth-Century Fiction.* London: MacMillan, 1967.

Schumpeter, Joseph. "The Sociology of Imperialisms." In Joseph Schumpeter, ed. *Imperialism and Social Classes.* Cleveland: Meridian Books, 1951.

Smith, Bonnie G. *Imperialism: A History in Documents.* New York: Oxford University Press, 2000.

Watts, S. J. *Epidemics and History: Disease, Power, and Imperialism.* New Haven: Yale University Press, 1997.

1808	Slave Trade Made Illegal in Great Britain	**1870**	**"Ottoman Decree"**
1810–38	Latin American Revolutions for Independence from Spain	1874	British Colonize Gold Coast
		1871	**"Emperor Meiji's Letter to President Grant"**
1819	Singapore Established by Stamford Raffles	1884	Berlin Conference
1830	First Public Railway Line between Liverpool and Manchester	**1887**	**"Queen Victoria's Golden Jubilee— Victorian Wallpaper"**
1831	French Take Algeria	**1890**	**Jules Ferry, *Tonkin and the Motherland***
1839–40	Opium War, China	1898	Spanish-American War
1851	**"The Indian Court at the Great Exhibition"**	**1899**	**Rudyard Kipling, "The White Man's Burden"**
1853	**Karl Marx, "The British Rule in India"**		**"Pears' Soap Advertisement"**
1854	"Opening" of Japan	1899–1902	Boer War
1857	**Mary Seacole, *Wonderful Adventures of Mrs. Seacole in Many Lands***	**1910**	**Balfour "Problems"**
			Mexican Revolution Begins
	Sepoy Rebellion	1914–18	World War I
1859	French Attack Vietnam	1920	League of Nations Founded
1861–65	United States Civil War	**1923**	**Joseph Conrad, "An Outpost of Progress"**
1864	**Herbert Spencer, *Illustrations of Universal Progress***	**1927**	**"Jungles To-day Are Gold Mines To-morrow"**
1869	Suez Canal Completed		

Entries in bold indicate sources.

Part I

The Imperialists

INTRODUCTION

The rapid and remarkable changes in patterns of global history in the nineteenth and twentieth centuries caused many observers to attempt to define or analyze what was going on around them. The period from the 1870s to the First World War (1914–18), in particular, brought wide-scale changes in political and economic relations. Historians and other scholars have defined this era as an age of "high" or "new" imperialism. The name is intended to recognize that although imperialistic relations had been a part of world historical patterns for centuries and even millennia, this period (1870s to 1920s or 1930s) was nevertheless marked by distinctively intense and broad-based colonial activity. European nations especially were heavily involved as colonial powers in Africa and Asia and also played a significant role in the economics and culture of South America. In Africa, for example, huge swaths of territory came under the direct political control of British, French, German, Belgian, or other European administrations. Although European nations did not acquire as much land directly in Asia as in Africa, they were nevertheless very active throughout the continent and especially in the Indian subcontinent, China, and Southeast Asia. Thus, by the end of the nineteenth century, European countries had become the political or economic overlords of most of Africa and either played that same role in many Asian lands or were at the very least involved in the economic and cultural affairs of many Asian peoples.

In the Americas, the situation was in some respects quite different, but patterns of global interdependence predominated here as well. In North America, the United States offered an interesting model of historical development; having won its war of independence from the British in the late eighteenth century and withstood a challenge to its very existence in a civil war, the United States emerged as a major economic, political, and cultural player by the second half of the nineteenth century. Indeed, the United States became a formal imperial power in its own right by the turn of the twentieth century and was increasingly involved in global affairs thereafter. At the same time, indigenous natives and people of African origin in the United States struggled with a wide range of legal, economic, and cultural problems and biases—a condition some have described as suffering from the effects of "domestic imperialism."

South American nations had freed themselves from the political and administrative grip of Spain and Portugal in the first half of the nineteenth century, but these same countries had become increasingly enmeshed in world economic patterns, which meant that they were in turn also progressively more deeply integrated into a larger global network. Because of the high degree of economic dependence of Latin American and Caribbean countries upon Europe and later increasingly upon the United States, many scholars have described this global relationship as *neocolonial* or *neo-imperial*. In this view, economic and sometimes cultural conditions in South America and the Caribbean were in some ways similar to those in areas being newly colonized in Africa and Asia.

Such dramatic shifts in the global balance of power and in economic and cultural patterns called for explanations and analyses. In this part of the reader, students will find arguments in favor of imperialism and colonialism. The texts and images are drawn primarily from the late nineteenth and early twentieth centuries. Rudyard Kipling's famous poem, "The White Man's Burden," is perhaps the classic statement on the subject of western involvement in the affairs of Asian and African people. The work and ideas of Herbert Spencer, a well-known social Darwinist, also contributed to pro-imperialist sentiment at the turn of the nineteenth century. These famous writings were, however, but a small sample of the range and style of arguments in favor of the new colonialism. Commentators from around the world and from a wide variety of perspectives attempted to justify or explain the dramatic changes in global politics, economics, and culture. Some of these explanations, like that of Karl Marx (a surprising supporter of British colonial policy in India), were primarily economic in character and focused on patterns of world development. Students should keep in mind, of course, that thinkers as dynamic as Spencer, Kipling, and Marx wrote on a wide variety of topics. Although they are grouped here in a section entitled "The Imperialists," they represented a very wide spectrum of opinion and perspective. They would have made strange bedfellows indeed if one could have brought them all together. Moreover, someone like Marx, while explaining and advocating for British overseas action in India, would probably chafe at the label "imperialist" applied to him.

Other observers, especially European apologists such as Jules Ferry, tended to describe the new imperial activity either as an important part of "great nation" status or as a type of "civilizing mission," religious or secular in nature. These types of arguments usually stressed either the political or moral dimension of colonialism. Within Europe, for example, there were various ways of promoting overseas expansion, from claims of the superiority of European culture and technology to the need for areas to develop trade or to settle immigrants. Pro-imperialists came from a wide variety of backgrounds and used an equally wide variety of media to press their arguments. Posters, advertisements, parliamentary speeches, and literature could all be employed to illustrate or convince people of the virtue or necessity of overseas colonies and imperial relationships. In this section of the reader, students will therefore find examples of visual images, political addresses, and literary works, all of which carried a pro-imperial slant.

Joseph Conrad, the Polish-born novelist who wrote in English, might be described as an ambivalent imperialist. In his writings, he was frequently critical of European motives and methods in colonizing Africa. Some of his writing is indeed a satire on European attitudes toward imperialism. At the same time, his writings often reflected some of those same attitudes by referring to Africa as a "dark" and uncivilized continent, which had corrupting influences upon Europeans. Conrad is represented in this part of the reader by a selection entitled "An Outpost of Progress." Arthur James Balfour was one of the most experienced politicians of the early twentieth century. His name is most often associated with a 1917 "declaration" that committed Great Britain to a policy of allowing Jewish migration to Palestine, a development that would lead to much conflict and controversy throughout the twentieth century and indeed to the present day. In the selection provided here, Balfour is addressing the British Parliament on the question of his nation's involvement in Egypt in particular and "the Orient" in general. He argues that one should recognize the historical greatness of a land like Egypt but still realize that "oriental" states have not produced self-government, a gift that comes from Europeans and which gives them the right to rule over Africans and Asians. Balfour's is a complex and subtle pro-imperialist statement. The selection from Mary Seacole's *Wonderful Adventures* offers a fascinating perspective on colonial activity in the nineteenth century. As a Creole woman from Jamaica, she might have been a critic of expanding European empires in the nineteenth century. Seacole, however, found herself supporting in general the extension of European influence around the globe.

As we have already seen, imperialism and colonialism were global phenomena in the late nineteenth and early twentieth centuries. States as diverse as Meiji Japan and the Ottoman Empire were concerned with either maintaining their hold over territories or acquiring new ones to fuel imperialist ambitions and often used western approaches to accomplish these goals. In the selection, "Emperor Meiji's Letter to President Grant on Iwakura Mission, 1871," we see how a strengthening Japan articulated its own pro-colonial aims. In the piece, "An Ottoman Government Decree Defines the Official Notion of the 'Modern' Citizen," we have an attempt by an older imperial state to employ contemporary rhetoric and definitions—"the modern citizen"—to shore up its control over subject peoples. Some historians have also seen the expansion of Russia and the United States as examples of land-based empires in the nineteenth and early twentieth centuries. Students should keep all of these issues in mind as they read the various pieces from Part I.

▲

Le Tonkin et la Mère-Patrie (Tonkin and the Motherland)

JULES FERRY

In the late nineteenth century, European commentators from a variety of backgrounds voiced their opinions about imperialism. Some of these commentators offered contemporary intellectual or cultural reasons to justify Europe's dramatic expansion into overseas territories, primarily in Africa and Asia. Jules Ferry (1832–93) was the French prime minister from 1880–81 and again from 1883–85, the period during which the age of high imperialism took off. Ferry was an ardent supporter of French colonial expansion and as such was a major participant in the Berlin Conference of 1885 (see Introduction). While prime minister, he oversaw France's expansion into Tunisia, Madagascar, central West Africa, and Indochina.

Following is an excerpt from Ferry's lengthy introductory chapter to a book about Indochina published in 1890. Ferry's chapter is first and foremost a defense of his policies while prime minister, policies that had since received some criticism in the public arena. The portion of the chapter reproduced here offers Ferry's explanation for why imperialism was inevitable and natural for industrialized nations.

▲

QUESTIONS

1. How, according to Ferry, are industrialization and colonial expansion related?
2. Note that Ferry uses the word *natural* more than once in this excerpt. Why do you think this might be?

[. . .] Colonial policy is the daughter of industrial policy. For rich states, where capital abounds and accumulates rapidly, where the manufacturing regime is on the path of continual growth, attracting to itself if not the majority, at least the most awake and lively among the population of manual workers, where the culture of the land is condemned to support industrialization, exports are an essential factor in public prosperity, and the use of capital, like the demand for work, is measured by the size of foreign markets. If there could be established among manufacturing nations something along the lines of a division of industrial labor, a methodical and rational allocation of industry according to ability and the economic, natural, and social conditions of the different producing countries—placing here the cotton and metallurgy industries, reserving for one alcohol and sugar, and for another wool and silk—Europe would not have to look beyond its own borders for outlets for its products. It was with this ideal in mind that they made the treaties of 1860. But today, everyone

Source: Jules Ferry. *Le Tonkin et la Mère-Patrie* [Tonkin and the Motherland]. (Trans., J. Megan Greene.) Paris: Victor-Havard, 1890. Pp. 40–43.

wants to spin and weave, forge and distill. All of Europe manufactures sugar in excess and wishes to export it. The arrival on the scene of the latest comers to industrialism—the United States on the one hand, Germany on the other, the advent of the small states, of sleepy and lazy people, of the regenerated Italy, of Spain enriched by French capital, and of Switzerland, so enterprising and informed—to the industrial life, has sent the entire Occident, except for Russia, which is still preparing and growing, on a slope that cannot be climbed back up.

From the other side of the Vosges, as from beyond the Atlantic, the protection system has multiplied manufactures, suppressed old outlets, and thrust on the European market a formidable competition. To defend one's perimeters by raising barriers is something, but it is not enough. Mister Torrens has well demonstrated, in his good book on the colonization of Australia, that a growth in manufacturing capital, if it is not accompanied by a proportional expansion of outlets abroad, will produce, simply through domestic competition, a general lowering of prices, profits, and wages. (Torrens, *Colonisation of South Australia*).

The protection system is a steam engine without a safety valve if it doesn't have as a corrective and a back up a healthy and serious colonial policy. An excess of capital committed to industry tends not only to diminish the profits of capital, it stops the rise of wages, even though that [rising wages] is a natural law and beneficial to modern societies. And that is not an abstract law, but a phenomenon made of flesh and blood, of passion and will, that moves, complains, and defends itself. Preservation of social harmony is, in humanity's industrial age, a question of outlets. The economic crisis that has weighed so heavily on the European working class since 1876 or 1877, the malaise that has followed it, of which frequent, long, and often ill advised, but always formidable strikes are the most painful symptoms, coincided in France, Germany, and England with a notable and persistent reduction in exports. Europe is like a business that wants, after a certain number of years, to diminish its sales revenue. European consumption is saturated and it [Europe] must now conjure up from other parts of the globe new groups of consumers or suffer the penalty of bankrupting modern society and preparing for the dawn of the twentieth century a social cataclysm of which we cannot know how to calculate the consequences. [. . .]

Jungles To-day Are Gold Mines To-Morrow

Artist: E. McKnight Kauffer

*This 1927 advertisement from the Empire Marketing Board makes vivid some of the economic
arguments for British expansion into sub-Saharan or tropical Africa. Considerations about
raw materials and overseas markets were central to debates surrounding imperialism. The ongoing industrial revolution required access to raw materials and markets for industrial products,
and some proponents of imperialism believed that Africa and Asia were good territory for both.
The Empire Marketing Board produced numerous advertisements that made effective use of both
language and images to convey to the British public the important role of empire in British economic development.*

Questions

1. What impressions of Africans and Africa might people viewing this promotional poster
   have formed?
2. Examine the statistics, words, and images in the poster. What messages about the benefits of empire did the Empire Marketing Board hope to convey?
3. Consider this advertisement in light of arguments made by Ferry, Marx, and Lenin (in
   Part II) about the economic components of imperialism.

Source: E. McKnight Kauffer, National Archives Image Library, UK.

The White Man's Burden

RUDYARD KIPLING

The poem "The White Man's Burden" is perhaps the classic defense of western imperialism in the late nineteenth century. In seven short stanzas, Rudyard Kipling outlined what he believed were the positive arguments for Europeans to be colonizing Africans and Asians. The poem's direct audience was the United States, however. Writing in 1899, Kipling dedicated the poem to the United States after its annexation of the Philippines. He was urging the emerging economic powerhouse to play its proper role in the world: educator, tamer, and civilizer of "new caught, sullen peoples, half devil and half child."

Although frequently cited and referred to in discussions of imperialism, Kipling's poem is not always fully understood. By arguing that white men's involvement overseas should be based primarily on moral and not political or economic considerations, he was making the entire colonizing project more palatable to a broad spectrum of people in Europe and the United States. Liberals and conservatives, high-born and low-born, could respond to his arguments to banish disease, to wage wars of peace, and to check famine. Finally, Kipling also provided Europeans with a reason for understanding resistance to their colonial aims: people emerging from the dark do not like to be brought into the light. The poem was a powerful and succinct defense of European imperialism at its height.

Kipling (1864–1936) was born in India and educated in England. In 1882, he returned to India, the "Jewel in the Crown" of the British Empire, and became a well-known journalist and writer.

QUESTIONS

1. How do you think such arguments as those presented in "The White Man's Burden" were received in Europe and North America?

2. What is the full range of positive arguments Kipling offers in his defense of imperialism?

3. Are arguments similar to Kipling's still found in discussions of world politics today?

Source: Rudyard Kipling. "The White Man's Burden." *Collected Verse*. Garden City, NY: Doubleday, 1907. Pp. 215–217.

The White Man's Burden

1899

Take up the White Man's burden—
Send forth the best ye breed—
Go bind your sons to exile
To serve your captives' need;
To wait in heavy harness
On fluttered folk and wild—
Your new-caught, sullen peoples,
Half devil and half child.

Take up the White Man's burden—
In patience to abide,
To veil the threat of terror
And check the show of pride;
By open speech and simple,
An hundred times made plain.
To seek another's profit,
And work another's gain.

Take up the White Man's burden—
The savage wars of peace—
Fill full the mouth of Famine
And bid the sickness cease;
And when your goal is nearest
The end for others sought,
Watch Sloth and heathen Folly
Bring all your hope to nought.

Take up the White Man's burden—
No tawdry rule of kings,
But toil of serf and sweeper—

The tale of common things.
The ports ye shall not enter,
The roads ye shall not tread,
Go make them with your living,
And mark them with your dead.

Take up the White Man's burden—
And reap his old reward:
The blame of those ye better,
The hate of those ye guard—
The cry of hosts ye humour
(Ah slowly!) toward the light:—
"Why brought ye us from bondage,
"Our loved Egyptian night?"

Take up the White Man's burden—
Ye dare not stoop to less—
Nor call too loud on Freedom
To cloak your weariness;
By all ye cry or whisper,
By all ye leave or do,
The silent, sullen peoples
Shall weigh your Gods and you.

Take up the White Man's burden—
Have done with childish days—
The lightly proffered laurel,
The easy, ungrudged praise.
Comes now, to search your manhood
Through all the thankless years,
Cold, edged with dear-bought wisdom,
The judgment of your peers!

∧

Pears' Soap Advertisement

The idea of the white man's burden gained wide currency and carried with it notions of civilization that made it suitable for marketing Western products such as soap. As early Western missionaries to the colonies preached, cleanliness was next to godliness. Although indigenous peoples in the colonies had their own cleansing practices, the combination of new nineteenth-century European

Source: From *Collier's*, October 4, 1899.

cleansing practices involving the use of relatively inexpensively manufactured soap and the rhetorical construction of native peoples as dirty savages that arose from attempts to legitimize imperialism paved the way for the marketing of soap as a civilizing product.

▲

QUESTIONS

1. How are language and images used in the advertisement to show the hierarchy of civilizations?
2. In what ways does the advertisement hint at ideas about a hierarchy of races?
3. What Western values are portrayed in this advertisement?
4. In what ways do economics and ideology appear to interplay here?

Illustrations of Universal Progress

Herbert Spencer

Among the many theories used to rationalize imperialism was that of social Darwinism, which drew on new ideas in the natural sciences by applying the ideas of evolution, natural selection, and survival of the fittest to the human landscape. Advocates of social Darwinism argued that people, races, and human institutions would survive only if they were fit enough to do so and that through competition the weak would be left behind. Although early social Darwinists, like Herbert Spencer, did not apply the theory to imperialism, the theory was nonetheless taken up by proponents of imperialism, who saw European and American domination of other parts of the globe as justified and legitimized by the idea of natural selection. Europeans and their descendants, according to the more extreme social Darwinists, were the fittest and thus best equipped to govern other parts of the world. Interestingly, this interpretation of social Darwinism was turned on its head by some victims of imperialism and white oppression, including East Asian and African American intellectuals, who believed that through competition and the struggle to survive, they, too, could compete and win.

A British journalist and writer, Herbert Spencer (1820–1903) was known for his pragmatic, liberal views on politics and economics, and his writings heavily influenced a number of British and American capitalists who were his contemporaries. The following excerpts come from Herbert Spencer's Illustrations of Universal Progress, *published in 1865. An early evolutionist, Spencer was a contemporary of Charles Darwin and has often been characterized as his rival.*

QUESTIONS

1. How does Spencer use biology to claim that there is a hierarchy of races?
2. What notions of progress does Spencer promote in this selection? How does he seem to define progress?
3. How might these ideas be employed to justify or explain imperialism?

[. . .] In respect to that progress which individual organisms display in the course of their evolution, this question has been answered by the Germans. The investigations of Wolff, Goethe, and Von Baer, have established the truth that the series of changes gone through during the development of a seed into a tree, or an ovum into an animal, constitute an advance from homogeneity of structure to heterogeneity of structure. In its primary stage, every germ consists of a substance that is uniform throughout, both in texture and chemical composition. The first step is the appearance of a difference between two parts of this substance; or, as the phenomenon is called in physiological language, a differentiation. Each of these differentiated divisions presently begins itself to exhibit some contrast

Source: Herbert Spencer. *Illustrations of Universal Progress.* New York: D. Appleton & Company, 1864. Pp. 2–3, 10–13.

of parts; and by and by these secondary differentiations become as definite as the original one. This process is continuously repeated—is simultaneously going on in all parts of the growing embryo; and by endless such differentiations there is finally produced that complex combination of tissues and organs constituting the adult animal or plant. This is the history of all organisms whatever. It is settled beyond dispute that organic progress consists in a change from the homogeneous to the heterogeneous.

Now, we propose in the first place to show, that this law of organic progress is the law of all progress. Whether it be in the development of the Earth, in the development of Life upon its surface, in the development of Society, of Government, of Manufactures, of Commerce, of Language, Literature, Science, Art, this same evolution of the simple into the complex, through successive differentiations, holds throughout. From the earliest traceable cosmical changes down to the latest results of civilization, we shall find that the transformation of the homogeneous into the heterogeneous, is that in which Progress essentially consists. [. . .]

Whether an advance from the homogeneous to the heterogeneous is or is not displayed in the biological history of the globe, it is clearly enough displayed in the progress of the latest and most heterogeneous creature—Man. It is alike true that, during the period in which the Earth has been peopled, the human organism has grown more heterogeneous among the civilized divisions of the species; and that the species, as a whole, has been growing more heterogeneous in virtue of the multiplication of races and the differentiation of these races from each other.

In proof of the first of these positions, we may cite the fact that, in the relative development of the limbs, the civilized man departs more widely from the general type of the placental mammalia than do the lower human races. While often possessing well-developed body and arms, the Papuan has extremely small legs: thus reminding us of the quadrumana, in which there is no great contrast in size between the hind and fore limbs.

But in the European, the greater length and massiveness of the legs has become very marked—the fore and hind limbs are relatively more heterogeneous. Again, the greater ratio which the cranial bones bear to the facial bones illustrates the same truth. Among the vertebrata in general, progress is marked by an increasing heterogeneity in the vertebral column, and more especially in the vertebrae constituting the skull: the higher forms being distinguished by the relatively larger size of the bones which cover the brain, and the relatively smaller size of those which form the jaw, &c. Now, this characteristic, which is stronger in Man than in any other creature, is stronger in the European than in the savage. Moreover, judging from the greater extent and variety of faculty he exhibits, we may infer that the civilized man has also a more complex or heterogeneous nervous system than the uncivilized man: and indeed the fact is in part visible in the increased ratio which his cerebrum bears to the subjacent ganglia.

If further elucidation be needed, we may find it in every nursery. The infant European has sundry marked points of resemblance to the lower human races; as in the flatness of the alæ of the nose, the depression of its bridge, the divergence and forward opening of the nostrils, the form of the lips, the absence of a frontal sinus, the width between the eyes, the smallness of the legs. Now, as the developmental process by which these traits are turned into those of the adult European, is a continuation of that change from the homogeneous to the heterogeneous displayed during the previous evolution of the embryo, which every physiologist will admit; it follows that the parallel developmental process by which the like traits of the barbarous races have been turned into those of the civilized races, has also been a continuation of the change from the homogeneous to the heterogeneous. The truth of the second position—that Mankind, as a whole, have become more heterogeneous—is so obvious as scarcely to need illustration. Every work on Ethnology, by its divisions and subdivisions of races, bears testimony to it. Even were we to admit the hypothesis that Mankind originated from several separate stocks, it would still remain true, that as, from each of these stocks, there have sprung many now widely different tribes, which are proved by philological evidence to have had a common origin, the race as a whole is far less homogeneous than it once was. Add to which, that we have, in the Anglo-Americans, an example of a new variety arising within these few generations; and that, if we may trust to the description of observers, we are likely soon to have another such example in Australia.

On passing from Humanity under its individual form, to Humanity as socially embodied, we find the general law still more variously exemplified. The change from the homogeneous to the heterogeneous is displayed equally in the progress of civilization as a whole, and in the progress of every tribe or nation; and is still going on with increasing rapidity. As we see in existing barbarous tribes, society in its first and lowest form is a homogeneous aggregation of individuals having like powers and like functions: the only marked difference of function being that which accompanies difference of sex. Every man is warrior, hunter, fisherman, tool-maker, builder; every woman performs the same drudgeries; every family is self-sufficing, and save for purposes of aggression and defence, might as well live apart from the rest. Very early, however, in the process of social evolution, we find an incipient differentiation between the governing and the governed. Some kind of chieftainship seems coeval with the first advance from the state of separate wandering families to that of a nomadic tribe. The authority of the strongest makes itself felt among a body of savages as in a herd of animals, or a posse of schoolboys. At first, however, it is indefinite, uncertain; is shared by others of scarcely inferior power; and is unaccompanied by any difference in occupation or style of living: the first ruler kills his own game, makes his own weapons, builds his own hut, and economically considered, does not differ from others of his tribe. Gradually, as the tribe progresses, the contrast between the governing and the governed grows more decided. Supreme power becomes hereditary in one family; the head of that family, ceasing to provide for his own wants, is served by others; and he begins to assume the sole office of ruling. [. . .]

The Indian Court at the Great Exhibition

Artist: Joseph Nash

The Great Exhibition of the Works of Industry of all Nations, 1851, held in the newly built Crystal Palace located in Hyde Park, London, was a showcase of both the technology of the industrial revolution and the exotic products of empire. The Crystal Palace itself was a display of new architectural techniques involving the combined use of iron and glass. Inside the building were endless displays of British products and machines and people and products from around the world, many from the growing British Empire. The Great Exhibition was the first of its kind and had a huge influence on British society. This image shows part of the India display.

Questions

1. How does the Crystal Palace show the power and status of Great Britain?
2. What items representing India do you see? What impression might you get of India from viewing them?

Source: Joseph Nash, Victoria & Albert Museum, UK.

The British Rule in India

Karl Marx

In the nineteenth century, pro-imperialist arguments could come from seemingly unlikely places. In this newspaper article from 1853, Karl Marx, the most famous socialist theoretician of the day, argued that Britain's colonial conquest of India was a necessary development if mankind was to "fulfill its destiny." In this piece, Marx was highly critical of India's social development before the English political takeover of the subcontinent. He offered a number of critiques of Hinduism in particular and Indian practices in general. Although he was equally unimpressed by English motives in acquiring India, he saw it as part of a historical process, namely, the bringing about of a social revolution in India. This interpretation was tied to Marx's fundamental idea that societies must move from a feudal to a bourgeois or capitalist stage before they are prepared to achieve a socialist revolution.

Marx (1818–83) wrote widely on a number of subjects—economics, politics, history, law, for example—in a long career, much of which was spent in exile from his native Germany. Marx was also a political activist who joined a number of progressive or radical organizations. In some European countries, most notably Germany and Russia, his ideas were adopted in outline to create political movements to challenge the political status quo. In the course of this development, his ideas were often simplified or adapted to fit changing political circumstances. Thus, his work and his contribution to intellectual debates and global developments have remained matters of intense debate and scrutiny.

Questions

1. What critiques of traditional India (India before English rule) does Marx offer?
2. What do you think Marx means by "oriental despotism"?

[. . .] Now, sickening as it must be to human feeling to witness those myriads of industrious patriarchal and inoffensive social organizations disorganized and dissolved into their units, thrown into a sea of woes, and their individual members losing at the same time their ancient form of civilization and their hereditary means of subsistence, we must not forget that these idyllic village communities, inoffensive though they may appear, had always been the solid foundation of Oriental despotism, that they restrained the human mind within the smallest possible compass, making it the unresisting tool of superstition, enslaving it beneath traditional rules, depriving it of all grandeur and historical energies. We must not forget the barbarian egotism which, concentrating on some miserable patch of land, had quietly witnessed the ruin of empires, the perpetration of unspeakable cruelties, the massacre of the population of large towns, with no other consideration bestowed upon them than on natural events, itself the helpless prey of any aggressor who deigned to notice it at all. We

Source: Karl Marx. "The British Rule in India." *New York Daily Tribune*. 25 June 1853.

must not forget that this undignified, stagnatory, and vegetative life, that this passive sort of existence evoked on the other part, in contradistinction, wild, aimless, unbounded forces of destruction, and rendered murder itself a religious rite in Hindostan [India]. We must not forget that these little communities were contaminated by distinctions of caste and by slavery, that they subjugated man to external circumstances instead of elevating man [to be] the sovereign of circumstances, that they transformed a self-developing social state into never changing natural destiny, and thus brought about a brutalizing worship of nature, exhibiting its degradation in the fact that man, the sovereign of nature, fell down on his knees in adoration of Kanuman, the monkey, and Sabbala, the cow [Hindu Gods].

England, it is true, in causing a social revolution in Hindostan, was actuated only by the vilest interests, and was stupid in her manner of enforcing them. But that is not the question. The question is, can mankind fulfil its destiny without a fundamental revolution in the social state of Asia? If not, whatever may have been the crimes of England she was the unconscious tool of history in bringing about that revolution. [. . .]

▲

Emperor Meiji's Letter to President Grant on Iwakura Mission, 1871

As part of its Pacific expansion, U.S. President Millard Fillmore sent Commodore Perry on two expeditions to Japan in 1853 and 1854. These expeditions had as their purpose the "opening" of Japan to America as a trading partner. Perry intimidated Japan with his naval power and forced it to sign an unequal treaty that gave the United States a series of unfair economic and diplomatic rights. This treaty was quickly followed by similarly unequal treaties with other Western nations that had interests in Japan and East Asia. Heavily criticized by many of Japan's leading samurai for having signed these treaties, the feudal Tokugawa government (1603–1868) gradually lost its hold on Japanese society and was eventually replaced by a new, centralized, imperial government supported by a powerful group of young samurai and led by the young Meiji emperor. The anti-Tokugawa, pro-imperial movement was motivated primarily by the desire to defend Japan against Western imperialism and to keep it from being colonized by the same Western countries that were already carving out "spheres of influence" in neighboring China.

The new Meiji government undertook to modernize the political, social, and economic systems of Japan so as to enable Japan to compete with the West. As part of this effort, the government sent missions abroad to study Western institutions and methods. One such expedition was the Iwakura Mission of 1871–73, led by Iwakura Tomomi, which had as one of its goals the renegotiation of the unequal treaties. The unequal treaties were not, however, immediately revoked, and the continuing quest to overturn them surely motivated Japan's imperialist ventures in the late nineteenth and early twentieth centuries.

▲

QUESTIONS

1. What strategies does the Meiji Emperor employ in his effort to encourage President Grant to consider revising the unequal treaties?

2. What seems to motivate Japanese plans to adopt Western institutions?

3. What sets Japan apart from other places that were facing imperialist threats in the late nineteenth century?

Mutsuhito, Emperor of Japan, etc., to the President of the United States of America, our good brother and faithful friend, greeting:

Mr. President: Whereas since our accession by the blessing of heaven to the sacred throne on which our ancestors reigned from time immemorial, we have not dispatched any embassy to the Courts and Governments of friendly countries. We have thought fit to select our trusted and honored minister, Iwakura Tomomi, the Junior Prime

Source: "Emperor Meiji's Letter to President Grant on Iwakura Mission, 1871." In David John Lu (Ed.), *Sources of Japanese History, Volume 2*. New York: McGraw Hill, 1974. Pp. 51–52.

Minister (*udaijin*), as Ambassador Extraordinary and have associated with him Kido Takayoshi, member of the Privy Council; Ōkubo Toshimichi, Minister of Finance; Itō Hirobumi, Acting Minister of Public Works; and Yamaguchi Masanao, Assistant Minister for Foreign Affairs Associate Ambassadors Extraordinary, and invested them with full powers to proceed to the Government of the United States, as well as to other Governments, in order to declare our cordial friendship, and to place the peaceful relations between our respective nations on a firmer and broader basis. The period for revising the treaties now existing between ourselves and the United States is less than one year distant. We expect and intend to reform and improve the same so as to stand upon a similar footing with the most enlightened nations, and to attain the full development of public rights and interest. The civilization and institutions of Japan are so different from those of other countries that we cannot expect to reach the declared end at once. It is our purpose to select from the various institutions prevailing among enlightened nations such as are best suited to our present conditions, and adapt them in gradual reforms and improvements of our policy and customs so as to be upon an equality with them. With this object we desire to fully disclose to the United States Government the condition of affairs in our Empire, and to consult upon the means of giving greater efficiency to our institutions at present and in the future, and as soon as the said Embassy returns home we will consider the revision of the treaties and accomplish what we have expected and intended. The Ministers who compose this Embassy have our confidence and esteem. We request you to favor them with full credence and due regard, and we earnestly pray for your continued health and happiness, and for the peace and prosperity of your great Republic.

In witness whereof we have hereunto set our hand and the great seal of our Empire, at our palace in the city of Tokyo, this fourth day of eleventh month, of fourth year of Meiji.

▲

An Outpost of Progress

Joseph Conrad

Joseph Conrad (1857–1924) was born in the Ukraine to exiled Polish parents. He sailed as a French and then British merchant marine from 1874 to 1894 before settling in England to write. Much of Conrad's literature was inspired by his travels, and both "An Outpost of Progress" (1898) and his best-known novel Heart of Darkness *(1899) drew heavily on Conrad's experience in the Congo in 1890. "An Outpost of Progress" was set in the Congo, which had been colonized over the course of the 1880s by Belgium's King Leopold. By 1890, Leopold's will to make the Congo profitable at the expense of its residents and natural environment was evident, and Conrad observed the excesses of Leopold's commercial regime at the time of his visit. Conrad wrote ironically of his reaction to the Congo in the introduction to a 1923 edition of* Tales of Unrest, *"Other men have found a lot of quite different things there {in Africa} and I have the comfortable conviction that what I took would not have been of much use to anybody else. And it must be said that it was but a very small amount of plunder." (Conrad,* Tales of Unrest, *p. ix)*

Tales of Unrest is about two white men, Kayerts and Carlier, who are sent by the Great Trading Company to a remote trading post up a river in Africa. It narrates the relationship between the two men and their relationship with Africa. The story begins with the two new arrivals coming to terms with their new environment. As the story progresses and the river boat, which had been supposed to return to supply them in six months, is delayed, the two men are increasingly affected by the climate, the threatening and unknown atmosphere, the isolation of "Africa" and their outpost, and their failure to engage enough with their environment to secure sufficient food to eat. They ultimately succumb to hunger, disease, and madness, and shed all vestiges of the "civilization" that they saw themselves as bringing to Africa. The following excerpt is from the first section of the story, in which the two men have only just arrived at their remote outpost and are adjusting to their new life.

▲

Questions

1. To what extent do Kayerts and Carlier actually seem to engage with Africa?

2. What are their attitudes toward Africa and toward their own roles there?

3. What has led these two men into the service of the Great Trading Company?

4. Do the contents of the article "Our Colonial Expansion" actually reflect their own experiences? To what extent are their views toward Africa shaped by the article?

Source: Joseph Conrad. "An Outpost of Progress." *Tales of Unrest.* New York: Doubleday, Page and Co., 1923. Pp. 88–95.

[. . .] Next day, some bales of cotton goods and a few cases of provisions having been thrown on shore, the sardine-box steamer went off, not to return for another six months. On the deck the director touched his cap to the two agents, who stood on the bank waving their hats, and turning to an old servant of the Company on his passage to headquarters, said, "Look at those two imbeciles. They must be mad at home to send me such specimens. I told those fellows to plant a vegetable garden, build new storehouses and fences, and construct a landing-stage. I bet nothing will be done! They won't know how to begin. I always thought the station on this river useless, and they just fit the station!"

"They will form themselves there," said the old stager with a quiet smile.

"At any rate, I am rid of them for six months," retorted the director.

The two men watched the steamer round the bend, then, ascending arm in arm the slope of the bank, returned to the station. They had been in this vast and dark country only a very short time, and as yet always in the midst of other white men, under the eye and guidance of their superiors. And now, dull as they were to the subtle influences of surroundings, they felt themselves very much alone, when suddenly left unassisted to face the wilderness; a wilderness rendered more strange, more incomprehensible by the mysterious glimpses of the vigorous life it contained. They were two perfectly insignificant and incapable individuals, whose existence is only rendered possible through the high organization of civilized crowds. Few men realize that their life, the very essence of their character, their capabilities and their audacities, are only the expression of their belief in the safety of their surroundings. The courage, the composure, the confidence; the emotions and principles; every great and every insignificant thought belongs not to the individual but to the crowd: to the crowd that believes blindly in the irresistible force of its institutions and of its morals, in the power of its police and of its opinion. But the contact with pure unmitigated savagery, with primitive nature and primitive man, brings sudden and profound trouble into the heart. To the sentiment of being alone of one's kind, to the clear perception of the loneliness of one's thoughts, of one's sensations—to the negation of the habitual, which is safe, there is added the affirmation of the unusual, which is dangerous; a suggestion of things vague, uncontrollable, and repulsive, whose discomposing intrusion excites the imagination and tries the civilized nerves of the foolish and the wise alike.

Kayerts and Carlier walked arm in arm, drawing close to one another as children do in the dark; and they had the same, not altogether unpleasant, sense of danger which one half suspects to be imaginary. They chatted persistently in familiar tones. "Our station is prettily situated," said one. The other assented with enthusiasm, enlarging volubly on the beauties of the situation. Then they passed near the grave. "Poor devil!" said Kayerts. "He died of fever, didn't he?" muttered Carlier, stopping short. "Why," retorted Kayerts, with indignation, "I've been told that the fellow exposed himself recklessly to the sun. The climate here, everybody says, is not at all worse than at home, as long as you keep out of the sun. Do you hear that, Carlier? I am chief here, and my orders are that you should not expose yourself to the sun!" He assumed his superiority jocularly, but his meaning was serious. The idea that he would, perhaps, have to bury Carlier and remain alone, gave him an inward shiver. He felt suddenly that this Carlier was more precious to him here, in the centre of Africa, than a brother could be anywhere else. Carlier, entering into the spirit of the thing, made a military salute and answered in a brisk tone, "Your orders shall be attended to, chief!" Then he burst out laughing, slapped Kayerts on the back and shouted, "We shall let life run easily here! Just sit still and gather in the ivory those savages will bring. This country has its good points, after all!" They both laughed loudly while Carlier thought: That poor Kayerts; he is so fat and unhealthy. It would be awful if I had to bury him here. He is a man I respect. . . . Before they reached the verandah of their house they called one another "my dear fellow."

The first day they were very active, pottering about with hammers and nails and red calico, to put up curtains, make their house habitable and pretty: resolved to settle down comfortably to their new life. For them an impossible task. To grapple effectually with even purely material problems requires more serenity of mind and more lofty courage than people generally imagine. No two beings could have been more unfitted for such a struggle. Society, not from any tenderness, but because of its strange needs, had taken care of those two men, forbidding them all independent thought, all initiative, all departure from routine; and forbidding it under pain of death. They could only live on condition of being machines. And now, released from the fostering care of men with pens behind the ears, or of men with gold lace on the sleeves, they were like those lifelong prisoners who, liberated after many years, do not know what use to make of their freedom. They did not know what use to make of their faculties, being both, through want of practice, incapable of independent thought.

At the end of two months Kayerts often would say, "If it was not for my Melie, you wouldn't catch me here." Melie was his daughter. He had thrown up his post in the Administration of the Telegraphs, though he had been for seventeen years perfectly happy there, to earn a dowry for his girl. His wife was dead, and the child was being brought up by his sisters. He regretted the streets, the pavements, the cafés, his friends of many years; all the things he used to see, day after day; all the thoughts suggested by familiar things—the thoughts effortless, monotonous, and soothing of a Government clerk; he regretted all the gossip, the small enmities, the mild venom, and the little jokes of Government offices. "If I had had a decent brother-in-law," Carlier would remark, "a fellow with a heart, I would not be here." He had left the army and had made himself so obnoxious to his family by his laziness and impudence, that an exasperated brother-in-law

had made superhuman efforts to procure him an appointment in the Company as a second-class agent. Having not a penny in the world he was compelled to accept this means of livelihood as soon as it became quite clear to him that there was nothing more to squeeze out of his relations. He, like Kayerts, regretted his old life. He regretted the clink of sabre and spurs on a fine afternoon, the barrack-room witticisms, the girls of garrison towns; but, besides, he had also a sense of grievance. He was evidently a much ill-used man. This made him moody, at times. But the two men got on well together in the fellowship of their stupidity and laziness. Together they did nothing, absolutely nothing, and enjoyed the sense of idleness for which they were paid. And in time they came to feel something resembling affection for one another.

They lived like blind men in a large room, aware only of what came in contact with them (and of that only imperfectly), but unable to see the general aspect of things. The river, the forest, all the great land throbbing with life, were like a great emptiness. Even the brilliant sunshine disclosed nothing intelligible. Things appeared and disappeared before their eyes in an unconnected and aimless kind of way. The river seemed to come from nowhere and flow nowhither. It flowed through a void. Out of that void, at times, came canoes, and men with spears in their hands would suddenly crowd the yard of the station. They were naked, glossy black, ornamented with snowy shells and glistening brass wire, perfect of limb. They made an uncouth babbling noise when they spoke, moved in a stately manner, and sent quick, wild glances out of their startled, never-resting eyes. Those warriors would squat in long rows, four or more deep, before the verandah, while their chiefs bargained for hours with Makola over an elephant tusk. Kayerts sat on his chair and looked down on the proceedings, understanding nothing. He stared at them with his round blue eyes, called out to Carlier, "Here, look! look at that fellow there—and that other one, to the left. Did you ever see such a face? Oh, the funny brute!"

Carlier, smoking native tobacco in a short wooden pipe, would swagger up twirling his moustaches, and surveying the warriors with haughty indulgence, would say—

"Fine animals. Brought any bone? Yes? It's not any too soon. Look at the muscles of that fellow—third from the end. I wouldn't care to get a punch on the nose from him. Fine arms, but legs no good below the knee. Couldn't make cavalry men of them." And after glancing down complacently at his own shanks, he always concluded: "Pah! Don't they stink! You, Makola! Take that herd over to the fetish" (the storehouse was in every station called the fetish, perhaps because of the spirit of civilization it contained) "and give them up some of the rubbish you keep there. I'd rather see it full of bone than full of rags."

Kayerts approved.

"Yes, yes! Go and finish that palaver over there, Mr. Makola. I will come round when you are ready, to weigh the tusk. We must be careful." Then turning to his companion: "This is the tribe that lives down the river; they are rather aromatic. I remember, they had been once before here. D'ye hear that row? What a fellow has got to put up with in this dog of a country! My head is split."

Such profitable visits were rare. For days the two pioneers of trade and progress would look on their empty courtyard in the vibrating brilliance of vertical sunshine. Below the high bank, the silent river flowed on glittering and steady. On the sands in the middle of the stream, hippos and alligators sunned themselves side by side. And stretching away in all directions, surrounding the insignificant cleared spot of the trading post, immense forests, hiding fateful complications of fantastic life, lay in the eloquent silence of mute greatness. The two men understood nothing, cared for nothing but for the passage of days that separated them from the steamer's return. Their predecessor had left some torn books. They took up these wrecks of novels, and, as they had never read anything of the kind before, they were surprised and amused. Then during long days there were interminable and silly discussions about plots and personages. In the centre of Africa they made acquaintance of Richelieu and of d'Artagnan, of Hawk's Eye and of Father Goriot, and of many other people. All these imaginary personages became subjects for gossip as if they had been living friends. They discounted their virtues, suspected their motives, decried their successes; were scandalized at their duplicity or were doubtful about their courage. The accounts of crimes filled them with indignation, while tender or pathetic passages moved them deeply. Carlier cleared his throat and said in a soldierly voice, "What nonsense!" Kayerts, his round eyes suffused with tears, his fat cheeks quivering, rubbed his bald head, and declared, "This is a splendid book. I had no idea there were such clever fellows in the world." They also found some old copies of a home paper. That print discussed what it was pleased to call "Our Colonial Expansion" in high-flown language. It spoke much of the rights and duties of civilization, of the sacredness of the civilizing work, and extolled the merits of those who went about bringing light and faith and commerce to the dark places of the earth. Carlier and Kayerts read, wondered, and began to think better of themselves. Carlier said one evening, waving his hand about, "In a hundred years, there will be perhaps a town here. Quays, and warehouses, and barracks, and—and—billiard-rooms. Civilization, my boy, and virtue—and all. And then, chaps will read that two good fellows, Kayerts and Carlier, were the first civilized men to live in this very spot!" Kayerts nodded, "Yes, it is a consolation to think of that." [. . .]

British Officer Reclining

Although the living situation of Kayerts and Carlier depicted by Conrad would probably not have been quite as comfortable as that depicted in this photograph, we can nonetheless imagine from their story something of the life of the British officer portrayed here. This photograph of a British officer reclining while being fanned and otherwise served by two Indian attendants offers us a glimpse of the colonial lifestyle. It also gives us a sense of race, class, and labor divisions in colonial India.

QUESTIONS

1. What impression of the relationship between the British and Indians do we get from this image?
2. What sort of lifestyle did the British in India appear to have?
3. What things do you notice about clothing, furniture, and architecture in this photograph?

Problems with Which We Have to Deal in Egypt

Arthur James Balfour

Arthur James Balfour's name is most often associated with a 1917 declaration that committed Great Britain to a policy of Jewish migration to Palestine. He was a man of remarkably wide political experience who served the British government in a number of capacities, including for a time as prime minister. He followed closely most of Britain's overseas colonial moves (Afghanistan, South Africa, the Sudan, Egypt, etc.) of the late nineteenth and early twentieth centuries.

In this speech to the House of Commons (13 June 1910), Balfour is defending the need for continuing British involvement in Egypt. Some of his contemporaries had begun to question the economic and sometimes political and cultural benefits of Britain's overseas colonies. Speaking with great authority and against the background of a long career of public service, Balfour sought to convince his colleagues of the importance of Britain's colonial efforts. In particular, he sought to rebut a challenge from J. M. Robertson, also a member of the House of Commons, who had posed the question, "What right have you to take up these airs of superiority with regard to people whom you choose to call Oriental?" Balfour's response was a fascinating defense of early twentieth-century imperialism. He acknowledged all of the importance of Egypt's storied past but still maintained that Europeans in general and the British in particular had to be involved in Africa and Asia, because in their long history the "Orientals" have never produced self-government (by which he means popular government). Thus, he argues that the Egyptians, and by extension all "Orientals," have it better under British rule than under their own despotic rulers.

Questions

1. What might be the accomplishments of Egyptian civilization to which Balfour is referring in his speech? Why does he claim that Englishmen would have been so familiar with these accomplishments?

2. What does Balfour mean when he says that "we are in Egypt not merely for the sake of the Egyptians, though we are there for their sake; we are there also for the sake of Europe at large"?

3. What do you make of the logic of Balfour's arguments? How do you think that imperialists of his convictions reconciled the idea of the benefits of "self-government" to colonized peoples?

Source: Arthur James Balfour. Speech to the House of Commons on the "Problems with which we have to deal in Egypt." 13 June 1910. *The Parliamentary Debates* (Official Report). Fifth Series, Volume XVII. London. Pp. 1140–41, 1142–44.

[. . .] I take up no attitude of superiority. But I ask those two hon[orable] Members and everybody else who has even the most superficial knowledge of history, if they will really try to look in the face the facts with which a British statesman has to deal when he is put in a position of supremacy over great races like the inhabitants of Egypt and countries in the East. We know the civilisation of Egypt better than we know the civilisation of any other country. We know it further back; we know it more intimately; we know more about it. It goes far beyond the petty span of the history of our own race, which is lost in the prehistoric period at a time when the Egyptian civilisation had already passed its prime. Look at all the Oriental countries. Do not talk about superiority or inferiority.

Look at the facts of the case. Western nations as soon as they emerge into history show the beginnings of those capacities for self-government, not always associated, I grant, with all the virtues or all the merits, but still having merits of their own. Nations of the West have shown those virtues from their beginning, from the very tribal origin of which we have first knowledge. You may look through the whole history of the Orientals in what is called, broadly speaking, the East, and you never find traces of self-government. All their great centuries—and they have been very great—have been passed under despotisms, under absolute government. All their great contributions to civilisation—and they have been great—have been made under that form of government. Conqueror has succeeded conqueror; one domination has followed another; but never in all the revolutions of fate and fortune have you seen one of those nations of its own motion establish what we, from a Western point of view, call self-government. That is the fact. It is not a question of superiority or inferiority. I suppose a true Eastern sage would say that the working government which we have taken upon ourselves in Egypt and elsewhere is not a work worthy of a philosopher—that it is the dirty work, the inferior work, of carrying on the necessary labour. Do let us put this question of superiority and inferiority out of our minds. It is wholly out of place. [. . .]

The point I am trying to press on the House is this. We have got, as I think, to deal with nations who, as far as our knowledge goes, have always been governed in the manner we call absolute, and have never had what we are accustomed to call free institutions or self-government. They have never had it; they have never, apparently, desired it. There is no evidence that until we indoctrinated them with the political philosophy, not always very profound, which has been in fashion in this country, they ever had the desire or the ambition which the hon[orable] Member opposite very naturally and properly wishes that they should have. The time may come when they will adopt, not merely our superficial philosophy, but our genuine practice. But after 3,000, 4,000, or 5,000 years of known history, and unlimited centuries of unknown history have been passed by these nations under a different system, it is not thirty years of British rule which is going to alter the character bred into them by this immemorial tradition.

If that be true, is it or is it not a good thing for these great nations—I admit their greatness—that this absolute Government should be exercised by us? I think it is a good thing. I think experience shows that they have got under it a far better government than in the whole history of the world they ever had before, and which not only is a benefit to them, but is undoubtedly a benefit to the whole of the civilised West. That has been pointed out by my honorable Friend and has not been denied by the Foreign Secretary. We are in Egypt not merely for the sake of the Egyptians, though we are there for their sake; we are there also for the sake of Europe at large. If this be the task which, as it has been thrown upon us we ought to take up, as it is a task which, at all events to the best of our knowledge and belief, is of infinite benefit to the races with whom we deal, what are the special difficulties attaching to it? The difficulties are very great and inevitable. There are those who talk as if the test of the excellence of our government were the gratitude which it elicited. A great reform in these countries, probably a great reform in any country, does elicit, usually, not always, gratitude at the moment of its inception. Certainly if you had consulted the fellaheen [Egyptian peasants] immediately following the period when we relieved them from the abominable treatment to which they were subjected before we went into Egypt, I have no doubt they would have expressed great and genuine gratitude. Generations pass. New men arise. Old memories vanish. Under a policy which casts pain and inconvenience on some members of the community ancient wrongs are forgotten, ancient benefits are forgotten likewise. All that remains are those complaints, sometimes just, most commonly, I believe, unjust, on which the agitator can work when he wishes to raise difficulties in his own interest or in the interests of some, as I think, impossible ideal. But if I am right, and if it is our business to govern, with or without gratitude, with or without the real and genuine memory of all the loss of which we have relieved the population, and no vivid imagination of all the benefits which we have given to them; if that is our duty, how is it to be performed, and how only can it be performed? We send out our very best to these countries. They work and strive, not for very great remuneration, not under very easy or very luxurious circumstances, to carry out

what they conceive to be their duty both to the country to which they belong and the populations which they serve. They carry out that work under difficulties which we sitting here quietly in Parliament can have no conception of. You place a single British official amidst tens of thousands of persons belonging to a different creed, a different race, a different discipline, different conditions of life. These officials can do that work, I believe, better then anybody, if they merely have the sense that they are being supported. If they lose that sense for a moment, rightly or wrongly—sometimes it is wrongly—their whole position is undermined. The base of their supplies, as it were, is cut off. They face a task which might well make anyone's courage fail under the happiest circumstances. They face it under circumstances which are most unhappy. Directly the native populations have that instinctive feeling that those with whom they have got to deal have not behind them the might, the authority, the sympathy, the full and ungrudging support of the country which sent them there, those populations lose all that sense of order which [is] the very basis of their civilisation, just as our officers lose all that sense of power and authority, which is the very basis of everything they can do for the benefit of those among whom they have been sent. [. . .]

▲

An Ottoman Government Decree Defines the Official Notion of the "Modern" Citizen, June 19, 1870

By the second half of the nineteenth century, the Ottoman Empire, which encompassed a large expanse of the Arab-Muslim world, was under increasing pressure internally and externally. An ancient empire dating from the fourteenth century and based in present-day Turkey, the Ottoman state was challenged by its subject peoples, domestic political and economic developments, and the adventurous international moves of European nations such as Great Britain and France. Under this set of pressures, some officials in the Ottoman Empire attempted to reform the state and society to make them more "modern." Their hope and aim was to preserve the political integrity and cultural authority of the Ottoman Empire and to promote an imperialist agenda.

This document makes clear one method for reshaping people—the Bedouins—living under the Ottoman state. By defining progress and productivity in terms of a settled way of life—the Bedouins were, after all, nomads—Ottoman officials hoped to "civilize" people living under their dominion and to create "modern," "useful" citizens. The document does more than outline arguments in favor of abandoning nomadic lifestyles; it also contains specific measures (tax, labor, and governance policies) intended to coerce the Bedouins into modernizing.

▲

QUESTIONS

1. What types of arguments are employed in the document to justify the notion of a modern citizen as a settled person? In particular, how were ideas about social evolution and religion used to justify the policies of the Ottoman Empire?

2. What territory specifically is addressed at the end of this document? What policies were supposed to go into effect in this territory?

To the model of proverbs and peers, His Excellency Firhan Pasha Zayd 'Alwa. It is known that if one compares the tribes and people who live in the lifestyle of Bedouins [nomadic tribes] with those urbane people who live in the cities and villages, one will note the complexity in the customs of city-folk. In contrast, it will be noted that in comparison to the original creation of man and his internal self, the way of life of Bedouins is simple. In fact, the primitive and original state of man is most likely the same as that of the Bedouin. However, God has graced human beings with a characteristic that is absent from any other [species]. According to this characteristic,

---

Source: "An Ottoman Government Decree Defines the Official Notion of the 'Modern' Citizen, 19 June 1870." In Akram Fouad Khater (Ed.), *Sources in the History of the Modern Middle East.* Boston: Houghton Mifflin, 2004. Pp. 19–21. Used with permission.

man cannot remain in his original state of creation but should prepare all that is needed for his food, drink, and clothing, and after this he must gather knowledge and develop commerce and other human necessities. He seeks to obtain other necessities as well, and every time he reaches a stage of acquisition, then he sees the need to advance and progress beyond what he had in the past. [. . .] Thus, it is apparent that even if the first state of man is to be a Bedouin, urbanity is a characteristic that cannot be separated from him. For the human being has become civilized [. . .] and the virtues of humanity cannot be attained except through the path of urbanization and civilization. Those who surpass their brethren and control all elements of this world, completely or partially, are those who live in the cities and who are civilized.

After proving that this is the case, we would like to explain and specify the reasons those people demand to remain in this state [of being Bedouins]. They remain in this state of deprivation of the virtues of humanity and the characteristics of civilization for several reasons. The first is that these people are ignorant of the state of the world and the nations. Because of their ignorance we have found our fathers desiring to stay unchanged in the state to which they were born. Secondly, the basis of the wealth of the tribes and clans is animals—in particular camels—and since it is difficult to manage and raise animals and camels in the cities—where they cannot find pasture—the people remain in their original state of being. [. . .] The third reason is that the mentioned peoples are like wild animals who enjoy what they have gotten used to in terms of stealing and raiding the property of others of their own people and killing them. This has become a reason for their wildness and their insistence on staying in the state of Bedouinism. It should be obvious that the first reason—which is ignorance and illiteracy—is an ugly and unacceptable characteristic in all the creatures of this world. And the second reason is the subordination [to tradition] characteristic of animals, and it is contrary to the image according to

which man was created, for God has created the human being to be the most honorable of all creatures, and He made all breathing creatures subservient to him. He who is a Bedouin has become accustomed to the opposite of this natural order, so that although he used to be over other creatures, he has become subservient.

The truth is that this fallen state is an insult to humanity, and accordingly if we investigate the immense harm these tribes cause to each other, we will find that it has no equivalence in magnitude. For the human being has been commanded to protect those of his kind and treat them well, and is not commanded to do the opposite. In fact, all the religions command this [good treatment of others], and in particular the Mohammedan Shari'a. After proving that this is contrary to what has been commanded and is prohibited in all religions and in the Mohammedan Shari'a, then anyone with intelligence will see that harming people and robbing them of their money and their cattle is contrary to humanity and Islam. He who dares to commit that which we have mentioned must be punished. In addition, we see that this implies that since living as a Bedouin [. . .] leads to these harmful results, then no one should stay in that state of being, especially since we have arrived at a time and epoch [. . .] where to stay in this fallen and immoral state of existence appears as an ugly habit in the eyes of the world. For these explained reasons, these people cannot stay even for a short period in this state, and these tribes and clans should be settled and gain good human characteristics. It is imperative upon the Sublime Government to facilitate the emergence of these moral characteristics. This is particularly the case since those tribes and clans that have been settled during the past two years have faced difficulties and material needs, and they have remained in their original state because they are deprived of access to agriculture and commerce. Thus, and in order to feed their children, they have dared to attack the fields belonging to the inhabitants of the cities and towns. And in that case the government will have to reimburse the farmers for their losses and to dispatch imperial troops to punish the perpetrators, all of which costs money. Thus, and before matters reach this state, we would advise to give the lands that extend from Tikrit [village in Iraq] to the borders of Mosul [main city in northern Iraq] and that are located east of the Tigris River to the Shamr clan. Furthermore, we recommend that these lands be designated as a Mutassarifiya [provincial government within the Ottoman Empire] and be named as Sandjak [province] of Shamr, and that they [the clan of Shamr] be settled in these lands until they dig the necessary canals to the Tigris and reclaim the lands and plant them like other people. Once it is apparent that they are settled, then this place should be designated as a Mutassarifiya, like the Mutassarifiya of al-Muntafak, and this Mutassarifiya should be placed under your authority, O Pasha! [. . .] Because those

[people] are used to being Bedouins, and because it will be difficult to sever those ties all at once, then we should grant some of them with animals a permit to pasture their animals on some of the lands, provided that they return to their places of residence. In order to encourage development of these lands, we should exempt those who reclaim the lands and dig the ditches and canals from all but the Miri tax. [. . .] Once this Sandjak is formed according to what has preceded, and a Mutassarifiya is subsequently established, then troops should be sent to keep the peace, and the Mutassarif should be assigned a deputy and a tax collector and all that he requires in terms of government officials. [. . .]

This official Ottoman decree has been issued by the ministry of the Vilayet of Baghdad, and let it be known to all.

Queen Victoria's Golden Jubilee—
Victorian Wallpaper

Although wallpaper had been printed in Britain since the 1500s, it was not until its mass production in the nineteenth century that it began to be found in middle- and working-class houses as well as in the homes of the aristocracy. By the late nineteenth century, manufacturers were commonly printing commemorative wallpapers to celebrate special events. This wallpaper, celebrating Queen Victoria's Golden Jubilee in 1887, uses exotic images of the empire to demonstrate the power of the Queen. It would probably have been used in hotels and inns rather than in private homes.

QUESTIONS

1. What elements of empire are represented by the wallpaper?
2. In what ways has empire been absorbed into domestic British culture?
3. What does the widespread production and use of such images suggest to you about British attitudes toward empire?

Source: Victoria and Albert Museum, UK, given by the Royal Scottish Museum, Edinburgh.

▲

Wonderful Adventures of Mrs. Seacole in Many Lands

MARY SEACOLE

Mary Jane Grant Seacole was born in Kingston, Jamaica, in the early nineteenth century, the daughter of a Scotch army officer and a free black woman. A Creole, Seacole described herself as "only a little brown—a few shades duskier than the brunettes whom you all {the British} admire so much" (p. 4). She clearly identified with her Scottish background and sought for herself a life of service to the British empire of which she felt herself to be a citizen. Seacole was an entrepreneur and a nurse. She learned "doctoring" from her mother, who ran a boarding house and did nursing on the side, and ministered to cholera and yellow fever victims in Panama and Jamaica before traveling to England in 1854 with the plan of assisting the British troops fighting in the Crimean War. As can be seen in the following selection, she petitioned a number of government and independent groups to join their nursing units but was turned away by all of them on what she suspected were racist grounds. As a result, Mrs. Seacole, who wanted nothing more than to "be useful to my own 'sons,'" (p. 74), as she called the British soldiers, set off on her own to open a hotel for invalids in the Crimea. Once in Balaclava, the site of the famous Charge of the Light Brigade, Mrs. Seacole set up the British Hotel, which offered rooms, cooked meals, goods, and medical services to British, French, and Turkish soldiers fighting in the Crimean War. By all accounts, her services proved invaluable to the troops, and although she was criticized for her entrepreneurship by Florence Nightingale, who also gained fame from nursing in the Crimean War, she nonetheless achieved considerable acclaim for her efforts, especially after the publication of her autobiography in 1857.

As a Creole who experienced racism in her efforts to serve the Empire's military efforts, Mrs. Seacole would seem an unlikely advocate of imperialism. Indeed, nowhere in her autobiography can one find an explicit statement of support for the empire. Yet so many of her actions and her very sense of duty toward the British military all suggest that she was a loyal imperial subject and an advocate of the imperial enterprise. The selection that follows describes her efforts to become a nurse in the Crimean War.

▲

QUESTIONS

1. In what ways does Mary Seacole differ from the other advocates of imperialism you have encountered in this chapter?

2. What might make you think that Mary Seacole supports the British empire?

[. . .] Need I be ashamed to confess that I shared in the general enthusiasm [for British efforts in the Crimea], and longed more than ever to carry my busy (and the reader will not hesitate to add experienced) fingers where the sword or bullet had been busiest, and pestilence most rife. I had seen much of sorrow and death elsewhere, but they had never daunted me; and if I could feel happy

Source: Mary Seacole. *Wonderful Adventures of Mrs. Seacole in Many Lands.* London: James Blackwood, 1857. Pp. 75–6, 77–80.

binding up the wounds of quarrelsome Americans and treacherous Spaniards, what delight should I not experience if I could be useful to my own "sons," suffering for a cause it was so glorious to fight and bleed for! [. . .] I made up my mind that if the army wanted nurses, they would be glad of me, and with all the ardour of my nature, which ever carried me where inclination prompted, I decided that I *would* go to the Crimea; and go I did, as all the world knows.

Of course, had it not been for my old strong-mindedness (which has nothing to do with obstinacy, and is in no way related to it—the best term I can think of to express it being "judicious decisiveness"), I should have given up the scheme a score of times in as many days; so regularly did each successive day give birth to a fresh set of rebuffs and disappointments. I shall make no excuse to my readers for giving them a pretty full history of my struggles to become a Crimean *heroine!*

My first idea (and knowing that I was well fitted for the work, and would be the right woman in the right place, the reader can fancy my audacity) was to apply to the War Office for the post of hospital nurse. Among the diseases which I understood were most prevalent in the Crimea were cholera, diarrhœa, and dysentery, all of them more or less known in tropical climates; and with which, as the reader will remember, my Panama experience had made me tolerably familiar. Now, no one will accuse me of presumption, if I say that I thought (and so it afterwards proved) that my knowledge of these human ills would not only render my services as a nurse more valuable, but would enable me to be of use to the overworked doctors. [. . .]

So I made long and unwearied application at the War Office, in blissful ignorance of the labour and time I was throwing away. I have reason to believe that I considerably interfered with the repose of sundry messengers, and disturbed, to an alarming degree, the official gravity of some nice gentlemanly young fellows, who were working out their salaries in an easy, off-hand way. But my ridiculous endeavours to gain an interview with the Secretary-at-War of course failed, and glad at last to oblige a distracted messenger, I transferred

my attentions to the Quartermaster-General's department. Here I saw another gentleman, who listened to me with a great deal of polite enjoyment, and—his amusement ended—hinted, had I not better apply to the Medical Department; and accordingly I attached myself to their quarters with the same unwearying ardour. But, of course, I grew tired at last, and then I changed my plans.

Now, I am not for a single instant going to blame the authorities who would not listen to the offer of a motherly yellow woman to go to the Crimea and nurse her "sons" there, suffering from cholera, diarrhœa, and a host of lesser ills. In my country, where people know our use, it would have been different; but here it was natural enough—although I had references, and other voices spoke for me—that they should laugh, good-naturedly enough, at my offer. War, I know, is a serious game, but sometimes very humble actors are of great use in it, and if the reader, when he comes in time to peruse the evidence of those who had to do with the Sebastopol drama, of my share in it, will turn back to this chapter, he will confess perhaps that, after all, the impulse which led me to the War Department was not unnatural.

My new scheme was, I candidly confess, worse devised than the one which had failed. Miss Nightingale had left England for the Crimea, but other nurses were still to follow, and my new plan was simply to offer myself to Mrs. H——— as a recruit. Feeling that I was one of the very women they most wanted, experienced and fond of the work, I jumped at once to the conclusion that they would gladly enroll me in their number. To go to Cox's, the army agents, who were most obliging to me, and obtain the Secretary-at-War's private address, did not take long; and that done, I laid the same pertinacious siege to his great house in ——— Square, as I had previously done to his place of business.

Many a long hour did I wait in his great hall, while scores passed in and out; many of them looking curiously at me. The flunkeys, noble creatures! marvelled exceedingly at the yellow woman whom no excuses could get rid of, nor impertinence dismay, and showed me very clearly that they resented my persisting in remaining there in mute appeal from their sovereign will. At last I gave that up, after a message from Mrs. H. that the full complement of nurses had been secured, and that my offer could not be entertained. Once again I tried, and had an interview this time with one of Miss Nightingale's companions. She gave me the same reply, and I read in her face the fact, that had there been a vacancy, I should not have been chosen to fill it.

As a last resort, I applied to the managers of the Crimean Fund to know whether they would give me a passage to the camp—once there I would trust to something turning up. But this failed also, and one cold evening I stood in the twilight, which was fast deepening into wintry night, and looked back upon the ruins of my last castle in the air. The disappointment seemed a cruel one. I was so conscious of the unselfishness of the motives which induced me to leave England—so certain of the service I could render among the sick soldiery, and yet I found it so difficult to convince others of these facts. Doubts and suspicions arose in my heart for the first and last time, thank Heaven. Was it possible that American prejudices against colour had some root here? Did these ladies shrink from accepting my aid because my blood flowed beneath a somewhat duskier skin than theirs? Tears streamed down my foolish cheeks, as I stood in the fast thinning streets;

tears of grief that any should doubt my motives—that Heaven should deny me the opportunity that I sought. Then I stood still, and looking upward through and through the dark clouds that shadowed London, prayed aloud for help. I dare say that I was a strange sight to the few passers-by, who hastened homeward through the gloom and mist of that wintry night. I dare say those who read these pages will wonder at me as much as they who saw me did; but you must all remember that I am one of an impulsive people, and find it hard to put that restraint upon my feelings which to you is so easy and natural.

The morrow, however, brought fresh hope. A good night's rest had served to strengthen my determination. Let what might happen, to the Crimea I would go. If in no other way, then would I upon my own responsibility and at my own cost. There were those there who had known me in Jamaica, who had been under my care; doctors who would vouch for my skill and willingness to aid them, and a general who had more than once helped me, and would do so still. Why not trust to their welcome and kindness, and start at once? If the authorities had allowed me, I would willingly have given them my services as a nurse; but as they declined them, should I not open an hotel for invalids in the Crimea in my own way? [. . .]

FURTHER RESOURCES

Cain, P. J., and A. G. Hopkins. *British Imperialism, 1688–2000.* New York: Longman, 2002.

Conrad, Joseph. *Heart of Darkness.* New York: Knopf, Random House, 1993.

Cook, Scott B. *Colonial Encounters in the Age of High Imperialism.* New York: Harper Collins, 1996.

Forster, E. M. *A Passage to India.* New York: Harcourt, Brace & World, 1969.

Hynes, William G. *The Economics of Empire: Britain, Africa and the New Imperialism, 1870–1895.* London: Longman, 1979.

Hobson, J. A. *Confessions of an Economic Heretic: The Autobiography of J. A. Hobson.* Hamden, CT: Harvester Press; Archon Books, 1976.

Hobson, J. A. *Imperialism: A Study.* Ann Arbor, MI: University of Michigan Press, 1965.

Kipling, Rudyard. *Kim.* Garden City, NY: Doubleday, 1901.

Meade, Teresa A., and Mark Walker. *Science, Medicine, and Cultural Imperialism.* New York: St. Martin's Press, 1991.

MacDonald, Robert H. *The Language of Empire: Myths and Metaphors of Popular Imperialism, 1880–1918.* Manchester, UK, and New York: Manchester University Press, 1994.

Pennycook, Alastair. *English and the Discourses of Colonialism.* New York: Routledge, 1998.

TIMELINE FOR PART II

1793	"Tippoo's Tiger"	1896	Philippine Revolution
1857	Sepoy Rebellion	**1909**	**Gandhi, "Civilization"**
1863	**Multatuli, *Max Havelaar***	1910	Union of South Africa created
1882	**al-Afghānī, "Lecture on Teaching and Learning"**	1914–18	First World War
1883–1902	**Britain's Scramble for Africa (Uzoigwe)**	**1916**	**Lenin, *Imperialism, the Highest Stage of Capitalism***
1885	Formation of Indian National Congress	1917	Russian Revolution
1887	**Chief Seattle's Oration Published**	**1918**	**Wilson, "Fourteen Points" Speech**
1887	**Rizal, *Noli Me Tangere***	1919	Lenin Image
1889	**Martí, "Mother America"**	**1920**	**Morel, *The Black Man's Burden***
1890s–1920s	Women's Suffrage Movements in Europe and the United States	**1922**	**Ho Chi Minh, "Equality!"**
		1950	**Césaire, *Discourse on Colonialism***

Entries in bold indicate sources.

Part II

The Anti-Imperialists

INTRODUCTION

Not all Westerners advocated imperialism, just as not all colonized peoples rejected it. There were a considerable number of people in both the metropoles and the colonies who argued that imperialism was wrong. This part presents a broad spectrum of condemnations of imperialism from the 1860s to the 1970s. Opponents of imperialism used a variety of media, including art, fiction, essays, poetry, newspapers, and books, to convey their message to readers in the colonies and in the West as well. The critiques of imperialism presented here range from criticisms of the methods and motivation of imperialists, on the one hand, to criticisms of the willingness of colonial subjects to adopt Western standards by which to measure themselves, on the other.

Opponents of imperialism were not all in complete agreement, nor did they universally oppose every aspect of it. Just how colonized peoples should cope with the influx of Western ideas, for example, was a critical question for opponents of imperialism. While some thinkers believed that Western ideas might be put to good use by colonized peoples in their effort to overthrow imperialism, others argued that to adopt any Western ways of thinking was to submit to oppression. In this part of the reader, therefore, we have the example of the Indian independence activist Mohandas K. (Mahatma) Gandhi, who hoped to persuade Indians and other colonial peoples to reject Western notions of civilization. At the same time, however, the founder of Islamic modernism, Sayyid Jamāl ad-Dīn al-Afghānī, called upon fellow Muslims to use elements of Western knowledge, in particular a foundation of Western scientific knowledge, to help construct a modern Islamic culture that could stand up to imperialism. Likewise, the Vietnamese Communist leader Ho Chi Minh drew upon Western conceptions of equality to build an anticolonial argument. No consensus was reached, therefore, among opponents of imperialism over whether Western ideas should be universally rejected, or alternatively, employed to reject imperialism.

If Western ideas were themselves to be rejected, then what ought to take their place? Gandhi and the Martiniquan poet Aimé Césaire offered perspectives on this question and proposed alternative paths for colonial peoples to take. With his philosophies of nonviolent resistance and self-reliance, Gandhi created a strategy by which Indians could achieve political and economic independence while drawing upon their native resources. Césaire, along with the Senegalese intellectual and politician Léopold Senghor and others, offered a concept—*négritude*—that embraced and celebrated blackness. Filipino nationalist José Rizal actively promoted a nativist independence movement in the Philippines by attempting to construct a sense of Filipino identity among his compatriots. The fight against imperialism thus inspired the development of a variety of indigenous movements and patterns of thinking, some of which are further discussed in later parts of this reader.

More common, perhaps, were critiques of the methods and motivation of imperialism. Economic, administrative, political, and religious motives for creating and controlling empires were all attacked on various grounds. Vladimir Lenin, a disciple of Marx and a leading figure in the Russian Revolution of 1917, viewed imperialism as the highest (and worst) form of capitalism and promoted a worldwide revolution of the working class to overthrow the capitalist imperialists. From his perspective, then, imperialism was bad because it enabled the capitalist classes to oppress workers and control markets around the world. The Nigerian scholar Godfrey Uziogwe, writing about sixty years after Lenin, carried the Leninist interpretation further by offering a more concrete exploration of precisely how the British drew Africa into the capitalist world. Césaire, Edward Morel, Multatuli (Eduard Douwes Dekker), and José Martí also wrote about economic exploitation and condemned the economic systems of imperialism on moral grounds. Martí, a Cuban writer and activist who has become a revolutionary icon throughout Latin America, wrote broadly about ways in which both Spain and the United States sought to control the economies of Latin America. Morel, a European journalist, argued that imperialism was morally wrong because it placed undue economic and social burdens on the backs of colonial peoples. Multatuli, the pen name of Eduard Douwes Dekker, a Dutch civil servant who had spent time in Dutch Indonesia, described the exploitative nature of a colonial administrative system that placed considerable coercive authority in the hands of local elites who were in charge of developing the economy for Dutch benefit. Both Morel and Multatuli were writing for a Western audience, attempting to open the eyes of the European public to the cruel inequities of the imperialist policies that they perhaps blindly supported.

This part of the reader also contains two very different documents from North America: a selection from Woodrow Wilson's "Fourteen Points" speech and Chief Seattle's famous oration. The former was intended primarily as a hopeful statement for international relations in the post–First World War era. Some of its points, however, could be seen as useful by colonials. The latter is a highly controversial piece; many scholars contend that the speech could not possibly have come originally from a Native American leader. It may well have been largely the product of a white newspaperman. Nevertheless, the speech has obtained near iconic status in some circles and offers an interesting nineteenth-century critique of the Western expansion of the United States.

Tippoo's Tiger

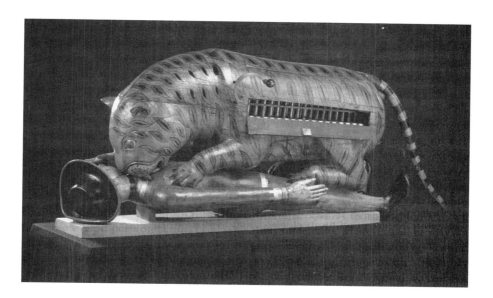

This mechanical organ, made of painted wood, was carved and manufactured in Mysore, India, around 1793. It offers a graphic representation of the reaction of many Indians to British control of India through the British East India Company, a control that had become increasingly formalized in the late eighteenth century. Inside the tiger is an organ, which can be accessed by a hatch in the side. Next to the hatch is a metal crank that, when turned, operates the organ.

QUESTIONS

1. Compare this image to the Victorian wallpaper in Part I. What do you think the tiger is intended to represent here?

2. Consider the positions of the tiger and the British soldier. What sorts of attitudes toward imperialism do you think are represented in this piece?

Source: Victoria & Albert Museum, UK.

Civilization

M. K. Gandhi

Mohandas Karamchand (Mahatma) Gandhi (1869–1948) was an Indian nationalist leader and also an important political philosopher. Born in India, Gandhi studied law in England from 1888 to 1891 and practiced law in Bombay for several years before moving to South Africa, where he lived between 1893 and 1915. While in South Africa, Gandhi became a prominent social activist, using passive resistance to protest the government's discriminatory policies against Indian settlers. From 1915 until his death, Gandhi lived in India, where he led a series of nonviolent protests against the colonial government and its policies and ultimately participated in the negotiations that led to Indian independence and the partition of India and Pakistan in 1947. He was assassinated in the following year during an intense period of Hindu and Muslim fighting.

The following excerpt comes from Gandhi's 1909 publication Hind Swaraj, *written during his time in South Africa. The volume was originally written in Gujarati, but Gandhi himself translated it into English in 1910. The volume is generally seen as the first full expression of Gandhi's philosophy. In addition to promoting Gandhi's now well-known philosophy of nonviolent resistance, the volume also critiques modern civilization and Indians for hoping that by adopting modern civilization they would be able to oust their British colonizers.*

QUESTIONS

1. According to Gandhi, what are the good and bad things about civilization?

2. What is immoral or irreligious about civilization?

READER: Now you will have to explain what you mean by civilization.

EDITOR: It is not a question of what I mean. Several English writers refuse to call that civilization which passes under that name. Many books have been written upon that subject. Societies have been formed to cure the nation of the evils of civilization. A great English writer has written a work called "Civilization: its Cause and Cure." Therein he has called it a disease.

READER: Why do we not know this generally?

Source: M. K. Gandhi. "Civilization." *Hind Swaraj, or Indian Home Rule* (Chapter VI). Madras: G. A. Natesan & Co., 1923. Pp. 25–30.

EDITOR: The answer is very simple. We rarely find people arguing against themselves. Those who are intoxicated by modern civilization are not likely to write against it. Their care will be to find out facts and arguments in support of it, and this they do unconsciously, believing it to be true. A man, whilst he is dreaming, believes in his dream; he is undeceived only when he is awakened from his sleep. A man labouring under the bane of civilization is like a dreaming man. What we usually read are the works of defenders of modern civilization, which undoubtedly claims among its votaries very brilliant and even some very good men. Their writings hypnotise us. And so, one by one, we are drawn into the vortex.

READER: This seems to be very plausible. Now will you tell me something of what you have read and thought of this civilization?

EDITOR: Let us first consider what state of things is described by the word "civilization." Its true test lies in the fact that people living in it make bodily welfare the object of life. We will take some examples. The people of Europe today live in better-built houses than they did a hundred years ago. This is considered an emblem of civilization, and this is also a matter to promote bodily happiness. Formerly, they wore skins, and used as their weapons spears. Now, they wear long trousers, and, for embellishing their bodies, they wear a variety of clothing, and, instead of spears, they carry with them revolvers containing five or more chambers. If people of a certain country, who have hitherto not been in the habit of wearing much clothing, boots, etc., adopt European clothing, they are supposed to have become civilized out of savagery. Formerly, in Europe, people ploughed their lands mainly by manual labour. Now, one man can plough a vast tract by means of steam-engines, and can thus amass great wealth. This is called a sign of civilization. Formerly, the fewest men wrote books that were most valuable. Now, anybody writes and prints anything he likes and poisons people's mind. Formerly, men travelled in waggons; now they fly though the air in trains at the rate of four hundred and more miles per day. This is considered the height of civilization. It has been stated that, as men progress, they shall be able to travel in airships and reach any part of the world in a few hours. Men will not need the use of their hands and feet. They will press a button, and they will have their clothing by their side. They will press another button, and they will have their newspaper. A third, and a motor-car will be waiting for them. They will have a variety of delicately dished up food. Everything will be done by machinery. Formerly, when people wanted to fight with one another, they measured between them their bodily strength; now it is possible to take away thousands of lives by one man working behind a gun from a hill. This is civilization. Formerly, men worked in the open air only so much as they liked. Now, thousands of workmen meet together and for the sake of maintenance work in factories or mines. Their condition is worse than that of beasts. They are obliged to work, at the risk of their lives, at most dangerous occupations, for the sake of millionaires. Formerly, men were made slaves under physical compulsion, now they are enslaved by temptation of money and of the luxuries that money can buy. There are now diseases of which people never dreamt before, and an army of doctors is engaged in finding out their cures, and so hospitals have increased. This is a test of civilization. Formerly, special messengers were required and much expense was incurred in order to send letters; to-day, anyone can abuse his fellow by means of a letter for one penny. True, at the same cost, one can send one's thanks also. Formerly, people had two or three meals consisting of home-made bread and vegetables; now, they require something to eat every two hours, so that they have hardly leisure for anything else. What more need I say? All this you can ascertain from several authoritative books. These are all true tests of civilization. And, if anyone speaks to the contrary, know that he is ignorant. This civilization takes note neither of morality nor of religion. Its votaries calmly state that their business is not to teach religion. Some even consider it to be a superstitious growth. Others put

on the cloak of religion, and prate about morality. But, after twenty years' experience, I have come to the conclusion that immorality is often taught in the name of morality. Even a child can understand that in all I have described above there can be no inducement to morality. Civilization seeks to increase bodily comforts, and it fails miserable even in doing so.

This civilization is irreligion, and it has taken such a hold on the people in Europe that those who are in it appear to be half mad. They lack real physical strength or courage. They keep up their energy by intoxication. They can hardly be happy in solitude. Women, who should be the queens of households, wander in the streets, or they slave away in factories. For the sake of a pittance, half a million women in England alone are labouring under trying circumstances in factories or similar institutions. This awful fact is one of the causes of the daily growing suffragette movement.

This civilization is such that one has only to be patient and it will be self-destroyed. According to the teaching of Mahomed this would be considered a Satanic civilization. Hinduism calls it the Black Age. I cannot give you an adequate conception of it. It is eating into the vitals of the English nation. It must be shunned. Parliaments are really emblems of slavery. If you will sufficiently think over this, you will entertain the same opinion, and cease to blame the English. They rather deserve our sympathy. They are a shrewd nation and I therefore believe that they will cast off the evil. They are enterprising and industrious, and their mode of thought is not inherently immoral. Neither are they bad at heart. I, therefore, respect them. Civilization is not an incurable disease, but it should never be forgotten that the English people are at present afflicted by it.

▲

Gandhi in Western Clothing

We are most accustomed to seeing images of Mahatma Gandhi from the period after he went to India and became involved in the home rule movement. In those pictures, he is typically shown wearing a traditional, minimalist outfit made of homespun cloth. Here, however, we see Gandhi in the Western clothes that he most typically wore while practicing law in South Africa.

▲

QUESTION

1. Think of Gandhi's piece "Civilization." In what ways does his attire seem compatible or incompatible with the values he is promoting in that article?

▲

Equality!

HO CHI MINH

Ho Chi Minh (1890–1969) was born Nguyen That Thanh in the northern part of Vietnam and was educated in a French and Vietnamese school. He worked first as a teacher and a seaman before moving to England in 1915, where he worked at a series of menial jobs. In 1917, he relocated to France, where he established himself as an anticolonial activist and became a founding member of the French Communist Party, believing that the international communist movement would be helpful to Vietnam in its quest for independence from the French. He went on to study in Moscow, which was to serve as his periodic base until his permanent return to Vietnam at the end of the Second World War. In 1930, while in Vietnam, he founded the Indochinese Communist Party, but was forced to return to Moscow after his arrest by the French in 1932. In the early 1940s, he founded the Viet Minh (the Vietnam League for Independence), which fought against the Japanese and later the French until their defeat in 1954 at Dien Bien Phu. Following that victory, Vietnam was partitioned at the seventeenth parallel, and Ho became president of North Vietnam in 1954. From there he supported the Viet Cong guerillas in South Vietnam until his death.

The following article is one of many on the same general theme published in French by Ho during his time in France between 1922 and 1926. "Equality!" was originally published in the journal Humanité *on June 1, 1922, under the name Nguyen Ai Quoc ("Nguyen, the patriot"), which, like Ho Chi Minh ("he who enlightens"), was a pseudonym.*

▲

QUESTIONS

1. What is the nature of Ho's critique of colonialism?
2. About what sort of equality is Ho writing?
3. For what audience do you think this essay was intended?
4. How do you think Ho hoped his audience would respond?

To mask the ugliness of its criminal exploitative regime, colonial capitalism always decorates its rotten coat of arms with the idealistic motto: Fraternity, equality, etc. . . .

Here is how the champions of equality put this into practice.

In the same workshop and doing the same work, the white worker is paid several times better than his brother of color.

Source: Ho Chi Minh. "Equality!" (Trans., J. Megan Greene.) *Humanité,* June 1, 1922.

In the administrative offices, in spite of length of service and in spite of their recognized aptitude, natives are paid starvation wages, while a newly appointed white man receives a higher salary for doing less work.

Young natives, having done their studies in the metropole and having obtained their degrees in medicine or law, cannot engage in their professions in their own countries if they are not naturalized (one knows how many difficulties and humiliations a native must suffer to obtain this naturalization).

Taken from their lands and their homes and forced to "volunteer," natives in the army quickly get to savor the exquisite meaning of this phantom "equality" that they must defend.

At the same rank, the white non-commissioned officer is almost always considered superior to the native non-commissioned officer. The latter must salute and obey the former. This "ethno-military" hierarchy is even more striking when white and colored soldiers travel together on a train or a boat. Let us take as an example the most recent such occasion:

In May, the steamer *Liger,* departing France for Madagascar, had 600 Malagasy soldiers on board. The native non-commissioned officers were piled up in the hold while their colleagues, the white non-commissioned officers, were comfortably installed in cabins.

May our brothers of color, warmed by the ship's boilers, if not by an ideal, and awakened by the noise of the propeller or by the voice of their conscience, reflect and understand that the good capitalism considers them, and always will consider them, as the dregs of society.

▲

Fourteen Points Speech

WOODROW WILSON

As the First World War drew to a close, European and American leaders hoped to construct a system of international governance that would prevent such a devastating war from happening again. The American President Woodrow Wilson made one of the most important statements on this subject when he articulated the "Fourteen Points" in a speech to a joint session of Congress on January 8, 1918, outlining his plans for the postwar world.

Many of Europe's colonial subjects had also participated in the war in Europe, some fighting, others working to support the war effort behind the scenes. As in the case of Ho Chi Minh, their experiences in Europe during this time could be disillusioning. They came to realize, once they made it to Europe, that the democratic ideals that countries like England and France claimed to embrace did not apply to them. Moreover, the horrors of the war demonstrated that the Europeans, who had long lectured their colonial subjects on what it meant to be "civilized," were no more civilized than anyone else and thus no more qualified to govern their colonies than the colonial peoples themselves. Wilson's articulation of a right to self-determination (the fifth point) was especially appealing, then, to colonial subjects who had witnessed the war, and it gave them hope that the great powers would begin to support their own calls for liberation from imperial control.

The following selection includes part of the opening section of Wilson's speech and the first five general points. All but one of the remaining points, not reproduced here, deal with specific matters of territorial settlement in Europe. The fourteenth point proposes the establishment of a general association of nations that would later be formed as the League of Nations.

▲

QUESTIONS

1. To what extent does Wilson appear to be concerned about colonial peoples?
2. How might colonial peoples have reacted to Wilson's fifth point?
3. What does Wilson think caused the First World War?

[. . .] It will be our wish and purpose that the processes of peace, when they are begun, shall be absolutely open and that they shall involve and permit henceforth no secret understandings of any kind. The day of conquest and aggrandizement is gone by; so is also the day of secret covenants entered into in the interest of particular governments and likely at some unlooked-for moment to upset the peace of the world. It is this happy fact, now clear to the view of every public man whose

Source: Woodrow Wilson. "Address by the President of the United States." *Congressional Record* 56, Part 1 (December 3, 1917–January 19, 1918). P. 680.

thoughts do not still linger in an age that is dead and gone, which makes it possible for every nation whose purposes are consistent with justice and the peace of the world to avow now or at any other time the objects it has in view.

We entered this war because violations of rights had occurred which touched us to the quick and made the life of our own people impossible unless they were corrected and the world secured once for all against their recurrence. What we demand in this war, therefore, is nothing peculiar to ourselves. It is that the world be made fit and safe to live in; and particularly that it be made safe for every peace-loving nation which, like our own, wishes to live its own life, determine its own institutions, be assured of justice and fair dealing by the other peoples of the world as against force and selfish aggression. All the peoples of the world are in effect partners in this interest, and for our own part we see very clearly that unless justice be done to others it will not be done to us. The programme of the world's peace, therefore, is our programme; and that programme, the only possible programme, as we see it, is this:

I. Open covenants of peace, openly arrived at, after which there shall be no private international understandings of any kind but diplomacy shall proceed always frankly and in the public view.

II. Absolute freedom of navigation upon the seas, outside territorial waters, alike in peace and in war, except as the seas may be closed in whole or in part by international action for the enforcement of international covenants.

III. The removal, so far as possible, of all economic barriers and the establishment of an equality of trade conditions among all the nations consenting to the peace and associating themselves for its maintenance.

IV. Adequate guarantees given and taken that national armaments will be reduced to the lowest point consistent with domestic safety.

V. A free, open-minded, and absolutely impartial adjustment of all colonial claims, based upon a strict observance of the principle that in determining all such questions of sovereignty the interests of the populations concerned must have equal weight with the equitable claims of the government whose title is to be determined. [. . .]

Britain and the Conquest of Africa

GODFREY N. UZOIGWE

With the scramble for Africa largely completed by the early years of the twentieth century, British activity in Africa shifted from conquest to governance as the British rulers sought to consolidate their colonies. In his book, Britain and the Conquest of Africa, *Godfrey N. Uzoigwe, a British-educated Nigerian, argues that the primary motivation for British imperialism was economic. British traders, Uzoigwe contends, were eager to fill the huge vacuum created by the cessation of the slave trade and replace it with a trade in "natural products."*

Uzoigwe supports the idea, initially advanced by Rosa Luxemburg and John A. Hobson, that imperialism was the final stage of capitalism. Admitting that noneconomic forces did play a part in imperial conquest and expansion, he nevertheless asserts that economic concerns were a major factor in the conquest of Africa. His book explains why the British pushed for the transition from the slave trade to the export of natural products by the 1880s and how the colonial system linked British Africa into capitalist world networks. Uzoigwe argues further that Africans did not all welcome this transformation.

QUESTIONS

1. According to Uzoigwe, what were the primary economic motivations for European imperialism?

2. How did media such as the newspaper *The Times* support and critique British imperialism?

3. How does Uzoigwe compare economic and moral arguments concerning British colonial activity in Africa?

Historically economic motives have always loomed large in processes of empire building. Every student of African history concedes the primacy of economic interests in the rise of the great empires during Africa's golden age. The historical explanations of their decline and fall have always had a strong economic orientation, but the correlation between economics and the rise of empires is not a phenomenon peculiar to African history: it is a general historical phenomenon. Since the beginning of history, Africa has faced an assortment of foreign conquerors all initially driven by stories of its enormous wealth—real or imaginary—to invade the continent. Whether similar impulses drove the European conquerors of Africa in the nineteenth century has ever since been a subject of great historical debate. [. . .]

Source: Godfrey N. Uzoigwe. *Britain and the Conquest of Africa: The Age of Salisbury.* Ann Arbor: The University of Michigan Press, 1974. Pp. 21, 24–28.

New British Markets and Foreign Competition

[. . .] Economic factors, social conditions, and politics are delicately connected. The historian who discusses the one in isolation of the others does so at his peril. To dismiss economic motivations as an unimportant factor in imperial expansion is as delusive as to argue that these motivations alone were the only justification for imperialism. The most surprising thing about the theory of economic imperialism or of any of the current theories, is its failure to take into consideration what the participants said, or implied, motivated their actions. What the opponents of economic imperialism are doing, in effect, is to use present-day knowledge in interpreting what happened in the past and under different circumstances. The reverse should be the case. Instead of posing the question: Was Africa worth having?, we should ask: Did contemporaries believe that it was worth having? And if so, why?

"New markets! New markets!", wrote Fredrick Greenwood, "is the constant cry of our captains of industry and merchant princes, and it is well that to them the ear of Government should willingly incline. It ought to do so, and it does." By new markets he meant primarily those regions yet unacquired by any European power, for example, western China, Tibet, and tropical Africa. The argument was that the acquisition of these markets—which implied the control of the countries themselves—would nullify the effects of hostile tariffs by creating an open door to world trade, and to British trade in particular, thereby helping to cure its economic ills. This argument was given more weight by the industrial unrest and unemployment which occurred in the early nineties. In 1891 Salisbury advocated African expansion as indispensable to British prosperity, employment, and world power. The British Chamber of Commerce declared: "there is practically no middle course for this country, between a reversal of free-trade policy to which it is pledged, on the

one hand, and a prudent but continuous territorial expansion for the creation of new markets." On subsequent occasions, Salisbury, Rosebery, and Chamberlain [British politicians] endorsed this view. In 1895 Salisbury warned that "at a period when the other outlets for the commercial energies of our countrymen were being gradually closed by the enormous growth of protectionist doctrines amongst other States it was our business in all these new countries to smooth the path of British enterprise and to facilitate the application of British capital."

In an important speech at Bradford, in the following May, he dwelt once more on the same theme. He spoke of "the dreary period of general depression and difficulty and distress through which we have passed for the last few years"; and he blamed it on hostile tariffs. To avoid repetition of such depression, he implored his audience "to make our way not only in the civilized, but in the uncivilized, markets of the world." This was the method, he said, their ancestors had adopted when Napoleon, by his Milan Declaration, had closed the outlets of British industry, and had triumphed in the end against the despot.

> It was that, one after another, you opened the less civilized portions of the world to your industry, and in proportion as Europe was closed to you, America and Africa and Asia were opened to you. But let us not forget the lessons which that experience taught us. Many men have dreamt that it would be a pleasant thing, so to speak, to close the capital account of the Empire and to add no further to its responsibilities. Many men have thought we have expanded far enough. "Let us draw the line," they say; "let us set up the temple of the god Terminus, and let us never go beyond it." But that is not the condition which fortune or the evolution of the world's causes has imposed upon the development of our prosperity. (Cheers.) If we mean to hold our own against the efforts of the civilized Powers of the world to strangle our commerce by their prohibitive finance we must be prepared to take the requisite measures to open

new markets for ourselves among the half-civilized nations of the globe, *and we must not be afraid if that effort, which is vital to our industries, should bring with it new responsibilities of empire and Government.* [Ozoigwe's italics.] (Cheers.) I feel that, in the present state of things in Africa and in the East, that consideration is not out of place. It is a consideration which ought never to be absent from the minds of the great captains of industry in towns such as this, where the forces of industry are centered upon what case we take—whether there is an adequate popular power behind in order to support those who wish to go on is the path which has won for England its splendid empire and its commercial supremacy, or in the path of those who wish to close the account and say that the growth of England has closed evermore. It will depend on you and on all who are interested in the trade of England, and I entreat you not to think it is a mere question of sentiment whether we should accept the openings which fortune gives to us in other lands. It is a question that involves our prosperity and our commercial existence to the last extent, and it is a question upon which the deciding voice of the commercial and industrial classes of this country will have to pronounce, whether our prosperity is to go on, as in the past, increasing, or whether from this moment it is to decline.

Chamberlain might as well had made this speech. Why then is Salisbury regarded as apathetic toward imperial ventures while Chamberlain is not?

When Salisbury returned to power a few months afterwards South African Chartered shares shot up from £1 to £8. From now on Chamberlain, ably supported by *The Times* [leading English newspaper] and the great majority of the press, as well as the Chambers of Commerce, became, as it were, the official spokesman for the need for new markets. But Salisbury had already made the points which Chamberlain was now to popularize; and with an effective and loquacious aide like the secretary of state for the Colonies, the prime minister was satisfied to stay in the background.

In November 1896 Chamberlain asserted that "commerce is the greatest of all political interests. . . . All the great offices of State are occupied with commercial affairs."

The Times, too, published an article entitled: "The Commercial Value of Africa." It showed that the immediate commercial value of tropical Africa was not startling, but admitted that given suitable conditions necessary for commercial development, the situation would drastically change. The same was true of India which, under British guidance, was now more valuable commercially than the whole of Africa. It concluded:

> The fact is that up to within the past few years Africa has hardly been needed by the rest of the world except as a slave market. But her turn has come, and the need for her co-operation in the general economy of the world will become greater and greater as the population increases, as industry expands, as commerce develops, as States grow ambitious, as civilization spreads. It is a discreditable anomaly that at this advanced stage in the progress of the race nearly a whole continent should still be given over to savagery. . . . We now take only what is most easily reached. . . .

In September *The Times* emphasized the dangers of foreign competition and renewed Salisbury's earlier call. "Some countries in which we once had a monopoly of the supply," it lamented, "have been learning of late to manufacture for themselves, and have become more or less independent of us. In others, the strain is caused by the competition of foreign traders, who contrive to draw themselves no small share of business which we have been in the habit of considering our own." A year later, it wondered whether British merchants ever bothered to read the Blue Books published for their benefit. "If the supremacy of British commerce is to be preserved," it warned, "our traders must bestir themselves betimes." Indeed, *The Times* proudly acknowledged that British imperialism was economic. So also did an economist, Miss Farraday. The *Pall Mall Gazette* affirmed that Britain desired Africa primarily for its trading needs, and even felt a tinge of pride in saying so. It wrote:

> Nor have we gone to the equatorial regions from religious or humanitarian motives. Missionaries and philanthropists, indeed, complain sometimes that their work is hampered by Downing Street regulations. Still less have we sought out the African in order to endow him with the vices (and virtues) of western civilization. The fact is that when what has been done through pure love of adventure and the pride of power has been eliminated, the dominating force which has taken us to Equatorial Africa is the desire for trade. We are in the tropical countries for our own advantage, and only incidentally for the good of the African. Nor is there in this anything immoral *per se,* though first to last, from the Guinea Coast Slave trade to gin and gun powder, we have done our share to demoralize the native. This has been the result rather than the intention of our trade and what we have now to do is so to rearrange our methods that while trade is further developed the African shall be protected from evils to which he has hitherto been exposed. . . . It reaffirmed its faith in the "gospel of trade." [. . .]

⋀

Mother America

José Martí

José Martí, 1853–1895, was a leader of the Cuban independence movement and an outspoken critic of Spanish and North American imperialism. He was especially critical of efforts by Europeans and European Americans to oppress and take advantage of the indigenous peoples of the Americas. A political activist and a prolific writer, Martí wandered through the Americas making a living as a journalist, diplomat, translator, and clerk. He wrote extensively about both North and South America. He died in a battle for Cuban independence against Spanish troops in 1895. His tragic and untimely death, fighting for the cause for which he had earlier been imprisoned and about which he had written extensively, quickly turned him into a martyr, and he has been treated as such by Latin American revolutionaries ever since.

The following selection does not explicitly mention imperialism, but it nonetheless offers a critique of attempts to control Latin America by both Spain and the United States. Although much of Latin America had become independent by 1889, the year in which this speech was given, Cuba remained under Spanish control, and so the subject of Spanish imperialism continued to be of singular importance for Martí, who was a leader of the Cuban independence movement.

⋀

QUESTIONS

1. What sorts of language does Martí use to describe Spain and the United States?
2. In what ways does Martí see Americans (that is, residents of both South and North America) as having been oppressed?
3. What sorts of things does Martí celebrate about the Americas?
4. How does he compare the history of North America to that of South America?

[. . .] In apostolic days North America was born from freedom at its fiercest. The new breed of light-crowned men were not willing to bow before any other. Impelled by the mind, the yoke of human reason that was vilified in empires created at sword's point, or with diplomacy, by the greatest power-crazed Republic, broke into pieces from everywhere in those nations born of an amalgamation of smaller nations. Modern rights sprang from the small and autochthonous regions that had formed their free character in continuous struggle, and they preferred independent caves to servile prosperity. A king who came told a man who addressed him familiarly and did not remove his hat in the presence to establish the Republic. The 41 souls from the *Mayflower* together with their women and children, defy the sea and on an oaken table of an anteroom establish their community. They carry loaded muskets to defend their planted fields; the wheat they eat, they plow. A land

Source: José Martí. "Mother America." In Deborah Shnookal and Merta Muñiz (Eds.), *José Martí Reader: Writings on the Americas*. New York: Ocean Press, 1999. Pp. 103–10. Used with permission.

without tyrants for the soul without tyrants is what they seek. In long jacket and felt hat comes the intolerant and irreproachable Puritan who despises luxury because men lie for it. In waistcoat and knee breeches come the Quaker, and with the trees he fells he builds schools. Then comes the Catholic, persecuted for his faith, and founds a State where nobody can be persecuted for his faith. The gentleman arrives in fine woolen cloth and plumed hat, and his very habit of commanding slaves gives him the insolence of a king wherewith to defend his freedom. One of them brings in his ship a group of Negroes to sell, or a fanatic who burns witches, or a governor who refuses to listen to anything about schools. The ships bring men of letters and university scholars, Swedish mystics, fervent Germans, French Huguenots, proud Scotsmen, thrifty Batavians. They bring plows, seeds, bolts of cloth, harps, psalms, books. The settlers live in houses built with their own hands, masters and servants of themselves. And as a recompense for the tiring task of contending with Nature, the brave colonist found satisfaction in seeing the old woman of the house, in hairnet and apron, come with blessing in her eyes and a tray of homemade sweets in her hand while one daughter opens a hymnal and another plays a prelude on the zither or the clavichord. School was taught by rote and with the lash, but going to it through the snow was the best kind of schooling. And when couples trudged along the road, faces to the wind—the men in leather jackets and carrying shotguns, the women in heavy flannels and carrying prayer books—they were usually bound for church to hear the new minister who refused to give the governor power in the personal aspects of religion, or they were on their way to elect their judges or call them to account. No unscrupulous breed of men came from outside. Authority belonged to all, and was given to whomever they desired. They elected their own magistrates and governors. If the governor was unwilling to convoke the council, the "free men" did so over his head. The taciturn adventurer there hunted both men and wolves in the woods and could sleep well only if he found a recently fallen tree trunk or a dead Indian for a pillow. And in the manorial mansions of the South, all was minuet and candlelight, and choruses of Negroes to greet their master as his coach drew up to the door, and silver goblets for the fine Madeira wine. But nothing in life was not food for freedom in the republican colonies that received certificates of independence from the king rather than royal charters. And when the Englishman, for granting them that independence in the capacity of master, levied a tribute which they resented, the glove that the colonies threw in his face was the selfsame one that the Englishman himself had put upon their hands. They led a horse to their hero's door. The nation that was later to refuse to help, accepted help. Triumphant freedom is like it: manorial and sectarian, with lace cuffs and a velvet canopy, more a matter of location than of human weakness, a selfish and unjust freedom teetering upon the shoulders of an enslaved race of men who before a century had passed hurled the litter to the ground with a crash. And ax in hand, out of the tumult and dust raised by the falling chains of a million emancipated men, emerged the woodcutter with the merciful eyes! Over the crumbling foundations of the stupendous convulsion rode Victory, proud and covetous. The factors that set the nation upon its feet appeared again, accentuated by war, and beside the body of the gentleman, dead among his slaves, were the Pilgrim (who refused to tolerate a master above him or a servant below him, or any conquests other than those made by the grain of wheat in the earth and by love in the heart) and the shrewd and grasping adventurer (born to acquire and to move forward in the forests, governed only by his own desires and limited only by the reach of his arm, a solitary and dreaded companion of leopards and eagles)—both Pilgrim and adventurer fighting for supremacy in the Republic and in the world.

And how can one fail to remember, for the glory of those who have known how to conquer, in spite of them, the confused and blood-soaked origins of Our America, although the faithful memory (more necessary now than ever) may be stained with untimely senility by the one whom the light of our glory—the glory of our independence—had hindered in the work of compromising or demeaning that America of ours? North America was born of the plow, Spanish America of the bulldog. A fanatical war took from the poetry of his aerial palaces the Moor weakened by his riches; and the remaining soldiers, reared to heresy on hate and sour wine and equipped with suits of armor and arquebuses, rushed upon the Indian protected by his breastplate of cotton. Ships arrived loaded with cavaliers in their half-cuirasses, disinherited second sons, rebellious lieutenants, hungry clergymen and university students. They brought muskets, shields, lances, thigh guards, helmets, backplates, and dogs. They wielded their swords to the four winds, took possession of the land in the name of the King, and plundered the temples of their gold. Cortés lured Montezuma into the palace he owed to the latter's wisdom or generosity, then held him prisoner there. The simple Anacaona invited Ovando to one of her festivities to show him her country's gardens, its joyful dances, and its virgins, whereupon Ovando's soldiers pulled their swords from beneath their disguises and seized Anacaona's land. Among the divisions and jealousies of the Indian people, the *conquistador* pushed on in America. Among Aztecs and Tlaxcaltecas, Cortés reached Cuauhtemoc's canoe. Among Quichés and Tzutuhils, Alvarado was victorious in Guatemala. Among the inhabitants of the Tunja and Bogotá, Quesada marched forward in Colombia. Among the warriors of Atahualpa and Huáscar, Pizarro rode across Peru. By the light of the burning temples the red banner of the Inquisition was planted in the breast of the last Indian. The women were carried off. When the Indian was free his roads were paved with stones, but after the Spaniard came he had nothing but cow paths used by the cow as she was sent nosing her way to the pasture, or by the Indian deploring how wolves had been turned into men. The Indian worked for what the Spanish commissioner ate. So many Indians died, like flowers that lose their aroma, that the mines had to shut down. Sacristans grew rich on the trimmings of their chasubles, and gentlemen went on walks, or burned the King's colors in a brazier, or watched heads fall in fights between viceroys and judges, or in rivalries among the commanders. When the head of a family wanted to mount his horse, he kept two Indian pages for the stirrups and two boys for the spurs. Viceroy, regent, and town council were appointed from Spain; when the town councils assembled, they were branded with branding irons. The mayor ordered the governor to stay out of the town because of the harm he did to the Republic, ordered the councilman to cross himself when entering the town council, and ordered 25 lashes for any Indian who galloped his horse. Children learned to read by means of bullfight posters and highwaymen's jingles; the schools of rank and prestige taught them "contemptible chimeras." And when groups of people gathered in the streets, it was to follow the old hags who carried proclamations, or to talk in hushed voices about the scandal of the judge and the heavily veiled woman, or to go to the burning of a Portuguese where a hundred pikes and muskets led the procession, and where the Dominicans with their white crosses and the grandees with their staffs and rapiers and gold-embroidered hoods ended it. There were trunks full of bones carried on the back and flanked by torches; the guilty with ropes around their necks, their sins written upon their head coverings; the stubborn with pictures of the enemy painted upon the *sanbenitos*. There were the distinguished gentlemen, the bishop, the higher clergy; and in the church, between two thrones brightly lit by candles, the black altar. Outside, the bonfire. At night, dancing. The glorious Creole falls bathed in blood every time he seeks a way out of his humiliation, with no guide or model but his honor, today in Caracas, tomorrow in Quito, thereafter with the common people of Socorro! Either he buys, hand to hand, the right to have Bolivian councilmen in Cochabamba, or he dies like the admirable Antequera, professing his faith on the scaffold in Paraguay, his countenance glowing with happiness; or growing weak at the foot of Chimborazo, he "exhorts the people to strengthen their dignity." The first Creole born to a Spaniard—the son of Malinche—was a rebel. Juan de Mena's daughter, in mourning of her father, dons her festive attire and all her jewels, for the day of Arteaga's death is a day of honor for all of humanity! What is happening so suddenly to make the whole world pause to listen and marvel and revere? From beneath the cowl of Torquemada comes the redeemed continent, bloody and with sword in hand! All the nations of America declare themselves free at the same time. Bolívar appears with his cohort of luminaries. Even the volcanoes acclaim him and publish him to the world, their flanks shaking and thundering. To your horses, all of America! And over plains and mountains, with all the stars aflame, redemptive hoof beats resound in the night. The Mexican clergy are now talking to their Indians. With lances held in their teeth, the Venezuelan Indians outdistance the naked runner. The battered Chileans march together, arm in arm with the half breeds from Peru. Wearing the Phrygian or liberty cap of the emancipated slave, the Negroes go singing behind their blue banner. Squads of *gauchos* in calfskin boots and swinging their *bolas* go galloping in triumph. The revived Pehuenches, hair flying and feathered lances held above their heads, put spurs to their horses. The war-painted Araucanians, carrying their cane lances tipped with colored feathers, come running at full gallop. And when the virgin light of dawn flows over the cliffs, San Martín appears there in the snow crossing the Andes in his battle cape—crest of the mountain and crown of the revolution. Where is America going, and who will unite her and be her guide? Alone and as one people she is rising. Alone she is fighting. Alone she will win.

And we have transformed all this venom into sap! Never was there such a precocious, persevering and generous people born out of so much opposition and unhappiness. We were a den of iniquity and we are beginning to be a crucible. We built upon hydras. Our railroads have demolished the pikes of Alvarado. In the public squares where they used to burn heretics, we built libraries. We have as many schools now as we had officers of the Inquisition before. What we have not yet done, we have not had time to do, having been busy cleansing our blood of the impurities bequeathed to us by our ancestors. The religious and immoral missions have nothing left but their crumbling walls where an occasional owl shows an eye, and where the lizard goes his melancholy way. The new American has cleared the path among the dispirited breeds of men, the ruins of convents, and the horses of barbarians, and he is inviting the youth of the world to pitch their tents in his fields. The handful of apostles has triumphed. What does it matter if, when emerging as free nations and with the book always in front of our eyes, we saw that the government of a hybrid and primitive land (molded from the residue of Spaniards and some grim and frightened aborigines, in addition to a smattering of Africans and Menceys) should understand, in order to be natural and productive, all the elements that rose in a marvelous throng—by means of the great politics inscribed in Nature—to establish that land? What does it matter if there were struggles between the city of the university and the feudal countryside? What difference if the servile marquis felt a warlike disdain for the half-breed workman? How important was the grim and stubborn duel between Antonio de Nariño and St. Ignatius Loyola? Our capable and indefatigable America conquers everything, and each day she plants her banner higher. From sunrise to sunset she conquers everything through the harmonious and artistic spirit of the land that emerged out of the beauty and music of our nature, for she bestows upon our hearts her generosity and upon our minds the loftiness and serenity of her mountains. She conquers everything through the secular influence with which this encircling grandeur and order has compensated for the treacherous mixture and confusing of our beginnings; and through the expensive and humanitarian freedom, neither local nor racial nor sectarian, that came to our republics in their finest hour, and later, sifted and purified, went out from the world's capitals. It was a freedom that probably has no more spacious site in any nation than the one prepared in our boundless lands for the honest effort, the loyal solicitude, and the sincere friendship of men. Would that the future might brand my lips!

Out of that troubled and sorely tried America, born with thorns upon her brow and with words and the heart's blood flowing out through the badly torn gag like lava, our eager strivings have brought us to Our America of the present, at once hard-working and heroic, frank and vigilant, with Bolívar on one arm and Herbert Spencer on the other. It is an America without childish jealousies or naive trust, fearlessly inviting all races to the fortunes of her home, because she knows she is the America of Buenos Aires' defense and of Callao's endurance, the America of Cerro de la Campanas and of the new Troy. And would she prefer the hates and appetites of the world instead of her own future, which is that of bringing equity and justice in an atmosphere of unrestricted peace, without a wolf's greed or a sacristan's admonitions? Would she rather disintegrate at the hands of her own children than undertake the grandiose task of becoming more firmly united? Would she desire to lie, because of neighboring jealousies, instead of following what is written by the fauna and stars and history? Or would she prefer to act as a legend to anyone who might offer her his services as a footboy, or go out into the world as a beggar to have her cup filled with terrible riches? Only self-created wealth and freedom earned by one's hand can endure, and it is for good. Whoever dares maintain that she would compromise, does not know Our America. Rivadavia, the man always seen in a white cravat, said that these countries would save themselves, and so they have. The sea has been plowed. Our America also builds palaces, and gathers the useful surplus from an oppressed world. She also contributes her forests and brings it the book, the newspaper, the town and the railroad. And Our America, with the sun on her brow, also rises over deserts crowned with cities. And when the elements that formed our nations reappear in this crisis of their elaboration,

the independent Creole is the one who prevails and asserts himself—not the beaten Indian serving as spur boy who holds the stirrup—and puts his own foot into it so that he can be higher than his master.

That is why we live here with such pride in Our America, to serve and honor her. We certainly do not live here as future slaves or dazzled peasants, but as people able and determined to help a man win esteem for his good qualities and respect for his sacrifices. The very wars that are thrown in her teeth by those who misunderstand her out of pure ignorance, are the seal of honor for our nations that have never hesitated to hasten the course of progress with the enriching sustenance of their blood, and that can display their wars like a crown. Devoid of the friction and daily stimulus of our struggles and passions that come to us from the soil where our children have not been reared—and from a great distance!—in vain does this country invite us with her magnificence, her life and its temptations, her heart and its cowardice, to indifference and forgetfulness. We are taking Our America, as host and inspiration, to where there is no forgetting and no death! And neither corruptive interests nor certain new fashions in fanaticism will let us be uprooted from her! We must show our soul as it is to these illustrious messengers who have come here from our nations, so they may see that we consider it faithful and honorable. We must convince these delegates that a just admiration and a usefully sincere study of other nations—a study neither too distant nor myopic—does not weaken the ardent, redemptive, and sacred love for what is our own. Let us allow them to see that for our personal good—if there is any good in the conscience without peace—we will not be traitors to that which Nature and humanity demand of us.

And thus, when each of them, content with our integrity, returns to the shores that we may never see again, he will be able to say to her who is our mistress, hope and guide: "Mother America, we found brothers there! Mother America, you have sons there!"

▲

Lecture on Teaching and Learning

Sayyid Jamāl ad-Dīn "al-Afghānī"

Sayyid Jamāl ad-Dīn al-Afghānī is considered to be the founding father of Islamic modernism that transformed Islam from a religious faith into an ideology of political activism in the late nineteenth and early twentieth centuries. The date and place of his birth are not known, but he was educated in Afghanistan, Iran, and India, and he traveled widely in Europe and the Middle East. He began writing his views of imperialism in 1882.

The teachings of al-Afghānī have had a deep impact on the Islamic world and continue to be a source of inspiration and controversy for many today. His Islamic modernism was based on his efforts to make traditional Islamic culture and the philosophical and scientific challenges of the modern west co-exist. At the same time, his program of pan-Islamism sought to mobilize Muslim nations in a fight against Western imperialism. Al-Afghānī's critics see the apparent contradiction between a desire to westernize and the need to avoid identification with the West. Others have suggested that he often adapted his ideas to two different audiences. To his Islamic adherents, al-Afghānī was passionately critical of Western science, which he saw as a tool of colonial conquest that strengthened Western imperialism in countries such as Afghanistan and Tunisia. He urged every government, however, including Islamic ones, to strive to lay a foundation of the sciences and to disseminate knowledge that would contribute to their greatness and power.

▲

Questions

1. Evaluate whether or not there is a link between al-Afghānī's denunciation of imperialism and modern Islamic fundamentalism.

2. What does al-Afghānī say about Western science? What is the relationship of Western science to Islamic philosophy?

3. What does he say about ulama, religiously trained Islamic learned men?

November 8 [1882], in Albert Hall, Calcutta

[. . .] Allow me to express my pleasure that so many Indian youths are here, all adorned with virtue and attainments, and all making great efforts to acquire knowledge. Certainly I must be happy to see such offspring of India, since they are the offshoots of that India that was the cradle of humanity. Human values spread out from India

Source: Sayyid Jamāl ad-Dīn "al-Afghānī." "Lecture on Teaching and Learning." In Nikki R. Keddie (Ed.), *An Islamic Response to Imperialism: Political and Religious Writings of Sayyid Jamāl ad-Dīn "al-Afghānī."* Berkeley and Los Angeles: University of California Press, 1968. Pp. 101–108. Used with permission.

to the whole world. These youths are from the very land where the meridian circle was first determined. They are from the same realm that first understood the zodiac. Everyone knows that the determination of these two circles is impossible until perfection in geometry is achieved. Thus we can say that the Indians were the inventors of arithmetic and geometry. Note how Indian numerals were transferred from here to the Arabs, and from there to Europe.

These youths are also the sons of a land that was the source of all the laws and rules of the world. If one observes closely, he will see the "Code Romain," the mother of all Western codes, was taken from the four *vedas* and the *shastras* [scriptures]. The Greeks were the pupils of the Indians in literary ideas, limpid poetry, and lofty thoughts. One of the pupils, Pythagoras, spread sciences and wisdom in Greece and reached such a height that his word was accepted without proof as an inspiration from heaven.

[The Indians] reached the highest level in philosophic thought. The soil of India is the same soil; the air of India is the same air; and these youths who are present here are fruits of the same earth and climate. So I am very happy that they, having awakened after a long sleep, are reclaiming their inheritance and gathering the fruits of their own tree.

Now I would like to speak of science, teaching, and learning. How difficult it is to speak about science. There is no end or limit to science. The benefits of science are immeasurable; and these finite thoughts cannot encompass what is infinite. Besides, thousands of eloquent speakers and sages have already expressed their thoughts to explain science and its nobility. Despite this, nature does not permit me not to explain its virtues.

Thus I say: If someone looks deeply into the question, he will see that science rules the world. There was, is, and will be no ruler in the world but science. If we look at the Chaldean conquerors, like Semiramis, who reached the borders of Tatary and India, the true conquerors were not the Chaldeans but science and knowledge.

The Egyptians who increased their realm, and Ramses II, called Sosestris, who reached Mesopotamia according to some and India according to others—it was not the Egyptians but science that did it. The Phoenicians who, with their ships, gradually made colonies of the British Isles, Spain, Portugal, and Greece—in reality it was science, not the Phoenicians, which so expanded their power. Alexander never came to India or conquered the Indians; rather what conquered the Indians was science.

The Europeans have now put their hands on every part of the world. The English have reached Afghanistan; the French have seized Tunisia. In reality this usurpation, aggression, and conquest has not come from the French or the English. Rather it is science that everywhere manifests its greatness and power. Ignorance had no alternative to prostrating itself humbly before science and acknowledging its submission.

In reality, sovereignty has never left the abode of science. However, this true ruler, which is science, is continually changing capitals. Sometimes it has moved from East to West, and other times from West to East. More than this, if we study the riches of the world we learn that wealth is the result of commerce, industry, and agriculture. Agriculture is achieved only with agricultural science, botanical chemistry, and geometry. Industry is produced only with physics, chemistry, mechanics, geometry, and mathematics; and commerce is based on agriculture and industry.

Thus it is evident that all wealth and riches are the result of science. There are no riches in the world without science, and there is no wealth in the world other than science. In sum, the whole world of humanity is an industrial world, meaning that the world is a world of science. If science were removed from the human sphere, no man would continue to remain in the world.

Since it is thus, science makes one man have the strength of ten, one hundred, one thousand, and ten thousand persons. The acquisitions of men for themselves and their governments are proportional to their science. Thus, every government for its own benefit must strive to lay the foundation of the sciences and to disseminate knowledge. Just as an individual who has an orchard must, for his own profit, work to level the ground and improve its trees and plants according to the laws of agronomy, just so rulers, for their own benefit, must strive for the dissemination of the sciences. Just as, if the owner of an orchard neglects to tend it according to the laws of agronomy, the loss will revert to him, so, if a ruler neglects the dissemination of the sciences among his subjects, the harm will revert to that government. What advantage is there to a Zulu king from ruling a society poor and barefoot, and how can one call such a government a government?

As the nobility of science has been somewhat clarified, we now wish to say some words about the relations between science, teaching, and learning. You must know that each science has a special subject and deals with nothing but the necessities and accidents of that special subject. For example, physics treats the special features of bodies that exist in the external world, and with its own special qualities, and does not enter into other matters that are necessary to the human world. *Kīmīyā,* or *chemistry* speaks of the special features of the bodies with regard to analysis and composition. Plant science or *botany* fixes only plants as the subject of its discussion. Arithmetic deals with separate quantities and geometry with interconnected quantities, and similarly the other sciences. None of these sciences deals with matters outside its own subject.

If we observe well, we will learn that each one of these sciences whose subject is a special matter is like a limb of the body of science. Not one of them can maintain its existence individually and separately, or be the cause of benefit for the human world. For, the existence of each one of these sciences is related to another science, like the relation of arithmetic to geometry.

This need of one science for other sciences cannot be understood from the one science itself. Thus it is that if that science were isolated, progress would not be achieved in it, nor would

it remain stable. Thus a science is needed to be the comprehensive soul for all the sciences, so that it can preserve their existence, apply each of them in its proper place, and become the cause of the progress of each one of those sciences.

The science that has the position of a comprehensive soul and the rank of a preserving force is the science of *falsafa* or philosophy, because its subject is universal. It is philosophy that shows man human prerequisites. It shows the sciences what is necessary. It employs each of the sciences in its proper place.

If a community did not have philosophy, and all the individuals of that community were learned in the sciences with particular subjects, those sciences could not last in that community for a century, that is, a hundred years. That community without the spirit of philosophy could not deduce conclusions from these sciences.

The Ottoman Government and the Khedivate of Egypt have been opening schools for the teaching of the new sciences for a period of sixty years, and until now they have not received any benefit from those sciences. The reason is that teaching the philosophical sciences was impossible in those schools, and because of the nonexistence of philosophy, no fruit was obtained from those sciences that are like limbs. Undoubtedly, if the spirit of philosophy had been in those schools, during this period of sixty years they themselves, independent of the European countries, would have striven to reform their kingdoms in accordance with science. Also they would not send their sons each year to European countries for education, and they would not invite teachers from there to their schools. I may say that if the spirit of philosophy were found in a community, even if that community did not have one of those sciences whose subject is particular, undoubtedly their philosophic spirit would call for the acquisition of all the sciences.

The first Muslims had no science, but, thanks to the Islamic religion, a philosophical spirit arose among them, and owing to that philosophical spirit they began to discuss the general affairs of the world and human necessities. This was why they acquired in a short time all the sciences with particular subjects that they translated from the Syriac, Persian, and Greek into theArabic language at the time of Mansūr Davānaqī.

It is philosophy that makes man understandable to man, explains human nobility, and shows man the proper road. The first defect appearing in any nation that is headed toward decline is in the philosophic spirit. After that deficiencies spread into the other sciences, arts, and associations.

As the relationship between the preeminence of philosophy and the sciences has been explained, we now wish to say something about the quality of teaching and learning among the Muslims. Thus, I say that the Muslims these days do not see any benefit from their education. For example, they study grammar, and the purpose of grammar is that someone who has acquired the Arabic language be capable of speaking and writing. The Muslims now make grammar a goal in itself. For long years they expend philosophic thought on grammar to no avail, and after finishing they are unable to speak, write, or understand Arabic.

Rhetoric, which they call *literature,* is the science that enables a man to become a writer, speaker, and poet. However, we see these days that after studying that science they are incapable of correcting their everyday speech.

Logic, which is the balance for ideas, should make everyone who acquires it capable of distinguishing every truth from falsehood and every right from wrong. However, we see that the minds of our Muslim logicians are full of every superstition and vanity, and no difference exists between their ideas and the ideas of the masses of the bazaar.

Philosophy is the science that deals with the state of external beings, and their causes, reasons, needs, and requisites. It is strange that our ulama [learned men] read *Ṣadrā* and *Shams al-bārī'a* and vaingloriously call themselves sages, and despite this they cannot distinguish their left hand from their right hand, and they do not ask: Who are we and what is right and proper for us? They never ask the causes of electricity, the steamboat, and railroads.

Even stranger, from early evening until morning they study the *Shams al-bārī'a* with a lamp placed before them, and they do not once consider why if we remove its glass cover, much smoke comes out of it, and when we leave the glass, there is no smoke. Shame on such a philosopher, and shame on such philosophy! A philosopher is someone whose mind is stimulated by all the events and parts of the world, not one who travels along a road like a blind man who does not know where its beginning and end are.

Jurisprudence among the Muslims includes all domestic, municipal, and state laws. Thus a person who has studied jurisprudence profoundly is worthy of being prime minister of the realm or chief ambassador of the state, whereas we see our jurisconsults after studying this science unable to manage their own households, although they are proud of their own foolishness.

The science of principles consists of the philosophy of the *shari'a,* or *philosophy of law.* In it are explained the truth regarding right and wrong, benefit and loss, and the causes for the promulgation of laws. Certainly, a person who studies this science should be capable of establishing laws and enforcing civilization. However, we see that those who study this science among the Muslims are deprived of understanding the benefits of laws, the rules of civilization, and the reform of the world.

Since the state of these ulama has been demonstrated, we can say that our ulama at this time are like a very narrow wick on top of which is a very small flame that neither lights its surroundings nor gives light to others. A scholar is a true light if he is a scholar. Thus, if a scholar is a scholar he must shed light on the whole world, and if his light does not reach the whole world, at least it should light up his region, his city, his village, or his home. What kind of scholar is it who does not enlighten even his own home?

The strangest thing of all is that our ulama these days have divided science into two parts. One they call Muslim science, and one European science. Because of this they forbid others to teach some of the useful sciences. They have not understood that science is that noble thing that has no connection with any nation, and is not distinguished by anything but itself. Rather, everything that is known is known by science, and every nation that becomes renowned becomes renowned through science. Men must be related to science, not science to men.

How very strange it is that the Muslims study those sciences that are ascribed to Aristotle with the greatest delight, as if Aristotle were one of the pillars of the Muslims. However, if the discussion relates to Galileo, Newton, and Kepler, they consider them infidels. The father and mother of science is proof, and proof is neither Aristotle nor Galileo. The truth is where there is proof, and those who forbid science and knowledge in the belief that they are safeguarding the Islamic religion are really the enemies of that religion. The Islamic religion is the closest of religions to science and knowledge, and there is no incompatibility between science and knowledge and the foundation of the Islamic faith.

As for Ghazālī, who was called the Proof of Islam, in the book *Deliverance from Error* he says

that someone who claims that the Islamic religion is incompatible with geometric proofs, philosophical demonstrations, and the laws of nature is an ignorant friend of Islam. The harm of this ignorant friend to Islam is greater than the harm of the heretics and enemies of Islam. For the laws of nature, geometric proofs, and philosophical demonstrations are self-evident truths. Thus, someone who says, "My religion is inconsistent with self-evident truths," has inevitably passed judgment on the falsity of his religion.

The first education obtained by man was religious education, since philosophical education can only be obtained by a society that has studied some science and is able to understand proofs and demonstrations. Hence we can say that reform will never be achieved by the Muslims except if the leaders of our religion first reform themselves and gather the fruits of their science and knowledge.

If one considers, he will understand this truth, that the ruin and corruption we have experienced first reached our ulama and religious leaders, and then penetrated the rest of the community. [. . .]

The Black Man's Burden

EDWARD D. MOREL

The Black Man's Burden (1920) was a direct critical response to Rudyard Kipling's defense of Western imperialism in Africa. In it, Edward D. Morel not only drew attention to colonial abuses but also attacked European imperial excesses in tropical Africa. The book was published at a time when it was unfashionable to be critical of Western imperialism in Africa, and its intended audience knew little of the evils meted out by European colonizers. Outraged by King Leopold's activities in the Congo in particular, Morel argued that it was the people of Africa who carried the black man's burden and experienced the destructive effects of European imperialism.

Morel was concerned about the economic and social impact of imperialism on Africa. He was among a small number of European writers who believed that the colonialism of the nineteenth century had the same economic objectives as slavery of the previous centuries: to seek the cheap labor and raw materials needed for the economic development of Europe. He argued further that even though the advent of European imperialism had led to the abolition of the slave trade, it was also causing the destruction of tribal life as European powers appropriated land. The Black Man's Burden was a powerful denunciation of the evils of imperialism that clearly made the case for opponents of European imperial exploitation in Africa. The appearance of The Black Man's Burden *helped spark an anti-imperialist movement in Europe that represented one of the most important human-rights campaigns of the twentieth century.*

Morel (1873–1924) was born in Paris and moved to Liverpool where he became a clerk of a shipping company and later a journalist.

QUESTIONS

1. Why does Morel contend that Black Africans are under such extreme pressure from Europeans in the early twentieth century? What has changed the essential relationship between Africans and Europeans?

2. How is climate a factor in Morel's argument?

It is with the peoples of Africa, then, that our inquiry is concerned. It is they who carry the "Black man's" burden. They have not withered away before the white man's *occupation*. Indeed, if the scope of this volume permitted, there would be no difficulty in showing that Africa has ultimately absorbed within itself every Caucasian and, for that matter, every Semitic invader too. In hewing out for himself a fixed abode in Africa, the white man has massacred the African in heaps. The African has survived, and it is well for the white settlers that he has.

In the process of imposing his political dominion over the African, the white man has carved

Source: Edward D. Morel. *The Black Man's Burden.* London: The National Labour Press, 1920. Pp. 7–11.

broad and bloody avenues from one end of Africa to the other. The African has resisted, and persisted.

For three centuries the white man seized and enslaved millions of Africans and transported them, with every circumstance of ferocious cruelty, across the seas. Still the African survived and, in his land of exile, multiplied exceedingly.

But what the partial occupation of his soil by the white man has failed to do; what the mapping out of European political "spheres of influence" has failed to do; what the maxim and the rifle; the slave gang, labour in the bowels of the earth and the lash, have failed to do; what imported measles, smallpox and syphilis have failed to do; what even the oversea slave trade failed to do, the power of modern capitalistic exploitation, assisted by modern engines of destruction, may yet succeed in accomplishing.

For from the evils of the latter, scientifically applied and enforced, there is no escape for the African. Its destructive effects are not spasmodic: they are permanent. In its permanence resides its fatal consequences. It kills not the body merely, but the soul. It breaks the spirit. It attacks the African at every turn, from every point of vantage. It wrecks his polity, uproots him from the land, invades his family life, destroys his natural pursuits and occupations, claims his whole time, enslaves him in his own home.

Economic bondage and wage slavery, the grinding pressure of a life of toil, the incessant demands of industrial capitalism—these things a landless European proletariat physically endures, though hardly. [. . .] The recuperative forces of a temperate climate are there to arrest the ravages, which alleviating influences in the shape of prophylactic and curative remedies will still further circumscribe. But in Africa, especially in tropical Africa, which a capitalistic imperialism threatens and has, in part, already devastated, man is incapable of reacting against unnatural conditions. In those regions man is engaged in a perpetual struggle against disease and an exhausting climate, which tells heavily upon child-bearing; and there is no scientific machinery for salving the weaker members of the community. The African of the tropics is capable of tremendous physical labours.

But he cannot accommodate himself to the European system of monotonous, uninterrupted labour, with its long and regular hours, involving, moreover, as it frequently does, severance from natural surroundings and nostalgia, the condition of melancholy resulting from separation from home, a malady to which the African is specially prone. Climatic conditions forbid it. When the system is forced upon him, the tropical African droops and dies.

Nor is violent physical opposition to abuse and injustice henceforth possible for the African in any part of Africa. His chances of effective resistance have been steadily dwindling with the increasing perfectibility in the killing power of modern armament. Gunpowder broke the effectiveness of his resistance to the slave trade, although he continued to struggle. He has forced and, on rare occasions and in exceptional circumstances beaten, in turn the old-fashioned musket, the elephant gun, the seven-pounder, and even the repeating rifle and the gatling gun. He has been known to charge right down repeatedly, foot and horse, upon the square, swept on all sides with the pitiless and continuous hail of maxims. But against the latest inventions, physical bravery, though associated with a perfect knowledge of the country, can do nothing. The African cannot face the high-explosive shell and the bomb-dropping aeroplane. He has inflicted sanguinary reverses upon picked European troops, hampered by the climate and by commissariat difficulties. He cannot successfully oppose members of his own race free from these impediments, employed by his white adversaries, and trained in all the diabolical devices of scientific massacre. And although the conscripting of African armies for use in Europe or in Africa as agencies for the liquidation of the white man's quarrels must bring in its train evils from which the white man will be the first to suffer, both in Africa and in Europe; the African himself must eventually disappear in the process. Winter in Europe, or even in Northern Africa, is fatal to the tropical or subtropical African, while in the very nature of the case anything approaching real European control in Africa, of hordes of African soldiery armed with weapons of precision is not a feasible proposition. The Black man converted by the European into a scientifically-equipped machine for the slaughter of his kind, is certainly not more merciful than the white man similarly equipped for like purposes in dealing with unarmed communities. And the experiences of the civilian population of Belgium, East Prussia, Galicia and Poland [First World War] is indicative of the sort of visitation involved for peaceable and powerless African communities if the white man determines to add to his appalling catalogue of past misdeeds towards the African, the crowning wickedness of once again, as in the day of the slave trade, supplying him with the means of encompassing his own destruction.

Thus the African is really helpless against the material gods of the white man, as embodied in the trinity of imperialism, capitalistic-exploitation, and militarism. If the white man retains these gods and if he insists upon making the African worship them as assiduously as he has done himself, the African will go the way of the Red Indian, the Amerindian, the Carib, the Guanche, the aboriginal Australian, and many more. And this would be at once a crime of enormous magnitude, and a world disaster.

An endeavor will now be made to describe the nature, and the changing form, which the burden inflicted by the white man in modern times upon the black has assumed. It can only be sketched here in the broadest outline, but in such a way as will, it is hoped, explain the differing causes and motives which have inspired white activities in Africa and illustrate, by specific and notable examples, their resultant effects upon African peoples. It is important that these differing causes and motives should be understood, and that we should distinguish between them in order that we may hew our way later on through the jungle of error which impedes the pathway to reform. Diffused generalities and sweeping judgments generate confusion of thought and hamper the evolution of a constructive policy based upon clear apprehension of the problem to be solved.

The history of contact between the white and black peoples in modern times is divisible into two distinct and separate periods: the period of the slave trade and the period of invasion,

political control, capitalistic exploitation, and, the latest development, militarism. Following the slave trade period and preceding the period of invasion, occurs the trade interlude which, indeed, had priority of both periods, as when the Carthagenians bartered salt and iron implements for gold dust on the West Coast. But this interlude concerns our investigations only when we pass from destructive exposure to constructive demonstration.

The first period needs recalling, in order to impress once more upon our memories the full extent of the African's claim upon us, the white imperial peoples, for tardy justice, for considerate and honest conduct.

Our examination of the second period will call for sectional treatment. The history of contact and its consequences during this period may be roughly sub-divided thus:

a. The struggle for supremacy between European invading *Settlers* and resident African peoples in those portions of Africa where the climate and other circumstances permit of Europeans rearing families of white children.

b. *Political action* by European Governments aiming at the assertion of sovereign rights over particular areas of African territory.

c. *Administrative policy,* sanctioned by European Governments, and applied by their local representatives in particular areas, subsequent to the successful assertion of sovereign rights.

These sub-divisions are, perhaps, somewhat arbitrary. The distinctiveness here given to them cannot be absolutely preserved. There is, for instance, a natural tendency for both *a* and *b* to merge into *c* as, through efflux of time, the originating cause and motive of contact is obscured by developments to which contact has given rise.

Thus racial contention for actual possession of the soil, and political action often resulting in so-called treaties of Protectorate thoroughly unintelligible to the African signees, are both landmarks upon the road leading to eventual administrative policy: *i.e.,* to direct government of the black man by the white. [. . .]

Discourse on Colonialism

AIMÉ CÉSAIRE

Aimé Césaire (1913–) was born in the French colony of Martinique where he grew up in a poor family. He was nonetheless able to attend a good secondary school in Fort-de-France, and from there went on to Paris where he continued to study in the 1930s. There he met other French colonial intellectuals, such as the African writer Léopold Senghor, and along with him and others founded a journal by the name of L'Étudiant noir *(The Black Student) that undertook to explore the concept of* négritude, *a term that they coined. For Césaire, négritude meant the awareness and appreciation by black people of their own color and of the importance of color in shaping them. In 1939, Césaire returned to Martinique where he continued to write poetry with social and political themes. From 1945 on, he was politically active in Martinique, serving as a delegate to the National Assembly in Paris and mayor of Fort-de-France. He was also a leading member of Martinique's Communist Party from 1945 until the late 1950s.*

Discourse on Colonialism (Discours sur le colonialisme) was first published in 1950. It is a long poem that has been described by one scholar as an act of revolution against the colonial enterprise.

QUESTIONS

1. Consider Césaire's comments on civilization. In what ways are they similar to or different those made by Gandhi in *Civilization?*

2. In what ways does the poem speak to or refute pro-imperialist arguments that you encountered in Part I of this reader?

3. What specific things does Césaire lament about the colonial enterprise? What results has it achieved?

A civilization that proves incapable of solving the problems it creates is a decadent civilization.

A civilization that chooses to close its eyes to its most crucial problems is a stricken civilization.

A civilization that uses its principles for trickery and deceit is a dying civilization.

The fact is that the so-called European civilization—"Western" civilization—as it has been shaped by two centuries of bourgeois rule, is incapable of solving the

Source: Aimé Césaire. *Discourse on Colonialism*. Translated by Joan Pinkham. New York: Monthly Review Press, 2000. Pp. 31–34, 42–43. Used with permission.

two major problems to which its existence has given rise: the problem of the proletariat and the colonial problem; that Europe is unable to justify itself either before the bar of "reason" or before the bar of "conscience"; and that, increasingly, it takes refuge in a hypocrisy which is all the more odious because it is less and less likely to deceive.

Europe is indefensible.

Apparently that is what the American strategists are whispering to each other.

That in itself is not serious.

What is serious is that "Europe" is morally, spiritually indefensible.

And today the indictment is brought against it not by the European masses alone, but on a world scale, by tens and tens of millions of men who, from the depths of slavery, set themselves up as judges.

The colonialists may kill in Indochina, torture in Madagascar, imprison in Black Africa, crack down in the West Indies. Henceforth the colonized know that they have an advantage over them. They know that their temporary "masters" are lying.

Therefore that their masters are weak.

And since I have been asked to speak about colonization and civilization, let us go straight to the principal lie that is the source of all the others.

Colonization and civilization?

In dealing with this subject, the commonest curse is to be the dupe in good faith of a collective hypocrisy that cleverly misrepresents problems, the better to legitimize the hateful solutions provided for them.

In other words, the essential thing here is to see clearly, to think clearly—that is, dangerously—and to answer clearly the

innocent first question: what, fundamentally, is colonization? To agree on what it is not: neither evangelization, nor a philanthropic enterprise, nor a desire to push back the frontiers of ignorance, disease, and tyranny, nor a project undertaken for the greater glory of God, nor an attempt to extend the rule of law. To admit once and for all, without flinching at the consequences, that the decisive actors here are the adventurer and the pirate, the wholesale grocer and the ship owner, the gold digger and the merchant, appetite and force, and behind them, the baleful projected shadow of a form of civilization which, at a certain point in its history, finds itself obliged, for internal reasons, to extend to a world scale the competition of its antagonistic economies.

Pursuing my analysis, I find that hypocrisy is of recent date; that neither Cortéz discovering Mexico from the top of the great teocalli, nor Pizzaro before Cuzco (much less Marco Polo before Cambuluc), claims that he is the harbinger of a superior order; that they kill; that they plunder; that they have helmets, lances, cupidities; that the slavering apologists came later; that the chief culprit in this domain is Christian pedantry, which laid down the dishonest equations *Christianity = civilization, paganism = savagery,* from which there could not but ensue abominable colonialist and racist consequences, whose victims were to be the Indians, the Yellow peoples, and the Negroes.

That being settled, I admit that it is a good thing to place different civilizations in contact with each other; that it is an excellent thing to blend different worlds; that whatever its own particular genius may be, a civilization that withdraws into itself atrophies; that for civilizations, exchange is oxygen; that the great good fortune of Europe is to have been a crossroads, and that because it was the locus of all ideas, the receptacle of all philosophies, the meeting place of all sentiments, it was the best center for the redistribution of energy.

But then I ask the following question: has colonization really *placed civilizations in contact?* Or if you prefer, of all the ways of *establishing contact,* was it the best?

I answer *no.*

And I say that between *colonization* and *civilization* there is an infinite distance; that out of all the colonial expeditions that have been undertaken, out of all the colonial statutes that have been drawn up, out of all the memoranda that have been dispatched by all the ministries, there could not come a single human value. [. . .]

I see clearly what colonization has destroyed: the wonderful Indian civilizations—and neither Deterding nor Royal Dutch nor Standard Oil will ever console me for the Aztecs and the Incas.

I see clearly the civilizations, condemned to perish at a future date, into which it has introduced a principle of ruin: the South Sea Islands, Nigeria, Nyasaland. I see less clearly the contributions it has made.

Security? Culture? The rule of law? In the meantime, I look around and wherever there are colonizers and colonized face to face, I see force, brutality, cruelty, sadism, conflict, and in a parody of education, the hasty manufacture of a few thousand subordinate functionaries, "boys," artisans, office clerks, and interpreters necessary for the smooth operation of business.

I spoke of contact.

Between colonizer and colonized there is room only for forced labor, intimidation, pressure, the police, taxation, theft, rape, compulsory crops, contempt, mistrust, arrogance, self-complacency, swinishness, brainless elites, degraded masses.

No human contact, but relations of domination and submission which turn the colonizing man into a classroom monitor, an army sergeant, a prison guard, a slave driver, and the indigenous man into an instrument of production.

My turn to state an equation: colonization = "thingification."

I hear the storm. They talk to me about progress, about "achievements," diseases cured, improved standards of living.

I am talking about societies drained of their essence, cultures trampled underfoot, institutions undermined, lands confiscated, religions smashed, magnificent artistic creations destroyed, extraordinary *possibilities* wiped out.

They throw facts at my head, statistics, mileages of roads, canals, and railroad tracks.

I am talking about thousands of men sacrificed to the Congo-Océan. I am talking about those who, as I write this, are digging the harbor of Abidjan by hand. I am talking about millions of men torn from their gods, their land, their habits, their life—from life, from the dance, from wisdom.

I am talking about millions of men in whom fear has been cunningly instilled, who have been taught to have an inferiority complex, to tremble, kneel, despair, and behave like flunkeys.

They dazzle me with the tonnage of cotton or cocoa that has been exported, the acreage that has been planted with olive trees or grape vines.

I am talking about natural *economies* that have been disrupted—harmonious and viable *economies* adapted to the indigenous population—about food crops destroyed, malnutrition permanently introduced, agricultural development oriented solely toward the benefit of the metropolitan countries; about the looting of products, the looting of raw materials. [. . .]

Noli me Tangere (The Social Cancer)

José Rizal

In looking at the age of high or new imperialism (circa 1870–1914), students of history some-times overlook a very old European colonizer: Spain. The Spanish had, of course, been heavily involved in the Americas since the late fifteenth century. They also acquired territories in other parts of the globe, including the Philippines. By the late nineteenth century, Spanish presence in this Asian country was not only centuries old, it was much resented.

In his novel Noli me Tangere *(the book was originally published in Spanish and the title would translate literally as* Do Not Touch Me, *but various translators have given the titles* The Lost Eden *and* The Social Cancer *to the book), José Rizal gave voice to this resentment and helped crystallize it into more active opposition to Spain's control over the Philippines. Pub-lished originally in 1887,* Noli me Tangere *painted a vivid and witty picture of colonial Manila shortly before the outbreak of revolution against Spain in 1896. The selection here is from the opening of the book and makes clear the type of social and ethnic distinctions made between Spanish and Filipinos. It also is a strong critique of the power of the Roman Catholic Church in the Philippines. The background for revolution is established in Rizal's fictional work.*

Rizal was also a political activist. In 1892, he helped create the Filipino League, an organization designed to provide a sense of unity and identity to the diverse peoples of the Philip-pine islands. He hoped for a national movement, headed by intellectuals (like himself) and the more well-to-do elements in Filipino society, to oppose Spanish political control. The publication of Noli me Tangere *and Rizal's political activities combined to earn him the hatred of the Span-ish authorities, who executed him in 1896.*

Ultimately, the Filipino revolution was overtaken by global events. After the defeat of the Spanish in the Spanish-American War of 1898, the United States demanded the Philippines as its colonial possession.

QUESTIONS

1. What was colonial Manila like according to Rizal? What differences are there in his descriptions of Spaniards and Filipinos [Indians]? Rich and poor?

2. How does Rizal portray Catholic churchmen in the Philippines?

A Social Gathering

On the last of October Don Santiago de los San-tos, popularly known as Capitan Tiago, gave a dinner. In spite of the fact that, contrary to his usual custom, he had made the announcement only that afternoon, it was already the sole topic of conversation in Binondo and adjacent districts,

Source: José Rizal, *The Social Cancer (Noli me Tangere)*. Manila: Philippine Education Company, 1912. Pp. 1–9.

and even in the Walled City, for at that time Capitan Tiago was considered one of the most hospitable of men, and it was well known that his house, like his country, shut its doors against nothing except commerce and all new or bold ideas. Like an electric shock the announcement ran through the world of parasites, bores, and hangers-on, whom God in His infinite bounty creates and so kindly multiplies in Manila. Some looked at once for shoe-polish, others for buttons and cravats, but all were especially concerned about how to greet the master of the house in the most familiar tone, in order to create an atmosphere of ancient friendship or, if occasion should arise, to excuse a late arrival.

This dinner was given in a house on Calle Anloague, and although we do not remember the number we will describe it in such a way that it may still be recognized, provided the earthquakes have not destroyed it. We do not believe that its owner has had it torn down, for such labors are generally entrusted to God or nature—which Powers hold the contracts also for many of the projects of our government. It is a rather large building, in the style of many in the country, and fronts upon the arm of the Pasig which is known to some as the Binondo River, and which, like all the streams in Manila, plays the varied rôles of bath, sewer, laundry, fishery, means of transportation and communication, and even drinking water if the Chinese water-carrier finds it convenient. It is worthy of note that in the distance of nearly a mile this important artery of the district, where traffic is most dense and movement most deafening, can boast of only one wooden bridge, which is out of repair on one side for six months and impassable on the other for the rest of the year, so that during the hot season the ponies take advantage of this permanent *status quo* to jump off the bridge into the water, to the great surprise of the abstracted mortal who may be dozing inside the carriage or philosophizing upon the progress of the age.

The house of which we are speaking is somewhat low and not exactly correct in all its lines:

whether the architect who built it was afflicted with poor eyesight or whether the earthquakes and typhoons have twisted it out of shape, no one can say with certainty. A wide staircase with green newels and carpeted steps leads from the tiled entrance up to the main floor between rows of flower-pots set upon pedestals of motley-colored and fantastically decorated Chinese porcelain. Since there are neither porters nor servants who demand invitation cards, we will go in, O you who read this, whether friend or foe, if you are attracted by the strains of the orchestra, the lights, or the suggestive rattling of dishes, knives, and forks, and if you wish to see what such a gathering is like in the distant Pearl of the Orient. Gladly, and for my own comfort, I should spare you this description of the house, were it not of great importance, since we mortals in general are very much like tortoises: we are esteemed and classified according to our shells; in this and still other respects the mortals of the Philippines in particular also resemble tortoises.

If we go up the stairs, we immediately find ourselves in a spacious hallway, called there, for some unknown reason, the *caida,* which tonight serves as the dining-room and at the same time affords a place for the orchestra. In the center a large table profusely and expensively decorated seems to beckon to the hanger-on with sweet promises, while it threatens the bashful maiden, the simple *dalaga,* with two mortal hours in the company of strangers whose language and conversation usually have a very restricted and special character.

Contrasted with these terrestrial preparations are the motley paintings on the walls representing religious matters, such as "Purgatory," "Hell," "The Last Judgment," "The Death of the Just," and "The Death of the Sinner." At the back of the room, fastened in a splendid and elegant framework, in the Renaissance style, possibly by Arévalo, is a glass case in which are seen the figures of two old women. The inscription on this reads "Our Lady of Peace and Prosperous Voyages, who is worshiped in Antipolo, visiting in the disguise of a beggar the holy and renowned Capitana Inez during her sickness." While the work reveals little taste or art, yet it possesses in compensation an extreme realism, for to judge from the yellow and bluish tints of her face the sick woman seems to be already a decaying corpse, and the glasses and other objects, accompaniments of long illness, are so minutely reproduced that even their contents may be distinguished. In looking at these pictures, which excite the appetite and inspire gay bucolic ideas, one may perhaps be led to think that the malicious host is well acquainted with the characters of the majority of those who are to sit at his table and that, in order to conceal his own way of thinking, he has hung from the ceiling costly Chinese lanterns; bird-cages without birds; red, green, and blue globes of frosted glass; faded air-plants; and dried and inflated fishes, which they call *botetes*. The view is closed on the side of the river by curious wooden arches, half Chinese and half European, affording glimpses of a terrace with arbors and bowers faintly lighted by paper lanterns of many colors.

In the sala, among massive mirrors and gleaming chandeliers, the guests are assembled. Here, on a raised platform, stands a grand piano of great price, which tonight has the additional virtue of not being played upon. Here, hanging on the wall, is an oil-painting of a handsome man in full dress, rigid, erect, straight as the tasseled cane he holds in his stiff, ring-covered fingers—the whole seeming to say, "Ahem! See how well dressed and how dignified I am!" The furnishings of the room are elegant and perhaps uncomfortable and unhealthful, since the master of the house would consider not so much the comfort and health of his guests as his own ostentation. "A terrible thing is dysentery," he would say to them, "but you are sitting in European chairs and that is something you don't find every day."

This room is almost filled with people, the men being separated from the women as in synagogues and Catholic churches. The women consist of a number of Filipino and Spanish maidens, who, when they open their mouths to yawn, instantly cover them with their fans and who murmur only a few words to each other, any conversation ventured upon dying out in monosyllables like the sounds heard in a house at night, sounds made by the rats and lizards. Is it perhaps the different likenesses of Our Lady hanging on the walls that force them to silence and a religious demeanor or is it that the women here are an exception?

A cousin of Capitan Tiago, a sweet-faced old woman, who speaks Spanish quite badly, is the only one receiving the ladies. To offer to the Spanish ladies a plate of cigars and *buyos*, to extend her hand to her countrywomen to be kissed, exactly as the friars do,—this is the sum of her courtesy, her policy. The poor old lady soon became bored, and taking advantage of the noise of a plate breaking, rushed precipitately away, muttering "*Jesús!* Just wait, you rascals!" and failed to reappear.

The men, for their part, are making more of a stir. Some cadets in one corner are conversing in a lively manner but in low tones, looking around now and then to point out different persons in the room while they laugh more or less openly among themselves. In contrast, two foreigners dressed in white are promenading silently from one end of the room to the other with their hands crossed behind their backs, like the bored passengers on the deck of a ship. All the interest and the greatest animation proceed from a group composed of two priests, two civilians, and a soldier who are seated around a small table on which are seen bottles of wine and English biscuits.

The soldier, a tall, elderly lieutenant with an austere countenance—a Duke of Alva straggling behind in the roster of the Civil Guard—talks little, but in a harsh, curt way. One of the priests, a youthful Dominican friar, handsome, graceful, polished as the gold-mounted eyeglasses he wears, maintains a premature gravity. He is the curate of Binondo and has been in former years a professor in the college of San Juan de Letran, where he enjoyed the reputation of being a consummate dialectician, so much so that in the days when the sons of Guzman still dared to match themselves in subtleties with laymen, the able disputant B. de Luna had never been able either to catch or to confuse him, the distinctions made by Fray Sibyla leaving his opponent in the situation of a fisherman who tries to catch eels with a lasso. The Dominican says little, appearing to weigh his words.

Quite in contrast, the other priest, a Franciscan, talks much and gesticulates more. In spite of the fact that his hair is beginning to turn gray, he seems to be preserving well his robust constitution, while his regular features, his rather disquieting glance, his wide jaws and herculean frame give him the appearance of a Roman noble in disguise and make us involuntarily recall one of those three monks of whom Heine tells in his "Gods in Exile," who at the September equinox in the Tyrol used to cross the lake at midnight and each time place in the hand of the poor boatman a silver piece, cold as ice, which left him full of terror. But Fray Damaso is not so mysterious as they were. He is full of merriment, and if the tone of his voice is rough like that of a man who has never had occasion to correct himself and who believes that whatever he says is holy and above improvement, still his frank, merry laugh wipes out this disagreeable impression and even obliges us to pardon his showing to the room bare feet and hairy legs that would make the fortune of a Mendieta in the Quiapo fairs.

One of the civilians is a very small man with a black beard, the only thing notable about him being his nose, which, to judge from the size, ought not to belong to him. The other is a rubicund youth, who seems to have arrived but recently in the country. With him the Franciscan is carrying on a lively discussion.

"You'll see," the friar was saying, "when you've been here a few months you'll be convinced of what I say. It's one thing to govern in Madrid and another to live in the Philippines."

"But—"

"I, for example," continued Fray Damaso, raising his voice still higher to prevent the other from speaking, "I, for example, who can look back over twenty-three years of bananas and *morisqueta,*

know whereof I speak. Don't come at me with theories and fine speeches, for I know the Indian [native people]. Mark well that the moment I arrived in the country I was assigned to a town, small it is true, but especially devoted to agriculture. I didn't understand Tagalog very well then, but I was soon confessing the women, and we understood one another and they came to like me so well that three years later, when I was transferred to another and larger town, made vacant by the death of the native curate, all fell to weeping, they heaped up gifts upon me, they escorted me with music—"

"But that only goes to show—"

"Wait, wait! Don't be so hasty! My successor remained a shorter time, and when he left he had more attendance, more tears, and more music. Yet he had been more given to whipping and had raised the fees in the parish to almost double."

"But you will allow me—"

"But that isn't all. I stayed in the town of San Diego twenty years and it has been only a few months since I—left it."

Here he showed signs of chagrin.

"Twenty years, no one can deny, are more than sufficient to get acquainted with a town. San Diego has a population of six thousand souls and I knew every inhabitant as well as if I had been his mother and wet-nurse. I knew in which foot this one was lame, and where the shoe pinched that one, who was courting that girl, what affairs she had had and with whom, who was the real father of the child, and so on—for I was the confessor of every last one, and they took care not to fail in their duty. Our host, Santiago, will tell you whether I am speaking the truth, for he has a lot of land there and that was where we first became friends. Well then, you may see what the Indian is: when I left I was escorted by only a few old women and some of the tertiary brethren—and that after I had been there twenty years!"

"But I don't see what that has to do with the abolition of the tobacco monopoly," ventured the rubicund youth, taking advantage of the Franciscan's pausing to drink a glass of sherry.

Fray Damaso was so greatly surprised that he nearly let his glass fall. He remained for a moment staring fixedly at the young man.

"What? How's that?" he was finally able to exclaim in great wonderment. "Is it possible that you don't see it as clear as day? Don't you see, my son, that all this proves plainly that the reforms of the ministers are irrational?"

It was now the youth's turn to look perplexed. The lieutenant wrinkled his eyebrows a little more and the small man nodded toward Fray Damaso equivocally. The Dominican contented himself with almost turning his back on the whole group.

"Do you really believe so?" the young man at length asked with great seriousness, as he looked at the friar with curiosity.

"Do I believe so? As I believe the Gospel! The Indian is so indolent!"

"Ah, pardon me for interrupting you," said the young man, lowering his voice and drawing his chair a little closer, "but you have said something that awakens all my interest. Does this indolence actually, naturally, exist among the natives or is there some truth in what a foreign traveler says: that with this indolence we excuse our own, as well as our backwardness and our colonial system. He referred to other colonies whose inhabitants belong to the same race—"

"Bah, jealousy! Ask Señor Laruja, who also knows this country. Ask him if there is any equal to the ignorance and indolence of the Indian."

"It's true," affirmed the little man, who was referred to as Señor Laruja. "In no part of the world can you find any one more indolent than the Indian, in no part of the world."

"Nor more vicious, nor more ungrateful!"

"Nor more unmannerly!"

The rubicund youth began to glance about nervously. "Gentlemen," he whispered, "I believe that we are in the house of an Indian. Those young ladies—"

"Bah, don't be so apprehensive! Santiago doesn't consider himself an Indian—and besides, he's not here. And what if he were! These are the nonsensical ideas of the newcomers. Let a few months pass and you will change your opinion, after you have attended a lot of fiestas and *bailúhan,* slept on cots, and eaten your fill of *tinola.*"

"Ah, is this thing that you call *tinola* a variety of lotus which makes people—er—forgetful?"

"Nothing of the kind!" exclaimed Fray Damaso with a smile. "You're getting absurd. *Tinola* is a stew of chicken and squash. How long has it been since you got here?"

"Four days," responded the youth, rather offended.

"Have you come as a government employee?"

"No, sir, I've come at my own expense to study the country."

"Man, what a rare bird!" exclaimed Fray Damaso, staring at him with curiosity. "To come at one's own expense and for such foolishness! What a wonder! When there are so many books! And with two fingerbreadths of forehead! Many have written books as big as that! With two fingerbreadths of forehead!" [. . .]

Imperialism, the Highest Stage of Capitalism

VLADIMIR LENIN

One of the most famous attempts at a comprehensive answer to the question, what is imperialism? was given by Vladimir Lenin, one of the core figures in the Russian Revolution of 1917. Lenin, a marxist theoretician, concluded in essence that the imperialism of the late nineteenth and early twentieth centuries was a product of finance or monopoly capitalism in Europe and the United States. He claimed that competition within the capitalist world had largely been replaced by the dominance of monopolies of cartels and banks. In his estimation, European countries and the United States were so aggressive in their overseas adventures because they were largely working in the interests of financial capitalists. Lenin was trying to find a systematic explanation for the dramatic territorial and political shifts associated with the period 1870 to 1914. For him, imperialism was a sign of the desperate state that European capitalism had reached as it moved into an era dominated by financial monopolies.

This selection, drawn from different sections of Lenin's Imperialism, the Highest Stage of Capitalism *(first published in 1916 in Zurich while Lenin was still in exile), contains his definition of imperialism and his claims about territorial and political shifts caused by imperialistic conquests.*

QUESTIONS

1. How does Lenin define and describe imperialism?

2. According to Lenin, how has monopoly capitalism led to imperialism? Which parts of the world have been most affected by imperialism in his view?

Imperialism, as a Special Stage of Capitalism

[. . .] Imperialism emerged as the development and direct continuation of the fundamental characteristics of capitalism in general. But capitalism only became capitalist imperialism at a definite and very high stage of its development, when certain of its fundamental characteristics began to change into their opposites, when the features of the epoch of transition from capitalism to a higher social and economic system had taken shape and revealed themselves all along the line. Economically, the main thing in this process is the displacement of capitalist free competition by capitalist monopoly. Free competition is the

Source: Vladimir Lenin. *Imperialism, the Highest Stage of Capitalism.* Moscow: Foreign Languages Publishing House, no date. Pp. 141–44, 121–25.

fundamental characteristic of capitalism, and of commodity production generally; monopoly is the exact opposite of free competition, but we have seen the latter being transformed into monopoly before our eyes, creating large-scale industry and forcing out small industry, replacing large-scale by still larger-scale industry, and carrying concentration of production and capital to the point where out of it has grown and is growing monopoly: cartels, syndicates and trusts, and merging with them, the capital of a dozen or so banks, which manipulate thousands of millions. At the same time the monopolies, which have grown out of free competition, do not eliminate the latter, but exist over it and alongside of it, and thereby give rise to a number of very acute, intense antagonisms, frictions and conflicts. Monopoly is the transition from capitalism to a higher system.

If it were necessary to give the briefest possible definition of imperialism we should have to say that imperialism is the monopoly stage of capitalism. Such a definition would include what is most important, for, on the one hand, finance capital is the bank capital of a few very big monopolist banks, merged with the capital of the monopolist combines of industrialists; and, on the other hand, the division of the world is the transition from a colonial policy which has extended without hindrance to territories unseized by any capitalist power, to a colonial policy of monopolistic possession of the territory of the world which has been completely divided up.

But very brief definitions, although convenient, for they sum up the main points, are nevertheless inadequate, since very important features of the phenomenon that has to be defined have to be especially deduced. And so, without forgetting the conditional and relative value of all definitions in general, which can never embrace all the concatenations of a phenomenon in its complete development, we must give a definition of imperialism that will include the following five of its basic features: 1) the concentration of production and capital has developed to such a high stage that it has created monopolies which play a decisive

role in economic life; 2) the merging of bank capital with industrial capital, and the creation, on the basis of this "financial capital," of a financial oligarchy; 3) the export of capital as distinguished from the export of commodities acquires exceptional importance; 4) the formation of international monopolist capitalist combines which share the world among themselves; and 5) the territorial division of the whole world among the biggest capitalist powers is completed. Imperialism is capitalism in that stage of development in which the dominance of monopolies and finance capital has established itself; in which the export of capital has acquired pronounced importance; in which the division of the world among the international trusts has begun; in which the division of all territories of the globe among the biggest capitalist powers has been completed. [. . .]

The Division of the World among the Great Powers

In his book, on "the territorial development of the European colonies," A. Supan, the geographer, gives the following brief summary of this development at the end of the nineteenth century:

PERCENTAGE OF TERRITORY BELONGING
TO THE EUROPEAN COLONIAL POWERS
(INCLUDING THE UNITED STATES)

	1876	1900	Increase or Decrease
In Africa	10.8%	90.4%	+79.6%
" Polynesia	56.8%	98.9%	+42.1%
" Asia	51.5%	56.6%	+5.1%
" Australia	100.0%	100.0%	—
" America	27.5%	27.2%	−0.3%

"The characteristic feature of this period," he concludes, "is, therefore, the division of Africa and Polynesia." As there are no unoccupied territories—that is, territories that do not belong to any state—in Asia and America, it is necessary to amplify Supan's conclusion and say that the characteristic feature of the period under review is the final partition of the globe—final, not in the sense that a *repartition* is impossible; on the contrary, repartitions are possible and inevitable—but in the sense that the colonial policy of the capitalist countries has *completed* the seizure of the unoccupied territory on our planet. For the first time the world is completely divided up, so that in the future *only* redivision is possible, i.e., territories can only pass from one "owner" to another, instead of passing as ownerless territory to an "owner."

Hence, we are passing through a peculiar epoch of world colonial policy, which is most closely connected with the "latest stage in the development of capitalism," with finance capital. For this reason, it is essential first of all to deal in great details with the facts, in order to ascertain as exactly as possible what distinguishes this epoch from those preceding it, and what the present situation is. In the first place, two questions of fact arise here: is an intensification of colonial policy, a sharpening of the struggle for colonies, observed precisely in the epoch of finance capital? And how, in this respect, is the world divided at the present time?

The American writer, Morris, in his book on the history of colonization, made an attempt to sum up the data on the colonial possessions of Great Britain, France and Germany during different periods of the nineteenth century. The following is a brief summary of the results he obtained:

For Great Britain, the period of the enormous expansion of colonial conquests is that between 1860 and 1880, and it was also very considerable in the last twenty years of the nineteenth century. For France and Germany this period falls precisely in these twenty years. We saw above that the development of pre-monopoly capitalism, of capitalism in which free competition was predominant, reached its limit in the 1860's and 1870's. We now see that it is *precisely after that period* that the tremendous "boom" in colonial conquests begins, and that the struggle for the territorial division of the world becomes extraordinarily sharp. It is beyond doubt, therefore, that capitalism's transition to the stage of monopoly capitalism, to finance capital, *is connected* with the intensification of the struggle for the partition of the world.

Hobson, in his work on imperialism, marks the years 1884–1900 as the epoch of intensified "expansion" of the chief European states. According to his estimate, Great Britain during these years acquired 3,700,000 square miles of territory with a population of 57,000,000; France acquired 3,600,000 square miles with a population of 36,500,000; Germany 1,000,000 square miles with a population of 14,700,000; Belgium 900,000 square miles with 30,000,000 inhabitants; Portugal 800,000 square miles with 9,000,000 inhabitants. The hunt for colonies by all the capitalist states at the end of the nineteenth century and particularly since the 1880's is a commonly known fact in the history of diplomacy and of foreign policy. [. . .]

COLONIAL POSSESSIONS

Year	Great Britain Area (mill. sq. m.)	Pop. (mill.)	France Area (mill. sq. m.)	Pop. (mill)	Germany Area (mill. sq. m.)	Pop. (mill.)
1815–30	?	126.4	0.02	0.5	—	—
1860	2.5	145.1	.2	3.4	—	—
1880	7.7	267.9	.7	7.5	—	—
1899	9.3	309.0	3.7	56.4	1.0	14.7

⋏

Lenin Giving a Speech

In this image we see Vladimir I. Lenin giving a speech in Moscow in 1919. Lenin was not only an intellectual but a political leader who governed the new Soviet Union in the years following the Russian Revolution. Here we see the massive crowds that would come out to hear him.

⋏

QUESTIONS

1. What image of Lenin is presented here?
2. How do media, such as photography, convey political messages in the twentieth century?

Source: FPG / Getty Images, Inc.—Taxi.

▲

Max Havelaar: Or the Coffee Auctions of the Dutch Trading Company

MULTATULI

Max Havelaar *was published in Holland in 1863 by a Dutch civil servant who had served for seventeen years in the Dutch East Indies (Indonesia). Eduard Douwes Dekker published the largely autobiographical novel under the pseudonym Multatuli. This attempt at anonymity failed, and his controversial critique of Dutch treatment of Indonesians quickly embroiled him in a debate over the veracity of his account. In the face of such attacks, some of his contemporaries defended his narrative as having understated rather than exaggerated the extent of the problem. By 1868, the novel had been translated into most other European languages, which served to broaden the criticism of European imperialism. As the translator of the 1868 English language edition, Baron Alphonse Nahuÿs dryly observed, "However perfect British rule may be, it cannot be so perfect that it has nothing more to learn" (p. ix). Nahuÿs further compared* Max Havelaar *to Harriet Beecher Stowe's* Uncle Tom's Cabin *for its exposure of the ill treatment of a subject people by men intent on economic gain.*

The main character, clearly modeled after the author, is a big-hearted and generous assistant in Java who genuinely wishes to improve the living conditions of the people in the area that he governs. The worst abuses described in the novel were committed not by the Dutch but by the regents (local elites empowered by the Dutch to help them rule). The following selection describes the system of government used by the Dutch in Java and explains how and why the regents abused their own people so mercilessly.

▲

QUESTIONS

1. According to the author, what led the regents to abuse their power so frequently? What is wrong with the structure of the colonial government?

2. What role were the regents supposed to play in the Dutch colonial system?

3. What effect do you think the author hoped this narrative would have on his Dutch readership?

[. . .] It is no uncommon thing to find Regents in pecuniary difficulties who have an income of two or three hundred thousand guilders. This is brought about by the princely indifference with which they lavish their money, and neglect to watch their inferiors, by their fondness for buying, and, above all things, the abuse often made of these qualities by Europeans. The revenue of the Javanese grandees may be divided into four parts. In the first place, their fixed monthly pay; secondly, a fixed sum as indemnification for their bought-up rights, which have passed to the Dutch

Source: Multatuli. *Max Havelaar: Or the Coffee Auctions of the Dutch Trading Company.* (Trans. Baron Alphonse Nahuÿs.) Edinburgh: Edmonston and Douglas, 1868. Pp. 66–73.

Government; thirdly, a premium on the productions of their regency,—as coffee, sugar, indigo, cinnamon, etc.; and lastly, the arbitrary disposal of the labour and property of their subjects. The two last-mentioned sources of revenue need some explanation. The Javanese is by nature a husbandman; the ground whereon he is born, which gives much for little labour, allures him to it, and, above all things, he devotes his whole heart and soul to the cultivating of his rice-fields, in which he is very clever. He grows up in the midst of his *sawahs,* and *gagahs,* and *tipars;* when still very young, he accompanies his father to the field, where he helps him in his labour with plough and spade, in constructing dams and drains to irrigate his fields; he counts his years by harvests; he estimates time by the colour of the blades in his field; he is at home amongst the companions who cut paddy with him; he chooses his wife amongst the girls of the *dessah,* who every evening tread the rice with joyous songs. The possession of a few buffaloes for ploughing is the ideal of his dreams. The cultivation of rice is in Java what the vintage is in the Rhine provinces and in the south of France. But there came foreigners from the West, who made themselves masters of the country. They wished to profit by the fertility of the soil, and ordered the native to devote a part of his time and labour to the cultivation of other things which should produce higher profits in the markets of Europe. To persuade the lower orders to do so, they only had to follow a very simple policy. The Javanese obeys his chiefs; to win the chiefs, it was only necessary to give them a part of the gain,—and success was complete.

To be convinced of the success of that policy we need only consider the immense quantity of Javanese products sold in Holland; and we shall also be convinced of its injustice, for, if anybody should ask if the husbandman himself gets a reward in proportion to that quantity, then I must give a negative answer. The Government compels him to cultivate certain products on his ground; it punishes him if he sells what he has produced to any purchaser but itself; and *it* fixes the price

actually paid. The expenses of transport to Europe through a privileged trading company are high; the money paid to the chiefs for encouragement increases the prime cost, and because the entire trade *must* produce profit, that profit cannot be got in any other way than by paying the Javanese just enough to keep him from starving, which would lessen the producing power of the nation.

To the European officials, also, a premium is paid in proportion to the produce. It is a fact that the poor Javanese is thus driven by a double force; that he is driven away from his rice-fields; it is a fact that famine is often the consequence of these measures; but the flags of the ships, laden with the harvest that makes Holland rich, are flapping gaily at Batavia, at Samarang, at Soorabaya, at Passarooan, at Bezookie, at Probolingo, at Patjitan, at Tjilatjap.

"FAMINE————? In Java, the rich and fertile, famine?"

—Yes, reader, a few years ago whole districts were depopulated by famine; mothers offered to sell their children for food, mothers also ate their own children.————But then the mother-country interfered. In the halls of the Dutch Parliament complaints were made, and the then reigning Governor had to give orders that THE EXTENSION OF THE SO-CALLED EUROPEAN MARKET SHOULD NO LONGER BE PUSHED TO THE EXTREMITY OF FAMINE.

"Oh! this angelic Parliament!————"

This I write with bitterness—what would you think of a person that could describe such things without bitterness?

I have yet to speak of the last and principal source of the revenues of the native chiefs, viz., their arbitrary disposal of the persons and property of their subjects. According to the general idea in nearly the whole of Asia, the subject, with all that he possesses, belongs to the prince. The descendants or relatives of the former princes like to profit by the ignorance of the people, who do not yet quite understand that their "Tommongong," "Adhipatti," or "Pangerang" [local leaders] is now a paid official, who has sold his own rights and theirs for a fixed income, and that thus the ill-requited labour of the coffee plantation or sugar field has taken the place of the taxes which they formerly paid their lords. Hence nothing is more common than that hundreds of families are summoned from far remote places to work, without payment, on fields that belong to the Regent. Nothing is more common than the furnishing of unpaid-for provisions for the use of the Court of the Regent; and if the Regent happens to cast a longing eye on the horse, the buffalo, the daughter, the wife of the poor man, it would be thought unheard-of if he refused the unconditional surrender of the desired object. There are Regents who make a reasonable use of such arbitrary powers, and who do not exact more of the poor man than is strictly necessary to uphold their rank. Some go a little further, and this injustice is nowhere entirely wanting. And it is very difficult, nay even impossible, entirely to destroy such an abuse, because it is in the nature of the population itself to induce or create it. The Javanese is cordial, above all things where he has to give a proof of attachment to his chief, to the descendant of those whom his forefathers obeyed. He would even think himself wanting in the respect due to his hereditary lord, if he entered his *Kratoon* without presents. These gifts are often of such small value, that to refuse them would be a humiliation, and the usage is rather more like the homage of a child who tries to give utterance to filial love by offering his father a little present, than a tribute to tyrannical despotism.

But the existence of such a good custom makes the abolition of a bad one very difficult.

If the *aloon-aloon* [square] in front of the residence of the Regent were in an uncultivated condition, the neighbouring population would be ashamed of it, and much force would be required to prevent them from clearing that square of weeds, and putting it in a condition suitable to the rank of the Regent. To give any payment for this would be considered as an insult to all. But near this 'aloon-aloon,' or elsewhere, there are 'sawahs' that wait for the plough, or a channel to bring water, often from a distance of many miles. Those 'sawahs' belong to the Regent. He summons the population of whole villages, whose 'sawahs' need labour as well as his.—There you have the abuse.

This is known to the Government; and whosoever reads the official papers, containing the laws, instructions, regulations, etc., for the functionaries, applauds the humanity and justice which seem to have influenced those who made them. Wherever the European is intrusted with power in the interior of Java, he is clearly told that one of his first obligations is to prevent the self-abasement of the people, and to protect them from the covetousness of the chiefs; and, as if it were not enough to make this obligation generally known, a special oath is exacted from the Assistant Residents that when they enter upon the government of a province, they will regard this fatherly care for the population as their first duty.

That is a noble vocation. To maintain justice, to protect the poor against the powerful, to defend the weak against the superior power of the strong, to recover the ewe-lamb from the folds of the kingly robber:—well, all this makes your heart glow with pleasure at the idea that it is your lot to have so noble a vocation;—and let any one in the interior of Java, who may be sometimes discontented with his situation or pay, consider the sublime duty which devolves upon him, and the glorious delight which the fulfilment of such a duty gives, and he will not be desirous of any other reward. But that duty is by no means easy. In the first place, one has exactly to consider where the *use* ends, to make room for *abuse;*—and where the abuse exists, where robbery has indeed been committed by the exercise of arbitrary power, the victims themselves are, for the most part, accomplices, either from extreme submission, or from fear, on from distrust of the will or the power of the man whose duty it is to protect them. Every one knows, that the European officer can be summoned every moment to another employment, and that the Regent, the powerful Regent, remains there. Moreover, there are so many ways of appropriating the property of a poor ignorant man. If a *mantrie* [overseer] says to him that the Regent wants his horse, the consequence is, that the wished-for animal is soon found in the Regent's stables; but this does not mean that the Regent does not intend to pay handsomely for it some time or other. If hundreds of people labour on the fields of a chief, without getting money for it, this is no proof that *he* makes them do so for his benefit. Might it not have been his intention to give them the harvest, having made the philanthropic calculation that his fields were more fertile than theirs, and would much better reward their labour?

Besides, where could the European officer get witnesses having the courage to give evidence against their lord the Regent? And, if he ventured to make an accusation without being able to prove it, where would be the relation of elder brother, who, in such a case, would have impeached his younger brother's honour? Where would he then find the favour of the Government, which gives him bread for service, but which would take that bread from him, which would discharge him as incapable, if he rashly accused so high a personage as an "Adhipatti" or "Pangerang?"

No, no, that duty is by no means easy! This can be proved by the fact—apparent to every one—that each native chief pushes too far the limit of the lawful disposal of labour and property; that all Assistant Residents take an oath to resist this, and yet that very seldom a Regent is accused for abuse of power or arbitrary conduct.

It seems also that there must be an insurmountable difficulty in *keeping the oath:* "TO PROTECT THE NATIVE POPULATION AGAINST EXTORTION AND TYRANNY."

Chief Seattle's Oration of the 1850s

One of the most famous and controversial pieces of North American literature is the oration of Chief Seattle (Sealth) reportedly delivered in the 1850s in the Puget Sound area in present-day Washington state. That Seattle was a historical character and leader of Native American peoples is not in doubt. That settlers were moving into his territory and seeking to acquire rights to land in the 1850s is also not in doubt. The origins and content of the oration attributed to him have, however, been hotly debated. Opinion ranges from the piece being wholly the work of a settler-doctor named H. A. Smith in the 1880s to being largely inspired by the words of the chief despite problems of recording his speech, translating it, or reporting it from memory several decades later. Smith published his version of the oration in the Seattle Sunday Star *on October 29, 1887, from recollections and notes of an oration that Seattle supposedly gave in December 1854. His notes have never been found, nor do governmental sources from the 1850s record the oration. There is apparently no other source or corroboration for the speech, and some have doubted that Seattle could or would have delivered such words, which since the 1880s have been rendered in many different forms. Most famously, a screenwriter in the early 1970s added the phrase "The earth does not belong to man; man belongs to the earth" to Chief Seattle's speech for a broadcast on environmental concerns of the day. The authority of a nineteenth-century Native American was thus appropriated to support twentieth-century ecological awareness and to make Seattle an environmental prophet.*

No matter whether it was a product of a Native American or of a white settler, the oration offers a moving articulation of an anti-imperialist sentiment of the mid- to late nineteenth century. At the same time, the controversial history of the document can tell us a great deal about the relationship between authors, translators, interpreters, and reading publics. Regardless of its author or authors, it is also a fascinating piece for contrasting views of religion and cosmology in late nineteenth-century North America.

This version of the text comes from the Museum of History and Industry in Seattle.

QUESTIONS

1. How does the oration distinguish between the religious and cosmological views of Native Americans and settlers of European descent?

2. Some commentators have argued that the flowery language of the oration is proof that it was largely, if not exclusively, authored by Smith, a man described by some sources as a poet. What do you make of the language of the oration, and how does it contribute to the arguments being made?

Source: Chief Seattle's Oration of the 1850s. (Reprinted by permission of the Museum of History and Industry, Seattle, Washington.) Used with permission.

3. One commentator, concluding that the oration is the product of Smith's imagination, has stated that the thoughts in the oration lose their nobility because they are based on a literary forgery. Do you agree?

4. Why do you think that Chief Seattle's oration has achieved legendary or iconic status in some circles in North America?

The white man's God cannot love his red children or he would protect them. They seem to be orphans and can look nowhere for help. How then can we become brothers? How can your father become our father and bring us prosperity and awaken in us dreams of returning greatness?

Your God seems to us to be partial. He came to the white man. We never saw Him; never even heard His voice; He gave the white man laws but He had no word for His red children whose teeming millions filled this vast continent as the stars fill the firmament. No, we are two distinct races and must ever remain so. There is little in common between us. The ashes of our ancestors are sacred and their final resting place is hallowed ground, while you wander away from the tombs of your fathers seemingly without regret.

Your religion was written on tables of stone by the iron finger of an angry God, lest you might forget it. The red-man could never remember nor comprehend it.

Our religion is the traditions of our ancestors, the dreams of our old men, given them by the great Spirit, and the visions of our sachems, and is written in the hearts of our people.

Your dead cease to love you and the homes of their nativity as soon as they pass the portals of the tomb. They wander far off beyond the stars, are soon forgotten, and never return. Our dead never forget the beautiful world that gave them being. They still love its winding rivers, its great mountains and its sequestered vales, and they ever yearn in tenderest affection over the lonely hearted living and often return to visit and comfort them.

Day and night cannot dwell together. The red man has ever fled the approach of the white man, as the changing mists on the mountain side flee before the blazing morning sun.

However, your proposition seems a just one, and I think my folks will accept it and will retire to the reservation you offer them, and we will dwell apart and in peace, for the words of the great white chief seem to be the voice of nature speaking to my people out of the thick darkness that is fast gathering around them like a dense fog floating inward from a midnight sea.

It matters but little where we pass the remainder of our days. There are not many.

The Indian's night promises to be dark. No bright star hovers about the horizon. Sad-voiced winds moan in the distance. Some grim Nemesis of our race is on the red man's trail, and wherever he goes he will still hear the sure approaching footsteps of the fell destroyer and prepare to meet his doom, as does the wounded doe that hears the approaching footsteps of the hunter. A few more moons, a few more winters and not one of all the mighty hosts that once filled this broad land or that now roam in fragmentary bands through these vast solitudes will remain to weep over the tombs of a people once as powerful and as hopeful as your own.

But why should we repine? Why should I murmur at the fate of my people? Tribes are made up of individuals and are no better than they. Men come and go like the waves of the sea. A tear, a tamanawus, a dirge and they are gone from our longing eyes forever. Even the white man, whose God walked and talked with him, as friend to friend, is not exempt from the common destiny. We may be brothers after all. We shall see.

We will ponder your proposition, and when we have decided we will tell you. But should we accept it, I here and now make this the first condition: That we will not be denied the privilege, without molestation, of visiting at will the graves of our ancestors and friends. Every part of this country is sacred to my people. Every hillside, every valley, every plain and grove has been hallowed by some fond memory or some sad experience of my tribe.

Even the rocks that seem to lie dumb as they swelter in the sun along the silent seashore in solemn grandeur thrill with memories of past events connected with the fate of my people, and the very dust under your feet responds more lovingly to our footsteps than to yours, because it is the ashes of our ancestors, and our bare feet are conscious of the sympathetic touch, for the soil is rich with the life of our kindred.

The sable braves, and fond mothers, and glad-hearted maidens, and the little children who lived and rejoiced here, and whose very names are now forgotten, still love these solitudes, and their deep fastnesses at eventide grow shadowy with the presence of dusky spirits. And when the last red man shall have perished from the earth and his memory among white man shall have become a myth, these shores shall swarm with the invisible dead of my tribe, and when your children's children shall think themselves alone in the field, the store, the shop, upon the highway or in the silence of the woods they will not be alone. In all the earth there is no place dedicated to solitude. At night, when the streets of your cities and villages shall be silent, and you think them deserted, they will throng with the returning hosts that once filled and still love this beautiful land. The white man will never be alone. Let him be just and deal kindly with my people, for the dead are not altogether powerless.

FURTHER RESOURCES

Fanon, Frantz. *The Wretched of the Earth.* New York: Grove Press, 1965.
Gandhi, M. K. *An Autobiography: Or the Story of My Experiments with Truth.* London: Penguin, 2001.
Gandhi, M. K. *Gandhi in India, in His Own Words.* Hanover, NH: Tufts University Press 1987.
Hetherington, Penelope. *British Paternalism and Africa, 1920–1940.* London: Frank Cass, 1978.
Ho Chi Minh. "The Struggle Lies in the Colonies." In Helmut Gruber (Ed.), *International Communism in the Era of Lenin.* Garden City, NY: Anchor Books, 1972.
Kenyatta, Jomo. *Facing Mount Kenya: The Tribal Life of the Gikuyu.* New York: Vintage Books, 1965.
Rodney, Walter. *How Europe Underdeveloped Africa.* London: Bogle-L'Ouverture, 1972.
Said, Edward. *Orientalism.* New York: Vintage Books, 1979.
Tinker, Hugh. *Men Who Overturned Empires: Fighters, Dreamers, and Schemers.* Madison: University of Wisconsin Press, 1987.

Film

José Martí and Cuba Libre. DVD. Directed by José Cruz Girona. Princeton, NJ: Films for Humanities and Sciences, 2001.

1800s	Westward Expansion in the United States (Coolies)	1872	United Fruit Company Begins to Develop Banana Plantations in Costa Rica
1814	Steam Powered Locomotive Invented		
1820s	**Britain Begins Financing Development in Liberated South America (Galeano)**	1880	Christlieb, *Protestant Foreign Missions: Their Present State*
1830s–80s	**Improving Western Military Technology (Adas)**	1884	Maxim Machine Gun Invented
		1884–85	Berlin Conference
1831	Telegraph Invented	1892	**Morgan Speaks on Compulsory Education at Lake Mohonk Conference**
1840	Opium War		
1840s	**Regular Use of Quinine by Europeans to Prevent Malaria (Headrick)**	1919	**Kita, "An Outline Plan for the Reorganization of Japan"**
1857–1914	**The Great Game, Competition for Control of Central Asia (Hopkirk)**	1921	**Cunningham, *Products of the Empire***
1861	**Japanese Woodcut Print of American Naval Vessel**	1930	**Display of East-African Transport Poster in London**
		1957	**Kimathi Executed (Ngugi)**
1863	**Barker, "The Secret of England's Greatness"**	1964	**Senghor, *Liberté 1: Négritude et Humanisme***

Entries in bold indicate sources.

Part III

Tools of Empire

Introduction

When we speak of tools of empire in world history, we should understand them in the broadest possible terms. Of course, direct military actions and political occupation of territory were important tools involved in colonialism in the late nineteenth and early twentieth centuries. Indeed, one of the hallmarks of the era of "high" or "new" imperialism was the change to formal systems of control in which colonial powers set up political, military, and judicial administrations in large and important new territories. A reaction to one of these developments is seen in the selection entitled "Kimathi on Law as a Tool of Oppression," about a famous Kenyan resistance figure whose protests throw into sharp relief how legal structures had been used as a tool of empire. Similarly, the selection by Peter Hopkirk shows how basic administrative tasks such as surveying, in this case conducted clandestinely, were a fundamental part of establishing imperial control and administration in new regions. Nevertheless, the tools of empire used in this period were often more subtle than guns, administrative structures, and the law. Much of the contact between colonizer and colonized was economic and cultural in nature and included important changes in trade, educational patterns, religious customs, and even language. These tools of empire transformed global patterns in the modern era even more profoundly and for the longer term than did military conquests and political occupations alone. Much of our contemporary world, with its cultural clashes and political and economic rivalries, was created in the often difficult colonial encounters of the nineteenth and twentieth centuries, which involved the use of a wide range of tools of empire.

The basic, although not complete, control of diseases and the application of certain advanced technologies, for example, allowed Europeans and North Americans to obtain direct or nominal control over important African and Asian lands and to play expanded roles in Latin America and throughout the globe. The relative containment of malaria and the consolidation of the fruits of industrialization (railways, ships, advanced weaponry, etc.) were crucially linked to the changing global political and economic landscape and were thus important tools of empire. Examples of these tools of empire can be seen in the selections by Daniel Headrick and Michael Adas as well as the images of Perry's ship, Coolies building a railroad bridge, and transport in East Africa. Eduardo Galeano also traces the profound influence of technology and capital as a tool of empire in South America. J. Clinton Cunningham gives us an interesting take on rubber as both an economic product and tool of empire. Further, he shows us how a science such as botany and plant cultivation in general could be put to use as part of the

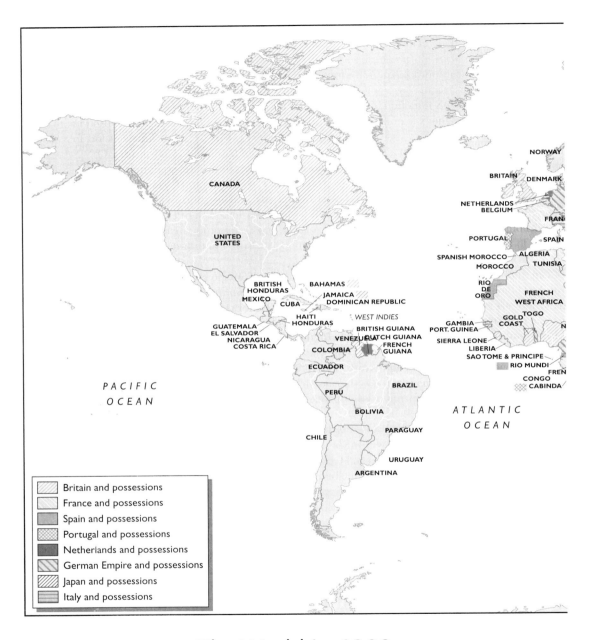

The World in 1900

Legend:
- Britain and possessions
- France and possessions
- Spain and possessions
- Portugal and possessions
- Netherlands and possessions
- German Empire and possessions
- Japan and possessions
- Italy and possessions

Map labels:

NORWAY
BRITAIN
DENMARK
NETHERLANDS
BELGIUM
FRAN[CE]
PORTUGAL
SPAIN
SPANISH MOROCCO
ALGERIA
MOROCCO
TUNISIA
RIO DE ORO
FRENCH WEST AFRICA
TOGO
GOLD COAST
GAMBIA
PORT. GUINEA
SIERRA LEONE
LIBERIA
SAO TOME & PRINCIPE
RIO MUNDI
FREN[CH] CONGO
CABINDA

CANADA
UNITED STATES
BRITISH HONDURAS
MEXICO
BAHAMAS
JAMAICA
DOMINICAN REPUBLIC
CUBA
HAITI
HONDURAS
WEST INDIES
GUATEMALA
EL SALVADOR
NICARAGUA
COSTA RICA
BRITISH GUIANA
DUTCH GUIANA
FRENCH GUIANA
VENEZUELA
COLOMBIA
ECUADOR
BRAZIL
PERU
BOLIVIA
PARAGUAY
CHILE
URUGUAY
ARGENTINA

PACIFIC OCEAN
ATLANTIC OCEAN

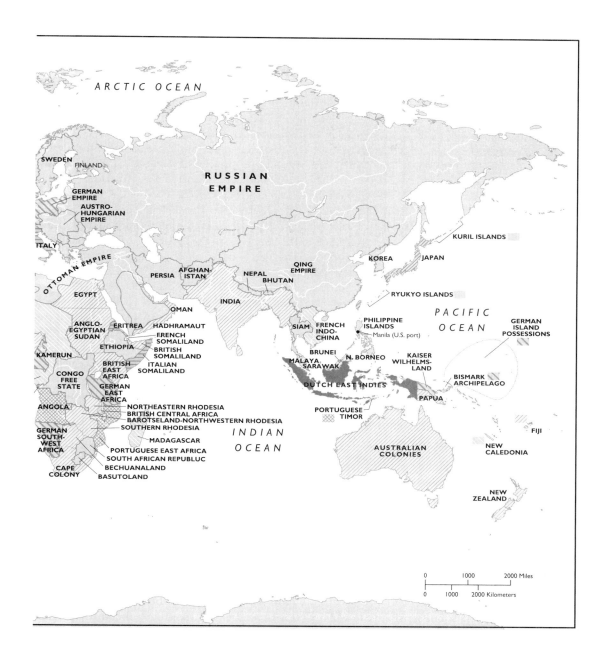

ARCTIC OCEAN

SWEDEN
FINLAND

GERMAN
EMPIRE
AUSTRO-
HUNGARIAN
EMPIRE

ITALY

OTTOMAN EMPIRE

EGYPT

ANGLO-
EGYPTIAN
SUDAN

ERITREA

ETHIOPIA

KAMERUN

BRITISH
EAST
AFRICA

CONGO
FREE
STATE

GERMAN
EAST
AFRICA

ANGOLA

GERMAN
SOUTH-
WEST
AFRICA

CAPE
COLONY

BASUTOLAND

BECHUANALAND

SOUTH AFRICAN REPUBLUC

PORTUGUESE EAST AFRICA

MADAGASCAR

SOUTHERN RHODESIA

BAROTSELAND-NORTHWESTERN RHODESIA

BRITISH CENTRAL AFRICA

NORTHEASTERN RHODESIA

OMAN

HADHRAMAUT

FRENCH
SOMALILAND

BRITISH
SOMALILAND

ITALIAN
SOMALILAND

RUSSIAN
EMPIRE

PERSIA

AFGHAN-
ISTAN

INDIA

NEPAL

BHUTAN

QING
EMPIRE

KURIL ISLANDS

KOREA

JAPAN

RYUKYO ISLANDS

SIAM

FRENCH
INDO-
CHINA

BRUNEI

MALAYA
SARAWAK

N. BORNEO

DUTCH EAST INDIES

PHILIPPINE
ISLANDS
Manila (U.S. port)

PACIFIC
OCEAN

GERMAN
ISLAND
POSSESSIONS

KAISER
WILHELMS-
LAND

PAPUA

BISMARK
ARCHIPELAGO

PORTUGUESE
TIMOR

INDIAN
OCEAN

AUSTRALIAN
COLONIES

FIJI

NEW
CALEDONIA

NEW
ZEALAND

| 0 | 1000 | 2000 Miles |
| 0 | 1000 | 2000 Kilometers |

colonial enterprise. In this selection, as in Headrick's piece on the use of quinine, we see science in the service of empire.

The establishment of schools and churches and the designation of official languages of administration were also important tools in the colonial process. These issues are addressed directly or indirectly in the selections from L. S. Senghor, Theodore Christlieb, and Thomas J. Morgan, and in the painting "The Secret of England's Greatness." Senghor demonstrates the influence of the French language in western Africa even as he champions its use by Africans to express *négritude,* or pride in being black. Christlieb reports on the spread in the Indian subcontinent of missionary Christianity activity and the obstacles to it presented by Hinduism. Morgan, an Indian Commissioner in the United States, argues that Native Americans must be forced to go to school so that they can be reformed and "civilized."

Colonial regimes also tried to regulate the everyday life of people living under their administration by modeling certain types of behaviors and habits, including dressing and grooming fashions. We see a subtle demonstration of this tendency in the picture of a Belgian administrator. Indeed, day-to-day contact between colonizers and the colonized allowed informal influence to be exercised in numerous ways. Even in areas that were not directly under colonial control, such as Latin America, European and North American economic and cultural patterns often had great impact upon people. Thus, in Latin America and the Caribbean, the tools of empire being used, following the logic of neo-imperialism, were usually economic and cultural in nature. Galeano's piece helps to show this point. In North America, the tools of empire were also usually cultural and economic in character as the United States, in particular, sought to expand its territory and to integrate a wide diversity of peoples into its society. Some of the most difficult issues involved in this process concerned the status of Native Americans and people of African origin. The selection from Morgan is instructive in this regard. Finally, ideology could be used as a tool of empire. Kita Ikki, a Japanese ultranationalist, argued that his nation should reject liberal political beliefs and assert itself as the leader of East Asia in opposition to Western colonial powers. In arguing thus, he was appropriating the rhetoric of nationalism, in an extreme form, to promote the new imperialistic ambitions of Japan. He was also none too subtly employing racial thinking—the superiority of the Japanese over other Asian peoples—to support his claims. Thus, there was a wide range of tools of empire in the late nineteenth and early twentieth centuries. Some of these tools were blunt and obvious; others were subtle and less well understood at the time by contemporaries. It is important to note that many of the tools of empire (education, nationalism, arguments about economic development, not to mention appeals to law and the use of guns) discussed in this part of the reader would later be used by the colonized as the empire's tools for liberation—a development treated in Part V.

Perry's Ship

This 1861 Japanese woodcut shows a modern steam clipper of the sort that Commodore Perry would have used to force Japan into signing an unequal treaty with the United States in 1854. European ships had dominated ocean trade routes since the sixteenth century, but with the industrial revolution, new technologies to power ships were invented that enabled faster travel that was less dependent on winds and ocean currents.

QUESTIONS

1. How did the industrial revolution of Europe and the United States facilitate imperialism?

2. Judging from this woodcut, what was the Japanese reaction to seeing the West's advanced technology?

Source: The Bridgeman Art Library International.

⋏

Machine as Civilizer

Michael Adas

One of the most direct examples of a tool of empire was the use of advanced technology—guns, ships, railroads—in the nineteenth and early twentieth centuries. Michael Adas, a leading global historian, discusses all of these technologies and their practical and ideological uses in colonial enterprises in his important book, Machines as the Measure of Men: Science, Technology, and Ideologies of Western Dominance. *In this selection from the book, he outlines the importance of comparative military development in India and China. Moreover, Adas shows how Europeans equated technical virtuosity, here represented in military capabilities, with moral superiority and therefore thought that their machines not only represented their power and wealth but could also be used to further European designs to "civilize" native peoples.*

⋏

Questions

1. How would you compare military development in India and China?
2. What conclusions about India and China did the British in particular draw on the basis of their military development?

[. . .] As in Africa, superiority in military technology and organization was one of the more obvious manifestations of the differences that Europeans believed distinguished their level of social development from that of the Indians. In contrast to their behavior in Africa, however, the Europeans made no attempt to employ rifles and revolvers or music boxes and cameras to dazzle or entertain the "natives." Extensive involvement in the internal affairs and political struggles of the subcontinent, extending back to the early decades of the eighteenth century, had left the British with no illusions about their ability to overawe the Marattas, Sikhs, or Rajputs with mere displays of the accuracy and firepower of their latest weapons. In land weaponry, the Europeans had begun their

rise to power in India in a state of rough parity with their Indian rivals. Through much of the eighteenth century the advantages the British and French enjoyed in warfare were primarily due to superb leadership, exemplified in such men as Robert Clive and Joseph Dupleix, plus superior discipline and organization. In applying the latter to struggles in the subcontinent, first the French and soon after them the British recruited Indian troops, called sepoys, into the European-led armies that vied for control with the larger but more unruly and poorly trained armies of Indian princes. In addition, Indian leaders—most successfully those of the Sikhs in the northwest—adopted European modes of training and organization and purchased large quantities of European arms in

Source: Reprinted from Michael Adas, *Machines as the Measure of Men: Science, Technology, and Ideologies of Western Dominance.* Copyright © 1990 by Cornell University. Used by permission of the publisher, Cornell University Press. Ithaca, New York, and London: Pp. 174–75, 186–87.

what eventually proved to be futile efforts to block the rise of British hegemony. Thus, the Indians had been exposed to British military technology long before the Industrial Revolution. They felt little or none of the shock of African peoples who were drawn—often quite abruptly—into conflict with European forces in a later era when Western military advantages had been greatly enhanced by the process of industrialization. In addition to large-scale sepoy recruitment, the intensive employment of Indians in the imperial bureaucracy, British mercantile and manufacturing concerns, and later in the railway, telegraph, and postal services meant that they had a greater familiarity with the latest advances in European applied science and European technology than any other non-Western people.

Military technology more often brought together than distanced the British and Indians on a day-to-day basis, but most nineteenth-century writers were quick to point out the ways in which the superiority of the Europeans was demonstrated by the fact that they were the inventors and manufacturers of modern weaponry. From James Mill early in the century to Fitzjames Stephen in the 1880s, British observers tended to subsume military technology within a broader category of military prowess that was seen as the key to the conquest and rule of the vast Indian subcontinent by a handful of intrepid Europeans. This myth of the stalwart few dominating the many hundreds of millions, which pointedly ignored the essential Indian military, administrative, and economic roles in the rise of British dominance, buttressed the claim of numerous writers that Britain had earned the right to rule India by virtue of conquest and martial excellence. In the 1860s John Crawfurd explored the links between better weapons and overall British superiority in some detail. Noting the Asians' failure to fully develop their early innovations in military organization and firearms, Crawfurd asserted that "the art of war is that which proclaims the loudest the incomparable superiority, both physical and intellectual, of the European over the Asiatic races."

He contrasted the stagnation of Indian military technology since the early eighteenth century with the Europeans' development in the same period of artillery that made Clive's cannons at the battle of Plassey in 1857 seem like "popguns." He noted that the sepoys were useless without British officers to train and command them. Echoing the sentiments of numerous nineteenth-century authors, Crawfurd declared that the technology and military skills that had allowed the British to conquer and rule the hundreds of millions of Indians provided "the most signal example of the superiority of the European races over the Asiatic." [. . .]

With the Opium Wars of 1839–42, the full meaning of China's military backwardness was brutally revealed. In a series of engagements on land and sea—rather modest confrontations by European standards—British ships and British-led Indian infantry routed the numerically superior Chinese forces. Britain's decisive military advantage was perhaps most dramatically demonstrated by clashes between the iron-clad paddle steamer *Nemesis* and the Chinese war junks. In addition to the most advanced naval artillery pieces, including two pivot-mounted thirty-two pounders, the newly built *Nemesis* was armed with a rocket launcher. In what proved to be the most memorable clash of the war, it singlehandedly engaged a fleet of fifteen Chinese war junks. The British ship took the initiative by reducing the lead junk to a roaring ball of smoke and fire with a Congreve missile. As the remaining junks fled or were hastily abandoned by their demoralized crews, the *Nemesis* continued up the coast, forced the panic-stricken inhabitants of a small town to evacuate their homes, sank a second war junk and captured another.

The contrast between the *Nemesis* and the Chinese junks—which with their mat sails and painted eyes struck one British officer as "apparitions from the Middle Ages"—cast further doubt on the already much contested image of China as a powerful and advanced civilization. These and later military setbacks convinced virtually all European observers that China was no match for Europe and reduced the Chinese in the eyes of the European public to the pitiful creatures ridiculed in an 1859 *Punch* jingle:

With their little pig-eyes and their large
    pig-tails
And their diet of rats, dogs, slugs, and snails,
All seems to be game in the frying-pan
Of that nasty feeder, *John Chinaman.*
Sing lie-tea, my sly *John Chinaman.*
No fightee, my coward *John Chinaman.*
John Bull has a chance—let him, if he can
Somewhat open the eyes of *John Chinaman.*

In order to imagine that China was Europe's equal, John Crawfurd mused nearly a decade later, "we must fancy a Chinese fleet and army capturing Paris and London, and dictating peace to the French and English."

Chinese ineptness at using up-to-date military technology provided the material for most of the anecdotes of bumbling "natives" which European commanders and travelers, like their counterparts in Africa, included in their memoirs to illustrate the great distance that separated the scientifically minded, industrializing Western peoples from all others. [. . .]

⋀

East African Transport, Old and New Style

ARTIST: ADRIAN ALLINSON

This double-paneled promotional poster was displayed by Britain's Empire Marketing Board from December 1930 to January 1931. It is notable for its before and after representation of the development of transportation, economy, and society in East Africa under British rule. The first panel shows East Africans on the move prior to European colonialism. The second panel shows the obvious economic benefits Europeans brought to East Africa. The presence of mechanized transport, bridges, and vibrant trade is immediately noticeable.

⋀

QUESTIONS

1. Consider the roles of African men and women as portrayed in these posters. How do these roles appear to shift from one poster to the other?

Source: National Archives Image Library, UK.

2. What conclusions about the African landscape, products, transportation, and trade can you draw from these two posters?

3. How is the European presented in the second poster? Compare him to the images of Africans in both panels.

Source: National Archives Image Library, UK.

Spies Along the Silk Road

PETER HOPKIRK

In their struggle for direct or indirect control of much of the globe in the late nineteenth century, European states also employed military means, survey teams, and spies as tools of empire. Although direct military encounters between imperial powers were relatively rare—more often they fought indigenous forces—Europeans were locked in a fierce and ongoing battle to survey, map, and gain intelligence about new territories that might in due course be brought into the informal orbit or official domain of a colonial empire. Imperial Russia and Great Britain were locked in one such contest for most of the nineteenth and into the twentieth century. The territorial expansion of Russia, on the one hand, and British interest in the Indian subcontinent, central Asia, and China, on the other, set the two imperial countries on a collision course in a vast stretch of central Asian territories from the Caucasus to China.

In his celebrated study The Great Game: The Struggle for Empire in Central Asia, *Peter Hopkirk, a British journalist, captured many important facets of the Russian–British contest for control. In this selection ("Spies Along the Silk Road"), he discusses the use of Indian spies, in particular, in exploring and mapping central Asian territories for the British. He tells of some ingenious techniques that were employed in the extension of colonial influence.*

QUESTIONS

1. Why did the British want to employ Indians as spies along the silk road?

2. What techniques did the British teach these spies for gathering information and mapping Central Asia?

3. Find out more about the "Great Game" between Russia and Great Britain. Which parts of the world were most caught up in this contest?

[. . .] The idea of using native explorers to carry out clandestine surveys of the lawless regions beyond India's frontiers had arisen as a result of the Viceroy's strict ban on British officers venturing there. Because of this the Survey of India, which had the task of providing the government with maps of the entire sub-continent and surrounding regions, found itself greatly hampered when it came to mapping northern Afghanistan, Turkestan and Tibet. Then a young officer working for the Survey, Captain Thomas Montgomerie of the Royal Engineers, hit upon a brilliant solution. Why not, he asked his superiors, send native explorers trained in secret surveying techniques into these forbidden regions? They were far less likely to be detected than a European, however

Source: Peter Hopkirk. *The Great Game: The Struggle for Empire in Central Asia.* New York: Kodansha America, 1994. Pp. 329–332. Reprinted by permission of Kodansha America, Inc.

good the latter's disguise. If they were unfortunate enough to be discovered, moreover, it would be less politically embarrassing to the authorities than if a British officer was caught red-handed making maps in these highly sensitive and dangerous parts.

Surprisingly perhaps, in view of the British and Indian governments' determination not to become entangled in Central Asia, Montgomerie's bold plan was approved, and over the next few years a number of Indian explorers, including Mirza Shuja, were dispatched in great secrecy across the frontier. All of them were hillmen, carefully chosen for their exceptional intelligence and resourcefulness. Because discovery, or even suspicion, would have spelt instant death, their existence and activities had to be kept as secret as possible. Even within the Survey of India they were known merely by a number or a cryptonym. They were trained personally by Montgomerie at Dehra Dun, the Survey's headquarters in the Himalayan foothills. Some of the techniques and equipment he devised were extremely ingenious.

Montgomerie first trained his men, through exhaustive practice, to take a pace of known length which would remain constant whether they walked uphill, downhill or on the level. Next he taught them ways of keeping a precise but discreet count of the number of such paces taken during a day's march. This enabled them to measure immense distances with remarkable accuracy and without arousing suspicion. Often they travelled as Buddhist pilgrims, many of whom regularly crossed the passes to visit the holy sites of the ancient Silk Road. Every Buddhist carried a rosary of 108 beads on which to count his prayers, and also a small wood and metal prayer-wheel which he spun as he walked. Both of these Montgomerie turned to his advantage. From the former he removed eight beads, not enough to be noticed, but leaving a mathematically convenient 100. At every hundredth pace the Pundit would automatically slip one bead. Each complete circuit of the rosary thus represented 10,000 paces.

The total for the day's march, together with any other discreet observations, had somehow to be logged somewhere safe from prying eyes. It was here that the prayer-wheel, with its copper cylinder, proved invaluable. For concealed in this, in place of the usual hand-written scroll of prayers, was a roll of blank paper. This served as a logbook, which could easily be got at by removing the top of the cylinder, and some of which are still preserved in the Indian State Archives. Then there was the problem of a compass, for the Pundit was required to take regular bearings as he journeyed. Montgomerie decided to conceal this in the lid of the prayer-wheel. Thermometers, which were needed for calculating altitudes, were hidden in the tops of pilgrims' staves. Mercury, essential for setting an artificial horizon when taking sextant readings, was hidden in cowrie shells and poured out into a pilgrim's begging bowl when required. Concealed pockets were added to the Pundits' clothing, and false bottoms, in which sextants could be hidden, were built into the chests which most native travellers carried. All this work was carried out in the Survey of India's workshops at Dehra Dun under Montgomerie's supervision.

The Pundits were also thoroughly trained in the art of disguise and in the use of cover stories. For in the lawless lands beyond the frontier their safety would depend on just how convincingly they could play the part of holy-man, pilgrim or Himalayan trader. Their disguise and cover had to stand the test of months of travelling, often in the closest intimacy with genuine pilgrims and traders. Some were away for years. One became the first Asiatic to be awarded the Royal Geographical Society's gold medal, having contributed 'a greater amount of positive knowledge to the map of Asia than any other individual of our time'. At least two never returned, while a third was sold into slavery, although he eventually escaped. In all, their clandestine journeys were to provide a wealth of geographical intelligence over some twenty years which Montgomerie and his fellow cartographers at Dehra Dun used to fill in many of the no-go areas on the British maps of Central Asia.

Just what drove men like Mirza Shuja to face such hardships and extreme dangers for their imperial masters has never been satisfactorily explained. Perhaps it was the inspirational leadership of Montgomerie, who took such a pride in their individual achievements, and who looked upon them as his sons. Or possibly it was the knowledge that they belonged to an élite, for each was aware that he had been hand-picked for this great task. Or maybe Montgomerie had managed to imbue them with his own patriotic determination to fill in the blanks on the Great Game map before the Russians did. In an earlier book, *Trespassers on the Roof of the World*, I have described some of the Pundits' more prodigious feats of exploration, which I shall not attempt to retell here. Sadly, very little is known of these men as individuals, for none of them left memoirs of any kind. However, it is in Kipling's masterpiece *Kim*, whose characters so clearly come from the shadowy world of Captain Montgomerie, that they have their just memorial.

⚔

Products of the Empire

J. CLINTON CUNNINGHAM

Products of the Empire *represents an effort to catalogue the natural resources of the British empire. The quest for raw materials in the form of plants and minerals that could only be found outside Europe was one of the major motivations for imperialism. In this excerpt on rubber, we can see exactly how British botanists and traders expanded cultivation of the Brazilian plant around the empire and through this process helped to both transform and consolidate British control over local economies. British-owned rubber plantations in Ceylon, Malaysia, and elsewhere enriched the homeland and connected remote parts of the empire more closely to the British economy. Rubber, in particular, served as a tool of empire both through its production and through its use in tires, electrical wiring, and other products that the British used to control and modernize the colonies.*

J. Clinton Cunningham's interest in botany seems to have motivated the writing of Products of the Empire, *which focuses principally, though not exclusively, on plants. Cunningham writes largely about what he calls "economic" plants, that is, plants that have economic value, such as cereals, sugar, tobacco, and cotton. The volume extends beyond plants, however, to consider the availability of and uses for other raw materials such as metals.*

⚔

QUESTIONS

1. By what process were rubber trees introduced to the British empire?
2. How did the study of botany help the British to enrich themselves?
3. In what sense might we consider plants or planting practices to be tools of empire?

Rubber (*Hevea brasiliensis*). We read that when Columbus was in Hayti he observed that the balls with which the children played bounced better than the windballs of the Spanish children at home, and it was found on inquiry that these West Indian balls were made of a substance which exuded from certain trees. They were in fact made of 'rubber', as ours are to-day, but rubber at that time had never been heard of in Europe, and the Spanish children had to be content with a very poor bounce to their balls.

In 1735, the distinguished French traveller, La Condamine, made a voyage to the Equator for the purpose of determining the dimensions of the earth. On his return he published an account of his ten years' journey, and among other marvels he described the rubber tree and its wonderful juice. The tree he called *He'vé*, and the solidified juice

Source: J. Clinton Cunningham. *Products of the Empire*. Oxford: Clarendon Press, 1921. Pp. 269, 270–71, 271–73, 276–77.

Cahuchu. These were both South American names. We called the solidified juice rubber, because it rubbed out pencil marks. [. . .]

There are a great many different kinds of trees which produce rubber, altogether about a hundred, and they all grow in hot climates. The forests of the Amazon Valley and of the Congo were for a long time the chief sources of supply.

The methods of the native collectors were primitive and extremely wasteful. More often than not the trees were killed, and the collectors had to probe more and more deeply into the forests to obtain supplies. (Some of the South American rubber has to travel 3,000 miles before it is put on board ship, and it does not reach us till a year after it has been gathered.)

The very best rubber of all is obtained from the tree called *Hevea brasiliensis.* It grows in the Amazon forests, and is especially vigorous and abundant on the plateau between the Tapajos and Madeira Rivers in Brazil.

Sir Joseph Hooker, at that time Director of Kew Gardens [Britain's Royal Botanical Garden], ardently desired to obtain some seeds of these trees, and to plant them in suitable regions of the empire, so that in course of time we might produce our own rubber.

It was a great idea, but almost insuperable difficulties stood in the way of its realization. To begin with, the seeds remain good only a short time after they fall from the tree (it is best to plant them within a week), and therefore it is not surprising to learn that great patience and perseverance were needed on the part of those who brought the seeds to England. [. . .]

At last, in 1876, a commission was given by the authorities at Kew to Mr. Wickham for the 'introduction of the tree which produced the true Para [a Brazilian state] rubber of commerce'.

Mr. Wickham [. . .] gives a fascinating account of how he successfully overcame every difficulty that stood in his way.

All around were the great hot forests, and in them, growing in glorious profusion, were the wonderful Hevea trees. The season for the ripening of their seeds was drawing near, and if they were not gathered now a whole year must elapse before anything further could be done. But it was useless to gather them, for the problem still remained, how to convey them quickly to England.

Just at that time the S.S. *Amazonas*, the first of the new Inman Line of steamers, had come up the river, and Mr. Wickham and a few other planters were invited to dinner on board. They passed a pleasant evening and the steamer proceeded on her way up the river.

The season for gathering the seeds, meanwhile, came nearer and nearer, and the problem of transport still remained unsolved. And then came his chance. News was brought down the river that the captain of the *Amazonas* was left stranded with the ship on his hands, and no chance of a return cargo, the men who were in charge of these matters having stripped the ship, and then abandoned her.

Mr. Wickham boldly chartered the ship in the name of the Indian Government, and arranged to meet the captain on a certain day at the junction of the Tapajos and Amazon. He engaged as many Indians as he could get and crossed the river into the pathless forests between the Tapajos and Madeira. Here day by day they ranged the forests, filling up their baskets with as heavy loads as their backs would bear, and at the appointed hour he arrived with his precious burden.

To his unspeakable relief he found the ship awaiting him. The seeds were safely stowed on board, and for the moment all anxiety was over. The weather was fine, and they made their way down the river quickly.

But then occurred a new difficulty. How were they to avoid delay at Pará? In all probability they would be detained here while inquiries were made of the authorities at Rio as to whether the ship should be allowed to proceed on her journey, and by the time the necessary permission was obtained the seeds would be spoiled. However, thanks to the exertions of our Consul, matters were speedily arranged with the Portuguese authorities, and the good ship *Amazonas* steered out into the ocean.

June 14, 1876, must always be regarded as a red-letter day in the history of British commerce, for on that day the *Amazonas* arrived at Liverpool docks with her precious freight of seven thousand rubber seeds. From Kew Gardens a night train was sent to meet the ship, and a fortnight later in the glass-houses of Kew row upon row of young Hevea plants gladdened the eyes of their owners.

Not all of these plants lived, but 1,919 of them were sent to Ceylon, and some few to Perak in the Malay Peninsula. Of those sent to Ceylon the greater number survived and flourished, while seven of the Perak ones were planted in the garden of the Residency at Kuala Kangsar. Later on plants were reared successfully at Singapore. It is from these small beginnings that the present enormous production of British rubber has sprung. [. . .]

Uses of Rubber.   It seems almost impossible to produce too much rubber, considering the great variety of uses to which it can be put. It is required for the great rubber tyres for motors [cars] of all kinds, and for the smaller tyres of other vehicles; even perambulators nowadays have rubber tyres. Rubber-soled shoes of various kinds use up large quantities. It is used in electrical, and scientific, and medical, and surgical apparatus. In electrical appliances it is especially valuable, as it is a non-conductor of electricity. In the future it is most probable its use will be greatly extended; floors will be covered with it, and footpaths paved with it. [. . .]

We cannot help feeling a deep debt of gratitude to those who introduced the tree into our empire and enabled us to be self-supporting in such a valuable commodity.

⅄

Malaria, Quinine, and the Penetration of Africa

DANIEL HEADRICK

In the last several decades, scholars have become aware of the critical roles played by "guns, germs, and steel" in global history. The uneven balance between peoples in regards to any of these three elements could, under certain circumstances, be decisive in world history. Moreover, the control of guns, germs, and steel played obvious and substantial roles in the patterns of modern colonialism. This was especially true during the European acquisition of African and Asian territory in the late nineteenth century.

In this selection, Daniel R. Headrick, a leading global historian, highlights how Europeans' use of quinine allowed them to penetrate the interior of Africa by reducing the risk of malaria. He reminds us of the importance of biological, medical, and environmental factors in human history. Some global historians, such as the pioneer in the field William McNeill, have argued that these factors should be understood as the *primary contours for understanding interactions and exchanges between peoples and nations. As Headrick points out, it is hard to imagine the success of European colonization in certain overseas areas without at least the relative control of a disease such as malaria.*

⅄

QUESTIONS

1. According to Headrick, what were the practical limits of the European occupation of Africa in particular before the widespread use of quinine to treat and prevent malaria?

2. How does the manufacture and use of quinine reveal a global pattern of trade and exchange of medical knowledge in the age of high imperialism? Where was a natural source of quinine found? Where was it eventually produced? And where was it principally used?

3. In a general sense, how do you weigh the importance of germs and their control in human history?

[. . .] In West Africa, too, the use of quinine became more common, while purgings and bleedings gradually fell into disfavor. By the mid-1840s, Europeans in the Gold Coast regularly kept a jar of quinine pills by their bedside, to be taken at the first sign of chills or fever. Yet this treatment, although beneficial against the *vivax* form of malaria prevalent in Algeria, was generally insufficient against *falciparum* malaria. To defeat the *Plasmodium falciparum*, the human

Source: Daniel Headrick. "Malaria, Quinine, and the Penetration of Africa." *The Tools of Empire: Technology and European Imperialism in the Nineteenth Century.* New York and Oxford: Oxford University Press, 1981. Pp. 67–73. Used with permission.

bloodstream had to be saturated with quinine before the onset of the first infection; in other words, throughout one's stay in *falciparum* areas, quinine had to be taken regularly as a prophylactic.

Two chance events led to this discovery. The first occurred in 1839, on board the *North Star* stationed off Sierra Leone. While serving on the ship, twenty crew members took cinchona bark daily and one officer did not; he alone died of malaria. The second incident took place two years later, when the British government sponsored the largest of all the Niger expeditions up to that time. With three new steamers—the 457-ton *Albert* and *Wilberforce* and the 249-ton *Soudan*—Capt. H. D. Trotter led 159 Europeans up the Niger to the confluence of the Benue. To avoid the health problems of previous missions every known precaution was taken. The crew was specially selected from among athletic young men of good breeding, the ships were equipped with fans to dispel bad air, and the expedition raced at top speed through the miasmic delta to reach the drier climate of the upper river as soon as possible. Nonetheless the first cases of fever appeared within three weeks, forcing the *Wilberforce* and the *Soudan* to return to the Atlantic as floating hospitals. Within two months, forty-eight of the Europeans had died, and by the end of the expedition another seven fell victim to the disease. Africa had regained its terrible reputation among the British.

Despite this disappointment, the Niger expedition of 1841 represents a major step toward a solution to the problem of malaria, for the physician on board one of the ships, Dr. T. R. H. Thomson, used the opportunity to experiment with various drugs. Some crew members received cinchona bark with wine, others got quinine; Dr. Thomson himself took quinine regularly and stayed healthy. He later wrote his observations on the matter in an article entitled "On the Value of Quinine in African Remittent Fever" which appeared in the British medical journal *The Lancet* on February 28, 1846. A year later, Dr. Alexander Bryson, an experienced naval physician, published his *Report on the Climate and Principal Diseases of the African Station* (London, 1847), in which he advocated quinine prophylaxis to Europeans in Africa. In 1848 the director-general of the Medical Department of the British Army sent a circular to all British governors in West Africa, recommending quinine prophylaxis.

Yet quinine prophylaxis was not immediately adopted. It took a spectacular demonstration to achieve this end. In 1854, Macgregor Laird, never cured of his fascination with Africa, proposed still another expedition to that continent. Under contract with the Admiralty, he had a ship called the *Pleiad* specially built. She was a 220-ton iron propeller-steamer rigged as a schooner, designed to pull two or three barges behind her on her way up the Niger. As was usually the case, she was armed with a 12-pounder pivot gun, four smaller swivel cannons, rifles, and muskets. The crew consisted of twelve Europeans and fifty-four Africans.

Before the ship sailed, Dr. Alexander Bryson wrote a set of instructions in which he described the clothing, diet, activities, and moral influences best suited to protect the health of the crew. To prevent fevers he recommended that each crew member take six to eight grains of quinine a day from the time the ship crossed the bar until fourteen days after she returned to the ocean. The captain of the ship, Dr. William Baikie, was himself a physician and saw to it that the crew followed this advice. The *Pleiad* stayed 112 days on the Niger and Benue rivers, and returned with all the European crew members alive. Thomas Hutchinson, a member of the expedition, attributed this to Dr. Bryson's suggestions; as he put it,

> Since my first visit to Africa in 1850, I have felt firmly convinced—and that conviction urges me to impress my faith on all who read this work—that the climate would not be so fatal as it has hitherto proved to Europeans, if a different mode of daily living, a proper method of prophylactic hygiene, and another line of therapeutic practice in the treatment of fevers, were adopted. Before, and beyond all others, is the preventive influence of quinine as it was used in the "Pleiad," in the mode here described. . . .

As the prophylactic use of quinine spread, and as purgings and bleedings vanished, the death rates fell significantly. Philip Curtin gives some statistics: In the Royal Navy's Africa Squadron, the mortality rate fell from 65 per 1,000 in 1825–45 to 22 per 1,000 in 1858–67; in 1874, during the two-month military expedition against Kumasi, only 50 of the 2,500 European soldiers died of disease; in 1881–97, among British officials in the Gold Coast, the rate was 76 per 1,000, and in Lagos it was 53 per 1,000. On the whole, the first-year death rates among Europeans in West Africa dropped from 250–750 per 1,000 to 50–100 per 1,000. To be sure, this was still five to ten times higher than the death rates for people in the same age bracket in Europe. Africa remained hostile to the health of Europeans. Yet psychologically the improvement was significant. No longer was tropical Africa the "white man's grave," fit for only the most ardent visionaries and the unluckiest recruits. It was now a place from which Europeans could reasonably hope to return alive. In Curtin's words, ". . . the improvement over the recent past was understood well enough in official and missionary circles to reduce sharply the most serious impediment to any African activity."

One immediate consequence of quinine prophylaxis was a great increase in the number and success of European explorers in Africa after the mid-century. Exploration, of course, remained a dangerous business, but no longer was it quasi-suicidal. With the prospect before them of fruitful discoveries, perhaps even glory and wealth, many more adventurous souls volunteered in the service of knowledge. David Livingstone, the most lionized of all the explorers, first heard of quinine prophylaxis while he was in Bechuanaland in 1843. During his march across southern Africa in 1850–56 he took quinine daily. By 1857 he was convinced that quinine was a preventive. In preparation for his Zambezi expedition of 1858 he made his European crew take two grains of quinine in sherry every day. Throughout the expedition, many suffered from malaria, but only three out of twenty-five died. Later he came to doubt the efficacy of quinine as a preventive, for it only lessened the impact of the disease. His favorite remedy for malaria was a concoction of quinine, calomel, rhubarb, and resin of julep which he called "Livingstone Pills."

In the footsteps of the explorers, lesser protagonists of European imperialism penetrated the African interior: missionaries, soldiers, traders, administrators, engineers, planters and their wives and children, and finally tourists. All of them needed their daily quinine. In India and other tropical areas, the influx of Europeans added to the growing demand for the drug.

Until the 1850s all the world's cinchona bark came from the forests of Peru, Bolivia, Ecuador, and Colombia, where the trees grew wild. As world demand increased, the bark exports of the Andean republics rose from two million pounds in 1860 to twenty million in 1881. At that point the Andean bark was swept from the world market by the competition of Indian and Indonesian bark, the result of deliberate efforts by Dutch and British interests.

The idea of growing cinchona in Asia had been discussed many times, but with little effect as long as demand was small. In the early 1850s, as demand grew, Dutch botanists and horticulturists in Java urged the Netherlands East Indies government to import cinchona seedlings. In 1853–54, Justus Charles Hasskarl, superintendent of the Buitenzorg Botanical Gardens in Java, traveled to the Andes under an assumed name and secretly collected seeds; most of them perished, however. In 1858–60, Clements Markham, a clerk at the India Office, aided by a gardener from the British Royal Botanic Gardens at Kew named Weir, traveled to Bolivia and Peru, again secretly, to collect seeds of the *Cinchona calisaya* tree. Simultaneously, the English botanist Richard Spruce and another Kew gardener, Robert Cross, collected 100,000 *C. succirubra* seeds and 637 young plants in Ecuador; of these, 463 seedlings reached India, forming the nucleus of the cinchona plantations at Ootacamund in the Nilgiri Hills near Madras.

There followed a period of intensive experimentation. At botanical gardens in Bengal,

Ceylon, Madras, and Java, horticulturists and quinologists exchanged seeds and information, and provided cheap seedlings and free advice to planters. A hybrid species, *C. calisaya Ledgeriana*, grafted onto the stem of a *C. succirubra* tree, formed the basis of the Javanese cinchona plantations after 1874. Techniques such as mossing (cutting strips of bark and wrapping the trees in moss) and coppicing (cutting trees to the ground every six or seven years) greatly increased the yield of alkaloids. While Peruvian bark had a two percent sulphate of quinine content, scientific breeding in Java raised the content to six percent by 1900, and later to eight or nine percent.

In the late nineteenth century, after the demise of the Andean bark industry, a compromise was worked out between the British and the Dutch. Plantations in India produced a cheaper, less potent bark from which chemists extracted totaquine, a mixture of antimalarial alkaloids. Almost the entire Indian production was destined to British military and administrative personnel in the tropics, and the excess was sold in India.

The Javanese industry, which produced the more potent and expensive pure quinine, captured over nine tenths of the world market by the early twentieth century. This world monopoly of cinchona resulted not only from scientific methods of cultivation, but also from a marketing cartel, the Kina Bureau of Amsterdam, which coordinated the purchase of bark and the price and quantity of quinine sold. Not until the Japanese conquest of Indonesia in World War Two and the development of synthetic malaria suppressants did this Dutch control over one of the world's most vital drugs come to an end.

Scientific cinchona production was an imperial technology par excellence. Without it European colonialism would have been almost impossible in Africa, and much costlier elsewhere in the tropics. At the same time, the development of this technology, combining the scientific expertise of several botanical gardens, the encouragement of the British and Dutch colonial governments, and the land and labor of the peoples of India and Indonesia, was clearly a consequence as well as a cause of the new imperialism.

▲

Open Veins of Latin America: Five Centuries of the Pillage of a Continent

Eduardo Galeano

Eduardo Galeano's Open Veins of Latin America, *originally published in 1971 in Mexico, remains one of the most articulate discussions of American and European economic imperialism in Latin America. Galeano, an early advocate of dependency theory and a strident critic of U.S. and European imperialism, argued that from the moment of European discovery of the Americas, Europe, and then North America, had imposed an unequal economic relationship upon Latin America. Latin America, he contended, had been deliberately underdeveloped, and it therefore was not, in the sense that people have commonly used the term in recent decades, a developing region.*

Born in Uruguay in 1940, Galeano made a career as a journalist and writer. Fear of persecution for his leftist sympathies caused him to flee the Uruguayan military government to Argentina in 1973 and then to leave Argentina for Spain in 1976. He spent a number of years in exile in Spain before returning to Uruguay in 1984.

The following selection argues that Europe and the United States employed the railroad system and loans for its construction to exploit Latin American economies and to keep them from developing.

▲

Questions

1. In what ways were the former Spanish colonies of Latin America economically "re-colonized" after they gained political independence in the early nineteenth century?

2. According to Galeano, how did Western powers use loans and debt to force Latin American nations to do their bidding?

3. In your estimation, can international finance be a tool of empire?

How Loans and Railroads Deformed the Latin American Economy

René Chateaubriand, France's foreign minister under Louis XVIII, wrote in presumably well-informed disgust: "In the hour of emancipation the Spanish colonies turned into some sort of British colonies." He cited some figures. Between 1822 and 1826, he said, Britain had extended to the liberated Spanish colonies ten loans for a nominal value of around £ 21 million, but after deduction of interest and middlemen's commissions scarcely

Source: Eduardo Galeano. *Open Veins of Latin America: Five Centuries of the Pillage of a Continent.* (Trans. Cedric Belfrage.) New York: Monthly Review Press, 1973. Pp. 216–219. Used with permission.

£ 7 million had actually reached Latin America. At the same time, more than forty limited stock companies had been created in London to exploit Latin America's natural resources— mines, agriculture—and to establish public service enterprises. Banks mushroomed in Britain: in one year, 1836, forty-eight were founded. British railroads appeared in Panama around mid-century, and the first streetcar line in Latin America was inaugurated by a British firm in 1868 in the Brazilian city of Recife. The Bank of England also directly financed government treasuries: Latin American public bonds actively circulated, with their crises and booms, in the British financial market. Their public services in British hands, the new states from their inception faced a flood of military expenditures and also had to cope with external payment deficits. Free trade involved a frenzied increase in imports, especially of luxury articles; governments contracted debts, which in turn called for new loans, so that a minority could live fashionably. The countries were mortgaging their future in advance, moving away from economic freedom and political sovereignty. Except in Paraguay (whose contrary effort was crushed), the process was similar throughout Latin America—and still is, although the creditors and the mechanisms are different. The need for external financing became, like the addict's need for morphine, indispensable. Holes were dug for the sake of filling them. Nor is the deterioration of commercial terms of exchange a phenomenon peculiar to our own day. According to Celso Furtado, the prices of Brazilian exports fell 40 percent between 1821 and 1830 and between 1841 and 1850, while foreign import prices remained stable: Latin America's vulnerable economies compensated for the decline with loans.

"The finances of these young states," writes Robert Schnerb, "are not sound . . . They must resort to inflation, which produces depreciation of the currency, and to onerous loans. These republics' history may be said to be that of the economic obligations they incur to the all-absorbing world of European finance." In fact, bankruptcies,

payment suspensions, and desperate refinancing were frequent. Pounds sterling ran out like water between the fingers. Of the £ 1 million loan that the Buenos Aires government negotiated with Baring Brothers in 1824, Argentina received only £ 570,000, and that not in gold (as stipulated) but in paper. The loan consisted of drafts on orders sent to British businessmen in Buenos Aires, who had no gold with which to pay since their real mission was to send all precious metals that came their way to London. So Argentina received paper but was required to pay in gold; it was not until early in this century that Argentina canceled the debt, which successive refinancings had inflated to £ 4 million. Buenos Aires province had been completely mortgaged—all its revenues, all its public lands—as guarantee of payment. As the finance minister in the period when the loan was contracted said: "We are not in a position to take measures against foreign trade, particularly British, because we are bound to that nation by large debts and would expose ourselves to a rupture which would cause much harm . . ." The use of debt as an instrument of blackmail is not, as we can see, a recent U.S. invention.

Such usurious operations put bars around free nations. By the middle of the nineteenth century, servicing of the foreign debt absorbed almost 40 percent of Brazil's budget, and every country was caught in the same trap. Railroads formed another decisive part of the cage of dependency: when monopoly capitalism was in flower, imperialist influence extended into the colonial economies' remote backyards. Many of the loans were for financing railroads to bring minerals and foodstuffs to export terminals. The tracks were laid not to connect internal areas one with another, but to connect production centers with ports. The design still resembles the fingers of an open hand: thus railroads, so often hailed as forerunners of progress, were an impediment to the formation and development of an internal market. The imperialist nations also achieved this in other ways, especially through a tariff policy cut to the British pattern. For example, freightage on articles processed in the Argentine interior was much higher than on unfinished goods. Railroad charges became a curse that made it impossible to manufacture cigarettes in tobacco-growing areas, to spin and weave in wool centers, or to finish wood in forest zones. True, the Argentine railroad developed the Santiago del Estero timber industry, but with such results that a local author groaned: "Oh, that Santiago had never had a tree!" The cross-ties were made of wood, and charcoal served as fuel; the lumber camps created by the railroad broke up rural communities, destroyed agriculture and cattle-farming by razing pastureland and shade trees, enslaved several generations of Santiagans in the forests, and furthered depopulation. The mass exodus has not stopped and today Santiago del Estero is one of Argentina's poorest provinces. When the railroads switched to fuel oil, the region was plunged into a deep crisis.

It was not British capital that laid the first tracks across Argentina, Brazil, Chile, Guatemala, Mexico, and Uruguay. Nor in Paraguay, as we have seen; but the railroads built by the Paraguayan state, with the help of European technicians, passed into

British hands after the defeat. The other countries' railroads went the same way without producing a single centavo of new investment; furthermore, the state contracts took care to assure the companies a minimum profit level, to avoid possible unpleasant surprises. Decades later, at the end of World War II, when the railroads yielded no more dividends and had fallen into relative disuse, the public authorities got them back. Almost all of the states bought the scrap iron from the British and thus nationalized the companies' losses.

When the railroads were booming, the British concerns had often obtained considerable land concessions on either side of the tracks, in addition to the railbeds themselves and the right to build new branch lines. The land was an additional business bonanza. A fabulous gift to the Brazilian railway in 1911 led to the burning of countless huts and the eviction or death of peasant families in the concession area. It was this that triggered off the "Contestado" revolt, one of the greatest outbursts of popular fury in Brazilian history.

▲

French—Language of Culture

Léopold S. Senghor

As colonies were constructed and empires expanded, colonial peoples were forced to learn the languages of the colonizers in order to be able to function within the new administrative, economic, and social structures. In the following selection, written after Senegal had achieved independence from France, Léopold Senghor constructs a rationale for the continued use of the French language by former French colonial subjects. In the same document, though not in this selection, he explores the concept of négritude, or blackness, and demonstrates his awareness of the racial divide between colonizer and colonized.

Born in the village of Joal, Senegal, Senghor attended the local Catholic Mission School. At seventeen, he went to the Catholic Seminary at Dakar and later attended Sorbonne University in Paris. He went on to prominence in both politics and literature, serving as President of Senegal from 1960 to 1981 and becoming one of Africa's best-known poets and the first African member of the French Academy (Académie Française). Though a staunch supporter of black African liberation from colonialism in general and French rule in particular, he hoped for the creation of an African federation and sought the continuation of close ties with France. He saw French as a natural means of communication in the modern world, of which Africa had become a part. In his article, "French—Language of Culture," Senghor emphasizes the use of French language as a tool that enabled him to benefit from the European cultural connection. He thus demonstrates the importance and ambivalence of language as a tool of empire.

▲

QUESTIONS

1. How does Senghor feel about the French language?
2. Why did he urge Francophonic Africans to continue to use French even after independence?

[. . .] But I must before ending reply to the question which was personally put to me. For the reasons are just as valid as the policies which primarily seek the economic and cultural development of their respective peoples, to go beyond well-being to achieve the ultimate happiness. *What does the use of French represent for me, a black writer?* The question deserves a much greater response than that which the *poet* makes here, having defined African languages as *'poetic languages.'* In replying I shall take up a statement of fact. I think in French; I express myself better in French than in my mother tongue.

There is also the fact that any child who is sent to a foreign country at an early age learns the language as easily as a native. This implies a plasticity

Source: Léopold S. Senghor. "French—Language of Culture." In J. Ayo Langley (Ed.), *Ideologies of Liberation in Black Africa 1856–1970*. London: Rex Collings, 1979. Pp. 382–84.

of the human mind, and that every language can be used as an expression of the human soul. It only emphasizes one or the other aspect of this soul besides interpreting it in its own way.

Now, as it happens, *French* is, contrary to what people say, *a highly poetic language.* Not through its clarity, but through its richness. Indeed, until the nineteenth century, it was a language of moralists, lawyers and diplomats: 'A language of good manners and courtesy'. But then Victor Hugo arrived, and upsetting Malherbe's strict noble enactment threw *'the old dictionary to the winds.'* At the same time, he let loose a multitude of forbidden words: concrete and abstract words, academic and technical words, popular and exotic words. And then a century later the surrealists, not content with putting the format for the *'poème-discours'* in the dustbin, with one blow got rid of all the 'hinge-words' leaving us with bare poems panting with the same rhythm of the soul. They had found the *black syntax of juxtaposition* again, focusing on words which burst out aflame with metaphors and symbolism. The scene was set for *black poetry in the French language.*

Of course, I am asked what advantage French was for those who had mastered an African Language. The advantage was essentially that of the richness of the vocabulary and the fact that French is the language of an *international audience.* We shall leave this last fact aside, since it is obvious enough not to need further explanation. The advantage of French was that it offered us a choice: 'The African', wrote André Davesne in *Croquis de Brousse,* 'is thus prepared through the oral tradition to distinguish two values in the words which the French language provides for him: one, its abstract and intellectual meaning; the other, its concrete and sensual musical quality. If, then, he incautiously attempts to learn our language, he imbibes a double series of words: some signifying something tangible, for example an object, which cannot lose its meaning; others, in more frequent use, whose meaning is too mysterious or too 'intellectual' to become the determining factor in the

context in which they are used, but which deserve to be used because of their tone and resonance.'

From what is instinctive for illiterates, we have been able to make a *'poièsis'*, a systematic method of creation. The problem, after all, is more complex than Davesne claims. These are all French words which, through violation and being turned inside out, can set alight the metaphor's flame. It suffices to uproot the most 'intellectual' words, through examining their etymology, to surrender them to the symbol's sunlight.

As we have seen, vocabulary does not account for all the qualities of the French language; stylistics, in particular, result in amazing gems. To return to the musical effect of the words, French offers a variety of sounds through which every effect can be captured: from the softness of the Alizés in the night among the palm trees, to the flashing violence of thunder in the tops of the baobab trees. It is not just the rhythms in French which provide unexpected resources. After all, the binary rhythm of classical verses can render the despotic breathing of the tom-tom. It suffices to speed it up gently to make syncopated notes emerge from the basic rhythm.

What should we conclude from all this except that we, as black politicians and writers, feel at least as free in the inner workings of French as in our mother tongue. Freer in fact, since *Freedom* should be measured against the power of the tool or the creating force.

It is not a question of disowning African languages. Over the centuries, for thousands of years perhaps, they will still be spoken, expressing the boundless depths of *Négritude.* We shall continue to fish for *archetypal images:* those fishes from the deepest waters. It is a question of expressing our *authenticity* as cross-cultural men of the twentieth century. At the moment when through *totalitarianism* and *socialisation* the *Universal Civilisation* is achieved, it is, in a word, a question of using this marvellous tool, found in the debris of the colonial régime: this tool is the French language.

Francophonie represents this *integrated Humanism* which weaves itself around the earth: this *symbiosis* of 'dormant energies' in all continents and all races, which wakes up to its complementary warmth. 'France', a representative of the F.L.N. [Algerian National Liberation Front] told me, 'it's you, it's me; it's French culture'. Let us turn the proposition upside down to make it complete: *Négritude, Arabisme* is also you, Frenchman of the Hexagon. *Our* values now throb within the books that you read and the language that you speak: *French*, the sun which shines beyond the Hexagon.

▲

Compulsory Education

THOMAS J. MORGAN

By the late nineteenth century, Native Americans from the eastern part of the United States had virtually all been forcibly relocated to the American West, and reservations were constructed on which they and western Indians were to live. Indians had thus been forced into the dependent position of being wards of the American state. Throughout this period, a growing group of Indian reformers, many of whom were white, and the Bureau of Indian Affairs sought strategies to make the Indian population less dependent. In general, these strategies involved education and the conversion to Christianity of Indians. Discussion of Indian reform occurred at the Lake Mohonk Conference of Friends of the Indian, which took place annually at Lake Mohonk, New York, between 1883 and 1929. Conference participants were mostly white men and women who had come into contact with Indians during military service in the American West or through Christian social reform activities.

Thomas J. Morgan was the son of a minister and served as Commissioner of Indian Affairs for the Bureau of Indian Affairs. He was also an ardent advocate of Indian reform through education. In this speech, delivered at the Lake Mohonk Conference of 1892, Morgan offered a forceful rationale for the compulsory education of Native Americans whether they wanted it or not. Education was a tool to shape Native American children as productive and responsible citizens and to deliver them from the "barbarian" lives that they would otherwise lead.

▲

QUESTIONS

1. In what ways does Morgan seek to reshape Native Americans?
2. Why does Morgan think the Native Americans should be "brought into relationship with the civilization of the nineteenth century?"

We must either fight the Indians, or feed them, or educate them. To fight them is cruel; to feed them is wasteful; to educate them is humane, economic, and Christian. We have forced upon them—I use the term not in any offensive sense—citizenship, and we are limiting severely the period of preparation. Unless they can be educated for the proper discharge of their duties and for the enjoyment of their privileges as citizens, they will fail to be properly benefited by the boon that we are conferring upon them. The government of the United States has at large expense provided accommodations for from twenty to twenty-five thousand of their children in schools maintained

Source: Thomas J. Morgan, "Compulsory Education," 1892. *Proceedings of the Tenth Annual Meeting for the Lake Mohonk Conference of Friends of the Indian, 1892.* Martha D. Adams (Ed.). Lake Mohonk Conference, 1892. Pp. 51–54.

wholly or in part by the government. The people will not long continue to expend these two and a quarter million dollars a year for the education of these children if those to whom it is offered are unwilling to accept it. If they refuse to send their children to school, these schools will be closed; and the people who have been made citizens will be thrown upon themselves, and be left to survive or perish, according to their individual inclination. A large body of them to-day are unwilling to send their children to school. The schools are open, they offer to them every facility for learning English, they offer them free board, free tuition, free clothing, free medical care. Everything is freely offered, they are urged to come, but they refuse; and there is growing up, under the shadow of these institutions of learning, a new generation of savages. We are confronted, then, with this simple proposition: Shall we allow the growth of another generation of barbarians, or shall we compel the children to enter these schools to be trained to intelligence and industry? That is practically the question that confronts the Indian Office now.

Let me illustrate: At Fort Hall in Idaho, where the Shoshones and the Bannacks are, there is a school population of about two hundred and fifty. The people are degraded. They wander about in the mountains. Their women do most of what little work is done. They live in a beastly way (I use the term thoughtfully, I have seen it); and they are refusing to send their children to school. We have spent thousands of dollars in making the school at Fort Hall one of the most attractive reservation schools that is anywhere to be found. We have two thousand acres under fence. We have a large herd of cattle, and we have a noble body of employees. We are pleading with these people to put their children in school on the reservation, almost within sight of their own homes, within twenty or thirty miles' ride of any part of the reservation; but they say "No. The medicinemen say it is bad medicine." Now, shall we compel them?

In Fort Yuma the Indians live in the sand, like lizards, and have till recently gone almost naked. They send their children to the school till they reach the age of ten or eleven years. Then they are out, the girls roaming at will in that vicinity, the boys loafing about the miserable village of Yuma, wearing their hair long and going back to the ways of the camp. One of the saddest things I ever attended was an Indian mourning feast on that reservation, within sight of that school. Now, the question for me is, Shall I compel those children to enter school, to receive a preparation for citizenship?

At San Carlos are the Apaches, who are regarded as the most vicious of the Indians with whom we have to deal. They are held practically as prisoners, the San Carlos Agency being under control of the military. For years there has been a military officer in command, supported by two or three companies of colored soldiers. The conditions on that reservation are simply deplorable, and I would not dare in this audience to more than allude to the conditions existing there. These people decline to send their children to school; but I have within the last twelve months taken from that reservation about two hundred of them. They are to-day well fed and properly clothed, are happy and contented, and making good progress. Did I do right?

VOICES.—Yes! Yes!

MORGAN.—I must illustrate by numerous other instances. We have provided these schools for the benefit of the children, not, primarily, for our own benefit. We have done it in order that they may be brought into relationship with the civilization of the nineteenth century. It is an expression of the sentiment that is generated here on these mountains. It comes, I believe, from God. Now, then, the question is simply, Shall we say that, after having made this abundant provision and having offered it to the children, we will allow those who are still savages in their instincts, barbarians in their habits, rooted to their conservatism—that we will allow them to keep their children out of these institutions of learning, in order that they may be prevented from becoming like white men and women?

I say, No; and I say it for these reasons: We owe it to these children to see to it that they shall have the advantages of these schools. We owe it to their children that are to come after them that they shall be born of educated parents, and not of savages. We owe it to the old people themselves. The most pitiful things that I have been confronted with on the Indian reservations are the old men and old women, wrinkled, blind, and wretched, living on the ash-heap, having no care, with no protection, turned out to die. The other day, as I stood by the side of that little Santee girl, her father said to me, as he pointed out an old wrinkled woman, "My mamma"; and a most horrible creature she was. We owe it to these people to educate their children, so that they can go back to their homes and take care of the fathers and mothers who are no longer able to take care of themselves. We owe it to ourselves. We have undertaken to do this work: we have laid aside sentiment; we have laid aside everything except regard for the welfare of the children, and simply said, This thing ought to be done. Now, I say the one step remaining is for us to say that it shall be done.

I would first make the schools as attractive as they can be made and would win these children, so far as possible, by kindness and persuasion. I would put them first into the schools near home, into the day schools, if there are any, or into the reservation boarding-schools, where there are such. Where it is practicable, I would allow them large liberty as to whether they shall go to a government school or a private school. I would bring to bear upon them such influences as would secure their acceptance voluntarily wherever it could be done. I would then use the Indian police if necessary. I would withhold from them rations and supplies where those are furnished, if that were needed; and when every other means was exhausted, when I could not accomplish the work in any other way, I would send a troop of United States soldiers, not to seize them, but simply to be present as an expression of the power of the government. Then I would say to these people, "Put your children in school"; and they would do it. There would be no warfare. At Fort Hall to-day, if there were present a sergeant or a lieutenant, with ten mounted soldiers, simply camped there, and I sent out to those Indians and told them that within ten days every child of school age must be in school, they would be there. Shall it be done? It *will* be done if public sentiment demands it: it will not be done if public sentiment does not.

⋏

Railroads and Coolies

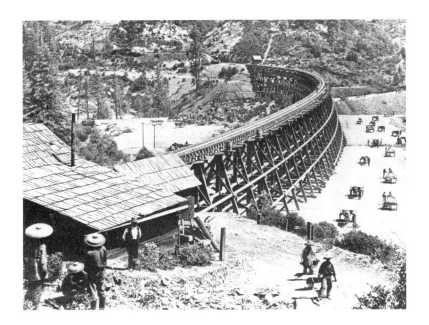

Railroads enabled imperial powers to consolidate control of territories and economies. Though native labor was often used to construct roads and railroads, in some cases labor was imported for this purpose. Such was the case in North America, where as the trade in African slaves was nearing its end, a trade in Chinese coolies sprung up to replace it. Coolies were contract laborers who were paid a very small wage for a defined period of work. They were transported to various destinations around the world, including South America, the Caribbean, and southern Africa, where they also worked on plantations and in mines. Some coolies succeeded in returning home after their contracts expired. Many, however, died of disease, injury, or malnutrition in the miserable working conditions they encountered. Still other coolies made their homes in their new locations at the end of their contracts.

⋏

Source: UPI/© Bettmann/Corbis.

QUESTIONS

1. In what ways can the movement of laborers be considered a tool of empire?

2. Why might imperialists have chosen to use imported rather than indigenous labor to complete labor-intensive building, planting, or mining projects?

3. Thinking ahead to the theme of the next part of the reader, how do labor migrations (forced or voluntary) lead to reconfigurations of empire?

▲

Protestant Foreign Missions: Their Present State

THEODORE CHRISTLIEB

Doctor Theodore Christlieb was professor of theology and university preacher in Bonn, Germany. In 1879, he presented to the Evangelical Alliance in Basel an extensive report that was subsequently published in German and rapidly translated into English, French, Dutch, and Swedish. The volume constitutes a comprehensive report on the state of Protestant missionary activity around the globe as Christlieb perceived it.

Perhaps the best indication of the approach that Christlieb took toward non-Christians can be found in the table of contents for the volume, in which he dedicated separate sections to "Work Among the Heathen" and "Work Among Civilized Peoples." Under the category of "heathen," by which he clearly meant "uncivilized" people, Christlieb included native peoples of Australia and the South Seas, the Americas, and Africa. The "Civilized Peoples," as he called them, included Moslems, Nestorians, Indians, Chinese, and Japanese—that is, people with organized religious beliefs and social customs that, while perhaps problematic for those with Christian sensibilities, were nonetheless recognizable to them as patterns of organization and systems of belief.

The following selection shows how missionary activity was employed by imperialists as a tool to re-order social and religious practices along Western lines and thus to "civilize" the colonial populations. This section focuses on the problems, as Christlieb saw them, with Hinduism and the obstacles that Hindu beliefs posed for the spread of Christianity in India.

▲

QUESTIONS

1. What did Christlieb find problematic about Hinduism?

2. In what ways does Christlieb hope to transform Indian society?

3. How might we view Christian missionary activity as a tool of empire?

[. . .] Five-sixths of the converts in all Indian missions belong to the lower classes of society, of inferior castes and of no caste. Converted Brahmins [high-caste Hindus] are found everywhere, but their number is still very small. This, therefore, is clear: the black aboriginal tribes with their pre-Brahminical devil worship, and the semi-Brahminism of Southern India, this compound of the Brahminic religion with that of the aboriginals, are much more accessible to the gospel than the Brahmins proper in the North. And, what is remarkable, these two most fruitful branches of

Source: Theodore Christlieb. *Protestant Foreign Missions: Their Present State. A Universal Survey.* (Trans. David Allen Reed.) Boston: Congregational Publishing Society, 1880. Pp. 166–71, 172–73.

the great missionary tree are related to each other in their languages. There are people of the Dravidian languages, stretching from Malay, Tamil, Telugu, &c., to Kola and Santal, opposed to whom Brahmin Hindooism stands with its Aryan languages. From this we perceive, that within this old civilized land the tribes and classes of people which are relatively least penetrated by heathen civilization are the most accessible to Christianity; while the real stronghold of the Hindoo religion and culture, the North with its Benares [a Hindu holy city], and the higher, more educated castes and lighter races of India generally, as a strong fortress still defy it, and, though besieged, are far from conquered.

But the process of undermining is in full progress, which in time must lead to their downfall, though we may not be able as yet to tell when that time will come. The axe of the gospel with a handle out of the tree of Hindooism itself, wielded by native agencies, will bring about this fall, as the thoughtful Hindoos now already perceive and openly confess. "After all, what did the Mohammedans do?" said a Hindoo to Mr. Leupolt. "They broke down a few bricks from the top of the house: these men (the missionaries) undermine its foundation by preaching and teaching, and, when once a great rain comes, the whole building will come down with a crash." The power which holds it together has long ceased to be the religious system itself with its inward wanderings; nor yet are the old and new literatures as such, with their many-colored compounds of old pious prayers, fantastical speculations, absurd and often terrible injunctions, composed of pantheistic, polytheistic, and even theistic elements, the power of heathen faith and thought; but the caste-system. As a system, Hindooism is becoming more and more a relic. It loses daily more of its influence over the spirit of the people. Polytheistic superstition is already overcome in the minds of the educated, although it has still many tenacious roots in the minds of the common people. The youth of India are withdrawing continually from its influences. But caste holds the old building

fast together: even liberals seldom have courage to break with it. "You know," said an accomplished Hindoo to Mr. Leupolt, "that, properly speaking, we have now no religious belief. Any one can believe what he likes, so long as he retains caste." In fact, Hindooism only clings to caste still, because caste in turn supports it. So much the more decisively must this caste be fought; for, if this be undermined, the whole religious edifice will fall in. That this great social fetter of the Hindoos must be broken off, there is no dispute among the evangelical missionary societies. But whether it is only to be continually restricted by those who are converted, and left to die out through the freeing activity of the evangelical spirit, or whether it is to be directly attacked, and a complete separation be demanded from the beginning of every one baptized, is the question.

In regard to this, the opinions of some, particularly of the Leipzig men, disagree with the majority. Without expecting in the least to solve this intricate and much-discussed question with a few general remarks, I still confess that I must hold the former practice as dangerous, because incompatible with a clear, proper execution of fundamental Christian ideas. And I have lately been much strengthened in this position by the article of Professor Monier Williams, of Oxford, an unbiased observer, upon "Modern India and the Indians" (1879). He says, "It is difficult for us Europeans to understand how the pride of caste, as a divine ordinance, interpenetrates the whole being of a Hindoo. He looks upon his caste as his veritable god; and those caste-rules which we believe to be a hinderance to his adoption of the true religion are to him the very essence of all religion, for they influence his whole life and conduct." One can fully acknowledge certain good services once accomplished by the caste laws of India, for example, protection against complete lawlessness; but these are far overbalanced, as Professor Williams shows, by the irreparable harm they bring to the physical, spiritual, and moral condition of the Hindoo people, by making marriage in early youth a religious duty, by the fetter of endogamy (marriage only within the caste, yea, within special divisions), by fencing in the family and home life with a wall of mysteries.

Go into the upper classes of the high schools in India, and you will find that half the boys are themselves already fathers! I ask: Do we not here front the explanation of the effeminacy of so many millions in India? Will not the children of children remain children throughout their whole life? and what is the cause of the childish character of the Indian women? Their awful exclusion through the caste-laws. Nothing can help in this but an entirely new ideal of womanhood, a complete renovation of the whole family life, through the emancipation of women from their prison-homes, yea, through a re-organization of the whole social building, from the foundation up. Therefore eradicate caste, this tap-root of the social evils of India, and, I must say, the more thoroughly the better! [. . .]

This great power in the social life of India begins to give way already here and there, though slowly. The contact with Christian civilization and morality, "the general extension of even a mere superficial knowledge of Christianity, is," as Sir Bartle Frere says, "the death-knell of caste. Generations may pass before the result is attained, but finally there can be no doubt of it." Already now and then there is a widow who marries again, with the applause of the young Indians. Even the railroad will be a sworn ally in the war against caste. Hindooism cannot accommodate itself to the progress of modern times, and therefore every thing works together for its destruction as a system. Reformed social ideas and customs make themselves felt involuntarily, wherever Hindoos are opposed to Christian family life; and caste will appear to them by degrees in its terrible unnatural limits, as anachronism. Because felt as a burden it will no longer be observed so closely; and with broken caste, the priests, in order not to lose all, will do every thing in their power to facilitate restoration. [. . .]

Belgian Territorial Agent

Representatives of empire had to work within the constraints of their environment. This meant living and working in buildings quite different from those at home and adjusting their attire to the climate. Nonetheless, they still found ways to maintain their authority over the indigenous peoples of the colonies. Clothing, posture, and the expectation that colonial subjects would defer to their authority all contributed to their effectiveness as agents of empire. This Belgian territorial agent could have been a model for Joseph Conrad's Kayerts and Carlier in Part I of this reader.

QUESTIONS

1. What conclusions do you draw from the attire of all of the men in this photograph?
2. What attitudes about dress, status, and power are on display in this image?
3. In what ways does the territorial agent serve as a tool of empire?

Source: Getty Images Inc.—Hulton Archive Photos.

An Outline Plan for the Reorganization of Japan

Kita Ikki

In the period after the First World War, Japan was at a crossroads. It was experiencing a time of political liberalism during which there was a proliferation of political parties and the vote was extended to all men. Nonetheless, there were Japanese thinkers who, blaming the First World War on the failure of weak democratic systems in Europe, believed that Japan would only weaken itself if it followed the path of further democratization. Among the critics of Japan's Taisho democracy (thus named because it occurred under the reign of the Taisho Emperor), were the ultranationalists whose ideas ultimately led to Japan's aggressive imperialism in Asia in the 1930s and 1940s.

Kita Ikki (1884–1937) was a leader of a group of outspoken Japanese ultranationalists in the 1920s and 1930s. He called for radical reform of Japanese society. He wrote "An Outline Plan for the Reorganization of Japan" in 1919, and his followers distributed it clandestinely through the early 1920s in defiance of police orders and censors, who had banned the book. This political manifesto called, among other things, for the implementation of martial law in Japan so as to strengthen the imperial polity and diminish the harmful effects of democracy. Inspired by a strong nationalist sentiment and an abhorrence of the imperialistic behavior of the West in Asia, Kita argued that Japan should lead Asia in the battle against the West, a path that Japan ultimately chose to follow in the 1930s and 1940s. Although Kita's book remained banned until the end of the Second World War, he continued throughout the 1920s and 1930s to push for the sorts of change he promoted in this publication, and he was ultimately executed for his part in an ultranationalist coup in 1936.

QUESTIONS

1. To what extent is Kita using notions of race and culture to argue for the unification of Asia under Japanese leadership?

2. According to Kita, why does Japan need to expand?

3. How can nationalism be used as a tool of empire?

At present the Japanese empire is faced with a national crisis unparalleled in its history; it faces dilemmas at home and abroad. The vast majority of the people feel insecure in their livelihood and they are on the point of taking a lesson from the collapse of European societies, while

---

Source: Kita Ikki. "An Outline Plan for the Reorganization of Japan." In Ryuska Tsunoda, Wm. Theodore de Bary, & Donald Keene (Eds.), *Sources of Japanese Tradition*, Vol. II. New York: Columbia University Press, 1958. Pp. 268–69. Reprinted with permission of the publisher.

those who monopolize political, military, and economic power simply hide themselves and, quaking with fear, try to maintain their unjust position. Abroad, neither England, America, Germany, nor Russia has kept its word, and even our neighbor China, which long benefited from the protection we provided through the Russo-Japanese War, not only has failed to repay us but instead despises us. Truly we are a small island, completely isolated in the Eastern Sea. One false step and our nation will again fall into the desperate state of crisis—dilemmas at home and abroad—that marked the period before and after the Meiji Restoration.

The only thing that brightens the picture is the sixty million fellow countrymen with whom we are blessed. The Japanese people must develop a profound awareness of the great cause of national existence and of the people's equal rights, and they need an unerring, discriminating grasp of the complexities of domestic and foreign thought. The Great War in Europe was, like Noah's flood, Heaven's punishment on them for arrogant and rebellious ways. It is of course natural that we cannot look to the Europeans, who are out of their minds because of the great destruction, for a completely detailed set of plans. But in contrast Japan, during those five years of destruction, was blessed with five years of fulfillment. Europe needs to talk about reconstruction, while Japan must move on to reorganization. The entire Japanese people, thinking calmly from this perspective which is the result of Heaven's rewards and punishments, should, in planning how the great Japanese empire should be reorganized, petition for a manifestation of the imperial prerogative establishing "a national opinion in which no dissenting voice is heard, by the organization of a great union of the Japanese people." Thus, by homage to the emperor, a basis for national reorganization can be set up.

Truly, our seven hundred million brothers in China and India have no path to independence other than that offered by our guidance and protection. And for our Japan, whose population has doubled within the past fifty years, great areas adequate to support a population of at least two hundred and forty or fifty millions will be absolutely necessary a hundred years from now. For a nation, one hundred years are like a hundred days for an individual. How can those who are anxious about these inevitable developments, or who grieve over the desperate conditions of neighboring countries, find their solace in the effeminate pacifism of doctrinaire socialism? I do not necessarily rule out social progress by means of the class struggle. But still, just what kind of so-called science is it that can close its eyes to the competition between peoples and nations which has taken place throughout the entire history of mankind? At a time when the authorities in the European and American revolutionary creeds have found it completely impossible to arrive at an understanding of the "gospel of the sword" because of their superficial philosophy, the noble Greece of Asian culture must complete her national reorganization on the basis of her own national polity. At the same time, let her lift the virtuous banner of an Asian league and take the leadership in a world federation which must come. In so doing let her proclaim to the world the Way of Heaven in which all are children of Buddha, and let her set the example which the world must follow. So the ideas of people like those who oppose arming the nation are after all simply childish.

Kimathi on Law as a Tool of Oppression

NGUGI WA THIONG'O

Colonial conquest was followed by the imposition of colonial laws intended to keep the conquered in their place. Under these laws, anyone involved in anticolonial activity could be arrested, tried, and imprisoned. Dedan Kimathi is now almost universally accepted as the *symbol of Kenya's liberation struggle for his fight with the Mau Mau against British colonial rule and his outspoken opposition to colonial laws. Since his death at the heart of the struggle, he has acquired, in the minds of many, legendary and mythical qualities.*

For his fierce opposition to colonial laws, Dedan Kimathi was arrested, tried, and executed. His trial, recounted here by Ngugi wa Thiong'o, a prominent Kenyan writer and nationalist, provided him with an opportunity to express his vehement opposition to colonial laws, which he viewed as a tool of colonialism and oppression. He was especially opposed to the British use of law to suppress the African liberation struggle led by the Mau Mau.

QUESTIONS

1. How does Kimathi react to the words of the judge? In what ways does he seem to see law as a tool of empire?

2. Why does Kimathi find the British use of law in Kenya to be problematic?

KIMATHI: *By what right dare you, a colonial judge, sit in judgment over me?*

JUDGE: *{playing with his glasses, oozing infinite patience}*
Kimathi, I may remind you that we are in a court of law.

KIMATHI: An imperialist court of law.

JUDGE: I may remind you that you are charged with a most serious crime. It carries a death sentence.

KIMATHI: Death . . .

JUDGE: Yes, death . . .

KIMATHI: To a criminal judge, in a criminal court, set up by criminal law: the law of oppression. I have no words.

JUDGE: Perhaps you don't understand. . . . I mean . . . we are here to deal fairly with you, to see that justice is done. Even handed justice.

KIMATHI: I will not plead to a law in which we had no part in the making.

JUDGE: Law is law. The rule of law is the basis of every civilized community. Justice is justice.

KIMATHI: Whose law? Whose justice?

JUDGE: There is only one law, one justice.

KIMATHI: Two laws. Two justices. One law and one justice protects the man of property, the man of wealth, the foreign exploiter. Another

Source: Ngugi wa Thiong'o. "Kimathi on law as a tool of oppression." *Barrel of a Pen: Resistance to Repression in Neo-Colonial Kenya.* Trenton, NJ: Africa World Press, 1983. Pp. 5–6. Used with permission.

law, another justice, silences the poor, the hungry, our people.

JUDGE: No society can be without laws to protect property . . . I mean protect our lives . . . Civilization . . . Investment . . . Christianity . . . Order.

KIMATHI: I despise your laws and your courts. What have they done for our people? What?
Protected the oppressor. Licensed the murderers of the people:
Our people,
whipped when they did not pick
your tea leaves
your coffee beans
Imprisoned when they refused
to "ayah"
your babies
and "boy" your houses and
gardens
Murdered when they didn't
rickshaw
your ladies and your gentlemen.
I recognize only one law, one
court:
the court and the law of those
who
fight against exploitation,
The toilers armed to say
We demand our freedom.
That's the eternal law of the
oppressed,
of the humiliated, of the injured,
the insulted!
Fight
Struggle
Change.

JUDGE: There's no liberty without law
and order.

KIMATHI: There is no order and law
without
liberty.
Chain my legs,
Chain my hands,
Chain my soul,
And you cry, law and justice?
And the law of the people bids
me:
Unchain my hands
Unchain my legs
Unchain my soul!

⋏

The Secret of England's Greatness

Thomas Jones Barker

This painting from circa 1863 depicts Queen Victoria, with Prince Albert standing behind her, presenting a bible to a man in African clothing. Behind the anonymous African stand two major British statesmen of the mid-nineteenth century, Lord Palmerston and Lord John Russell, both of whom were active in pushing an aggressive and expansionist British foreign policy. The painting was reproduced as an engraving in 1864 with the title "The Bible: The Secret of England's Greatness."

⋏

QUESTIONS

1. Why might the Bible have been described as the secret of England's greatness?
2. Look closely at the African man. What do you notice about him? Compare him to the other people represented in the painting.

Source: Thomas Jones Barker. Circa 1863. Copyright ©National Portrait Gallery, London.

FURTHER RESOURCES

Anderson, David, and David Killingray (Eds.). *Policing the Empire: Government, Authority, and Control, 1830–1940.* New York: St. Martin's Press, 1991.

Cohen, Benjamin J. *The Question of Imperialism: The Political Economy of Dominance and Dependence.* New York: Basic Books, 1973.

Crosby, Alfred W. *Ecological Imperialism: The Biological Expansion of Europe, 900–1900.* New York: Cambridge University Press, 1986.

Diamond, Jared. *Guns, Germs, and Steel.* New York: W. W. Norton, 2005.

Fieldhouse, D. K. *Economics and Empire, 1830–1914.* Ithaca, NY: Cornell University Press 1973.

Gallagher, John. *The Decline, Revival, and Fall of the British Empire: The Ford Lectures and Other Essays.* New York: Cambridge University Press, 1982.

Herbertson, A. J. (Ed.). *The Oxford Survey of the British Empire.* Oxford: Clarendon, 1914.

Hobson, J. A. *The Evolution of Modern Capitalism: A Study of Machine Production.* New York: Allen and Unwin, 1949.

Lomax, Eric. *The Railway Man: A POW's Searing Account of War, Brutality, and Forgiveness.* New York: W. W. Norton, 1995.

MacLeod, Roy M., and Milton James Lewis. *Disease, Medicine, and Empire: Perspectives on Western Medicine and the Experience of European Expansion.* New York: Routledge, 1988.

McNeill, William. *Plagues and People.* Garden City, NY: Anchor Press, 1976.

Meade, Teresa A., and Mark Walker. *Science, Medicine and Cultural Imperialism.* New York: St. Martin's Press, 1991.

Miller, Helen. *French Imperialism in the Congo Basin.* Berkeley: University of California Press, 1930.

Naipaul, V. S. *Reading and Writing: A Personal Account.* New York: New York Review of Books, 2000.

Olumwullah, Osaak A. *Disease in the Colonial State: Medicine, Society, and Social Change among the AbaNyole of Western Kenya.* Westport, CT: Greenwood Press, 2002.

Radnitzky, Gerard, and Peter Bernholz. *Economic Imperialism: The Economic Approach Applied Outside the Field of Economics.* New York: Paragon House Publishers, 1987.

Schumpeter, Joseph. *The Economics and Sociology of Capitalism.* Princeton, NJ: Princeton University Press, 1991.

Schweitzer, Albert. *More From the Primeval Forest.* London: A. & C. Black, 1956.

Films

Breaker Morant. DVD, Directed by Bruce Beresford. New York, NY: Wellspring Media, 2004.

Gallipoli. DVD. Directed by Peter Weir. Hollywood, CA: Paramount, 1999.

Lawrence of Arabia. VHS. Directed by David Lean. Burbank, CA: Columbia Tristar Home Video, 1998.

Queen Victoria's Empire. VHS (2 videocassettes). Directed by Paul Bryers and Paul Burgess. London, England: Brook Lapping Productions, 2001.

1871	Barker, *Station Life in New Zealand*
1868–1912	**Japan's Meiji Reforms (Meiji Emperor)**
1870s–1900s	**Events of "Portrait of the Hard Life of a Woman"**
1884–85	Berlin Conference
1880–1914	British Empire at Its Territorial Height
1885–1908	Worst Excesses in the Belgian Congo
1890	Salisbury Rhodesia Founded
1904	**Liang, "Inaugural Statement for the Eastern Times"**
1910	Japanese Annexation of Korea
1913–17	***The Red Man***
1914	**"Advertisement for the Sontag Hotel"**
1915	Population of Shanghai Reaches 1,500,000
1917	**"Advertisement for the African and Oriental Bureau and Buying Agency"**
1919	**"Summary of Orders"**
1920s	**"Child Marriage Restraint Act"**
1920s	**Mariátegui, "Outline of the Economic Evolution"**
1931	**Lulofs, *Rubber***
1939	**Cary, *Mister Johnson***
1950s	**"Beautiful Maria in the Act of True Love"**
1965	**Memmi, *The Colonizer and the Colonized***
1975	**Achebe, "Named for Victoria, Queen of England"**

Entries in bold indicate sources.

Part IV

Reconfigurations:
The Colonial World

INTRODUCTION

Part IV takes up the theme of tools of empire explored in Part III and examines ways in which these tools reshaped people and landscapes. With the new imperialism, not only did the map of the world change, but cultural, political, economic, and social practices of people in the new colonies were transformed. To a lesser extent, this transformation was also taking place in the lives of the citizens of the imperial powers themselves and of everyone around the globe. The readings in this part consider ways in which the social, political, economic, cultural, and environmental landscapes of the colonies were reconfigured. Perhaps the best known and most intentional exploration of this topic of reconfiguration is Chinua Achebe's novel *Things Fall Apart*, which carefully and deliberately introduces the reader to Igbo society as it existed prior to the British colonization of Nigeria and then explores the impact of British colonization on this society. The intent of this part of the reader is to follow Achebe's lead by selecting texts from Africa, Asia, the Americas, and the Pacific that explore some of the many ways in which societies were reconfigured by imperialist practices.

Education and religion were two of the most effective tools of empire that led to significant changes in the social and cultural landscape of the colonies. As new belief systems and educational standards were disseminated, so too were new ideas about what it meant to be civilized. These new systems encouraged colonial peoples to measure themselves against the yardsticks of civilization that were used by their colonial rulers, and this led in some cases to the adoption of the values of the colonizers. These shifts in values affected gender roles, ideas about the social order, notions of what constituted the legitimate basis for power, and much more. The "Portrait of the Hard Life of a Woman" by Attiya Hanim Saqqaf, as well as the "Child Marriage Restraint Act" and "Beautiful Maria in the Act of True Love," for example, all examine the reconfiguration of ideas about gender, love, and marriage in legal and social terms.

New ideas about the social order gained currency in the colonies as white imperialists asserted their political, cultural, and social superiority in part on the basis of race. The readings from *The Red Man* and Achebe's "Named for Victoria" examine ways in which social order could be transformed. The selection from Cary's *Mister Johnson* considers this theme too, through a caricature of an eager colonial subject. Albert Memmi takes this analysis a step further by considering how imperialism transforms the self-perception of the colonized and produces racial and cultural stereotypes.

Foreign Imperialism in East Asia

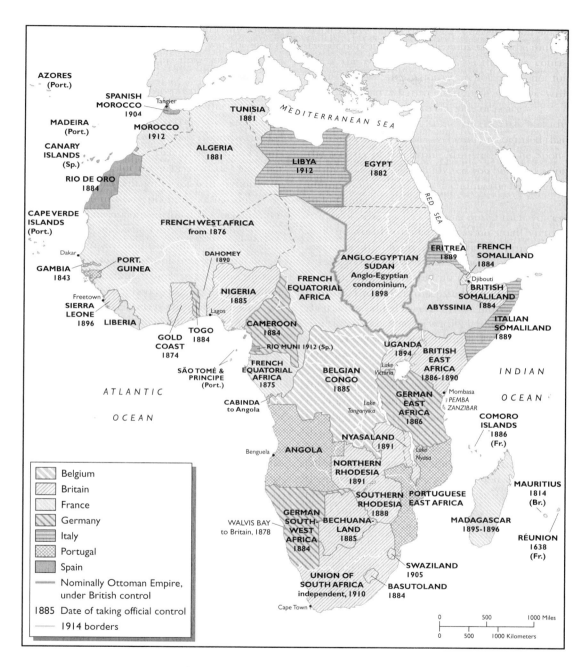

AZORES
(Port.)

SPANISH
MOROCCO
1904 Tangier

MADEIRA
(Port.)

MOROCCO
1912

CANARY
ISLANDS
(Sp.)

RIO DE ORO
1884

CAPE VERDE
ISLANDS
(Port.)

TUNISIA
1881

MEDITERRANEAN SEA

ALGERIA
1881

LIBYA
1912

EGYPT
1882

RED SEA

FRENCH WEST AFRICA
from 1876

Dakar

GAMBIA
1843

PORT.
GUINEA

DAHOMEY
1890

Freetown
SIERRA
LEONE
1896

LIBERIA

GOLD
COAST
1874

TOGO
1884

SÃO TOMÉ &
PRINCIPE
(Port.)

NIGERIA
1885

Lagos

FRENCH
EQUATORIAL
AFRICA

CAMEROON
1884

RIO MUNI 1912 (Sp.)

ANGLO-EGYPTIAN
SUDAN
Anglo-Egyptian
condominium,
1898

ERITREA
1889

FRENCH
SOMALILAND
1884

Djibouti
BRITISH
SOMALILAND
1884

ABYSSINIA

ITALIAN
SOMALILAND
1889

UGANDA
1894

Lake
Victoria

BRITISH
EAST
AFRICA
1886-1890

INDIAN

OCEAN

ATLANTIC

OCEAN

FRENCH
EQUATORIAL
AFRICA
1875

CABINDA
to Angola

BELGIAN
CONGO
1885

Lake
Tanganyika

GERMAN
EAST
AFRICA
1886

Mombasa
PEMBA
ZANZIBAR

COMORO
ISLANDS
1886
(Fr.)

NYASALAND
1891

Lake
Nyasa

Benguela

ANGOLA

NORTHERN
RHODESIA
1891

SOUTHERN
RHODESIA
1888

PORTUGUESE
EAST AFRICA

MAURITIUS
1814
(Br.)

WALVIS BAY
to Britain, 1878

GERMAN
SOUTH-
WEST
AFRICA
1884

BECHUANA-
LAND
1885

MADAGASCAR
1895-1896

RÉUNION
1638
(Fr.)

SWAZILAND
1905

UNION OF
SOUTH AFRICA
independent, 1910

BASUTOLAND
1884

Cape Town

Belgium
Britain
France
Germany
Italy
Portugal
Spain
Nominally Ottoman Empire,
under British control
1885 Date of taking official control
1914 borders

0   500   1000 Miles
0   500   1000 Kilometers

The Scramble for Africa

In spite of these race barriers to social advancement, changing educational and political systems led upwardly mobile colonial people to educate themselves in the languages as well as the values of the colonizers. Readings in this chapter by Chinua Achebe and Liang Qichao and the example of "Beautiful Maria" further illuminate these phenomena and show how both language and values influenced and were made use of by the colonized and by people such as the Chinese, who sought to modernize in order to prevent colonization. In Liang Qichao's piece, therefore, we see one way in which the imperialism of the late nineteenth century effectively forced changes even in societies, cultures, and polities that were not directly under foreign control.

Law and administration, like other structures that regulate society, were also transformed by the colonial experience. The "Child Marriage Restraint Act" illustrates ways in which laws could be used to transform traditional customs. The "Summary of Orders" for the implementation of martial law in the Punjab shows just how deeply colonial law could penetrate into society. By contrast, in the excerpts from *The Red Man*, we see the attempts of Native Americans to find ways of negotiating with and participating in government in the early twentieth-century United States.

New technologies and economic practices transformed the landscapes of the colonies. The roads and railroads mentioned in Part III led to a different sort of interconnectedness across space than had previously existed. As with education and religion, roads and railroads brought with them "civilization," but from the perspective of the local residents, civilization was not necessarily entirely positive. New modes of transportation altered patterns of social interaction and transformed the geography and economy of the colonies. Urbanization also changed the physical landscapes of the colonies, as we see in the maps of Singapore and Cairo.

The physical landscape was also reconfigured by new agricultural practices, as we see in the short selection from Madelon Lulofs' novel *Rubber*, which is set on a plantation in Indonesia. The small-scale agriculture and nomadic practices of indigenous peoples in Africa, Asia, the Americas, and the Pacific were to a large extent replaced by large-scale and plantation agriculture, which yielded greater economic benefits to landowners, many of whom were white imperialists. Plantations not only changed the physical landscape, replacing small fields and forests with large areas of carefully planted trees, bushes, or other plants, as we see in the image of the Colombian coffee plantation, but they also affected the human landscape. Plantations that had been populated by slaves before the abolition of that institution in Europe and the Americas later made use of coolie and contract labor through which large numbers of Chinese and South Asian laborers were transported around the globe. In addition, colonial empires and the new transportation networks within them combined to facilitate migration within empires, and so we see a resulting diversification of populations throughout the new empires. The human geography of some parts of empire, such as North America, Australia, and New Zealand, was transformed through settlement, as we see in the example provided by Lady Barker.

Colonial economies were transformed not only in terms of agricultural practices, as mentioned previously, but also with respect to buying habits. The advertisements, for the African and Oriental Bureau and Buying Agency and the Sontag Hotel in Seoul both demonstrate this transformation. Imperialist economic practices were not, however, confined to formal empires, as we see in the piece by José Carlos Mariátegui, who is writing about Latin American countries that had already achieved political independence from Spain but whose economies were still being shaped by the economic designs of the major empires.

Eventually, many of these reconfigurations put colonial peoples in a position to be able to argue and even fight for their independence in terms that were familiar to the Western world. This reworking of the "tools of empire" is explored in Part V.

▲

Meiji Emperor

Japan's Meiji Emperor oversaw Japan's transformation from a weak country ruled in a feudal, samurai tradition that was in danger of being imperialized to an imperialist nation in its own right. Though Japan did not undertake a wholesale adoption of Western models, it was nonetheless substantially reconfigured by its late nineteenth-century interactions with the imperialist powers. This process was perhaps most immediately apparent in the change in clothing and hairstyles sported by elite Japanese. The young Meiji Emperor led the way by cutting off his topknot and adopting Western, military-style dress, clearly modeled on the attire then popular in Prussia.

▲

QUESTIONS

1. How does the Meiji Emperor's attire reflect the cultural reconfiguration of Japan?
2. Japan was never colonized; it instead became an imperialist nation in its own right. Even so, do you think that Japan was affected by imperialism?

Source: Library of Congress.

The Colonizer and the Colonized

Albert Memmi

European nations sometimes resorted to extreme violence to sustain their colonial governments and to enforce colonial rule on African and Asian subjects. In response to such violence, Africans were left with two choices: to resist or to seek ways of adapting to their conditions. In his study The Colonizer and the Colonized, *Albert Memmi theorized that people subjected to colonial conditions adapt to them in order to survive. He concluded that the colonizer had no choice but to resort to violence to legitimize his oppression. Only in this way can he claim to have authority over the colonized. Unable to liberate himself from the oppressive conditions imposed on him, the colonized, on the other hand, is left with only one choice—to adapt so that he can survive. Memmi described this work as "portraits of the two protagonists of the colonial drama and the relationship that binds them." In his conceptualization of the relationship between colonizer and colonized, we can see reconfigurations of the mentality of both actors that enable them to play their roles.*

Memmi defined the colonizer as a person who imposes his culture—a way of life that includes government, education, and a socioeconomic system—on another in total disregard of the latter's culture. In the process of colonization, the colonizer becomes "an illegitimately privileged usurper." Although Memmi, who was born in Tunisia and later studied at the University of Algiers and at the Sorbonne in France, based his examples on events in North Africa, the dynamics he described are similar to those of any colonial system.

Questions

1. In what ways, according to Memmi, did the colonizers perceive and describe the colonized?
2. How did these descriptions affect the colonized?

Just as the bourgeoisie proposes an image of the proletariat, the existence of the colonizer requires that an image of the colonized be suggested. These images become excuses without which the presence and conduct of a colonizer, and that of a bourgeois, would seem shocking. But the favored image becomes a myth precisely because it suits them too well.

Let us imagine, for the sake of this portrait and accusation, the often-cited trait of laziness. It seems to receive unanimous approval of colonizers from Liberia to Laos, via the Maghreb. It is easy to see to what extent this description is useful. It occupies an important place in the dialectics exalting the colonizer and humbling the colonized. Furthermore, it is economically fruitful.

Nothing could better justify the colonizer's privileged position than his industry, and nothing could better justify the colonized's destitution than his indolence. The mythical portrait of the colonized therefore includes an unbelievable laziness, and that of the colonizer, a virtuous taste for action. At the same time the colonizer suggests that employing the colonized is not very profitable, thereby authorizing his unreasonable wages.

It may seem that colonization would profit by employing experienced personnel. Nothing is less true. A qualified worker existing among the colonizers earns three or four times more than does the colonized, while he does not produce three or four times as much, either in quantity or in quality. It is more advantageous to use three of the colonized than one European. Every firm needs specialists, of course, but only a minimum of them, and the colonizer imports or recruits experts among his own kind. In addition, there is the matter of the special attention and legal protection required by a European worker. The colonized, however, is only asked for his muscles; he is so poorly evaluated that three or four can be taken on for the price of one European.

From listening to him, on the other hand, one finds that the colonizer is not so displeased with that laziness, whether supposed or real. He talks of it with amused affability, he jokes about it, he takes up all the usual expressions, perfects them, and invents others. Nothing can describe well enough the extraordinary deficiency of the colonized. He becomes lyrical about it, in a negative way. The colonized doesn't let grass grow under his feet, but a tree, and what a tree! A eucalyptus, an American centenarian oak! A tree? No, a forest!

But, one will insist, is the colonized truly lazy? To tell the truth, the question is poorly stated. Besides having to define a point of reference, a norm, varying from one people to another, can one accuse an entire people of laziness ? It can be suspected of individuals, even many of them in a single group. One can wonder if their output is mediocre, whether malnutrition, low wages, a

closed future, a ridiculous conception of a role in society, does not make the colonized uninterested in his work. What is suspect is that the accusation is not directed solely at the farm laborer or slum resident, but also at the professor, engineer or physician who does the same number of hours of work as his colonizer colleagues; indeed, all individuals of the colonized group are accused. Essentially, the independence of the accusation from any sociological or historical conditions makes it suspect.

In fact, the accusation has nothing to do with an objective notation, therefore subject to possible changes, but of an institution. By his accusation the colonizer establishes the colonized as being lazy. He decides that laziness is constitutional in the very nature of the colonized. It becomes obvious that the colonized, whatever he may undertake, whatever zeal he may apply, could never be anything but lazy. This always brings us back to racism, which is the substantive expression, to the accuser's benefit, of a real or imaginary trait of the accused.

It is possible to proceed with the same analysis for each of the features found in the colonized.

Whenever the colonizer states, in his language, that the colonized is a weakling, he suggests thereby that this deficiency requires protection. From this comes the concept of a protectorate. It is in the colonized's own interest that he be excluded from management functions, and that those heavy responsibilities be reserved for the colonizer. Whenever the colonizer adds, in order not to fall prey to anxiety, that the colonized is a wicked, backward person with evil, thievish, somewhat sadistic instincts, he thus justifies his police and his legitimate severity. After all, he must defend himself against the dangerous foolish acts of the irresponsible, and at the same time—what meritorious concern!—protect him against himself! It is the same for the colonized's lack of desires, his ineptitude for comfort, science, progress, his astonishing familiarity with poverty. Why should the colonizer worry about things that hardly trouble the interested party? It would be, he adds with dark and insolent philosophy, doing him a bad turn if he subjected him to the disadvantages of civilization. After all, remember that wisdom is Eastern; let us accept, as he does, the colonized's wretchedness. The same reasoning is also true for the colonized's notorious ingratitude; the colonizer's acts of charity are wasted, the improvements the colonizer has made are not appreciated. It is impossible to save the colonized from this myth—a portrait of wretchedness has been indelibly engraved.

It is significant that this portrait requires nothing else. It is difficult, for instance, to reconcile most of these features and then to proceed to synthesize them objectively. One can hardly see how the colonized can be simultaneously inferior and wicked, lazy and backward.

What is more, the traits ascribed to the colonized are incompatible with one another, though this does not bother his prosecutor. He is depicted as frugal, sober, without many desires and, at the same time, he consumes disgusting quantities of meat, fat, alcohol, anything; as a coward who is afraid of suffering and as a brute who is not checked by any inhibitions of civilization, etc. It is additional proof that it is useless to seek this consistency anywhere except in the colonizer himself. At the basis of the entire construction, one finally finds a common motive; the colonizer's economic and basic needs, which he substitutes for logic, and which shape and explain each of the traits he assigns to the colonized. In the last analysis, these traits are all advantageous to the colonizer, even those which at first sight seem damaging to him.

The point is that the colonized means little to the colonizer. Far from wanting to understand him as he really is, the colonizer is preoccupied with making him undergo this urgent change. The mechanism of this remolding of the colonized is revealing in itself. It consists, in the first place, of a series of negations. The colonized is not this, is not that. He is never considered in a positive light; or if he is, the quality which is conceded is the result of a psychological or ethical failing: Thus it is with Arab hospitality, which

is difficult to consider as a negative characteristic. If one pays attention, one discovers that the praise comes from tourists, visiting Europeans, and not colonizers, i.e., Europeans who have settled down in the colony. As soon as he is settled, the European no longer takes advantage of this hospitality, but cuts off intercourse and contributes to the barriers which plague the colonized. He rapidly changes palette to portray the colonized, who becomes jealous, withdrawn, intolerant and fanatical. What happens to the famous hospitality? Since he cannot deny it, the colonizer then brings into play the shadows and describes the disastrous consequences.

This hospitality is a result of the colonized's irresponsibility and extravagance, since he has no notion of foresight or economy. From the wealthy down to the fellah [peasants], the festivities are wonderful and bountiful: but what happens afterward? The colonized ruins himself, borrows and finally pays with someone else's money! Does one speak, on the other hand, of the modesty of the colonized's life? Of his not less well known lack of needs? It is no longer a proof of wisdom but of stupidity—as if, then, every recognized or invented trait had to be an indication of negativity.

Thus, one after another, all the qualities which make a man of the colonized crumble away. The humanity of the colonized, rejected by the colonizer, becomes opaque. It is useless, he asserts, to try to forecast the colonized's actions ("They are unpredictable!" "With them, you never know!"). It seems to him that strange and disturbing impulsiveness controls the colonized. The colonized must indeed be very strange, if he remains so mysterious after years of living with the colonizer.

Another sign of the colonized's depersonalization is what one might call the mark of the plural. The colonized is never characterized in an individual manner; he is entitled only to drown in an anonymous collectivity ("They are this." "They are all the same."). If a colonized servant does not come in one morning, the colonizer will not say that she is ill, or that she is cheating, or that she is tempted not to abide by an oppressive contract.

(Seven days a week; colonized domestics rarely enjoy the one day off a week granted to others.) He will say, "You can't count on them." It is not just a grammatical expression. He refuses to consider personal, private occurrences in his maid's life; that life in a specific sense does not interest him, and his maid does not exist as an individual.

Finally, the colonizer denies the colonized the most precious right granted to most men: liberty. Living conditions imposed on the colonized by colonization make no provision for it; indeed, they ignore it. The colonized has no way out of his state of woe—neither a legal outlet (naturalization) nor a religious outlet (conversion). The colonized is not free to choose between being colonized or not being colonized.

What is left of the colonized at the end of this stubborn effort to dehumanize him? He is surely no longer an alter ego of the colonizer. He is hardly a human being. He tends rapidly toward becoming an object. As an end, in the colonizer's supreme ambition, he should exist only as a function of the needs of the colonizer, i.e., be transformed into a pure colonized.

The extraordinary efficiency of this operation is obvious. One does not have a serious obligation toward an animal or an object. It is then easily understood that the colonizer can indulge in such shocking attitudes and opinions. A colonized driving a car is a sight to which the colonizer refuses to become accustomed; he denies him all normality. An accident, even a serious one, overtaking the colonized almost makes him laugh. A machine-gun burst into a crowd of colonized causes him merely to shrug his shoulders. Even a native mother weeping over the death of her son or a native woman weeping for her husband reminds him only vaguely of the grief of a mother or a wife. Those desperate cries, those unfamiliar gestures, would be enough to freeze his compassion even if it were aroused. An author was recently humorously telling us how rebelling natives were driven like game toward huge cages. The fact that someone had conceived and then dared build those cages, and

even more, that reporters had been allowed to photograph the fighting, certainly proves that the spectacle had contained nothing human.

Madness for destroying the colonized having originated with the needs of the colonizer, it is not surprising that it conforms so well to them, that it seems to confirm and justify the colonizer's conduct. More surprising, more harmful perhaps, is the echo that it excites in the colonized himself. Constantly confronted with this image of himself, set forth and imposed on all institutions and in every human contact, how could the colonized help reacting to his portrait? It cannot leave him indifferent and remain a veneer which, like an insult, blows with the wind. He ends up recognizing it as one would a detested nickname which has become a familiar description. The accusation disturbs him and worries him even more because he admires and fears his powerful accuser. "Is he not partially right?" he mutters. "Are we not all a little guilty after all? Lazy, because we have so many idlers? Timid, because we let ourselves be oppressed." Willfully created and spread by the colonizer, this mythical and degrading portrait ends up by being accepted and lived with to a certain extent by the colonized. It thus acquires a certain amount of reality and contributes to the true portrait of the colonized.

This process is not unknown. It is a hoax. It is common knowledge that the ideology of a governing class is adopted in large measure by the governed classes. Now, every ideology of combat includes as an integral part of itself a conception of the adversary. By agreeing to this ideology, the dominated classes practically confirm the role assigned to them. This explains, *inter alia*, the relative stability of societies; oppression is tolerated willy-nilly by the oppressed themselves. In colonial relationships, domination is imposed by people upon people but the pattern remains the same. The characterization and role of the colonized occupies a choice place in colonialist ideology; a characterization which is neither true to life, or in itself incoherent, but necessary and inseparable within that ideology. It is one to which the colonized gives his troubled and partial, but undeniable, assent.

There is only a particle of truth in the fashionable notions of "dependency complex," "colonizability," etc. There undoubtedly exists—at some point in its evolution—a certain adherence of the colonized to colonization. However, this adherence is the result of colonization and not its cause. It arises after and not before colonial occupation. In order for the colonizer to be the complete master, it is not enough for him to be so in actual fact, but he must also believe in its legitimacy. In order for that legitimacy to be complete,

it is not enough for the colonized to be a slave, he must also accept this role. The bond between colonizer and colonized is thus destructive and creative. It destroys and re-creates the two partners of colonization into colonizer and colonized. One is disfigured into an oppressor, a partial, unpatriotic and treacherous being, worrying only about his privileges and their defense; the other, into an oppressed creature, whose development is broken and who compromises by his defeat.

Just as the colonizer is tempted to accept his part, the colonized is forced to accept being colonized.

▲

Summary of Orders (For Martial Law in the Districts of Lahore and Amritsar, India)

ISSUED BY THE BRITISH-CONTROLLED GOVERNMENT OF INDIA

In the years immediately following the First World War, Indian independence activists, inspired on the one hand by Gandhi's social movement and on the other hand by Wilsonian ideals of self-determination, called increasingly for greater autonomy. In response to these calls, the British passed in 1919 the Government of India Act, also known as the Montagu-Chelmsford Reforms, establishing an elected bicameral Parliament that had no power to check the actions of the British Viceroy. This act went only halfway toward giving Indians the autonomy that they sought and was met with even more demonstrations. To counter this response, the government of India passed the Rowlatt Anti-Sedition Bills, sparking off even more massive protests across India by members of all social classes. Fearful of the disruptive influences of such protests, Sir Michael O'Dwyer, Lieutenant Governor of the Punjab, ordered the implementation of martial law in April 1919.

The summary of orders to implement martial law that follows demonstrates in considerable detail just how many facets of everyday life in colonial India could be controlled by the state. Martial law, of course, was used only in extraordinary times. Nonetheless, that the state had the power and resources to implement such a penetrating series of provisions at short notice speaks to the exceptional authority of the state even during ordinary times. The daily lives of people in the Punjab were affected economically, socially, and politically by the laws enacted by the British-controlled government of India.

▲

QUESTIONS

1. In what ways could people's lives be affected by colonial administration under these orders?

2. What coercive strategies did the colonial administration employ to force people to comply with its orders?

3. How does this approach to colonial government seem inconsistent with the domestic political ideals of the United Kingdom in the early twentieth century (insofar as you understand them)?

No. 1

Whereas the Government of India has for good reasons proclaimed Martial Law in the districts of Lahore and Amritsar; and

Whereas superior military authority has appointed me to command troops and administer Martial Law in a portion of the Lahore district, . . . and whereas Martial Law may be briefly described

Source: "Summary of Orders." Reprinted in Lajpat Rai, *The Political Future of India.* New York: B. W. Huebsch, 1919. Pp. xxii–xxvii.

as the will of the Military Commander in enforcing law, order and public safety:

I make known to all concerned that until further orders by me the following will be strictly carried out:

1. At 20·00 hours (8 o'clock) each evening a gun will be fired from the Fort, and from that signal till 05·00 hours (5 o'clock) on the following morning no person *other than a European* or a person in possession of a military permit signed by me or on my behalf will be permitted to leave his or her house or compound or the building in which he or she may be at 20 hours. During these prohibited hours no person other than those excepted above will be permitted to use the streets or roads, and any person found disobeying this order will be arrested, and if any attempt is made to evade or resist that person will be liable to be shot.

This and all other orders which from time to time I may deem necessary to make will be issued on my behalf from the water-works station in the city, whither every ward will keep at least four representatives from 6 A.M., till 17·00 hours (5 P.M.) daily to learn what orders, if any, are issued and to convey such orders to the inhabitants of their respective wards. *The onus of ascertaining the orders issued by me will rest on the people through their representatives.*

2. Loyal and law-abiding persons have nothing to fear from the exercise of Martial Law.

3. In order to protect the lives of his Majesty's soldiers and police under my command, I make known that if any firearm is discharged or bombs thrown at them the most drastic reprisals will instantly be made *against property surrounding the scene of the outrage.* Therefore it behooves all loyal inhabitants to see to it that no evil-disposed agitator is allowed on his premises.

4. During the period of Martial Law I prohibit all processions, meetings or other gatherings of more than 10 persons without my written authority, and any such meetings, gatherings or processions held in disobedience of this order will be broken up by force without warning.

5. I forbid any person to offer violence or cause obstruction to any person desirous of opening his shop or conducting his business or proceeding to his work or business. Any person contravening this order will be arrested, tried by a summary court and be liable to be shot.

6. At present the city of Lahore enjoys the advantage of electric lights and a water-supply; but the continuance of these supplies will depend on the good behaviour of the inhabitants and their prompt obedience to my orders.

No. 2

All tongas and tum-tums, (horse carriages) whether licensed for hire or otherwise, will be delivered up to the Military Officer appointed for that purpose at the Punjab Light Horse ground by 17·00 (5 P.M.) to-day—Tuesday, 15th April. Drivers will receive pay and horses be rationed.

No. 3

All motor-cars or vehicles of any descriptions will be delivered to the Military Officer appointed for that purpose at the Punjab club by 17·00 (5 P.M.) this day.

No. 4

By virtue of the powers vested in me I have prohibited the issue of third or intermediate class tickets at all railway stations in the Lahore Civil Command, *except only in the case of servants travelling with their European masters or servants or others in the employ of the Government.*

No. 5

Whereas, from information received by me, it would appear that shops, generally known as Langars, for the sale of cooked food, are used for the purpose of illegal meetings, and for the dissemination of seditious *propaganda*, and whereas I notice that all other shops (particularly in Lahore city) have been closed as part of an organized demonstration against his Majesty's Government, now, therefore, by virtue of the powers vested in me under Martial Law, I order that all such Langars or shops for the sale of cooked food in the Lahore civil area, except such as may be granted an exemption in writing by me shall close and cease to trade by 10·00 hours (10 A.M.) tomorrow, Wednesday, the 16th April, 1919.

Disobedience to this order will result in the confiscation of the contents of such shop and the arrest and trial by summary procedure of the owner or owners. [. . .]

No. 7

Whereas I have reason to believe that certain students of the D. A. V. College in Lahore are engaged in spreading seditious *propaganda* directed against his Majesty's Government, and whereas I deem it expedient in the interests of the preservation of law and order to restrict the activities of such students, I make the following order:—

All students of the said college now in this Command area will report themselves to the Officer Commanding Troops at the Bradlaugh Hall daily at the hours specified below and remain there until the roll of such students has been called by the principal or some other officer approved by me acting on his behalf, and until they have been dismissed by the Officer Commanding Troops at Bradlaugh Hall.

07·00 hours. (7 A.M.)
11·00 hours. (11 A.M.)
15·00 hours. (3 P.M.)
19·30 hours. (7.30 P.M.)

No. 8

Whereas some evilly-disposed persons have torn down or defaced notices and orders which I have caused to be exhibited for information and good government of the people in the Lahore (Civil) Command.

In future all orders that I have to issue under Martial Law *will be handed to such owners of property as I may select and it will be the duty of such owners of property to exhibit and keep exhibited and undamaged in the position on their property selected by me all such orders.*

The duty of protecting such orders will therefore devolve on the owners of property and failure to ensure the proper protection and continued exhibition of my orders will result in severe punishment.

Similarly, I hold responsible the owner of any property on which seditious or any other notices, proclamations or writing not authorized by me are exhibited. [. . .]

No. 13

Whereas information laid before me shows that a martial law notice issued by me and posted by my orders on a property known as the Sanatan Dharam College Hostel on Bahawalpur road, has been torn or otherwise defaced, in contravention of my Martial Law Notice No. 8.

Now, therefore, by virtue of the powers vested in me under martial law, I order the immediate arrest of *all male persons domiciled in the said hostel and their internment in the Lahore Fort* pending my further orders as to their trial or other disposal.

No. 14

Whereas practically every shop and business establishment in the area under my command has been closed in accordance with the *hartal* [strike] or organized closure of business directed against his Majesty's Government.

And whereas the continuance or resumption of such *hartal* is detrimental to the good order and governance of the said area.

And whereas I deem it expedient to cause the said *hartal* to entirely cease:

Now therefore by virtue of the powers vested in me by martial law I make the following order, namely:—

By 10·00 hours (10 A.M.) tomorrow (Friday), the 18th day of April, 1919, every shop and business establishment (except only *langare* [shops] referred to in martial law notice No. 5, dated 15th April, 1919) in the area under my command, shall open and carry on its business *and thereafter daily shall continue to keep open and carry on its business* during the usual hours up to 20·00 hours (8 P.M.) in exactly the same manner as before the creation of the said *hartal*.

And likewise I order that every skilled or other worker will from 10·30 hours (10.30 A.M.) tomorrow, resume and continue during the usual hours his ordinary trade, work or calling.

And I warn all concerned that if at 10·00 hours (10 A.M.) tomorrow, or at any subsequent time I find this order has been without good and valid reason disobeyed, the persons concerned will be arrested and tried under the summary procedure of martial law, and shops so closed will be opened and kept open by force, any resultant loss arising from such forcible opening will rest on the owners and on occupiers concerned.

And I further warn all concerned that this order must be strictly obeyed in spirit as well as in letter, that is to say, that to open a shop and then refuse to sell goods and to charge an exorbitant or prohibitive rate, will be deemed a contravention of this order.

[Note: Shops had evidently remained closed for seven days.]

No. 15

Whereas it has come to my knowledge that the present state of unrest is being added to and encouraged by the spreading of false, inaccurate or exaggerated reports or rumours:

Now, therefore, by virtue of the powers vested in me by martial law I give notice that *any person* found guilty of publishing, spreading or repeating, false, inaccurate or exaggerated reports in connection with the military or political situation, will be arrested and summarily dealt with under martial law.

No. 16

Whereas I have reason to believe that certain students of the Dyal Singh College in Lahore are engaged in spreading seditious propaganda directed against his Majesty's Government and whereas I deem it expedient in the interest of the preservation of law and order to restrict the activities of such students, I make the following order:—

All students of the said college now in this command area will report themselves to the officer commanding troops at the telegraph office daily at the hours specified below and remain there until the roll of such students has been called by the principal or some other officer approved by me acting on his behalf, and until they have been dismissed by the Officer Commanding Troops at the telegraph office:—

07·00 hours. (7 A.M.)
11·00 hours. (11 A.M.)
15·00 hours. (3 P.M.)
19·00 hours. (7 P.M.)

First parade at 11·00 hours (11 A.M.) on the (?) April, 1919.

"The latest order under martial law passed today makes it unlawful for more than two persons to walk abreast on any constructed or clearly defined pavement or side-walk in such area. Disobedience to this order will be punished by special powers under martial law. It shall also be illegal for any male person to carry or be found in possession of an instrument known as a *lathi* [a long bamboo stick sometimes with a metal end that could be used as a weapon]. All persons disobeying this order will be arrested and tried by summary proceedings under martial law." [. . .]

No. 24

Whereas I deem it expedient to make provision for the preservation of health and the greater comfort of British troops stationed in the area under my command,

And whereas a number of electric fans and lights are required in the buildings in which some of such troops are quartered,

Now therefore by virtue of the powers vested in me by martial law I authorize any officer appointed by me for that purpose to enter any college, public building, hostel, hotel, private or other residence or building and remove such number of electric lights and fans required for the purpose aforesaid,

And any attempt to obstruct such removal, or to hide, or to damage or to impair the immediate efficiency of any such fans or lights, will be summarily dealt with under martial law,

But nothing in this order shall authorize the removal of any fan or light from a room usually inhabited by a woman. [. . .]

⋏

Child Marriage Restraint Act

Government of India

India's marriage practices had long been a subject of concern to Western missionaries, civil servants, and observers who deemed arranged marriage, child marriage, dowries, and the Hindu ideas about widowhood, particularly the practice of suttee—burning a widow to death on her husband's funeral pyre—to be backwards and uncivilized. As increasing numbers of Indian boys and girls were educated in Western-style schools, they came to share many of these concerns, and Indian activists began to call for new legislation to reform some of India's traditional social customs. Following the Government of India Act of 1919 (see introduction to the previous reading) and the establishment of a native parliament, the Government of India grew to include among its ranks numerous educated Indians who had assimilated Western notions of propriety enough to be willing to sponsor the following bill, which prohibited marriages of girls younger than twelve and boys younger than fifteen.

In this selection we see an indigenous attempt to reconfigure Indian marriage practices to make them conform more closely to Western norms. Note that the new legal limit of fourteen remained low and thus reflects an attempt to respond to a modernizing impulse while at the same time not completely outlawing local custom.

⋏

Questions

1. What sorts of indigenous influences and what sorts of external influences do we see in this text?

2. What arguments in favor of restricting the age of marriage does the document present? Whom is the bill intended to protect?

Whereas it is expedient to restrain the solemnisation of child marriages: It is hereby enacted as follows:

1. (1) This Act may be called the Child Marriage Restraint Act, 1928. (2) It extends to the whole of British India, including British Baluchistan and the Santhal Parganas. (3) It shall come into force on the 1st day of April, 1930.

2. In this Act, unless there is anything repugnant in the subject or context,—(a) "child" means a person who, if a male, is under eighteen years of age, and if a female, is under fourteen years of age; (b) "child marriage" means a marriage to which either of the contracting parties is a child; (c) "contracting party" to a marriage means either of the parties whose marriage is thereby solemnised;

Source: "A Bill to Restrain the Solemnisation of Child Marriages." In Radha Kumar, *The History of Doing.* London: Verso, 1993. Pp. 70–71. Reprinted with permission.

and (d) "minor" means a person of either sex who is under eighteen years of age.

3. Whoever, being a male above eighteen years of age and below twenty-one, contracts a child marriage shall be punishable with fine which may extend to one thousand rupees.

4. Whoever, being a male above twenty-one years of age, contracts a child marriage shall be punishable with simple imprisonment which may extend to one thousand rupees, or with both.

5. Whoever performs, conducts or directs any child marriage shall be punishable with simple imprisonment which may extend to one month, or with fine which may extend to one thousand rupees, or with both, unless he proves that he had reason to believe that the marriage was not a child marriage.

6. (1) Where a minor contracts a child marriage, any person having charge of the minor, whether as parent or guardian or in any other capacity, lawful or unlawful, who does any act to promote the marriage or permits it to be solemnised, or negligently fails to prevent it from being solemnised, shall be punishable with simple imprisonment which may extend to one month, or with fine which may extend to one thousand rupees, or with both: Provided that no woman shall be punishable with imprisonment. (2) For the purposes of this section, it shall be presumed, unless and until the contrary is proved, that, where a minor has contracted a child marriage, the person having charge of such minor has negligently failed to prevent the marriage from being solemnised.

7. Notwithstanding anything contained in section 25 of the General Clauses Act, 1897, or section 64 of the Indian Penal Code, a Court sentencing an offender under section 3 shall not be competent to direct that, in default of payment of the fine imposed, he shall undergo any term of imprisonment.

8. Notwithstanding anything contained in section 190 of the Code of Criminal Procedure, 1898, no Court other than that of a Presidency Magistrate or a District Magistrate shall take cognizance of, or try, any offence under this Act.

9. No Court shall take cognizance of any offence under this Act save upon complaint made within one year of the solemnisation of the marriage in respect of which the offence is alleged to have been committed.

10. The Court taking cognizance of an offence under this Act shall, unless it dismisses the complaint under section 203 of the Code of Criminal Procedure, 1898, either itself make an inquiry under section 202 of that Code, or direct a Magistrate of the first class subordinate to it to make such inquiry.

11. (1) At any time after examining the complainant and before issuing process for compelling the attendance of the accused, the Court shall, except for reasons to be recorded in writing, require the complainant to execute a bond, with or without sureties, for a sum not exceeding one hundred rupees, as security for the payment of any compensation which the complainant may be directed to pay under section 250 of the Code of Criminal Procedure, 1898; and if such security is not furnished within such reasonable time as the Court may fix, the complaint shall be dismissed. (2) A bond taken under this section shall be deemed to be a bond taken under the Code of Criminal Procedure, 1898, and Chapter XLII of that Code shall apply accordingly.

This Bill was passed at a meeting of the Legislative Assembly on the 23rd day of September, 1929.

V.J. Patel,
President, Legislative Assembly
The 25th September, 1929.

STATEMENT OF OBJECTS AND REASONS

1. The object of the Bill is twofold. The main object, by declaring invalid the marriages of girls below 12 years of age, is to put a stop to

such girls becoming widows. The second object, by laying down the minimum marriageable ages of boys and girls, is to prevent, so far as may be, their physical and moral deterioration by removing a principal obstacle to their physical and mental development.

2. According to the Census Report of 1921 A.D., there were in that year 612 Hindu widows who were less than one year old, 2,024 who were under 5 years, 97,857 who were under 10 years, and 332,024 who were under 15 years of age. The deplorable feature of the situation, however, is that the majority of these child widows are prevented by Hindu custom and usage from remarrying. Such a lamentable state of affairs exists in no country, civilised or uncivilised, in the world. And it is high time that the law came to the assistance of these helpless victims of social customs, which whatever their origin or justification in old days, are admittedly out of date and are the source of untold misery and harm at the present time.

3. According to the Brahmanas, the most ancient and the most authoritative book containing the laws of the Hindus, the minimum marriageable age of a man is 24 and a woman 16. And if the welfare of the girl were the only consideration in fixing the age, the law should fix 16 as the minimum age for the valid marriage of a girl. But amongst the Hindus, there are people who hold the belief that a girl should not remain unmarried after she attains puberty. And as in this country,

some girls attain puberty at an age as early as 12, the Bill fixes 12 as the minimum age for the valid marriage of a Hindu girl.

4. In order, however, to make the Bill accessible to most conservative Hindu opinion, provision is made in the Bill that for conscientious reasons, the marriage of a Hindu girl would be permissible even when she is 11 years old. No Hindu Sastra enjoins marriage of a girl before she attains puberty, and the time has arrived and public opinion sufficiently developed, when the first step towards the accomplishment of the social reform so necessary for the removal of a great injustice to its helpless victims and so essential to the vital interests of a large part of humanity, should be taken, by enacting a law declaring invalid the marriages of girls below 11 years of age.

5. With regard to boys, the Sastras do not enjoin marriage at a particular age. Thoughtful public opinion amongst the Hindus would fix 18 as the minimum marriageable age for a boy. But as some classes of the Hindus would regard such legislation as too drastic, the Bill takes the line of least resistance by providing 15 years as the age below which the marriage of a Hindu boy shall be invalid. Even in England, where child marriages are unknown and early marriages are exceptions, it has been found necessary to fix the ages below which boys and girls may not marry.

M. HARBILAS SARDA.

⚚

Portrait of the Hard Life of a Woman

Attiya Hanim Saqqaf

The lives of women were greatly affected by global developments in the nineteenth and twentieth centuries. Traditional and modern ideas about their roles in society, the family, and marriage, for example, often combined to create a complex set of demands upon women. In areas such as education, religion, sexuality, child rearing, politics, and more, women found that they were frequently involved in complicated negotiations about their roles in a globalizing world.

In her remarkable memoir The Harem Years, *Huda Shaarawi (1879–1947) writes of her journey from the harem to involvement in international feminist politics, beginning in the immediate post–First World War era. She remained committed to feminist causes until her death. Born in Egypt to upper-class parents, she negotiated the spaces between traditional Muslim ideas about the proper role of women in society and her own increasingly independent and political outlook. In this selection, "Portrait of the Hard Life of a Woman," Shaarawi's friend, Attiya Hanim Saqqaf, recounts her struggles with her husband and their marriage. Further, Attiya tells of her travels in the Arabian Peninsula to visit Madina and Mecca, two of the holiest Muslim cities.*

⚚

QUESTIONS

1. What problems is Atiyya Hanim Saqqaf having with her husband? Do husband and wife seem to have compatable notions of marriage and child rearing?

2. What does Atiyya Hanim Saqqaf's journey to Madina and Mecca reveal about the role of Turkish authorities in the Arabian Peninsula?

3. What was the relationship between Turkish rulers and indigenous people in the Arabian peninsula? What rules and laws toward women, marriage, and child rearing did Turkish authorities create or attempt to enforce?

I was born of a Circassian mother and a Turkish father. My father, who was wealthy, married my mother after his first wife had failed to bear him children. My mother gave him a boy and a girl. Later, he died after losing his fortune, leaving only the large house where we lived and the garden. My mother was a young woman at her wits' end. After some time she was introduced to a suitable man whom she soon married. He treated her well and cared for us like a father.

There was a neighbouring family of ordinary means who had a bright young son, a little older

Source: Attiya Hanim Saqqaf, "Portrait of the Hard Life of a Woman," in Huda Shaarawi. *Harem Years: The Memoirs of an Egyptian Feminist (1879–1924)*, translated and edited by Margot Badran. Translation copyright © 1986 by Margot Badran. Reprinted with the permission of the Feminist Press at the City University of New York, www.feministpress.org. Pp. 70–76.

than I. He began to grow fond of me. My mother used to say, 'I shall arrange a marriage between Atiyya and him.' We grew up expecting this. When he finished school, he began to work for the government and was posted outside Stamboul. Afterwards, I no longer saw him. Some time later my mother heard he was going to marry a girl in the town where he worked. She became angry.

Then one day my step-father arrived with a dark-skinned stranger who asked for my hand in marriage. After ascertaining that he was not already married and would not oblige me to leave her side and live abroad, my mother consented.

When news of the impending marriage reached our neighbour's son, he hastened to Stamboul. He tried to dissuade her from going through with the plans for my marriage. He confessed that he had been married only briefly. He said he had never stopped loving me. His love was so strong that if my mother deprived him of me he would take his life. I, for my part, still loved the man and wished to marry him. The two of us concocted a plan. At nightfall on the eve of my wedding, I was to jump out of the bathroom window which was close to the ground. Unfortunately, my attempted escape was discovered and I was brought back to the house again.

I cannot describe my anxieties and how much I feared my husband the night of our wedding. I believed dark men ate white people. Nevertheless, he gained my affection and later when he decided to return home to Arabia, I insisted upon going with him. My mother accompanied us as well. Once in the Hidjaz, it was indeed confirmed that my husband did not have another wife. My mother, forebodings eased, returned after some time home to Stamboul. My husband and I lived in harmony for three years. I gave birth to a girl, although he preferred a son.

My husband went to Mecca every year for the *haj* (pilgrimage). One year when he lingered I became suspicious. I began to open his letters, struggling to read them despite my poor Arabic. I learned that he had taken another wife. When he returned, I confronted him. In anger, I returned to

my mother in Stamboul. I discovered after my marriage that our neighbour's son had fallen ill and eventually died. I was told he had never ceased to think of me, saying 'Tell her I shall never forget her.' I was deeply saddened.

My anger against my husband who had been unfaithful and not cared that I had pledged my life to him continued to rage. He had disregarded that I was young and a stranger to his country. The following summer, my husband arrived in Turkey. He made great efforts to achieve a reconciliation. He explained that he had married the daughter of a wealthy uncle to save the family patrimony from being broken up. Eventually, I consented to return with him to Madina and later gave birth to a boy.

However, it became clear before long that he would not be satisfied with one wife, or even two. I was told he had worked as a young man on ships owned by an uncle, a prosperous merchant in Indonesia. During the annual *haj* season he worked on the pilgrim ships bound for Arabia. He would marry a woman aboard ship and divorce her upon arrival. His marriages were so numerous he couldn't count them nor did he know the number of children he had. Meanwhile, I found him going after servant girls, in the house. Once when I caught him outright he began to beat the girl, pretending she had assaulted him.

Life continued like that for some time when he became gravely ill and everyone—even the doctors—eventually withdrew from him. I spent months at his side, nursing him day and night. He once asked how he could reward me for all I was doing whereupon I asked him to take me to visit the tomb of the Prophet, God bless him and upon him be salvation, when he recovered and he gave me his word.

No sooner was my husband able to stand on his feet again, not without the support of a cane, however, than he journeyed alone to Mecca to remain there with his second wife. I was badly shaken. After some time, he summoned me to make the journey to the holy shrine at Madina. Yet when I arrived in Mecca, my husband ignored me and the children. We made the journey to

Madina as planned but when we reached our destination I did not dismount the camel with my husband but proceeded with the children to the house of an aunt. I sent him a letter requesting a divorce and insisted that our infant son stay with me until he was weaned. My husband concurred. The children remained with me for the stipulated period. I then delivered them to my husband's *wakil* [agent] and the agent gave them to their father.

Next I made preparations for my departure and hired two camels for myself and my maid. A caravan of Turkish soldiers taking the mail agreed to let us travel with them to Mecca on condition we dress like men. My aunt urged me to stay in Madina, warning of bedouin attacks on the caravans. In my despair and suffering, I was determined to leave at all costs. We set out from Madina and after covering several leagues by nightfall pitched camp outside the walls of a large dwelling. The master informed us the bedouin had closed off the mountain pass because the Turkish government had failed to pay them their customary tribute. The soldiers turned to me and said, 'We shall take you back to Madina before continuing as we cannot guarantee your safety.' I replied, 'Let us go forward. Whatever befalls you, befalls me.' That night as dinner was being prepared, a group of veiled bedouin passed by our encampment. We invited them to partake of our meal but they rode on without answering. This was an unfriendly gesture that confirmed what we had heard about their hostility.

The following morning we arose before dawn and set out. We had been crossing the desert for some time when we met a party of bedouin who shouted orders to stop. The Turkish soldiers asked if I could gallop. I gave free rein to my camel as gun shots signalled the battle was on. In an instant, what seemed like thousands of bedouin appeared on the high plateau and descended upon us like lightning. They had forced us to a standstill and had begun to direct their fire at us when I shouted out to the Turkish soldiers, 'Stop! There are two women with you! Do not sacrifice them!' A soldier shouted back, 'How can we sacrifice our

honour and the purse and weapons of the Ottoman government?' By imploring them to stop I revealed my fear of death. The soldiers painfully surrendered and were divested of their weapons and money.

When the bedouin recognized two women, they made us dismount. They opened my saddle bag and removed the silver coins I had brought for expenses, as well as a string of fake pearls which appeared valuable in the glistening sun. They ordered us to follow them. When I asked where they were taking us they said, 'To our tents to pay you honour and that you may partake of our repast.' One of them added, 'We are going to devour you!'

When I feigned fright, the chief said, 'Do not fear, oh *Sharifa*, we wish to honour you and receive your *baraka* [blessing].' When examining my possessions they had discovered my seal and my children's seals carrying the name of my former husband, a descendant of the Prophet, may God bless him and upon him be salvation. The bedouin revere the descendants of the Prophet. My former husband had also always been generous with them.

Unable to tread the stones and thorns, I was carried to the encampment on the back of my servant. The chief led us to his tent where his women welcomed me. They gathered round me and touched me all over exclaiming, 'How beautiful you are!' I understood they wanted to know if anything was concealed under my garments. When they came upon a solid object I told them it was the Holy Koran which was always with me. To prove I was speaking the truth, they asked me to remove it and read some *ayas* [verses] to them, which I did. The bedouin slaughtered animals for us and fêted us lavishly.

Early the next morning, the chief appeared to wish me good day and said, 'Oh, *Sharifa*, you have honoured us. You and your companions may now go in peace.' I replied, 'How can we proceed when you have taken all we possess? I fear we shall be halted along the way by bedouin not as noble and kind as you and your people.'

He answered, 'Our home is your home. You may remain with us as long as you wish.' I said,

'I am awaited in Mecca and my relations will grow anxious if I do not appear.' He asked, 'What then can I do for you?' and I answered, 'Ride with us and protect us.' He laughed and asked, 'Do you wish to deliver me over to the Turkish authorities who have put a price on my head?' I told him, 'I shall be responsible for your safety. I give my promise that no harm shall befall you.' He replied, 'I pledge to protect you, I am at your service.' I asked him to bring enough money for the journey, which I would repay upon arrival in Mecca. I also requested the return of the mail pouches and unloaded rifles to the soldiers so the Ottoman authorities would not discipline them.

With the bedouin chief as our guide, the caravan set out once more. Whenever we approached an encampment he would hasten forward in greeting and in an instant we would be welcomed with drums and flutes. The nomads would seek my blessing, holding out their ailing children for me to touch, as they had great faith in the miraculous powers of the descendants of the Prophet. Near Mecca, the chief dismounted and dug a hole in a small hillock. A Turkish soldier told me he had buried a rifle—undoubtedly one of the recently pilfered ones—and he intended to report it immediately upon arrival in Mecca. 'Do not,' I said, 'I have promised him protection. If it were not for his trust in me, you and your companions would not be alive now.' I made him swear he would not reveal what he had seen. As we made our entry into Mecca, the chief disappeared from sight.

After returning to my house, I collected a bundle of clothing and other items, including the garlic I had promised the bedouin women. At nightfall there came a knock on the door. The bedouin chief had come to settle accounts for the journey and to collect the promised gifts. When I paid him his due, he thanked me, wished me well, and pledged to remain forever in my service. He excused the deeds of his tribesmen by explaining they were poor. When the Turkish government cut off payments of money and grain, they were forced to block the caravan routes to put pressure on the authorities. Otherwise, they would die of starvation. The chief took his leave. On the following day I left for Jeddah and thence to Egypt.

Beautiful Maria in the Act of True Love

FELIX N. STEPHEN

As the colonial powers imposed their own languages and systems of education on the colonies, reading, writing, and publishing habits changed. By the early twentieth century, there was a vast reading public in English-speaking West Africa in general and in Nigeria in particular, which sought access to English-language reading material. Onitsha Market Literature, as it is commonly called, describes a large array of novels and pamphlets that were published and distributed in the Onitsha Market through the early to mid-twentieth century. Onitsha had a large population of students in secondary and commercial schools and a vast number of printing presses. These features, combined with the presence of one of the largest markets in East Africa, made Onitsha into a publishing powerhouse in the mid-twentieth century.

The emphasis of the Onitsha Market Literature was on educating the people in a broad sense, so many of the Onitsha publications sought to teach people to live a moral life. Popular themes in the publications were the evils of witchcraft, maladjustment of social status, generational problems, the changing status of women in society, sexual mores, and so on. Many of the Onitsha printing firms were staffed with poorly educated personnel, and the publications were poorly proofread. Moreover, most of the characters were underdeveloped, the themes were quite superficial, and the literature was typically written in a pidgen English. In spite of these apparent flaws, Onitsha Market Literature was wildly successful with the local audience because of the closeness of the authors to their subjects and their audience. Reader requests, in fact, often dictated the sorts of topics about which authors wrote. This selection addresses issues of courtship and love.

QUESTIONS

1. Why might this story have appealed to a broad reading audience?
2. What values does this story promote?

Act I Scene 2

The Love Tutelage

MARIA: I have been approached by many suitors, but I find it quite difficult, to take a decision.

THERESA: Does it simply go to mean that none of them measures up to expectation?

MARIA: Most of them are presentable. But in fact Theresa I only want to make sure that he to whom I shall agree to give my hand will not disappoint me later on. It is for this sake that I am of the opinion to give trials to many men. He who succeeds will do so, out of the gravity of love that he has on me.

Source: Felix N. Stephen. "Beautiful Maria in the Act of True Love." Onitsha: Michael Allan Ohaejesi, no date. Pp. 8–10.

THERESA: Can you at this stage not guess of any man that is languishing for not being able to have secured your love?

MARIA: I have heard of one Emmanuel. Really I can not just tell if he is serious. I want to give him a tough time first. If I do not do so, he will deem me very cheap. His boy often comes here.

THERESA: Has that Emmanuel made you any presents[?]

MARIA: I am one of those who firmly believe that presents cannot get lady convinced against her will. At any rate, I am sure that if I had given an expression of interest in his presents, he could have even exhausted himself to see that I am kept happy over him. Right now I owe him nothing and so it will be very possible for me to speak to him any how. He might only take an offence which I suspect might not be of long duration.

THERESA: Why not get presents from him and still be on what you are after?

MARIA: That will degrade me very much before him. Again it will expose me to public scandal. Every other man will think that it is my custom. You remember this, men always discuss women whenever they are holding a friendly discussion. I want my person to be respected.

THERESA: For my part I believe in cheating foolish men because I did not force them to come and seek my love.

MARIA: Men are not really foolish when they get about looking for female friends. For a person to be alone is a type of sickness—a great one too. Many factors give rise to it. There might be the conclusion that especially on the part of women the person is not beautiful. In these rosy days of ours we must be up and doing to get partners who will still be with us when beauty fades.

THERESA: Personally I have many male friends. I do not like to keep to one. That is why it appears that I have got some good amount of money.

MARIA: Do you think that all of them who come to you pay the money joyfully?

THERESA: Whether they do or not is not my real concern. It is my policy that without their money I do not give out my love.

MARIA: Can that be taken as true love?

THERESA: That is why I can say [it] is the best way for a woman to follow men. They are deceitful. If you are soft with them, they become very insultive to you.

MARIA: I will also like to have my own sound experience of men. But I shall like to experiment on one man only. [. . .]

Named for Victoria, Queen of England

Chinua Achebe

Chinua Achebe's efforts, described in the following selection, to reclaim his African identity exemplify a strategy employed by colonial peoples to shed the identities that had been imposed upon them through colonization. "If I were God," Chinua Achebe wrote in 1963 in the famous essay "The Novelist as a Teacher," "I would regard as the very worst our acceptance, for whatever reason, of racial inferiority." He went on to define his role as a writer as that of an educator trying to help "my society regain belief in itself and put away the complexes of the years of denigration and self-denigration." In his essay "Named for Victoria, Queen of England," Chinua Achebe tells us that his initial motivation to write came from his encounter with Western novels about Africa, including Joseph Conrad's Heart of Darkness *and Joyce Cary's* Mister Johnson, *that he found appalling for their failure to adequately describe African identities. He decided that "the story we had to tell could not be told for us by anybody else no matter how gifted or well intentioned."*

Born in Ogidi, in the eastern part of Nigeria in 1930, Achebe was, as he informs us in the autobiographical essay that follows, originally christened Albert Chinualumogu. His father was an evangelist and church teacher, although many of his relatives and neighbors adhered to the Igbo religion and customs. Thus, Achebe wrote, he grew up "at the crossroads of cultures." He took upon himself the mission of describing and reconstructing in literature Igbo identity as opposed to British-African identity.

QUESTIONS

1. How did education shape identity in colonial settings?
2. How did Achebe use his writing as a tool to shape African identity?

[. . .] I was baptized Albert Chinualumogu. I dropped the tribute to Victorian England when I went to the university, although you might find some early acquaintances still calling me by it. The earliest of them all—my mother—certainly stuck to it to the bitter end. So if anyone asks you what her Britannic Majesty Queen Victoria had in common with Chinua Achebe, the answer is, They both lost their Albert! As for the second name, which in the manner of my people is a full-length philosophical statement, I simply cut it in two, making it more businesslike without, I hope, losing the general drift of its meaning.

Source: Chinua Achebe. "Named for Victoria, Queen of England." In *Morning Yet on Creation Day: Essays.* Garden City, NY: Anchor Press, 1975. Pp. 118–124. Copyright © 1975 by Chinua Achebe. Used by permission of Doubleday, a division of Random House.

I have always been fond of stories and intrigued by language—first Igbo, spoken with such eloquence by the old men of the village, and later English which I began to learn at about the age of eight. I don't know for certain but I have probably spoken more words in Igbo than English, but I have definitely written more words in English than Igbo. Which I think makes me perfectly bilingual. Some people have suggested that I should be better off writing in Igbo. Sometimes they seek to drive the point home by asking me in which language I dream. When I reply that I dream in both languages they seem not to believe it. More recently I have heard an even more potent and metaphysical version of the question, In what language do you have an orgasm? Which should settle the matter if I knew!

We lived at the crossroads of cultures. We still do today, but when I was a boy one could see and sense the peculiar quality and atmosphere of it more clearly. I am not talking about all that rubbish we hear of the spiritual void and mental stresses that Africans are supposed to have, or the evil forces and irrational passions prowling through Africa's heart of darkness. We know the racist mystique behind a lot of that stuff and should merely point out that those who prefer to see Africa in those lurid terms have not themselves demonstrated any clear superiority in sanity or more competence in coping with life.

But still the crossroads does have a certain dangerous potency; dangerous because a man might perish there wrestling with multiple-headed spirits, but also he might be lucky and return to his people with the boon of prophetic vision.

On one arm of the cross, we sang hymns and read the Bible night and day. On the other, my father's brother and his family, blinded by heathenism, offered food to idols. That was how it was supposed to be anyhow. But I knew without knowing why that it was too simple a way to describe what was going on. Those idols and that food had a strange pull on me in spite of my being such a thorough little Christian that often at Sunday services at the height of the grandeur of "Te Deum laudamus" I would have dreams of a mantle of gold falling on me as the choir of angels drowned our mortal song and the voice of God Himself thundered: This is my beloved son in whom I am well pleased. Yes, despite those delusions of divine destiny I was not past taking my little sister to our neighbor's house when our parents were not looking and partaking of heathen festival meals. I never found their rice and stew to have the flavor of idolatry. I was about ten then. If anyone likes to believe that I was torn by spiritual agonies or stretched on the rack of my ambivalence, he certainly may suit himself. I do not remember any undue distress. What I do remember was a fascination for the ritual and the life on the other arm of the crossroads. And I believe two things were in my favor—that curiosity and the little distance imposed between me and it by the accident of my birth. The distance becomes not a separation but a bringing together like the necessary backward step which a judicious viewer may take in order to see a canvas steadily and fully.

I was lucky in having a few old books around the house when I was learning to read. As the fifth in a family of six children, and with parents so passionate for their children's education, I inherited many discarded primers and readers. I remember *A Midsummer Night's Dream* in an advanced stage of falling apart. I think it must have been a prose adaptation, simplified and illustrated. I don't remember whether I made anything of it. Except the title. I couldn't get over the strange beauty of it. A Midsummer Night's Dream. It was a magic phrase—an incantation that conjured up scenes and landscapes of an alien, happy, and unattainable land.

I remember also my mother's *Ije Onye Kraist* which must have been an Igbo adaptation of *Pilgrim's Progress*. It could not have been the whole book; it was too thin. But it had some frightening pictures. I recall in particular a most vivid impression of *the valley of the shadow of death*. I thought a lot about death in those days. There was another little book which frightened and fascinated me. It had drawings of different parts of the human body. But I was primarily interested in what my elder sister told me was the human heart. Since there is a slight confusion in Igbo between heart and soul, I took it that that strange thing, looking almost like my mother's iron cooking pot turned upside down, was the very thing that flew out when a man died and perched on the head of the coffin on the way to the cemetery.

I found some use for most of the books in our house but by no means all. There was one arithmetic book I smuggled out and sold for half a penny which I needed to buy the tasty *mai-mai* some temptress of a woman sold in the little market outside the school. I was found out and my mother who had never had cause till then to doubt my honesty—laziness, yes; but not theft—received a huge shock. Of course she redeemed the book. I was so ashamed when she brought it home that I don't think I ever looked at it again, which was probably why I never had much use for mathematics.

My parents' reverence for books was almost superstitious, so my action must have seemed like a form of juvenile simony. My father was much worse than my mother. He never destroyed any paper. When he died we had to make a bonfire of all the hoardings of his long life. I am the very opposite of him in this. I can't stand paper around me. Whenever I see a lot of it I am seized by a mild attack of pyromania. When I die my children will not have a bonfire.

The kind of taste I acquired from the chaotic literature in my father's house can well be imagined. For instance I became very fond of those aspects of ecclesiastical history as could be garnered from *The West African Churchman's Pamphlet*—a little terror of a booklet prescribing interminable Bible readings morning and night. It had the date of consecration for practically every Anglican bishop who ever served in West Africa, and, even more intriguing, the dates of their death. Many of them didn't last very long. I remember one pathetic case (I forget his name) who arrived in Lagos straight from his consecration at St. Paul's Cathedral and was dead within days, and his wife a week or two

after him. Those were the days when West Africa was truly the white man's grave, when those great lines were written, of which I was at that time unaware:

Bight of Benin! Bight of Benin!
Where few come out though many go in!

But the most fascinating information I got from *Pamphlet*, as we called it, was this cryptic entry:

Augustine, Bishop of Hippo, died 430.

It had that elusive and eternal quality, a tantalizing unfamiliarity which I always found moving.

I did not know that I was going to be a writer because I did not really know of the existence of such creatures until fairly late. The folk stories my mother and elder sister told me had the immemorial quality of the sky and the forests and the rivers. Later, when I got to know that the European stories I read were written by known people, it still didn't help much. It was the same Europeans who made all the other marvelous things like the motorcar. We did not come into it at all. We made nothing that wasn't primitive and heathenish.

The nationalist movement in British West Africa after the Second World War brought about a mental revolution which began to reconcile us to ourselves. It suddenly seemed that we too might have a story to tell. "Rule Britannia!" to which we had marched so unselfconsciously on Empire Day now stuck in our throats.

At the university I read some appalling novels about Africa (including Joyce Cary's much praised *Mister Johnson*) and decided that the story we had to tell could not be told for us by anyone else, no matter how gifted or well-intentioned.

Although I did not set about it consciously in that solemn way I now know that my first book, *Things Fall Apart*, was an act of atonement with my past, the ritual return and homage of a prodigal son. But things happen very fast in Africa. I had hardly begun to bask in the sunshine of reconciliation when a new cloud appeared, a new estrangement.

Political independence had come. The nationalist leader of yesterday (with whom it had not
been too difficult to make common cause) had
become the not so attractive party boss. And then
things really got going. The party boss was chased
out by the bright military boys, new idols of the
people. But the party boss knows how to wait,
knows by heart the counsel Mother Bedbug gave
her little ones when the harassed owner of the bed
poured hot water on them. "Be patient," said she,
"for what is hot will in the end be cold." What is
bright can also get tarnished, like the military boys.

One hears that the party boss is already conducting a whispering campaign. "You done see us

chop," he says. "Now you see *dem* chop. Which one
you like pass?" And the people are truly confused.

In a little nondescript coffee shop where I
sometimes stop for a hamburger in Amherst, there
are some unfunny inscriptions hanging on the
walls, representing a one-sided dialogue between
management and staff. The unfunniest of them
all reads—poetically:

Take care of your boss
The next one may be worse.

The trouble with writers is that they will often
refuse to live by such rationality.

▲

Inaugural Statement for the Eastern Times

Liang Qichao

Liang Qichao was a classically trained scholar who was among China's early advocates of large-scale political, social, and cultural reform. He was also publisher of one of China's earliest modern political newspapers, the Eastern Times. *Earlier Western-style newspapers had existed in China's major urban areas, but they tended to concentrate on commerce. In the wake of China's military defeat by Japan in 1895, a new press that called for political reform of the outdated Chinese imperial system also began to flourish, though it went into a period of decline after 1898 when the reformers were defeated at court. The* Eastern Times *came into being during a second wave of reform in the wake of the failed Boxer Uprising of 1900. A mere five years after its inauguration, the newspaper had the largest circulation of any journal in Shanghai.*

In this inaugural statement for the first issue, published June 12, 1904, Liang considers the role to be played by this new medium in transforming the political and social culture of China. The newspaper, in Liang's view, could educate its readers about the issues of the day and foster the development of public opinion, something that would be essential for the democratic China that Liang hoped to see come into being.

▲

Questions

1. What purpose does Liang think the *Eastern Times* can serve?
2. Does Liang believe that Western knowledge can help China to reform? If so, what role can the *Eastern Times* play in this process?

[. . .] Why publish the *Eastern Times* (*Shibao*)? The *Record of Rites* says, "A gentleman acts according to the golden mean." It also says, "A man of profound self-cultivation and high learning uses his knowledge appropriately." Therefore, in regulating the state and ordering society, nothing is more valuable than timeliness. It is not the Chinese teachings alone that emphasize this. In the West, Darwin first developed the principle of natural selection and the triumph of the strong. Spencer later replaced this principle with the theory of survival of the fittest. According to this theory, which constitutes the field of victory and defeat, that which is of superior quality but not adapted to the environment will eventually become inferior and that which is of inferior quality but adapted to the environment will eventually become superior. Therefore, although the fur of a fox is very warm, it is of no use in the heat of summer, and although fine satin is very beautiful, it cannot protect against the cold of winter. That which is not appropriate to the time will certainly fail.

Source: Liang Qichao. "Inaugural Statement for the Eastern Times." In Wm. Theodore de Bary and Richard Lufrano (Eds.), *Sources of Chinese Tradition*. Vol. 2. New York: Columbia University Press, 2000. Pp. 300–302. Copyright © 2000 Columbia University Press. Reprinted with permission of the publisher.

In China today, those in lofty and powerful positions and those who are reclusive hermits are all unaware of the general world situation. They believe that thousand-year-old politics and thousand-year-old learning are appropriate to the changes of today. According to an assessment of present conditions, however, this is not possible; one could knit one's brow in worry for a whole day and still not be able to solve today's problems with yesterday's methods. As a result, when heroic young activists hear that Western nations have such and such a method of regulating chaos, such and such a method of self-strengthening, they all run and shout, "We too must do it this way! We too must do it this way!" While no one would deny that these methods are the reason the West can regulate chaos and strengthen itself, we simply do not know if these methods are appropriate to our times. As Confucius said, "To go beyond is as wrong as to fall short." To fall short and apply methods that are no longer fitting to the times is a waste; every day corruption would increase and there would be no way to save the nation. At the same time, to go beyond the present situation and apply methods that are too advanced for the times, to yell and shout and wildly push forward, would not accomplish anything either. Moreover, proceeding in this way could give rise to new problems, and the nation would become unsalvageable. In sum, if the country should be lost, both kinds of people [conservatives and Western-oriented radicals] would be equally responsible.

There are also intelligent, broad-minded, and steadfast individuals who are committed to listening to both sides but choosing the middle course in order to plan the orderly progress of the people. It seems, however, that because their general knowledge is insufficient, their understanding of scientific theory weak, and their concrete investigations of the current situation lacking, when they speak in terms of general principles they have no tangible proof, when they try to manage matters they cannot manage them successfully, and when they want to implement their ideas they are bewildered and do not know how to

proceed. They vigorously apply themselves to do one or two things but because their methods are mistaken, they incessantly fail. Because everyone is aware of this and admonished by it they do not dare speak of reform again. Alas! Although there are numerous kinds of publicists and politicians in the nation, upon scrutiny all of them follow one of these three paths [of conservatives, radicals, or impractical reformists].

Alas! This is a dangerous time and we are deeply concerned. Therefore in founding this newspaper, we have named it *shi*—The Times (*Shibao*). While we of course wish to revere the essence of the nation, we believe that that which is not appropriate to the present should be put aside and forgotten. And while we of course admire Western civilization, we believe that that which is not appropriate to the level of Chinese development must be temporarily put aside. We will exert our knowledge to the highest possible level in order to resolve the major political and scholarly problems that arise in China and abroad. Using fair and honest discussions, we will analyze the positive and negative, advantageous and disadvantageous aspects of these problems. We will also investigate methods for delivering the nation from danger and coping with the current situation, while cooperating with the government and conferring with the citizens.

It is the duty of newspapers in advanced nations to report on the facts in the news, to follow the trend of international public opinion, to investigate conditions in the interior of the nation, to develop knowledge of politics and the arts, to introduce new ideas, and to provide materials for leisurely reading. We must drive ourselves on. We will use our writings to define and convey the will of the nation. We must also, however, take note of the saying of Western philosophers that "perfect things must be produced in perfect times." Today, given that our nation is still young in terms of development, I realize that it is not appropriate for us to wish to place ourselves among the great newspapers of all of the nations in the world. But by taking one step after another, a distance of one thousand miles can eventually be overcome, and by joining together one hundred streams, the four seas could eventually be formed. It is certain that, sooner or later, our newspaper's trajectory will not only follow but parallel the progress of the nation. This is what we will assiduously work toward every day.

Our nation can take the highest position among the nations of the world. Therefore, this newspaper must seek to take the highest position among all of the newspapers in the world. The favor that the people of our nation will owe us is unlimited! The favor that the people of our nation will owe us is unlimited!

Mister Johnson

JOYCE CARY

Joyce Cary was born in Northern Ireland, and his experiences there and in Nigeria shaped his perspective on the colonial enterprise. In his twenties, Cary settled in Africa, where he joined the British colonial civil service in Nigeria, and it was there that he based his novel Mister Johnson *(1939).* Mister Johnson *portrays the fate of an African clerk, who is delighted with the prestige of his clerkship but tragically flawed by his inability to take routine seriously.* Mister Johnson *is a humorous novel that has as its main theme the changes taking place in colonial Nigeria, changes that put an African like Johnson in a no-man's land between two cultures, one too backward for his modern tastes and the other too rule-oriented for his nonconformist ways. Johnson likes white men's possessions; he embezzles, steals, commits fraud, and finally murders. He is a pawn in the hands of Europeans, who make use of him, and then having tempted him, execute him. The novel's protagonist is an excellent example of the reconfigurations that took place in colonial settings; he takes an English name, wears European-style clothes, and refers to England, where he has never been, as home.*

QUESTIONS

1. In what ways does the character of Mister Johnson appear to have been reconfigured by the colonial experience?

2. Why does the English colonial administrator describe some black Africans as "romantic reactionaries"?

[. . .] Johnson walks up and down in the compound and every moment his walk becomes grander; it is like the walk of the royal guard, but a guard of poets fresh from a triumph of loyalty. Johnson slaps himself on the chest. "I belong for de King—I 'gree for de King. I Mister Rudbeck's frien'."

Beer is going round in large calabashes, all the clerks and servants are talking at the top of their voices and the words, "King," "home," "England," "royal" are heard. Everybody is excited by the idea of patriotism. Every now and then, as Johnson walks among his guests, he makes a few dance steps, and sings through his nose, "England is my country, dat King of England is my King."

Then Ajali chimes in with a bass "Oh, England is my home, all on de big water."

At one in the morning all boys and clerks have gone except one small boy. But half a dozen townspeople are still gossiping in the shadows. Johnson is walking restlessly in the compound. He has taken off all his clothes except his bright shoes. A thin moon glitters on the shoes, on an empty gin bottle and the dregs of beer in scattered calabashes. Johnson is singing softly with quick changes of pitch and tone:

Source: Joyce Cary. *Mister Johnson*. New York: New Directions Books, 1989. Pp. 35–38. By permission of the Trustees of the Joyce Cary Estate.

'England is my country.

Oh, England, my home all on de big water.

Dat King of England is my King,

De bes' man in de worl', his heart is too big.

Oh, England, my home all on de big water.'

Two of the gossipers dimly seen in the shadow are clapping softly while they talk about their own affairs; an old Yoruba trader in the corner, very drunk, with an English cloth cap on his head, sings the chorus with Johnson, and utters loud sobs. God knows what the word "England" means to him, but he is an old man who probably learned his English at some English mission.

'Oh, England, my home, away der on de big water.

England is my country, dat King of England is my King.

His heart is big for his children—

Room for everybody.'

Johnson sings along, falsetto, dancing with peculiar looseness as if all his joints are turned to macaroni.

'I say hallo, I act de fool.

I spit on de carpet of his great big heart.'

"Oh, England my home," the old Yoruba sings with a loud sob, "Away, away, over de big water."

'Hi, you general dar, bring me de cole beer,

I, Mister Johnson, from Fada, I belong for King's service,

Hi, you judge dar, in yo' crinkly wig,

Roll me out dat bed, hang me up dat royal net.'

The clapping grows louder and someone throws in a syncopation. Four or five voices hum and wail the tune with the effect sometimes of clarinets, sometimes of kazoos. Johnson's dance

grows even looser, his legs seem to bend in every part, as he sways and sings, clearly but softly:

'Hi, you coachy man with you peaky hat,

Bring me dat gold pot for I make my night water.

I, Mister Johnson from Fada, I big man for Fada,

De King, he tired, he work all day, it's mail day.

He wanna sleep. He feel me dar like hot pain in his bress.

He say Doss some fool chile in my bress

Runnin through my bress like he was drunk.

De Pramminister he come running from his clerk-office.

He shout out to de King, Up on top; you majesty, I see um,

I see um like lil black ting no more big than stink bug.

He drunk, he play de fool, he black trash,

He no care for nobody. He bad dirty boy,

He spit all over de carpet of you great big heart.

All right, you majesty, I go catch him now,

I go trow him right out right over de top of Pallament right

In de river Thames, kersplash.

De King, he say, oh no, Mr. Pramminister, don't do so,

I know dat Johnson from Fada, he my faithful clerk from Fada,

He drunk for me, he drunk for love of his royal King,

He drunk becas he come here, he doanno how to be so happy,

He got no practice in dem great big happiness,

Why, what he do now, he laugh. Poot, what's de good to laugh.

He dance. Poot. What's de good to dance.

He walk on his han's.'

Johnson makes an attempt to walk on his hands and falls back on his knees.

'What's the good of walking on his han's.
Dat's why he drunk, Mister Pramminister.
Dat's why he play around like he low black trash.
He spit on my carpet because he wanna die for me.
He————'

At this moment a furious voice bawls across the bush, "Who's that? What the hell are you playing at, there?"

Johnson stands in a trance of astonishment with eyes like a hare's. He licks his lips and cries in a trembling voice, "Johnson, sah—I sing small small, sah."

"Johnson? Who's Johnson? Oh, you mean Johnson. Are you drunk, Johnson?"

"Oh, no, sah, I never————"

"Oh, go to bed, go to bed, Johnson."

"Yes, Mister Rudbeck. Goo' night, Mister Rudbeck."

"Oh, the hell, good night, damn it all."

The guests are already in the bush. Johnson goes to bed still in a trance of surprise. How, he wonders, should Mr. Rudbeck hear him at two o'clock. How should he be awake at such a time? [. . .]

Rubber

MADELON H. LULOFS

Madelon Lulofs (1899–1953) was born and grew up in the Dutch East Indies, where her father worked for the Dutch colonial government. At nineteen, she married a Dutch planter and went to live with him on a rubber plantation in Sumatra. While on the plantation, she fell in love with another planter, and her elopement with him and divorce of her first husband caused such a scandal that she was forced to go to the Netherlands in disgrace. There she spent her life writing a series of novels set in colonial Indonesia. Rubber, *the most recent edition of which has the subtitle "The 1930s novel which shocked European society," was largely autobiographical, telling the story of a young planter's wife, stuck on a rubber plantation, falling in love with a man who was not her husband.*

Large areas of Southeast Asia were replanted as plantations under the colonial economic systems brought by the Dutch, British, and French in the eighteenth and nineteenth centuries. Prior to the advent of the plantation economy, places like Indonesia, Malaysia, Indochina, and Ceylon were already inhabited by people with well-established agricultural economies in the hands of smaller landowners, though much virgin forest remained. The colonial powers brought with them new plants, new populations of workers, and a new approach to agriculture. The selection that follows describes the physical and human landscape of an Indonesian rubber plantation, showing ways in which the environment was transformed by the development of plantations.

QUESTIONS

1. How is the rubber plantation transforming the landscape?
2. Who works on the rubber plantation?
3. What is John's attitude toward the work he is undertaking?

[. . .] He gazed dreamily in front of him. There, in one long strip, was the naked land. The first thousand acres ready to be planted! The first thousand of the four thousand which would form Tumbuk Tinggih, the new plantation of the Sumatra Hevea Company. It was all to happen very quickly, with American swiftness, no matter what the cost might be. Rubber had a future.

The markets were clamouring for increased production.

The evening was falling rapidly. The glare had gone from the sky, which was colourless as it awaited the approaching night. From the front veranda, the road and the coolie compounds with their brown roofs and walls were visible. A few coolies could be seen running about with their

Source: Madelon H. Lulofs. *Rubber*. (Trans., G. J. Renier and Irene Clephane.) Singapore: Oxford University Press, 1989. Pp. 15–17.

typical half-trot. They were carrying water from the river that flowed below the level of the road. Their brown bodies, almost naked, matched the brown environment and the shadows of dusk. Malays from the campong were arriving with fruit, vegetables, sweets, and the mats for playing dice. They carried little paraffin lamps or smoking torches to find their way back home. From the river came the sound of the voices of women bathing and doing the washing at the same time, now that their day's task was over.

It's heavy work, reflected John, but at least it's interesting. It's better than the monotonous control of a tapping section. This will grow and remain. One's own work, one's own achievement.

Soon the virgin forest would have been cut away, and a piece of civilization substituted. There would be a fine head-quarters with short cropped lawns and a wealth of cultivated flowers. The road would be metalled, and later, when the motor lorries arrived to fetch the latex for the factory, then he would be able to point to it all and say: "This is the piece I have reclaimed and planted. I have taken it from the forest."

Now there was only a stretch of bare ground burned clean. There were two compounds, the huts of the Chinese, and the two houses of Van der Meulen and himself. Everything was still provisional.

High on their piles, the houses of the Europeans were like square boxes divided into four smaller squares by half walls of unplaned, oiled planks. The living-room was shut in with mosquito netting. Above one's head one could see the beams tied together with ratan. Nailed down here and there with an immense nail, the roof of leaves rested on the beams. In the dusk the rats were chasing each other. Wall lizards stuck to the walls, waiting for the mosquitoes that were still buzzing round in wide circles.

When a gust of wind passed over the roof, a black cloud of tenuous dust fell over everything—the table, the plate, the glass—and also over one's hair, one's hands, one's bed. It could not harm the furniture: a couple of tables, a bed, chairs, and, most essential of all, a water filter, sufficed for a bachelor's needs. A creaky stair descended from the bedroom to a musty damp recess with a slippery floor containing an old cement barrel from which one dipped water to pour over oneself: that was the bathroom, and when one used it, one suspended the towels over the splits in the wall to avoid being seen by the whole world.

In the front veranda and in the living-room hung paraffin lamps whose glasses were always a little black because with every sigh of the wind the lamps smoked. Underneath the house stood tubs full of cement and chalk. There lived centipedes and scorpions, and sometimes a hen that had been missing for days re-appeared from there, proudly leading half a dozen young chicks.

Now it was evening. In the compounds the reddish flames of oil lamps flickered. Here and there a fire in the open sent up its smoke. The breeze that came from across the hills swept the smoke like a fluid veil past the buildings. That was the way the coolies protected themselves against mosquitoes.

The Chinese were chattering loudly. Their voices, shouting harsh monosyllables, always seemed quarrelsome. One knew that it meant nothing—the Chinese are a noisy lot. How different the Javanese, slow, silent Mohammedans! Their thoughts, their words, their deeds were heavy. They were primitive sages, unaware of their wisdom, serious children whose sudden lapses from self-control alone revealed that they were not grown up. Sometimes a laugh or a shriek, usually a woman's, could be distinguished, and occasionally a child whimpered. [. . .]

⋏

Coffee Plantation

PHOTOGRAPHER: JERRY FRANK

The short excerpt from Lulofs' novel describes the transformation of the Indonesian landscape through the creation of rubber plantations. Other products were planted on a large scale in other parts of the world. Crops such as coffee not only shaped agricultural economies by linking them to global networks but also reconfigured landscapes and the environment, as we see in this photograph of a Colombian coffee plantation.

⋏

QUESTIONS

1. What do you imagine this landscape might have looked like prior to the adoption of plantation-style farming techniques? How has the natural environment been reconfigured by this coffee plantation?

2. How might the economy of Colombia have been affected by a shift from small-scale to plantation-style farming?

Source: United Nations/DPI/Jerry Frank.

▲

Station Life in New Zealand

LADY BARKER

Mary Anne Stewart Barker Broome, who wrote under the name of Lady Barker, was born in England in 1831 and lived until 1911. Both of her husbands, George Barker and Frederick Napier Broome, were active participants in Britain's colonial enterprise in the nineteenth century. George Barker served in India during the Indian Mutiny of the 1850s and died at Simla in the Punjab. Shortly after her marriage to her second husband, Lady Barker moved with him to New Zealand, where Broome had bought a sheep farm. They remained there for several years in the 1860s and then returned to England. In the 1870s, Broome entered the colonial civil service, and his wife moved with him while he was posted to such places as South Africa, Mauritius, Australia, Barbados, and Trinidad.

Station Life in New Zealand was Lady Barker's first book, originally published in 1870. She subsequently authored a number of other books about her life in the colonies. This volume chronicles her life in New Zealand as an elite settler and describes in considerable detail the natural and human landscape that she encountered there. Interestingly, other than a few passing references to Maori customs, the only mention of New Zealand's indigenous population in the book refers to a reservation near Christchurch to which the relatively small number of Maoris living on New Zealand's South Island had been relocated. Her narrative, therefore, focuses entirely on the British settlers of New Zealand. In fact, by the 1860s the European population of New Zealand already outnumbered the Maori population. The first Maori census of New Zealand, taken in 1857, revealed a population of just over 56,000 Maoris, whereas by the following year there were already nearly 60,000 Europeans residents, and the number of Europeans continued to grow rapidly thereafter. The human geography of some colonies, therefore, was substantially reconfigured through settlement.

The following selection offers Lady Barker's description of a settlement of lower-class immigrants in New Zealand.

▲

QUESTIONS

1. In what ways did the settlers that Lady Barker describes reconfigure the landscape of New Zealand?

2. What sorts of institutions did the settlers bring with them?

[. . .] In one of our rides the other day, after crossing a low range of hills, we suddenly dropped down on what would be called in England a hamlet, but here it is designated by the extraordinary name of a "nest of cockatoos." This expression puzzled me so much when I first heard it,

Source: Lady Barker. *Station Life in New Zealand.* London: Macmillan, 1871. Pp. 109–13.

that I must give you as minute an explanation as I myself found necessary to the comprehension of the subject.

When a shepherd has saved a hundred pounds or the better class of immigrant arrives with a little capital, the favourite investment is in freehold land, which they can purchase, in sections of twenty acres and upwards, at 2*l.* the acre. The next step is to build a sod hut with two rooms on their property, thatching it with Tohi, or swamp-grass; a door and a couple of window-frames all ready glazed are brought from Christchurch in the dray [cart] with the family and the household goods. After this rough and ready shelter is provided, the father and sons begin fencing their land, and gradually it all assumes a cultivated appearance. Pigsties and fowl-houses are added; a little garden, gay with common English flowers, is made in front of the house, whose ugly walls are gradually hidden by creepers, and the homestead looks both picturesque and prosperous. These small farmers are called Cockatoos in Australia by the squatters or sheep-farmers, who dislike them for buying up the best bits of land on their runs; and say that, like a cockatoo, the small freeholder alights on good ground, extracts all he can from it, and then flies away to "fresh fields and pastures new." But the real fact is, that the poor farmer perhaps finds his section is too far from a market, so he is forced to abandon it and move nearer a town, where the best and most productive land has been bought up already and he has to begin again at a disadvantage. However, whether, the name is just or not, it is a recognized one here; and I have heard a man say in answer to a question about his usual occupation, "I'm a Cockatoo."

This particular "nest" appeared to me very well off, comparatively speaking; for though the men complained sadly of the low price of their wheat and oats, still there was nothing like poverty to be seen. Ready money was doubtless scarce, and an extensive system of barter appeared to prevail; but still they all looked well fed and well clothed; sickness was unknown among them, and it did one's heart good to see the children—such

sturdy limbs, bright fearless eyes, and glowing faces. They have abundance of excellent food. Each cottager has one or two cows, and the little ones take these out to pasture on the hills, so they are in the open air nearly all day: but their ignorance is appalling! Many of them had never even been christened; there was no school or church within thirty miles or more, and although the parents seemed all tidy, decent people, and deplored the state of things, they were powerless to help it. The father and elder sons work hard all day; the mother has to do everything, even to making the candles, for the family; there is no time or possibility of teaching the children. The neighbouring squatters do not like to encourage settlers to buy up their land, therefore they carefully avoid making things pleasant for a new "nest," and the Cockatoos are "nobody's business;" so, as far as educational advantages go, they are perfectly destitute.

When I mentioned my discovery of this hamlet and my dismay at the state of neglect in which so many fine intelligent-looking children were growing up, every one warned me not to interfere, assuring me the Cockatoo was a very independent bird, that he considered he had left all the Ladies Bountiful and blanket and coal charities behind him in the old country; that, in short, as it is generally put, "Jack is as good as his master" out here, and any attempt at patronage would be deeply resented. But I determined to try the effect of a little visiting among the cottages, and was most agreeably surprised at the kind and cordial welcome I received. The women liked to have some one to chat to about their domestic affairs, and were most hospitable in offers of tea, &c. and everywhere invitations to "come again" were given; so the next week I ventured to invite the men over to our Sunday services. Those who were fond of reading eagerly accepted the offer to join the book-club, and at last we started the educational subject. Many plans were discussed, and finally we arranged for one woman, who had received an excellent education and was quite fitted for the post, to commence a day-school; but this entailed so much loss of her valuable time that the terms she is obliged to ask seem disproportionately high to the people's means. She wants *2s. 6d.* a week with each child, and this is terribly heavy on the head of a family who is anxious and willing to give them some "schooling." However, the plan is to be tried, and I have promised to start them with books, slates, copybooks, &c. It was quite touching to hear their earnest entreaties that F——— would come over on Sunday sometimes and hold a service there, but I tried to show them this could not be managed. The tears actually came into their eyes when I talked of the happiness it would be to see a little church and school in their midst; and the almost invariable remark was, "Ah, but it'll be a far day first." And so I fear it will—a very far day; but I have often heard it said, that if you propose one definite object to yourself as the serious purpose of your life, you will accomplish it some day. Well, the purpose of my life hence-forward is to raise money somehow or somewhere to build a little wooden school-room (licensed for service, to be held whenever a missionary clergyman comes by), and to pay the salary of a schoolmaster and mistress, so that the poor Cockatoo need not be charged more than threepence a week for each child. The Board of Education will give a third of the sum required, when two-thirds have been already raised; but it is difficult to collect subscriptions, or indeed to induce the squatters to listen to any plan for improving the condition of the small farmers, and every year which slips away and leaves these swarms of children in ignorance adds to the difficulty of training them. [. . .]

The African and Oriental Bureau and Buying Agency (Advertisement)

132   THE AFRICAN TIMES AND ORIENT REVIEW.   JUNE, 1917.

The African & Oriental Bureau & Buying Agency.

("African Times and Orient Review" Trading Department.)

TO AFRICANS & ORIENTALS:

WE ARE NOW IN TOUCH WITH THE PRINCIPAL MANUFACTURERS AND WHOLESALE AND RETAIL DEALERS IN GREAT BRITAIN.

We will buy you a Box of Pins or a Motor Car.

Nothing is Too Small.   Nothing is Too Large.

We supply Competent Guides who speak English, French and Arabic, and will take you over London at a small cost.

If you Want Information on any Subject

or if you want to get anything from Europe, write to THE AFRICAN AND ORIENTAL BUREAU, stating your requirements, clearly and concisely, in English, French, Arabic, or any other language, enclosing with your inquiry a Postal Order for 2s., and address it to—

The Manager,
AFRICAN & ORIENTAL BUREAU,
158, Fleet Street, London, E.C., England.

If these instructions are complied with, the Bureau will answer your inquiry on any subject, or will put you into communication with the proper channel.

The Bureau will also Effect Purchases

If the orders are accompanied by a Postal Order for 2s., and remittance to cover cost and carriage, and including a commission of 5 per cent. to cover expenses.

Estimates and Catalogues obtained and forwarded free of charge.

Please mention "The African Times and Orient Review."

As the architects of late-nineteenth-century empires had hoped, new colonies created markets for Western-manufactured goods. This advertisement demonstrates how new services were developed to cater to a variety of material and other needs that colonial elites might have had. The African and Oriental Bureau set itself up as both a guide to European goods and culture and a middleman for virtually any purchase that a colonial subject might wish to make.

QUESTIONS

1. To whom does this advertisement seem to be targeted? Why would these people require the services that it offers?

2. What does this advertisement suggest about the reconfiguration of colonial economies and values?

Source: The African Times and Orient Review, 1912. Courtesy of University of Kansas Libraries.

Outline of the Economic Evolution

José Carlos Mariátegui

Perhaps the most demonstrative example of global reconfigurations in the late nineteenth and early twentieth centuries came in the area of economics. New territories were acquired by European countries and the United States for the control of minerals, markets, and merchants. In addition, many politically independent countries, such as those in Latin America, found themselves caught up in global economic patterns over which they did not seem to have much control.

In this selection from his Seven Interpretive Essays on Peruvian Reality *(written in the mid-1920s), José Carlos Mariátegui, a Peruvian journalist, intellectual, and activist, outlines in clear paragraphs some of the most profound economic changes that had affected his native land by the early decades of the twentieth century. In response to these economic realities and the dictatorial government in Peru, Mariátegui became increasingly radicalized in his own politics. He also has become well known in Latin America for proposing indigenous solutions to some of its economic problems.*

QUESTIONS

1. For Mariátegui, what were some of the most profound shifts that had transformed Peru's economy?

2. According to Mariátegui, in what ways was Peru being drawn into the economic orbit of the United States?

3. Can you discern global patterns of trade and development in Mariátegui's presentation of economic conditions?

[. . .] The fundamental aspects of this chapter, in which our economy, recuperating from its postwar crisis, slowly organized itself on less lucrative but more solid bases than those of guano and nitrates, can be outlined by the following facts:

1. The appearance of modern industry. The establishment of factories, plants, transport, et cetera, which has transformed life on the coast. The formation of an industrial proletariat with a growing natural tendency to adopt a class ideology, thereby blocking one of the traditional paths of caudillo proselytism and changing the terms of the political struggle.

2. The role of finance capital. The emergence of national banks which finance various industrial and commercial enterprises but which are very limited in scope because of their subservience to foreign capital and large

agricultural properties; and the establishment of branches of foreign banks serving the interests of North American and English finance.

3. The shorter distance and increased traffic between Peru and the United States and Europe. As a result of the opening of the Panama Canal, Peru's geographical position has notably improved and its incorporation into Western civilization has accelerated.

4. The gradual substitution of North American for British ascendancy. The Panama Canal seems to have brought Peru closer to the United States than to Europe. The participation of North American capital in the exploitation of Peru's copper and petroleum, which have become two of its most important products, furnishes a broad and enduring base for the growing influence of the United States. Exports to England, which in 1898 made up 56.7 percent of total exports, by 1923 came only to 33.2 percent. In the same period, exports to the United States rose from 9.5 percent to 39.7 percent. And this trend was even more striking in imports: whereas in that twenty-five year period, imports from the United States went up from 10.0 percent to 38.9 percent, those from Great Britain dropped from 44.7 percent to 19.6 percent.

5. The development of a capitalist class no longer dominated by the old aristocracy. Although agricultural property owners retain their power, the authority of families with viceregal names has declined. The bourgeoisie has grown stronger.

6. The rubber illusion. In its halcyon days, Peru thought it had found El Dorado in its tropical forests, which temporarily acquired enormous value in the economy. They especially caught the imagination of the country and attracted hordes of "hardy adventurers." This illusion—tropical in origin and tone—faded with the fall in the price of rubber.

7. The excess profits of the European period. The boom in Peruvian products caused a rapid increase in domestic private wealth. The hegemony of the coast in the Peruvian economy was reinforced.

8. The policy on borrowing. The reestablishment of Peruvian credit abroad has enabled the government once again to use loans to carry out its public works program. North America also has replaced Great Britain as creditor. Overflowing with gold, the New York market offers the best terms. North American bankers study the possibilities of lending capital to Latin American governments. And they are careful, of course, that such investments benefit North American industry and commerce.

These would appear to be the principal aspects of the economic evolution of Peru in its postwar period. This series of comments does not permit a thorough study of the foregoing statements or propositions. I have sought only to sketch some of the essential characteristics of the formation and development of the Peruvian economy.

I shall make a final observation: the elements of three different economies coexist in Peru today. Underneath the feudal economy inherited from the colonial period, vestiges of the indigenous communal economy can still be found in the sierra. On the coast, a bourgeois economy is growing in feudal soil; it gives every indication of being backward, at least in its mental outlook. [. . .]

Advertisement for the Sontag Hotel

Along with trade, imperialism also facilitated tourism. As the Japanese developed the Korean economic infrastructure by building ports, expanding modern transportation networks, and constructing Western-style buildings, they simultaneously made Korea more hospitable to Western tourists. This advertisement for a European-run hotel shows the extent to which Seoul had become a modern city and a cosmopolitan center under Japanese control.

QUESTIONS

1. What services did the Sontag Hotel offer to its guests? In what ways would these services have been appealing to Europeans and Asians alike?

2. In what ways did the Japanese apparently modernize Korea?

3. Examine the advertisement carefully. What do you make of the architecture, landscape, and overall physical impression of the hotel?

Source: Advertisement for the Sontag Hotel. In T. Philip Terry, *Terry's Japanese Empire.* London: Constable & Company, LTD, 1914. Courtesy of Kansas State University.

▲

Selections from *The Red Man:*
An Illustrated Magazine Printed by Indians

For Native Americans in the United States, the period from the late nineteenth century into the early decades of the twentieth century was largely one of learning to accommodate to American society. Open conflict with U.S. military forces had ended and the reservation system was firmly in place. In educational institutions, Native Americans discussed how best to adapt to their changed circumstances. On the one hand, they wanted their fundamental social, economic, and political grievances addressed. On the other, they also sought ways to integrate themselves into mainstream American society and to escape their marginal status.

The following selections are from The Red Man, *a Native American journal published at Carlisle, Pennsylvania's famous Indian School before and during the First World War. The first piece is a poem about North America before European settlement. The second article is a resolution passed at a national meeting of Native Americans and outlines some of their key grievances with the U.S. government and society. The last selection discusses different models for incorporating Native Americans into the U.S. military during the First World War.*

▲

QUESTIONS

1. According to the poem, what were conditions like for Native Americans "before the white man came"?

2. According to the resolution passed at the national meeting, what were some of the major problems of Native Americans in U.S. society at this time?

3. What competing models were discussed for integrating Native Americans into the United States military during the First World War?

Before the White Man Came

R. H. Adams

Many suns had kissed the morning, many
    moons adorned the night,

Come and gone full many winters, and as many
    summers bright.

The while across the broad prairies, through the
    forests deep and still

O'er the plains and up the mountains roamed
    the Red Man at his will.

Warrior, Chieftains, men of fame,

Long before the White man came.

'Neath the pine tree's friendly shadows, on the
    shore of lake or stream;

Here he pitched his humble wigwam, near the
    water's crystal gleam;

Source: The Red Man: An Illustrated Magazine printed by Indians. R. H. Adams, "Before the White Man Came," (March 1915): 252–53; Arthur C. Parker, "Cedar Rapids Platform," (November 1916): 79–80; and "General Pratt Dissents to Separate Indian Organizations for the Army," (March–April 1917): 189–90. Taken from original microfilm, Gettysburg College.

And swan-like glide across the water, in his
light birch-bark canoe.

Catching fish and trapping game,

Long before the White Man came.

Reared he here his sons and daughters, nature's
children plain and free,

Temperate, moral, true, and honest, he knew no
law but liberty.

Bound by no confederation, scarcely knowing of
its worth,

Yet the Indians were the sovereigns of the greatest land on earth.

Possession being their sovereign claim,

Long before the White Man came.

He heard the voice of the "Great Spirit" in the
thunder's rumbling sound,

While whispering winds brought him a message
from the "Happy Hunting Ground."

By suns and moons and winters counted he the
days and months and years,

And in the spirit of the water read he all his
hopes and fears.

Read destiny in drops of rain,

Long before the White Man came.

Thus they dwelt for generations in their own
dear native land,

From sea to sea an earthly Eden, with fish and
game at every hand;

Countless birds sang in the forest, anthems rang
from all the trees,

And the wild flowers in profusion scented every
wind and breeze.

Paradise, or much the same,

Long before the White Man came.

The Cedar Rapids Platform

Arthur C. Parker

The society of American Indians assembled in the Sixth Annual Conference in the city of Cedar Rapids, Iowa, September 26 to September 30, 1916, more conscious than ever of the complex situation in which a kindly and benevolent Government has placed the Indian of the United States, and appealing to the people, the Congress, and the Executive officers of the Nation for such sympathetic counsel and assistance as may be necessary in working out a plan for a legal, educational and administrative policy, which, when adopted, shall contemplate the speedy and just settlement of all causes of Indian discontent, by placing them on an equal footing with other Americans, do adopt the following platform:

1. *Closing the Indian Bureau.*—We believe the time has come when we ought to call upon the country and upon Congress to look to the closing of the Indian Bureau, so soon as trust funds, treaty rights and other just obligations can be individualized, fulfilled or paid. It should be clearly seen that the Indian Bureau was never intended as a permanent part of the Interior Department, but merely to perform a temporary function. With the progress and education of Indians, they should be invested with the full privileges of citizens without burdensome restrictions. As its jurisdiction is removed, the books of the Bureau should be closed until there is a final elimination. As citizens and taxpayers struggling side by side with other Americans, we are willing to entrust our liberties, and fortunes to the several communities of which we form a part.

2. *Schools for Citizenship.*—It is believed that the preparation and introduction in Indian schools of the new vocational courses of study marks an epoch in Indian education. Furthermore, we can not urge too strongly upon the Congress that provision should be made, and Indian pupils encouraged, to make use of the Federal schools merely as stepping stones to attendance of white schools, where contact with other American youth makes for patriotic, competent citizenship. Furthermore, we believe that all Indian pupils over 21 years of age, having completed a prescribed course of study, should be deemed fully competent, given control of their property and thrown upon their own resources.

3. *Liquor Traffic an Evil.*—We commend the efforts of the officials of the Bureau for the suppression of the liquor traffic among Indians and we urge upon our own people the adoption of habits of total abstinence which we are convinced are conducive of happiness and prosperity. We urge unequivocally upon Congress the passage of the Gandy bill to prohibit the commerce in and use of peyote among our people because of its known baneful effects upon the users in mind and morals.

4. *Health Conditions on Reservations.*—We commend the efforts to improve sanitary and health conditions on the reservations and to save the lives of the Indian babies, which efforts have already resulted in greatly reducing the death rate. We trust that the health campaign will continue unabated until the baneful effects of reservation life and ignorance shall have been wiped out for both infants and adults.

5. *Former Principles Reaffirmed.*—We reaffirm the principles so ardently and justly urged by former conferences of this society. We reiterate our

pleas made in our Denver, Madison, and Lawrence platforms calling for (*a*) a definition of the legal status of the Indians; (*b*) for the individualization of trust funds; (*c*) and the early adjudication of all tribal claims. We renew our appeal as made in our memorial to the President of the United States, December 11, 1914.

Again we call upon our own people to the exercise of all manly and womanly virtues, fighting with courage the battles of life, thoroughly imbued with the spirit of progress, so essential to the ultimate salvation of our race.

General Pratt Dissents to Separate Indian Organizations for the Army

R. H. PRATT

One of the Indian school papers gives a proposition by Mr. Ayer, a member of the Board of Indian Commissioners, to raise regiments of Indian soldiers. Allow me to dissent from Mr. Ayer's method:

In the nineties, under the Secretary of War Proctor, a scheme to have a company of Indian soldiers in a number of our regular regiments was inaugurated. Some of us opposed, giving as our reasons that it was not recognizing the manhood and ability of the Indians and was continuing to make him an exception in the American family. That it was creating Indian reservations in each regiment where such Indian company was incorporated. That it was a continuation of the segregating Indian system. There were other patent reasons, but these are sufficient. These companies were disbanded within two years and the system pronounced a failure. I had previously urged the adjutant general to take Indians into army service as individual men and put no two Indians in the same company. After this failure my suggestion was accepted and my influence used and fifty were enlisted. There were no failures. Several of them distinguished themselves in the Philippine and China wars. One, an Osage, did so well in the Ninth Infantry that he was advanced to first sergeant in his company. Twice during his enlistment he had special mention for gallantry. Another was one of the body guard of General Lawton when he was killed and who shot out of a tree the Filipino who had killed his general.

The Indians should furnish their full quota of our national defenders but should be taken into regular companies as individual men and never as purely Indian organizations. This would wipe out, instead of strengthening, racial prejudice. It would also make real soldiers out of the Indians and abolish exploitation of the race, which is one of the evils they have been subject to all the years.

Segregating, reservating, has been the bane of Indian management from the beginning and will continue to be so long as it prevails. Those who assume to advise as to what should be done with the Indians need larger vision.

By all means let us have a full proportion of Indians in the army, but no special Indian organizations. If practicable it would be better that no two Indians be placed in the same company.

Instead of keeping them near their reservations, as Mr. Ayer recommends and as was provided in the Indian companies in the nineties, they should be sent away from home and treated in all respects the same as all other men in the army. Even three or four Indians in one company would be an Indian reservation, in that company.

I belonged to a colored regiment for more than thirty years—the Tenth United States Cavalry. It was against the best interests of the negro that he was put in the army as a separate organization, and yet the negroes should furnish their full quota of national defenders. The creation of four regiments of negroes in the regular army was a tremendous prejudice builder and a clear violation of the constitutional amendment which provides that there shall be no distinction on account of race, color, or previous condition of servitude. Indian regiments would be equally unconstitutional and equally prejudice builders.

If the army is increased to half a million men the Indians' proportion would be less than 1,700. That number of most efficient Indians can easily be found and enlisted in a month, and I know there is hearty welcome for them in the regular companies.

Do what you can to prevent the accomplishment of Indian organizations in the army, but do all you can to have the Indians furnish their full proportion of men required for our national defense.

Maps of Cairo and
Singapore in the Mid-Nineteenth Century

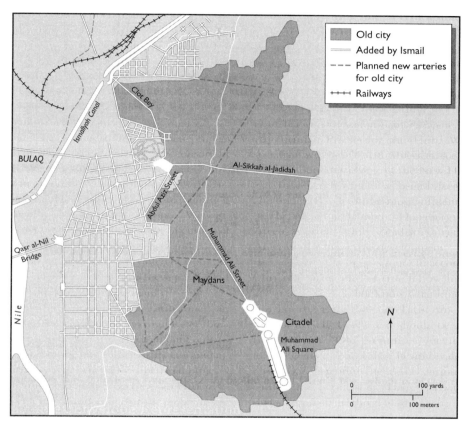

Legend:
- Old city
- Added by Ismail
- Planned new arteries for old city
- Railways

Map labels: Ismailyan Canal, Clot Bey, BULAQ, Al-Sikkah al-Jadidah, Abdul Aziz Street, Qasr al-Nil Bridge, Muhammad Ali Street, Nile, Maydans, Citadel, Muhammad Ali Square, N

Scale: 0 — 100 yards / 0 — 100 meters

Cairo

Imperialism had a transformative effect on urban as well as rural landscapes. In this pair of maps we see examples of two distinct but common patterns of urbanization in the nineteenth and twentieth centuries. Singapore was a planned city designed and built by Sir Stamford Raffles after 1819. It was constructed on the site of a small fishing village that happened to be located on a good natural harbor. The new city was divided into three sections to house people of different ethnicities (Chinese, European, and South Asian), many of whom were encouraged by the British to migrate to Singapore. Cairo, on the other hand, had been a thriving metropolis for many centuries prior to the nineteenth century. Although Cairo was at various times under the control of the Ottoman, French, and British empires, the expansion and modernization of the city took place under the leadership of Khedive Ismail in the 1860s and 1870s. Ismail sought

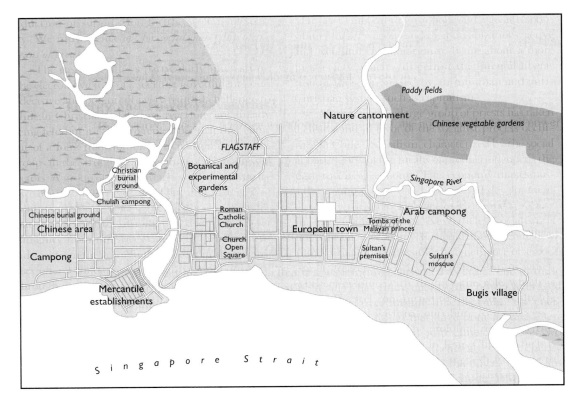

Map labels (reading across):

Paddy fields

Nature cantonment

Chinese vegetable gardens

FLAGSTAFF

Christian burial ground

Botanical and experimental gardens

Singapore River

Chulah campong

Chinese burial ground

Roman Catholic Church

Arab campong

Chinese area

Tombs of the Malayan princes

European town

Church Open Square

Campong

Sultan's premises

Sultan's mosque

Mercantile establishments

Bugis village

S i n g a p o r e   S t r a i t

Singapore

to reconstruct Cairo along the lines of a European city, with wide boulevards, gardens, and European looking architecture.

QUESTIONS

1. What features do you notice about these two cities?
2. In what ways do they appear to have been influenced by Western ideas of urban planning?

FURTHER RESOURCES

Achebe, Chinua. *Things Fall Apart.* New York: Anchor Books, 1994.

Allen, Charles. *Plain Tales from the Raj. Images of British India in the Twentieth Century.* New York: St. Martin's, 1976.

Allman, Jean Marie, Susan Geiger, and Nakanyike Musisi. *Women in African Colonial Histories.* Bloomington, IN: Indiana University Press, 2002.

De Kretser, Michelle. *The Hamilton Case.* New York: Little, Brown, 2004.
Ghosh, Amitav. *The Glass Palace.* New York: Random House, 2001.
Lulofs, Madelon. *Coolie.* Singapore: Oxford University Press, 1982.
Memmi, Albert. *Dependence: A Sketch for a Portrait of the Dependent.* Boston: Beacon Press, 1984.
Moane, Geraldine. *Gender and Colonialism: A Psychological Analysis of Oppression and Liberation.* New York: St. Martin's, 1999.
Naipaul, V. S. *A Bend in the River.* New York: Knopf, 1979.
Ramabai, Pandita. *The High-Caste Hindu Woman.* New York: Fleming H. Revel Company, 1901.
Scott, Paul. *The Raj Quartet,* Vol. 1: *The Jewel in the Crown.* Chicago: University of Chicago Press, 1998.
Strobel, Margaret. *Gender, Sex, and Empire.* Washington, DC: American Historical Association, 1993.

Films

Indochine, VHS. Directed by Régis Wargnier, Burbank, CA: Columbia Tristar Home Video, 1993.
Mister Johnson, DVD. Directed by Bruce Beresford. Charlotte, NC: VAV Corp., 1997.
The Jewel in the Crown, VHS (8 videocassettes). Directed by Christopher Morahan and Jim O'Brien. New York, NY: A & E Home Video, 1993.

TIMELINE FOR PART V

1897	Liliuokalani Protests Annexation of Hawaii
1906–1914	Gandhi Leads Satyagraha Campaign in South Africa
1911	Casely Hayford, "Race Emancipation"
1912	McKay, "Passive Resistance"
1914–18	World War I
1915–47	Protests Against British Rule of India (Madras Protest, Sahgal)
1917	Lenin creates the Comintern
1917	Li, "The Victory of Bolshevism"
1918	Faduma, "African Negro Education"
1920s	Thuku, "Nairobi"
1923	Atatürk Begins to Modernize Turkey
1938–45	World War II
1939	Buber, "Open Letter"
1943–75	Vietnam Struggles for Independence from Japanese, French, United States (Truong)
1949	Chinese Communist Revolution Ends in Establishment of People's Republic of China
1952–59	Mau Mau Rebellion in Kenya
1954–62	French Algerian War (Algerian Women Fighters)
1955	Bandung Conference (Soekarnu)
1959	Cuban Revolution
1967	Che Guevara Dies
1983	United States Invades Grenada (Cuban Protest)

Entries in bold indicate sources.

Part V

Empire's Tools for Liberation

INTRODUCTION

By the end of the First World War, colonial peoples had become starkly aware of their positions within various empires and were beginning to construct strategies to promote independence. As they did so, they frequently used the very same methods that European and North American empire-builders had used to force them into submission in the first place. Thus, the colonized very often employed the tools of the colonizer in their own efforts to achieve political, economic, and cultural independence.

The First World War was a watershed event for colonial peoples. As citizens of European empires, large numbers of colonial peoples were called upon to serve the war effort, sometimes as soldiers, sometimes in other capacities, and many of them did so willingly. In Europe, they encountered racism and other demeaning behavior that served only to remind them that they would never be treated as equals within the imperial order. At the same time, however, colonial peoples serving in Europe were also exposed to Western notions of nationalism, democracy, and self-determination, all of which inspired them to believe that there might be broad support among Westerners for their own independence movements. In fact, the Western powers had no intention of extending these political ideals to the colonies. Instead, the colonial powers colluded to support each other. Not only did the European powers not interfere in each other's affairs, the United States also "respected" their claims overseas and continued to extend its own influence in the Americas. Forgotten were the colonized people who were left to develop their own tools to express their anticolonial sentiments.

Independence movements were waged by peasants, workers, women, youth, and the urban poor as well as by elites who had had the opportunity to see Europe and the United States for themselves. They struggled against the economic deprivation and social injustice of colonialism through military uprisings and nonviolent protest (as illustrated by the images included in this part), the construction of new institutions, and the use of education and the written word to disseminate ideologies of liberation.

As the twentieth century progressed, colonial intellectuals increasingly put their educations to work for the cause of nationalist and independence movements. Most often using the languages of the colonizers, they crafted articulate and compelling arguments against colonial domination. Although many of the pieces in Part V in one respect or another reflect this process, we see it most clearly in Claude McKay's poem and in the works of Orishatuke Faduma, Li Dazhao, Martin Buber, and Mahatma Gandhi. Written works such as these provided a method of disseminating a wide variety of ideologies of liberation, such as the patriotism of McKay, the cultural nationalism of Faduma, the international communism of Li, the Zionism of Buber, and the nonviolent resistance of Gandhi. Ideology was, in fact, an effective organizing tool for the liberation of the colonized, as is evident in Manmohini Zutshi Sahgal's discussion of both feminism and nonviolent resistance, Buber's discussion of Zionism, and Li's discussion of Bolshevism.

Organization was required for independence movements to gain steam, and we see examples of varying approaches to the construction of new organizations and institutions in the writings of Henry Thuku and J. E. Casely Hayford. Both of these men constructed new local and regional institutions such as the East Africa Association and the National Congress of British West Africa to represent the voice of the African people. These structures fought colonial rule by organizing protests, as was the case with the East African Association, and through the formal representation of African popular voices, as in the National Congress of British West Africa.

New institutions and organizations were emerging on an international level as well, including the Comintern, or Communist International, and the Non-Aligned Movement. The Comintern was a Soviet-led international communist movement formed shortly after the Bolshevik revolution that offered organizational, technical, military, and financial assistance to nascent communist parties around the world. Although Li Dazhao makes no reference to it in the reading that follows, a few years after the publication of his piece, the Comintern would help his Marxist study group form a Communist Party in China. The Non-Aligned Movement came into being in the wake of the Bandung Conference. It was a movement to represent the interests of newly independent states that chose not to ally themselves with either the Western powers or the Soviet bloc.

Protest and violent revolution were other means through which colonial peoples sought independence. Protests were sometimes formal, as in the case of Queen Lilioukalani's official protest of the United States' attempts to annex Hawaii. Other times, as in the case of the protest images in this part, they involved nonviolent action. Gandhi, Sahgal, and McKay all contended that to fight imperialism with violence was to be no better than the imperialists themselves and that nonviolent resistance would therefore be both more effective and more morally correct. Many independence movements, however, made use of Western military strategies to undermine colonial (or, in the case of Che Guevara, postcolonial) authority. Both Truong Nhu Tang and Che Guevara serve as examples of the use of guerilla warfare strategies to overthrow imperialist forces, as does the image of the Algerian women fighters. As we shall see in Part VI, guerilla warfare and nonviolent resistance were both effective in different decolonizing contexts.

▲

Nairobi

Harry Thuku

The First World War provided an important catalyst for liberation movements in the colonies, and it was in the years immediately following the war that Harry Thuku launched his critique of British colonial land policies in Kenya. While more than 100,000 Kenyan Africans voluntarily served in the British Army during the war, the British colonial government oversaw a land grab by demobilized officers and other white settlers. When African soldiers returned to Kenya, they found that they had lost their landholdings during their absence. In a speech made in 1922, Harry Thuku openly accused the colonial government of stealing African land. Thuku's criticism of colonial land policy culminated in the rise of African nationalism and new patterns of indigenous political mobilization in Kenya. He did not advocate national independence, but in organizing Africans to agitate for their rights, he established a model for struggle against colonial rule that subsequent organizations emulated with varying degrees of effectiveness. Although he was not a radical, the European community in Kenya reacted sharply against Thuku's agitation by arresting him.

Harry Thuku was born in Kenya in 1895 into a prominent Kikuyu family. After four years at an American missionary school, he moved to Nairobi where he held various clerical jobs. In 1921 he joined the Kikuyu Association, a political organization that was battling against British colonial rule. Then, to appeal to wider loyalties, he helped to found the East African Association and became the first Kenyan national leader.

▲

QUESTIONS

1. What was the difference in the treatment of demobilized black and white members of the King African Rifles after the war?

2. What methods of resistance did Thuku and his cohort use?

[. . .] The War ended, and after it, things began to warm up in the British East Africa Protectorate (that was Kenya's old name). First there were many thousands of porters who came back from very very difficult conditions in the East Africa Campaign, and found that they would not get any gratuity. Instead the government under General Northey decided that the white soldiers, and especially the officers, should be rewarded. So they alienated many thousands of acres in the area round Kericho for a Soldier Settlement Scheme. Also in my own Kiambu area, more land was taken at this time and given to white settlers. However, I want to make one thing clear about this land business; back at that time we Africans who were a little educated were not saying that all

Source: Harry Thuku. "Nairobi." In *An Autobiography*. Nairobi: Oxford University Press, 1970. Pp. 18–24. Copyright © 1970 by Oxford University Press. Reprinted with the permission of Oxford University Press East Africa, Nairobi, Kenya.

Europeans should leave the country, or that we should get self-government. There was no idea of that. What we objected to was that the Europeans did not treat us as we had treated the Dorobos. I mean, we bought our land from the Dorobo according to agreed prices, and as I said earlier, we planted *itoka* lilies to confirm these sales. We did not simply claim land without the Dorobo knowing anything about it. And I am not saying that one or two Europeans did not do things in a proper manner. Take the way Mr. Krieger bought his farm from a Kikuyu, Gichinga, just nearby here at Thembigwa. He paid him 70 female goats in the presence of Mr. Knapp, and I always told my people that they should not fight to get that piece back, for it was not taken secretly or by force.

Not all the Africans who fought in the War were treated badly. The ones in the Carrier Corps (the present Kariakor market in Nairobi was named after their camp) had the hardest time, and often after the war they did not like to discuss what they had seen because so many of their friends had died. But then there were the Mission Volunteers who served under missionaries like Dr. Arthur and Mr. Hooper. Many from around Kambui joined them, even my later political fighter, George Mugekenyi, who had been working with me at the *Leader*. I saw all of them on their way to Tanganyika once when I was going by train to Mombasa.

The second thing that was making Africans angrier after the War was this thing called *kipande*. This was Swahili for a container in which a registration paper was carried. Now General Northey, Kenya's Governor after the War, decided in 1919 to implement the recommendations of an earlier committee which had suggested that Africans be registered. The ordinary people did not understand what this registration was, but even more educated ones like me did not oppose it to begin with, for we knew that many countries asked their citizens to register. So we did not object until we found out that it was a very different business in Kenya. First of all you had to wear this quite heavy metal box round your neck on a string all

the time; then in the columns on the paper inside there were many things that were against Africans. There was one space where the employer had to sign when he engaged you and also when you left. You could not leave employment without permission, and if you did, you could be taken to the D.C.'s court. Also, no other employer would take you if the space for discharge was not filled up. Another thing in the early kind of *kipande* was a space for remarks; and here, if an employer did not like you, he could spoil your name completely by putting 'lazy', 'disobedient,' or 'cheeky'. That column made me very angry. *Kipande* was only for Africans; and in 1919, at that old building still standing opposite Nairobi General Post Office, I collected my one.

There was also the question of rising tax for Africans. It kept on going up even though we did not see anything like schools or clinics which we get nowadays for our high taxes. The reason for it was to pull African workers out of their houses to work for the European settlers; you see, they could not get the money to pay their tax unless they left their homes and worked for some months. Then also there was confusion when the currency changed from Indian rupees to shillings. Colonel Grogan, Lord Delamere, and Mr. Archer, the settler leaders, brought this change because they thought that the Indians were secretly exporting rupees to India—hidden in large tins of ghee [Indian butter]! The new rate was one old rupee equals two shillings, but many people tried to give Africans one shilling for one rupee. I was allright, for in my government job, I had got 70 rupees, and this now gave me sh. 140/-.

The final thing was when we heard that the settlers were going to reduce African wages by one third. Many of us got very angry, and we called a meeting in Pangani on 7 June 1921 to see if we could form a Young Kikuyu Association. The reason we called it 'Young' was this. For a long time in Nairobi I had know Baganda people. There was one Muganda called Ssentongo who had his own newspaper, *Sekanyolya,* and there were clerical workers. Then there was a Buganda football team which used to come through and play us in Nairobi. Indeed a little later on it was through football that I met Prince Suna of Buganda—he was the uncle of Kabaka Daudi Chwa. He had come to Nairobi accompanying his team; his secretary came and found me, and Suna and I had our photograph taken together. From some of these people I learnt that they had a body called the Young Baganda Association in their country. 'Does that mean,' I asked them, 'that only young people can join it?' 'No!' they told me, 'even men of seventy years old, for it is the Association which is young and not the members!' So we thought of doing the same.

I have mentioned people like Tairara, Waiganjo and Mugekenyi; they were all with me in thinking about this, and there were others such as Job Muchuchu and Ishmael Mungai. They worked together selling bread in a little shop in River Road; it belonged to Mr. Torr of the old Torr Hotel near the present Ottoman Bank.

Now while we were wondering about our new Association we heard that the Kikuyu Association, which had been formed some time earlier, had got a petition which they were going to present to government. What had happened was that some of the chiefs and younger men in the country areas had asked Mr. Barlow of the Scottish Mission to draw up a list of grievances. Government had agreed to hear the petition at Dagoretti, near Chief Kinyanjui's village, on 24 June 1921. Accordingly, I left the night before with some friends on my bicycle and rode to the CMS station at Kabete. I wanted to find out from Matthew Njoroge whether other Christians were going to go, or if it was only for government servants and chiefs. I found it was going to be attended by all people, since it was not only the chiefs who were angry. So we spent the night in Njoroge's house and left the next morning for Dagoretti.

When we got there, many people were present from all over Kiambu country—not from Fort Hall or Nyeri. Also many high officials were there, including the Acting Chief Native Commissioner (C.N.C.), D.C. Kiambu, and others. The meeting was held in front of the District Officer's (D.O.) house, and Mr. Usher, the D.O., was asked to organize things. Then Kinyanjui, Waruhiu, Philipo Karanja James and other prominent Kikuyu went into a committee for a short time; we younger people did not know what was being discussed. They came back and waited until all the European officers were settled. At this point Kinyanjui rose up and came over to my left side. He had a black fly whisk in his hand—not white like Kenyatta's. With it he touched my shoulder, and told the Europeans, 'This is the man we have chosen to be secretary of the meeting. If you want to tell us anything, tell him.'

Mr. Usher then ordered a small table to be brought in front of me with a chair, and a copy of the Barlow Memorandum was placed on it. So we started with the first point and went through all the agenda. There was discussion after each point with Mr. Barlow as interpreter. One point was particularly interesting. It concerned a long list of charges being brought against my friend, Waiganjo wa Ndotono, the chief tribal retainer. I soon saw as we dealt with these accusations that he would get a bad case, for people began to believe he really was guilty. So when everyone had finished talking, I suggested that the matter be dealt with by D.C. Campbell at Kiambu; he could investigate the charges and report to the Provincial Commissioner (P.C.). I suggested this because I knew Campbell was on good terms with Waiganjo, and felt that things would work out in his favour. I was proved right, for Waiganjo was not punished, simply he was asked to resign; and then he was able to join my Association.

However, when we had gone through all the points of the Memorandum, I realized what the Kikuyu chiefs wanted to do (quite different from me); they would have liked to send their petition to England through the traditional channels—that is, first to D.C. Kiambu, then P.C. Nyeri, then from P.C. to the C.N.C., and from him to the Chief Secretary of Government. He would send it on to the Governor, and eventually the

Governor might send it to England. But I knew that each man on the way would add his comments to the Memorandum, and I could guess what some of them might be—not in our favour certainly! I decided to do things quite another way, and fortunately they had left a copy of the Memorandum in my hands.

Once I got back to Nairobi, I began to have discussions with my friends. We saw clearly that if we sent anything coming from the Kikuyu tribe alone, we would carry no weight. But if we could show that it came from all tribes—the Maasai, the Kamba, etc., then we should have a great voice. At the same time, over the next few days, we continued our discussions for the proper name for our Association, and finally decided that we should change it from the Young Kikuyu to the East African Association (EAA), so that anyone in the whole area could join. This we agreed in committee on 1 July.

To acquaint the people of Nairobi with our plans, I called a meeting on Sunday, 10 July, 1921, for all Africans. The site was where the present Arya Samaj Girls' School is, near Ngara Road, and we had an attendance of about 2,000. I was voted into the Chair, and we had a long discussion on our grievances. I do not remember all the speakers, but I do remember two men in particular— how powerfully James Mwanthi from Kamba country spoke; and also how a Luo, Abednego, jumped up on the table and gave a fiery speech. By the end we had passed a number of resolutions on the Indians, forced labour, taxation and education, and the mass meeting agreed that we should send the substance of our resolutions direct to the Colonial Office in London.

Our Committee afterwards drafted all the main ideas into a telegram, and then I think I took it along to my friend, Mr. Desai. He corrected the English, and suggested the names of further people in England who were pro-African to whom we could also address the telegram—I mean people like Lord Islington, and Captain

Wedgewood in the House of Commons. I returned two days later to show the committee the final version. Actually at our meeting, Jimmy Jones had brought Ssentongo along, and I think Ssentongo took a copy of the telegram, for he published it in his paper a day or so later. Fortunately, however, we got the telegram off to England first. I simply collected some money from the committee, added some of my own, then sent it from the Post Office. It cost us 43 rupees. And I even put as my own Post Office Box, the Treasury number! A few days later I sent directly to the Kenya Government a full text of the resolutions and also the Barlow Memorandum, with a request for them to be sent to the Secretary of State for the Colonies.

Very shortly everybody—government, missionaries and settlers—knew that we had sent a telegram to the Prime Minister in England. They were very angry, and especially because the first thing we had said was 'next to missionaries Indians were our best friends'. Now the reason I had put that first was this. Just recently Lord Delamere, Colonel Grogan and Mr. Archer (President of the European Convention of Associations) had gone to London to tell the government that Africans did not like Indians to be in Kenya. They had been told by the Colonial Office that if they went to Kenya and produced a letter from Africans to that effect, their case would be considered. But before they had sailed back to Kenya, I had got this news, and therefore put that statement about Indians at the front of our resolutions. After all, Indians had not taken any of our land by force; they had no power and were only traders. Further, Africans were able to buy from Indians what they could not get from European shops. You see, European shops were very expensive, and they would not sell to an African if he only wanted to buy something for two pice, or one rupee; but the Indian would sell to you even if you wanted a very small thing. Apart from that, we were both fighting for equal rights in Kenya with Europeans. [. . .]

▲

Race Emancipation—Particular Considerations: African Nationality

J. E. CASELY HAYFORD

Joseph Ephraim Casely Hayford was born September 29, 1866, in Cape Coast. The son of the Reverend Joseph de Graft Hayford, he studied law at Fourah Bay College, Freetown, in Sierra Leone. In 1892, he went to London, where he entered the Inner Temple to study law. Upon his return to the Gold Coast, he set up his chambers and established a busy and lucrative practice. In the Gold Coast, Casely Hayford joined with other Africans in organizing the Aborigines Rights Protection Society (the first African nationalist organization) to protect their rights in land use and ownership. Casely Hayford threw himself into the work of many African nationalist organizations. In 1920, he went on to play a leading role in founding the National Congress of British West Africa. His efforts in constructing indigenous African institutions that were in many respects modeled on Western institutions demonstrated just how such institutions could be used as tools for liberation.

In addition to his organizational activities, Casely Hayford wrote extensively. His publications included Ethiopia Unbound, *which delineated the basic social, political, and economic institutions of the peoples of the Gold Coast by stressing the inherent virtues of indigenous institutions and practices. In the following selection, Casely Hayford considers the role that culture and identity could play in the racial uplift of both Africans (or as he often calls them, Ethiopians) and African Americans. He argues that Africans and African Americans should embrace and celebrate indigenous African cultural practices and through this process strengthen themselves.*

▲

QUESTIONS

1. What cultural model does Casely Hayford propose for Africans?
2. In what ways does Casely Hayford see Africans and African Americans as connected?

In the name of African nationality the thinker would, through the medium of *Ethiopia Unbound,* greet members of the race everywhere throughout the world. Whether in the east, south, or west of the African Continent, or yet among the teeming millions of Ethiopia's sons in America, the cry of the African, in its last analysis, is for

scope and freedom in the struggle for existence, and it would seem as if the care of the leaders of the race has been to discover those avenues of right and natural endeavour which would, in the end, ensure for the race due recognition of its individuality.

The race problem is probably most intense in the United States of America, but there are

Source: J. E. Casely Hayford. "Race Emancipation—Particular Considerations: African Nationality." In *Ethiopia Unbound: Studies in Race Emancipation.* London: C.M. Phillips, 1911. Pp.167–177.

indications that on the African Continent itself it is fast assuming concrete form. Sir Arthur Lawley, the present Governor of Madras, before leaving the Governorship of the Transvaal, is reported in a public address to have said that the "black peril" is a reality, and to have advised the whites to consolidate their forces in presence of the potential foe. The leaders of the race have hitherto exercised sound discretion and shown considerable wisdom in advising the African to follow the line of least resistance in meeting any combination of forces against him. The African's way to proper recognition lies not at present so much in the exhibition of material force and power, as in the gentler art of persuasion by the logic of facts and of achievements before which all reasonable men must bow.

A two-fold danger threatens the African everywhere. It is the outcome of certain economic conditions whose method is the exploitation of the Ethiopian for all he is worth. He is said to be pressed into the service of man, in reality, the service of the Caucasian. That being so, he never reaps the full meed of his work as a *man*. He materially contributes to the building of pavements on which he may not walk—take it as a metaphor, or as a fact, which way you please. He helps to work up revenues and to fill up exchequers over which, in most cases, he has no effective control, if any at all. In brief, he is labeled as belonging to a class apart among the races, and any attempt to rise above his station is terribly resented by the aristocracy of the races. Indeed, he is reminded at every turn that he is only intended to be a hewer of wood and a drawer of water. And so it happens that those among the favoured sons of men who occasionally consider the lot of the Ethiopian are met with jeers and taunts. Is it any wonder, then, that even in the Twentieth Century, the African finds it terribly difficult to make headway even in his own country? The African may turn socialist, may preach and cry for reform until the day of judgment; but the experience of mankind shows this, that reform never comes to a class or a people unless and until those concerned have worked out

their own salvation. And the lesson we have yet to learn is that we cannot depart from Nature's way and hope for real success.

And yet, it would seem as if in some notable instances the black man is bent upon following the line of greatest resistance in coping with the difficulties before him. Knowledge is the common property of mankind, and the philosophy which seeks for the Ethiopian the highest culture and efficiency in industrial and technical training is a sound one. It is well to arrest in favour of the race public opinion as to its capability in this direction. But that is not all, since there are certain distinctive qualities of race, of country, and of peoples which cannot be ignored without detriment to the particular race, country or people. Knowledge, deprived of the assimilating element which makes it natural to the one taught, renders that person but a bare imitator. The Japanese, adopting and assimilating Western culture, of necessity commands the respect of Western nations, because there is something distinctly Eastern about him. He commands, to begin with, the uses of his native tongue, and has a literature of his own, enriched by translations from standard authors of other lands. He respects the institutions and customs of his ancestors, and there is an intelligent past which inspires him. He does not discard his national costume, and if, now and again, he dons Western attire, he does so as a matter of convenience, much as the Scotch, across the border, puts away, when the occasion demands it, his Highland costume. It is not the fault of the black man in America, for example, that he suffers to-day from the effects of a wrong that was inflicted upon him years ago by the forefathers of the very ones who now despise him. But he can see to it that as the years go by it becomes a matter of necessity for the American whites to respect and admire his manhood; and the surest way to the one or the other lies not so much in imitation as in originality and natural initiative. Not only must the Ethiopian acquire proficiency in the arts and sciences, in technical and industrial training, but he must pursue a course of scientific enquiry which would reveal to him the good things of the treasure house of his own nationality.

There are probably but a few men of African descent in America who, if they took the trouble by dipping into family tradition, would not be able to trace their connection and relationship with one or other of the great tribes of West Africa; and now that careful enquiry has shown that the institutions of the Aborigines of Africa are capable of scientific handling, what would be easier than for the great centres of culture and learning in the hands of Africans in the United States to found professorships in this relation? In the order of Providence, some of our brethren aforetime were suffered to be enslaved in America for a wise purpose. That event in the history of the race has made it possible for the speedier dissemination and adoption of the better part of Western culture; and to-day Africa's sons in the East and in the West can do peculiar service unto one another in the common cause of uplifting Ethiopia and placing her upon her feet among the nations. The East, for example, can take lessons from the West in the adoption of a sound educational policy, the kind of industrial and technical training which would enable aboriginals to make the best use of their lands and natural resources. And, surely, the West ought not to be averse to taking hints from the East as regards the preservation of national institutions, and the adoption of distinctive garbs and names, much as obtains among our friends the Japanese. While a student in London, a thrill of Oriental pride used to run through the writer when he brushed against an Asiatic in a garb distinctively Eastern. They aped no one. They were content to remain Eastern. For even when climatic conditions necessitated the adoption of European habiliments, they had sense enough to preserve some symbol of nationality. On the contrary, Africans would seem never to be content unless and until they make it possible for the European to write of them thus:

"How extraordinary is the spectacle of this huge race—millions of men—without land or language

of their own, without traditions of the country they came from, bearing the very names of the men that enslaved them! . . .

"The black element is one which cannot be 'boiled down' into the great cosmopolitan American nation—the black man must always be tragically apart from the white man"—

and so on and so forth.

Now, if there is aught in the foregoing which is true to life, it bears but one meaning, namely, this, that the average Afro-American citizen of the United States has lost absolute touch with the past of his race, and is helplessly and hopelessly groping in the dark for affinities that are not natural, and for effects for which there are neither national nor natural causes. That being so, the African in America is in a worse plight than the Hebrew in Egypt. The one preserved his language, his manners and customs, his religion and household gods; the other has committed national suicide, and at present it seems as if the dry bones of the vision have no life in them. Looking at the matter closely, it is not so much *Afro-Americans* that we want as *Africans* or *Ethiopians,* sojourning in a strange land, who, out of a full heart and a full knowledge can say: If I forget thee, Ethiopia, let my right hand forget its cunning! Let us look at the other side of the picture. How extraordinary would be the spectacle of this huge Ethiopian race—some millions of men—having imbibed all that is best in Western culture in the land of their oppressors, yet remaining true to racial instincts and inspiration, customs and institutions, much as did the Israelites of old in captivity! When this more pleasant picture will have become possible of realisation, then, and only then, will it be possible for our people in bondage "metaphorically to walk out of Egypt in the near future with a great and a real spoil."

Someone may say, but, surely, you don't mean to suggest that questions of dress and habits of life matter in the least. I reply emphatically they do. They go to the root of the Ethiopian's self-respect. Without servile imitation of our teachers in their get-up and manner of life, it stands to reason that the average white man would regard the average black man far more seriously than he does at present. The adoption of a distinctive dress for the cultured African, therefore, would be a distinct step forward, and a gain to the cause of Ethiopian progress and advancement. Pray listen to the greatest authority on national life upon this matter, "Behold I have taught you statutes and judgments even as the Lord God commanded me that ye should do in the land whither ye go to possess it. Keep, therefore and do them: for this is your wisdom and your understanding in the sight of the nations which shall hear these statutes and say, surely, this great nation is a wise and understanding people." Yes, my people are pursuing knowledge as for a hidden treasure, and have neglected wisdom and true understanding, and hence are they daily a laughing stock in the sight of the nations.

Here, then, is work for cultured West Africans to start a reform which will be world-wide in its effects among Ethiopians, remembering as a basis that we, as a people, have our own statutes, the customs and institutions of our fore-fathers, which we cannot neglect and live. We on the Gold Coast are making a huge effort in this direction, and though European habits will die hard with some of our people, the effort is worth making; and, if we don't succeed quite with this generation, we shall succeed with the next. That the movement is gaining ground may well be gathered from the following extract from the *Gold Coast Leader* of 24th February, 1907, reporting the coronation of Ababio IV., *Mantse*, that is King, of "British Accra." Says the correspondent:

> "For the first time I realised that the Gold Coast would be more exhilarating and enjoyable indeed if the educated inhabitants in it would hark back to the times of old and take a few lessons in the art and grace of the sartorial simplicity and elegance of their forebears. The 'scholars' looked quite noble and full of dignity in the native dress. There was not one ignoble or mean person among them, and so for the matter of that did the ladies."

Then I should like to see *Ethiopian Leagues* formed throughout the United States much in the same way as the *Gaelic League* in Ireland for the purpose of studying and employing Fanti, Yoruba, Hausa, or other standard African language, in daily use. The idea may seem extraordinary on the first view, but if you are inclined to regard it thus, I can only point to the examples of Ireland and Denmark, who have found the vehicle of a national language much the safest and most natural way of national conservancy and evolution. If the Dane and Irish find it expedient in Europe, surely the matter is worthy of consideration by the Ethiopian in the United States, in Sierra Leone, in the West Indies, and in Liberia.

A distinguished writer, dwelling upon the advantages of culture in a people's own language said: "These are important considerations of a highly practical kind. Ten years ago, we had in Ireland a people divorced, by half a century of education conducted along alien lines, from their own proper language and culture. We also had in Ireland a people seemingly incapable of rational action, sunk in hopeless poverty, apparently doomed to disappear. We have in Ireland to-day the beginnings of a system of education in the national language and along national lines; and we have at the same time, and in the places where this kind of education has been operative, an unmistakable advance in intellectual capacity and material prosperity." Now, if the soul that is in the Ethiopian, even in the United States, remains Ethiopian, which it does, to judge from the coon songs which have enriched the sentiment of mankind by their pathos, then, I say, the foregoing words, true as everyone must admit they are, point distinctly to the impossibility of departing from *nature's* way with any hope of lasting good to African nationality. I do sincerely trust these thoughts will catch the eye of such distinguished educationists as Mr. Booker T. Washington and others of the United States and in the West Indies as also the attention of similar workers in West Africa, who have the materials ready at hand. It is a great work, but I do believe that my countrymen have the heart and the intelligence to grapple with it successfully.

African Negro Education

Orishatuke Faduma

Education was an especially powerful tool of empire, but it could also be turned around and employed as a tool to promote cultural nationalism and colonial independence. Writing when the only means of acquiring education was through Christian missionary schools, Orishatuke Faduma warned the people of Sierra Leone and his fellow Africans across the continent not to permit themselves to be wholly shaped by missionary education. Although he encouraged his fellow Africans to seek as much education as the missionaries could provide, he cautioned them against wholesale Westernization. In this brief article, Faduma argues that Africans need to define education for themselves.

Orishatuke Faduma was born William J. Davies of Yoruban parents in Freetown, Sierra Leone, in the early 1870s. He was educated in Sierra Leone and obtained a Bachelor of Divinity at Yale University in 1894. After holding several teaching and other positions in the United States, he retired to his native Sierra Leone in 1915, where he remained until 1935. He returned to the United States in that year and died in the early 1940s.

Questions

1. What does Faduma see as the advantages and drawbacks of European education for Africans?
2. Explain how Africans could make use of European education.
3. How are Faduma's ideas about culture different from Casely Hayford's?

Eclectic Education for Negro

In an age of scientific progress it is dangerous to cling tenaciously to one system of thought. No system is the perfect one because of its age or lack of age. Truth is independent of both and is its own authority. The true theology is the sum of all theologies and refuses to be denominational. Educational methods must not be hide-bound but should be the product of all that is best in present day methods. Pestalozzi, Froebel, Herbart, Comenius, Montessori and many other leaders of educational methods need careful study but not wholesale adoption. Each of them needs careful pruning and intelligent sifting, an addition here and a subtraction there. The reason for this judicious study and selection of methods is that in dealing with mind to which these methods are applied, you are dealing not with dead matter but with a living organism. The chemistry of mind—whether European, Asiatic, African or American mind—is organic and spiritual. You cannot dump anything and everything into it without imperilling its action. A system or method might have worked well at a certain period but unworkable at another period, because the growing mind has

Source: Orishatuke Faduma. "African Negro Education." *Weekly News*, 31 August 1918.

outgrown it: it is a Procrustean system of education which tolerates no change of methods of procedure. When new and fresh facts are discovered, our old conclusions must be changed. It is here that the too conservative mind, club, state, or religious society becomes a stumbling block to progress and must be fought to a finish to prevent fossilization because when a false premise is allowed, truth is suppressed. *Suggestio falsi suppression veri.*

A few years ago very little was heard of the study of Tropical Diseases in European or American Medical Schools. The unsystemized native knowledge of Tropical herbs was laughed at as superstitious. To-day the resources of the Tropics for the well-being of the world are better known. The native African went to foreign countries to study medicine but knew little or nothing of native herbal remedies. Europeans paid dearly in lives for their residence in malarial districts. Civilised governments are now specialising in Tropical Diseases and their medicinal plants. Medicos whether foreign or native who specialise in Tropical Diseases are more serviceable to people in the tropics than those who are not. The eclectic medical practitioner is likely to be far more successful than the man of one school of thought. In Medicine, Law, Theology, Education there must be election, selection, combination and separation to reach success.

In the vegetable as well as in the lower animal kingdom, life is maintained by judicious selection of plant or animal food. When the environments of plants are normal, they are able to absorb organic or inorganic materials suitable to their growth. Cattle do not live on the same food as birds. Each has its own food peculiar to its class and will die if fed otherwise. Each animal knows instinctively what leaf it should eat. All flesh is not the same flesh. Among higher animals, human beings, the same law holds good. What suits the Chinaman may not suit the Englishman, what suits the Englishman may not suit the African and so on, though there may be the same things which may suit all. Just as there are plant

idiosyncrasies so there are racial idiosyncrasies which may be modified by some process of grafting. It takes a skilled grafter to change a plant's life, for if violence is done to the transplanted or grafted plant, it dies under the change.

In the education of the African it should be remembered that he has a life of his own, that he is characteristically a native—physically, morally, spiritually. It should be remembered that he has a soul with an outward and visible clothing and an inward and invisible life, and that a true interpretation of the man African must be an interpretation of his inner consciousness. The only true interpreter of the man African must be an African, one like himself with similar yearnings, hopes, and aspirations. All that the foreigner can do in the line of education for the African is to lead him in the line of progress to see and know himself so that he may faithfully interpret his own to other people. This thought I may later on expand.

The African should have the advantage of all that is best in the educational methods of the twentieth century. *He should not slavishly imitate but should carefully adopt and adapt* what has been found good for the Englishman so that in addition to being a native he may have the doggedness and love of justice of the typical Englishman. To these qualities he needs the ruggedness of character and the breadth and depth of thought of the Scotchman, the practicalness and many sidedness of the American, the concentration, organization and scientific precision of the German, the esthetics, politeness, and good manners of the French.

Evolution of a New African

The scaffolding work of education must be laid by the foreigner and . . . be completed by the Negro himself. The foreigner is needed, the Englishman and others with a developed civilization the sum total of which will produce the New African Negro, who must be neither English, Scottish, German, French or American, but an

African Negro with a cosmopolitan spirit and a broadened mental horizon. The effect of such an education will be the production of an African Negro of a superior type, an African still, a lover of his people and other peoples, free from narrow race prejudice, an imitator and conservator of all that is excellent in the foreigner, and a retainer of all that is best in his own people.

In this work of evolution, the Church, the State, and native society, must co-operate. The Church working from within, the State working from without, and native society co-operating with both, these component forces will effect what each apart from the rest cannot.

If mind and matter are divine in their origin, then they are both sacred and should be treated as such. The spiritual and the physical were not created as antagonistic forces but could be made so through human ignorance. The knowledge of things material side by side with things spiritual must get a firm grip of the African Negro, with emphasis on the spiritual, because this is abiding. If man shall not live by bread alone it is equally true that the physical side of man must live on bread. The New African must be more than a spiritual man. His development must be all round. The new school in a new age for the New African must be one that allows freedom of thought and soul, must be one in which the wisdom of the past and of the present combine, must be one which regards the industry of the hand as divine. The African is still in bondage, a prey to himself and others unless dominated with these ideas. In fine, the New African which the new school must produce is the "man of muscle and brain, and power, fit to cope with everything," from the digging of a ditch, to the carrying of a hod, the building of a bridge, the planting of a seed, the healing of diseases, the interpreting of laws human and divine, to the production of a masterpiece in verse, prose or music.

▲

The Victory of Bolshevism

Li Dazhao

Li Dazhao (1888–1927) was a professor at Peking (Beijing) University and a founding member in 1921 of the Chinese Communist Party. An active member of the Chinese youth movement of the 1910s, Li mentored many aspiring Marxists, including Mao Zedong, through a study group that he founded. In 1918, China faced numerous domestic as well as international crises. After its first republican government disintegrated in the wake of the death of Yuan Shikai, the first president of the Republic of China, it essentially had no central government. Moreover, China's domestic weaknesses put it at a great disadvantage with respect to foreign powers, which treated it as a semicolony.

The following document shows the enthusiasm that some Chinese intellectuals had for Bolshevism, which appeared to be a reasonable model for China. The Bolshevik Revolution, which had taken place in Russia in 1917, served as a beacon for left-leaning intellectuals around the world. Russia's imperial government had been overthrown by a new political movement that claimed to represent the interests of the masses. The Bolsheviks demonstrated the power of the masses in the face of imperial tradition and modern capitalism, both of which appeared to be obstacles to Russia's development in the early twentieth century. China's situation, though not identical to Russia's, bore enough similarities that Bolshevism spoke to many Chinese youths in 1917 and after. Moreover, Bolshevism was an international movement, and on that basis it seemed only logical that Chinese Marxists should find it appealing. In fact, only a few years after the publication of this piece, the Soviet-led Comintern (Communist International) assisted members of Li's Marxist study group to found the Chinese Communist Party.

▲

Questions

1. What does Li find appealing about Bolshevism?

2. In what ways does this article resonate with the earlier piece in Part II by Lenin?

3. How might Bolshevism serve as an ideological tool for liberation?

"Victory! Victory! The Allies have been victorious! Surrender! Surrender! Germany has surrendered!" These words are on the national flag bedecking every doorway, they can be seen in color and can be indistinctly heard in the intonation of every voice. Men and women of the Allied powers run up and down the street in celebration of the victory, and in the city of Peking

Source: Li Dazhao. "The Victory of Bolshevism." In Teng Ssu-yü and John K. Fairbank (Eds.), *China's Response to the West: A Documentary Survey, 1839–1923*. Cambridge: Harvard University Press, 1954. Pp. 246–49. Reprinted by permission of the publisher. Copyright © 1954, 1979 by the President and Fellows of Harvard College. Copyright renewed 1982 by Ssu-yu Teng and John King Fairbank.

the soldiers of these nations loudly blast forth their triumphal songs. Now and then, echoed amid the noises of celebration and rejoicing, you hear the tinkling sounds of some German merchant's shop window being shattered, or that of the bricks and tiles taken off the von Ketteler Memorial Arch [a memorial to the German Minister killed by the Boxers]. It is indeed needless to describe the happiness of the people of the Allied powers who are living in our country . . .

But let us think carefully as small citizens of the world; to whom exactly does the present victory belong? Who has really surrendered? Whose is the achievement this time? And for whom do we celebrate? If we ponder over these questions, then not only will our non-fighting generals' show of strength and our shameless politicians' grasping of credit become senseless, but also the talk of the Allied nations, that the end of the war was brought about by their military forces defeating the military force of Germany, and their mad celebrations will be entirely without significance. And not only are their celebrations and boasts meaningless, but even the fate of their political system will probably [. . .] be the same as that of German militarism, and vanish with the latter in the near future.

For the real cause of the ending of the war was not the vanquishing of the German military power by the Allied military power, but the vanquishing of German militarism by German socialism. It was not the German people who surrendered to the armed forces of the Allied powers, but the German Kaiser, militarists and militarism who surrendered to the new tides of the world. It was not the Allied nations but the awakened minds of the German people that defeated German militarism; and the failure of German militarism was the failure of the Hohenzollern [Chinese text here inserts "Bolshevism" in English, by error] German imperial family and not that of the German nation. The victory over German militarism does not belong to the Allied nations; even less does it belong to our factious military men who used participation in the war only as an excuse [for engaging in civil war], or to

our opportunistic, cunningly manipulative politicians. It is the victory of humanitarianism, of pacifism; it is the victory of justice and liberty; it is the victory of democracy; it is the victory of socialism; it is the victory of Bolshevism [Chinese text inserts "Hohenzollern" by error]; it is the victory of the red flag; it is the victory of the labor class of the world; and it is the victory of the twentieth century's new tide. Rather than give Wilson and others the credit for this achievement, we should give the credit to Lenin [These names are inserted in English], Trotzky, Collontay [Alexandra Kollontai], to Liebknecht, Scheidemann, and to Marx . . .

Bolshevism is the ideology of the Russian Bolsheviki. What kind of ideology is it? It is very difficult to explain it clearly in one sentence. If we look for the origin of the word, we see that it means "majority." An English reporter once asked Collontay, a heroine in that [Bolshevik] party [. . .], what the meaning of "Bolsheviki" was. The heroine answered . . . "Its meaning will be clear only if one looks at what they are doing." According to the explanation given by this heroine, then, "Bolsheviki means only what they are doing." But from the fact that this heroine had called herself a Revolutionary Socialist in western Europe, and a Bolshevika in eastern Europe, and from the things they have done, it is clear that their ideology is revolutionary socialism; their party is a revolutionary socialist party; and they follow the German socialist economist Marx as the founder of their doctrine. Their aim is to destroy the national boundaries which are obstacles to socialism at present, and to destroy the system of production in which profit is monopolized by the capitalist. Indeed, the real cause of this war was also the destruction of national boundaries. Since the present national boundaries cannot contain the expansion of the system of production brought about by capitalism, and since the resources within each nation are inadequate for the expansion of its productive power, the capitalist nations all began depending on war to break down these boundaries, hoping to make of all parts of the globe one single, coördinated economic organ.

So as far as the breaking down of national boundaries is concerned, the socialists are of the same opinion with them. But the purpose of the capitalist governments in this matter is to enable the middle class in their countries to gain benefits; they rely on world economic development by one class in the victor nations, and not on mutual coöperation among humanitarian, reasonable organizations of the producers of the world. This war will cause such a victor nation to advance from the position of a great power to that of a world empire. The Bolsheviki saw through this point; therefore they vigorously protested and proclaimed that the present war is a war of the Tsar, of the Kaiser, of kings and emperors, that it is a war of capitalist governments, but it is not their war. Theirs is the war of classes, a war of all the world's proletariat and common people against the capitalists of the world. While they are opposed to war itself, they are at the same time not afraid of it. They hold that all men and women should work. All those who work should join a union, and there should be a central administrative soviet in each union. [. . .] Such soviets then should organize all the governments of the world. There will be no congress, no parliament, no president, no prime minister, no cabinet, no legislature, and no ruler. There will be only the joint soviets of labor, which will decide all matters. All enterprises will belong to those who work therein, and aside from this no other possessions will be allowed. They will unite the proletariat of the world, and create global freedom with their greatest, strongest power of resistance: first they will create a federation of European democracies, to serve as the foundation of a world federation. This is the ideology of the Bolsheviki. This is the new doctrine of the twentieth-century revolution.

In a report by Harold Williams in the London *Times,* Bolshevism is considered a mass movement. He compares it with early Christianity, and finds two points of similarity: one is enthusiastic partisanship, the other is a tendency to revelation. He says, "Bolshevism is really a kind of mass movement, with characteristics of religion . . ."

Not only the Russia of today, but the whole world of the twentieth century probably cannot avoid being controlled by such religious power and swayed by such a mass movement.

[. . .] In the *Fortnightly Review* Frederic Harrison says: "Savage, impossible, and anti-social as Bolshevism is, we must realize that it is also an emotional disturbance that is very solid, very wide, and very deep . . ."

In his book *Bolshevism and World Peace,* Trotzky writes: "In this new revolutionary era a new organization shall be created by unlimited proletarian socialist methods. The new organization will be as great as the new task. Amid the mad roar of the cannon, the crash of temples and shrines, and the wild blast of patriotic songs from wolf-like capitalists, we ought to be the first to undertake this new task. With the death-music of hell about us, we should maintain our clarity of mind, and clearly perceive and realize that ours will be the one and only creative force in the future . . ."

From this passage it is plain that Trotzky holds that the Russian revolution is to serve as a fuse to world revolution. The Russian revolution is but one [. . .] of the world revolutions; numerous revolutions of other peoples will successively arise . . .

The above are all statements made before the end of the war, and before the outbreak of the socialist revolutions in Germany and Austria. Today Trotzky's criticisms have been justified. The comments made by Messrs. Williams and Harrison have also been upheld. There are the Austrian revolution—the German revolution—the Hungarian revolution—and recently there have been reports also of the rise of vigorous revolutionary socialist parties in Holland, Sweden, and Spain. The pattern of the revolutions generally develops along the same line as that in Russia. The red flag flies everywhere, the soviets are established one after another. Call it revolution entirely *á la Russe,* or call it twentieth-century revolution. Such mighty rolling tides are indeed beyond the power of the present capitalist governments to prevent or to stop, for the mass movement of the twentieth century combines the whole of mankind into one great mass. The efforts of each individual within this great mass, following the example of some of them, will then be concentrated and become a great, irresistible social force. Whenever a disturbance in this worldwide social force occurs among the people, it will produce repercussions all over the earth, like storm clouds gathering before the wind and valleys echoing the mountains. In the course of such a world mass movement, all those dregs of history which can impede the progress of the new movement—such as emperors, nobles, warlords, bureaucrats, militarism, capitalism—will certainly be destroyed as though struck by a thunderbolt. Encountering this irresistible tide, these things will be swept away one by one. . . [. . .] Henceforth, all that one sees around him will be the triumphant banner of Bolshevism, and all that one hears around him will be Bolshevism's song of victory. The bell is rung for humanitarianism! The dawn of freedom has arrived! See the world of tomorrow; it assuredly will belong to the red flag! . . . The revolution in Russia is but the first fallen leaf warning the world of the approach of autumn. Although the word "Bolshevism" was created by the Russians, the spirit it embodies can be regarded as that of a common awakening in the heart of each individual among mankind of the twentieth century. The victory of Bolshevism, therefore, is the victory of the spirit of common awakening in the heart of each individual among mankind in the twentieth century.

⋀

From an Open Letter
to Mahatma Gandhi (1939)

MARTIN BUBER

One of the most vexing political issues of the last century has been the question of Palestine. Arabs and Jews have both claimed the territory for a wide range of historical, political, and religious reasons. Clearly, the struggle for possession of this territory has gone on until today and has been marked by warfare and violence.

Part of the background to this struggle over Palestine was the rise of Zionism, a movement to represent Jewish views and positions in the modern world. Zionists represented a wide variety of perspectives, but many of them were concerned with creating a Jewish homeland. The most compelling choice for this homeland was Palestine. Zionists often advocated and sponsored migration to Palestine. In the first half of the twentieth century, this policy brought them into conflict with the local Arab population in Palestine and, for a time, with the British, who held a political mandate to oversee the territory. After the Second World War, an independent Jewish state, Israel, was created in the territory, but the conflict between Arabs and Jews in the region has continued and erupted into open warfare on a number of occasions. From the Jewish perspective, Zionism was a political tool for liberation.

The famed Jewish theologian Martin Buber was a moderate Zionist who before the Second World War advocated a binational solution to the question of Palestine. While representing Jewish interests, Buber optimistically believed that cooperation between Arabs and Jews was possible. In this selection, an open letter to Mahatma Gandhi (who had earlier expressed himself on the issue of Palestine), Buber laid out some of his main arguments concerning Palestine and Jewish–Arab coexistence.

⋀

QUESTIONS

1. How does Buber challenge Gandhi's claim that Palestine belongs to the Arabs? What does Buber have to say about conquest, settlement, and possession of a land or territory?

2. What does Buber say about the cultivation of desert land? Why does he think that this type of cultivation can be a good example of Jewish–Arab cooperation?

YOU, MAHATMA GANDHI, who know of the connection between tradition and future, should not associate yourself with those who pass over our cause without understanding or sympathy.

Source: Martin Buber. "From an Open Letter to Mahatma Gandhi (1939)." In Arthur Hertzberg (Ed.), *The Zionist Idea: A Historical Analysis and Reader.* New York: The Jewish Publication Society of America, 1959. Pp. 463–65. Copyright © 1959 by Arthur Hertzberg. Reprinted with the permission of the publisher.

But you say—and I consider it to be the most significant of all the things you tell us—that Palestine belongs to the Arabs and that it is therefore "wrong and inhuman to impose the Jews on the Arabs."

Here I must add a personal note in order to make clear to you on what premises I desire to consider your thesis.

I belong to a group of people who from the time Britain conquered Palestine have not ceased to strive for the concluding of a genuine peace between Jew and Arab.

By a genuine peace we inferred and still infer that both peoples together should develop the land without the one imposing its will on the other. In view of the international usages of our generation, this appeared to us to be very difficult but not impossible. We were and still are well aware that in this unusual—yes, unprecedented—case it is a question of seeking new ways of understanding and cordial agreement between the nations. Here again we stood and still stand under the sway of a commandment.

We considered it a fundamental point that in this case two vital claims are opposed to each other, two claims of a different nature and a different origin which cannot objectively be pitted against one another and between which no objective decision can be made as to which is just, which unjust. We considered and still consider it our duty to understand and to honor the claim which is opposed to ours and to endeavor to reconcile both claims. We could not and cannot renounce the Jewish claim; something even higher than the life of our people is bound up with this land, namely its work, its divine mission. But we have been and still are convinced that it must be possible to find some compromise between this claim and the other, for we love this land and we believe in its future; since such love and such faith are surely present on the other side as well, a union in the common service of the land must be within the range of possibility. Where there is faith and love, a solution may be found even to what appears to be a tragic opposition.

In order to carry out a task of such extreme difficulty—in the recognition of which we have had to overcome an internal resistance on the Jewish side too, as foolish as it is natural—we have been in need of the support of well-meaning persons of all nations, and have hoped to receive it. But now you come and settle the whole existential dilemma with the simple formula: "Palestine belongs to the Arabs."

What do you mean by saying a land belongs to a population? Evidently you do not intend only to describe a state of affairs by your formula, but to declare a certain right. You obviously mean to say that a people, being settled on the land, has so absolute a claim to that land that whoever settles on it without the permission of this people has committed a robbery. But by what means did the Arabs attain the right of ownership in Palestine? Surely by conquest, and in fact a conquest with intent to settle. You therefore admit that as a result their settlement gives them exclusive right of possession; whereas the subsequent conquests of the Mamelukes and the Turks, which were conquests with a view to domination, not to settlement, do not constitute such a right in your opinion, but leave the earlier conquerors in rightful ownership. Thus settlement by conquest justifies for you a right of ownership of Palestine; whereas a settlement such as the Jewish—the methods of which, it is true, though not always doing full justice to Arab ways of life, were even in the most objectionable cases far removed from those of conquest—does not justify in your opinion any participation in this right of possession. These are the consequences which result from your axiomatic statement that a land belongs to its population. In an epoch when nations are migrating you would first support the right of ownership of the nation that is threatened with dispossession or extermination; but were this once achieved, you would be compelled, not at once, but after a suitable number of generations had elapsed, to admit that the land "belongs" to the usurper. . . .

It seems to me that God does not give any one portion of the earth away, so that the owner may say as God says in the Bible: "For all the earth is

Mine" (Exodus 19:5). The conquered land is, in my opinion, only lent even to the conqueror who has settled on it—and God waits to see what he will make of it.

I am told, however, I should not respect the cultivated soil and despise the desert. I am told, the desert is willing to wait for the work of her children: she no longer recognizes us, burdened with civilization, as her children. The desert inspires me with awe; but I do not believe in her absolute resistance, for I believe in the great marriage between man (*adam*) and earth (*adamah*). This land recognizes us, for it is fruitful through us: and precisely because it bears fruit for us, it recognizes us. Our settlers do not come here as do the colonists from the Occident to have natives do their work for them; they themselves set their shoulders to the plow and they spend their strength and their blood to make the land fruitful. But it is not only for ourselves that we desire its fertility. The Jewish farmers have begun to teach their brothers, the Arab farmers, to cultivate the land more intensively; we desire to teach them further: together with them we want to cultivate the land—to "serve" it, as the Hebrew has it. The more fertile this soil becomes, the more space there will be for us and for them. We have no desire to dispossess them: we want to live with them. We do not want to dominate them: we want to serve with them. . . .

▲

Satyagraha in South Africa

M. K. GANDHI

Following the colonization of South Africa by the British and Dutch, large numbers of Indi-
ans were imported as coolie laborers in the late nineteenth century. Over time, as many of these
contract laborers returned to India, a new wave of free Indian immigration to South Africa
occurred. These new Indian immigrants made their living primarily through trade, and many
of the early traders provided goods for the coolies. By the early 1890s, the white residents of South
Africa, feeling increasingly threatened by the merchant activities of this new wave of Indian
immigrants, began to establish laws, regulations, and taxes to restrict Indian merchant activ-
ity and further immigration. Indians increasingly found their civil liberties diminished by new
legislation that restricted their right to vote, forced them to register with the government and to
live in separate areas, and specified other rules for public behavior.

It was against this backdrop that Mohandas K. Gandhi, a British-trained Indian lawyer
living in South Africa, initiated the satyagraha *campaign, which took place between 1906 and*
1914. This strategy met with at least some success in South Africa, and in 1915 Gandhi
returned to India to initiate a satyagraha *campaign against the British Raj. The basic ideas*
of satyagraha, *or nonviolent resistance, are explained in the selection that follows, which was*
originally published in the 1920s.

▲

QUESTIONS

1. What is *satyagraha?*
2. How does Gandhi distinguish between *satyagraha* and passive resistance?

Satyagraha v. Passive Resistance

As the movement advanced, Englishmen too began to watch it with interest. Although the English newspapers in the Transvaal generally wrote in support of the Europeans and of the Black Act, they willingly published contributions from well-known Indians. They also published Indian representations to Government in full or at least a summary of these, sometimes sent their reporters to important meetings of the Indians, and when such was not the case, made room for the brief reports we sent them.

These amenities were of course very useful to the community, but by and by some leading Europeans came to take interest in the movement as it progressed. One of these was Mr Hosken, one of the magnates of Johannesburg. He had always been free from colour prejudice but his interest in the Indian question deepened after the starting of Satyagraha. The Europeans of Germiston, which is something like a suburb of Johannesburg, expressed a desire to hear me. A meeting was held, and introducing me and the movement I stood for to the audience, Mr Hosken observed, "The Transvaal Indians have had recourse to passive resistance when all other

Source: M. K. Gandhi. *Satyagraha in South Africa.* Ahmedabad: Navajivan Publishing House, 1928. Pp. 111–15.

means of securing redress proved to be of no avail. They do not enjoy the franchise. Numerically, they are only a few. They are weak and have no arms. Therefore they have taken to passive resistance which is a weapon of the weak." These observations took me by surprise, and the speech which I was going to make took an altogether different complexion in consequence. In contradicting Mr Hosken, I defined our passive resistance as 'soul force.' I saw at this meeting that a use of the phrase 'passive resistance' was apt to give rise to terrible misunderstanding. I will try to distinguish between passive resistance and soul force by amplifying the argument which I made before that meeting so as to make things clearer.

I have no idea when the phrase 'passive resistance' was first used in English and by whom. But among the English people, whenever a small minority did not approve of some obnoxious piece of legislation, instead of rising in rebellion they took the passive or milder step of not submitting to the law and inviting the penalties of such non-submission upon their heads. When the British Parliament passed the Education Act some years ago, the Non-conformists offered passive resistance under the leadership of Dr Clifford. The great movement of the English women for the vote was also known as passive resistance. It was in view of these two cases that Mr Hosken described passive resistance as a weapon of the weak or the voteless. Dr. Clifford and his friends had the vote, but as they were in a minority in the Parliament, they could not prevent the passage of the Education Act. That is to say, they were weak in numbers. Not that they were averse to the use of arms for the attainment of their aims, but they had no hope of succeeding by force of arms. And in a well-regulated state, recourse to arms every now and then in order to secure popular rights would defeat its own purpose. Again some of the Non-conformists would generally object to taking up arms even if it was a practical proposition. The suffragists had no franchise rights. They were weak in numbers as well as in physical force. Thus their case lent colour to Mr Hosken's observations. The suffragist

movement did not eschew the use of physical force. Some suffragists fired buildings and even assaulted men. I do not think they ever intended to kill any one. But they did intend to thrash people when an opportunity occurred, and even thus to make things hot for them.

But brute force had absolutely no place in the Indian movement in any circumstance, and the reader will see, as we proceed, that no matter how badly they suffered, the Satyagrahis never used physical force, and that too although there were occasions when they were in a position to use it effectively. Again, although the Indians had no franchise and were weak, these considerations had nothing to do with the organization of Satyagraha. This is not to say, that the Indians would have taken to Satyagraha even if they had possessed arms or the franchise. Probably there would not have been any scope for Satyagraha if they had the franchise. If they had arms, the opposite party would have thought twice before antagonizing them. One can therefore understand, that people who possess arms would have fewer occasions for offering Satyagraha. My point is that I can definitely assert that in planning the Indian movement there never was the slightest thought given to the possibility or otherwise of offering armed resistance. Satyagraha is soul force pure and simple, and whenever and to whatever extent there is room for the use of arms or physical force or brute force, there and to that extent is there so much less possibility for soul force. These are purely antagonistic forces in my view, and I had full realization of this antagonism even at the time of the advent of Satyagraha.

We will not stop here to consider whether these views are right or wrong. We are only concerned to note the distinction between passive resistance and Satyagraha, and we have seen that there is a great and fundamental difference between the two. If without understanding this, those who call themselves either passive resisters or Satyagrahis believe both to be one and the same thing, there would be injustice to both leading to untoward consequences. The result of our using the phrase 'passive resistance' in South Africa was, not that people admired us by ascribing to us the bravery and the self-sacrifice of the suffragists but we were mistaken to be a danger to person and property which the suffragists were, and even a generous friend like Mr Hosken imagined us to be weak. The power of suggestion is such, that a man at last becomes what he believes himself to be. If we continue to believe ourselves and let others believe, that we are weak and helpless and therefore offer passive resistance, our resistance would never make us strong, and at the earliest opportunity we would give up passive resistance as a weapon of the weak. On the other hand if we are Satyagrahis and offer Satyagraha believing ourselves to be strong, two clear consequences result from it. Fostering the idea of strength, we grow stronger and stronger every day. With the increase in our strength, our Satyagraha too becomes more effective and we would never be casting about for an opportunity to give it up. Again, while there is no scope for love in passive resistance, on the other hand not only has hatred no place in Satyagraha but is a positive breach of its ruling principle. While in passive resistance there is a scope for the use of arms when a suitable occasion arrives, in Satyagraha physical force is forbidden even in the most favourable circumstances. Passive resistance is often looked upon as a preparation for the use of force while Satyagraha can never be utilized as such. Passive resistance may be offered side by side with the use of arms. Satyagraha and brute force, being each a negation of the other, can never go together. Satyagraha may be offered to one's nearest and dearest; passive resistance can never be offered to them unless of course they have ceased to be dear and become an object of hatred to us. In passive resistance there is always present an idea of harassing the other party and there is a simultaneous readiness to undergo any hardships entailed upon us by such activity; while in Satyagraha there is not the remotest idea of injuring the opponent. Satyagraha postulates the conquest of the adversary by suffering in one's own person.

These are the distinctions between the two forces. But I do not wish to suggest that the merits, or if you like, the defects of passive resistance thus enumerated are to be seen in every movement which passes by that name. But it can be shown that these defects have been noticed in many cases of passive resistance. Jesus Christ indeed has been acclaimed as the prince of passive resisters but I submit in that case passive resistance must mean Satyagraha and Satyagraha alone. There are not many cases in history of passive resistance in that sense. One of these is that of the Doukhobors of Russia cited by Tolstoy. The phrase passive resistance was not employed to denote the patient suffering of oppression by thousands of devout Christians in the early days of Christianity. I would therefore class them as Satyagrahis. And if their conduct be described as passive resistance, passive resistance becomes synonymous with Satyagraha. It has been my object in the present chapter to show that Satyagraha is essentially different from what people generally mean in English by the phrase 'passive resistance.'

While enumerating the characteristics of passive resistance, I had to sound a note of warning in order to avoid injustice being done to those who had recourse to it. It is also necessary to point out that I do not claim for people calling themselves Satyagrahis all the merits which I have described as being characteristic of Satyagraha. I am not unaware of the fact that many a Satyagrahi so called is an utter stranger to them. Many suppose Satyagraha to be a weapon of the weak. Others have said that it is a preparation for armed resistance. But I must repeat once more that it has not been my object to describe Satyagrahis as they are but to set forth the implications of Satyagraha and the characteristics of Satyagrahis as they ought to be.

In a word, we had to invent a new term clearly to denote the movement of the Indians in the Transvaal and to prevent its being confused with passive resistance generally so called. I have tried to show in the present chapter the various principles which were then held to be a part and parcel of the connotation of that term.

▲

Madras Protest

This demonstration in Madras, India, called for the boycott of the Simon Commission of 1927. The Simon Commission had been established to report to the British government on the political situation in British India, a situation that was becoming more unpredictable as increasing numbers of educated Indians were calling for home rule (that is, autonomy). The Simon Commission was boycotted because none of its members were Indian, and thus many Indians felt that it would not make fair or accurate reports.

▲

QUESTIONS

1. What strategies are the people pictured here using to gain a political voice?
2. What tools for liberation are these protesters employing?

Source: Getty Images Inc.—Hulton Archive Photos.

Passive Resistance

CLAUDE MCKAY

Poetry could also be used as a tool of liberation. Just as Rudyard Kipling had called on the United States to take up its "white man's burden" at the end of the nineteenth century, Claude McKay, in "Passive Resistance" (1912), called upon Jamaicans to free themselves from those who oppressed them. In strong, direct language McKay demonstrated how passive resistance could work. For him, its eventual promise was a "vic'try day."

McKay (1889–1948) was a Jamaican-born poet who lived and traveled in many parts of the world: the Caribbean, the United States, Europe, and North Africa. He was a founding figure in New York's Harlem Renaissance and in his lifetime completed a fascinating personal ideological journey from communism to Catholicism.

QUESTIONS

1. According to McKay, what types of activities will be held in check by passive resistance?
2. Who do you think would be "given worry," as McKay puts it, by passive resistance?

Passive Resistance

There'll be no more riotin',
Stonin' p'lice an' burnin' car;
But we mean to gain our rights
By a strong though bloodless war.

We will show an alien trust
Dat Jamaicans too can fight
An' dat while our blood is hot,
They won't crush us wi' deir might.

Hawks may watch us as dey like,
But we do not care a pin;
We will hold "the boys" in check,
There'll be no more riotin'.

We are sorry, sorry much
For the worry given some;
But it will not last for aye,—
Our vic'try day shall come.

There are aliens in our midst
Who would slay us for our right;
Yet though vipers block the way
We will rally to the fight.

We'll keep up a bloodless war,
We will pay the farthings-fare
An' we send the challenge forth,
"Only touch us if you dare!"

Source: Claude McKay. "Passive Resistance." In William J. Maxwell (Ed.), *Complete Poems*. Urbana: University of Illinois Press, 2004. P. 13. Copyright © 2004 by University of Illinois Press. Courtesy of the Literary Representative for the Works of Claude McKay, Schomburg Center for Research in Black Culture, The New York Public Library, Astor, Lenox and Tilden Foundations.

⬤

An Indian Freedom Fighter
Recalls Her Life

MANMOHINI ZUTSHI SAHGAL

*Manmohini Zutshi Sahgal, born 1909, was a member of the Nehru family, a politically
prominent Brahmin family from Kashmir. Her mother became politically active, supporting, in
particular, feminist causes, during Manmohini's youth. This feminism was distinct from the
missionary-inspired approach that we saw manifested in the child marriage law in Part IV.
Rather than faulting Indian culture for its barbarism and trying to reform it along Western
or Christian lines, Manmohini's mother taught her daughters to seek the same sorts of reforms
that Western women sought at that time: to cast off the bonds of patriarchal society and to create leadership opportunities in the public realm for women. This feminism shaped Manmohini,
who, along with her sisters, was among the first generation of Indian women to enroll in what
had previously been all-men's colleges.*

*An advocate of Gandhi's strategy of nonviolent struggle and an opponent of the British Raj,
Manmohini Sahgal became in her college years deeply involved in the organization of strikes and
protests. She was quickly recognized by young women as well as men as having a particular gift
for protest and was sought out by students as a protest leader. She continued to protest the British
Raj as a graduate student and was imprisoned three times during the 1930s. After Gandhi
called off the protest movement in 1935, she turned to teaching. In 1947, she started working
as a volunteer with refugees from newly established Pakistan and continued to be an activist
for social causes in India after independence. The selection that follows shows how Sahgal used
both nonviolent protest and feminism as tools to promote Indian independence.*

⬤

QUESTIONS

1. Why does Manmohini Sahgal actively desire to be arrested?

2. How is her approach to protest a reflection of the ideas promoted by Gandhi in the selection earlier in this part of the reader?

3. In what ways does she appear to be using feminist arguments as a tool of liberation?

[. . .] When I left home on the morning of October 8, 1930, I had a strong feeling that I would
not be returning home that day. My elder sister
Janak left for college as usual. She was a lecturer
in English at Lahore College for Women, a government institution. I sent my younger sister
Shyama to get our friend Swadesh Kumari from
her house, go to the district office, collect all the

Source: Manmohini Zutshi Sahgal. *An Indian Freedom Fighter Recalls Her Life*. Edited by Geraldine Forbes. Armonk,
New York: M. E. Sharpe, 1994. Pp. 68–74. Copyright © 1994 by Manmohini Zutshi Sahgal. Reprinted with
permission of M. E. Sharpe, Inc.

women assembled there, and post them at the three colleges. I would join her at Government College for Men as soon as I was free. When I got to Mr. Kapur's residence, he informed me that the District Congress Committee felt that the *hartal* [strike], to be effective, needed more organizing. One night's notice was not sufficient, so the committee decided to call for a *hartal* on October 9. I replied that since the student union had announced a *hartal* for October 8, we would go ahead with our program and the Congress could organize the general strike for the next day.

I asked Mr. Kapur to go to the District Congress Office and ask six male volunteers to meet me as soon as possible at Government College, New Hostel Gate. I then proceeded to Government College to find that Shyama and Swadesh had already posted women volunteers at Forman Christian College, the Law College, and Government College.

Picketing was in full swing and the roads were swarming with people. The student community is the same the world over. Any excitement is enough to keep them away from their lectures, and here was excitement with a vengeance. Never in the history of any university in India had educational institutions been picketed by a group of young women while the male students stood by to cheer them. When I got to the Government College, I found that I was the "odd man out," so to say, so I spent my time going from one gate of the college to the other, trying to keep the roads clear for traffic. On the side road was the entrance to the District Courts, but the boundary wall was crowded with people. I do not think any work was done in court that morning.

My principal, Mr. H.L.O. Garrett, had just returned from a long leave of absence. He had been rejoicing that the troublesome Miss Zutshi [the author] was no longer in college, when word was sent to his residence that she had returned to create even more trouble by picketing the college. Mr. Garrett left whatever he was doing and rushed to the college. When he saw me standing there he remarked, "So, you are back!" I am told that he

then telephoned the police and asked them to take away Miss Zutshi, who was making a nuisance of herself. In their rush to get there, the police could not lay their hands on an official transport, so they commandeered a car to drive them to Government College. The male volunteers had just arrived, and I had left the gate to post them at strategic points. The police did not recognize me and were never known to be very intelligent in making inquiries. They had been told to arrest Miss Zutshi, who was standing at the gate opposite the new hostel. They found two young women there, and, presuming one of them to be me, promptly arrested them both. When I heard of their arrest, I went and stood alone at the gate, challenging the students to enter the college if they dared. As the day wore on, the excitement and enthusiasm became more intense. The roads all around the college were packed with students. I was inundated by requests to come and organize picketing at a number of other colleges. I replied that I was already so involved with one college that I had no time to go elsewhere. I urged the students to organize picketing in their own colleges. But this was quite unnecessary. With so many students absent, it was unlikely that classes were held in their colleges.

Meanwhile, the principal was getting annoyed. Where were the police? The reply came that Miss Zutshi had already been arrested and was on her way to prison. The principal was dancing mad. Miss Zutshi was still at the gate, he roared at the police authorities. Who had they arrested? They had no idea. Presuming that Miss Zutshi was a dangerous person, they were taking no risks. This time they sent a prison van with a large posse of police to arrest me. To cover up their mistake, they decided to arrest everyone picketing the colleges. So the young women from Forman Christian College and the Law College were rounded up. But the real excitement and the real challenge was at Government College. I was arrested. Meanwhile, Shyama and Swadesh were warned by friends to be ready, as their turn would be coming soon.

All Congress workers had been instructed by the local High Command not to carry any valuables (money, jewelry, even fountain pens) in their purses or bags, as they could be confiscated by the police in lieu of fines that would be imposed. Raj Rani, one of the two girls mistakenly arrested at the gate, was wearing a gold necklace and gold bangles. She left these with me. I had some cash and my fountain pen, which, with the gold jewelry, added up to a tidy sum. When the police came for me with the prison van, the crowd increased tenfold and became very resistant. They did not like the idea of a young woman being taken away in a prison van so the police were anxious to do their duty and hurry away. But I would not leave until I had handed over my purse to someone I knew well. Meanwhile, I refused to budge. Finally, one of my colleagues from the student union, Lajpat Rai, came, and I handed him the purse. I then allowed myself to be arrested and boarded the police van. The prison van was an oblong steel structure on wheels with two very narrow benches (only about six inches wide) attached to each side, running the length of the van. The door, also made of steel, was padlocked from the outside. The only air came from a four-inch-wide steel network opening, which extended along the walls just above the benches. On the driver's side were two steel network partitions that enabled the police to keep an eye on the prisoners inside. I had the honor of being the first woman to be arrested and to travel in this van. Soon after my arrest, Shyama and Swadesh were also arrested. When there were no more women, the young men took over the picketing. The Law College closed early, so no attention was paid to it. Forman Christian College did not merit any attention either. The principal there had refrained from calling in the police, so all the resentment of the young men was concentrated on Government College. The authorities at Government College escalated tension by calling in the police; otherwise, this might have been a peaceful demonstration. After all, if there were no classes for one day, no one would lose very much, but to call in the

police just to have one young woman removed angered the student community.

The police had to come again and again in their effort to put a stop to this. Tempers ran high on both sides. Finally the police had to resort to a *lathi*-charge [riot control using bamboo batons] to disperse the crowd. By 2:30 P.M., sixteen women and thirty-five men, mostly college students, had been arrested. Never had Lahore witnessed so many arrests in one day.

Soon after my arrest, Lajpat Rai telephoned Janak at her college to relay the news and to tell her that Shyama would soon follow. Janak asked her principal, Miss Harrison, for leave for the rest of the day, explaining what had happened and the fact that mother was already in prison. She would have to make the arrangements to send our clothes and food to the jail and inform Father, in Allahabad, about what happened. Miss Harrison curtly refused her request. Janak was so upset that she promptly wrote out her resignation from the college, handed it to her principal, and walked out. She came home and packed a few things for me, Shyama, and herself as well, because she had now decided to court arrest. She then wrote a telegram for Father, left it with the servants with instructions to send it if she did not return home by 4:00 P.M., and left the house. Janak reached Government College just as Shyama and Swadesh were being taken away. She announced to the assembled crowd that since her two younger sisters had been arrested she had come to court arrest. The authorities were in no mood to discriminate as to who had been involved in the actual picketing and who had not. Before she knew what was happening, she was whisked away in a car and driven straight to the office of the district magistrate, Mr. Edgar Lewis. Unknown to her, I was sitting in the prison van waiting for the arrest warrants to be signed. Shyama and Swadesh had already been taken inside the office to have their formalities completed. I was deemed to be too dangerous to be allowed to leave the van, even with a police guard. After the formalities were over, Shyama and Swadesh joined me in the van, but for some reason it did not move. I supposed that the police were waiting to see how many more women would be arrested, and we were surprised when the door was unlocked and in stepped Janak. Having had a glimpse of a posh car out on the road, we presumed that she had come to see us, but she calmly informed us that she had resigned her job and had also been arrested. And so we were all brought to the female jail.

While waiting in the prison van I began worrying about what was happening at Government College. I felt responsible for organizing the picketing and began to worry that some untoward incident might happen. My main concern was contacting Mr. Jawan Lal Kapur. I could not leave the van to telephone him. After scanning the crowd for many anxious moments, I saw a lone bicyclist. I shouted to him to stop and asked him to carry a message to Mr. Jawan Lal Kapur at 3 Begum Road. He was to tell Mr. Kapur that all the young women picketing Government College had been arrested and that he needed to go immediately to the college. The intensity of public sympathy could be gauged by the fact that although this young man could not see me, he could hear a woman's voice from a stationary prison van and guessed what had happened. He listened to my plea and delivered the message. Later, Mr. Kapur told me that a young man had come to bring the news of the wholesale arrest of women at Government College.

After Janak's arrest, Lajpat Rai called *Anand Bhavan* at Allahabad and informed Mrs. Kamla Nehru of our arrest. He was not able to contact my father directly as we had no telephone. Mrs. Nehru went over to our house, smilingly congratulated my father, and gave him the message. Pandit Motilal and Jawaharlal were already in prison. On learning of our arrest, Motilal remarked that he was very happy that three generations of his family were then in jail. The Uttar Pradesh government was not resorting to such harsh measures at that time. It was not until January 1931 that the Uttar Pradesh authorities made their first arrest of women, beginning with

Mrs. Kamla Nehru. After that, others were arrested: Mrs. Vijayalakshmi Pandit, her sister Krishna, and Mrs. Uma Nehru.

We were excited and enthusiastic about being taken to prison. We felt as if a great honor had been conferred on us. We shouted slogans and sang national songs while waiting for the formalities to be completed. In fact, the three of us, my sisters and I, dearly hoped to be imprisoned three times so we would be termed "habitual offenders."

Word had already reached Mother and the other women inside the prison that a fresh batch of young women had been arrested and that Shyama and I were among them. Each new entrant, whether people knew her or not, was cheered by those already in prison. Not only did it add spice to the otherwise dull and monotonous existence in prison; it was evidence for us that the *satyagraha* movement was alive and confirmation that our sacrifices had not been made in vain. When we arrived, the women were gathered near the big black iron gate, trying to see the new arrivals. Mother was worried that poor Janak would be left all alone in the house.

Meanwhile, we were outside the prison office waiting to be processed. The prison office was a small, unimpressive building just outside the main prison. In front of it was a huge iron gate with bars and at the back a huge black sheet of solid iron serving as another gate. This rectangular building housed the jailor's office, another small room adjacent to it, and the store rooms for uniforms and supplies. A narrow verandah served as the visitors' room. A warden sat just inside the front gate acting as a sort of timekeeper. His duty was to sound the passing of every hour and half-half hour on a gong.

As we sang songs and shouted slogans, our voices echoed and reechoed in the narrow confines of the office block. The poor jailor, Bakshi Suggarmal, was so distracted that he rushed out of his office and implored us to be quiet so that he could take us into custody. The police were anxious to be off. Until then, Bakshi Suggarmal had led a very peaceful life. Mother had been arrested in August, Pooran Devi in September, and only a few other women from Delhi and other places. Suddenly, he had to take charge of sixteen women, most of whom were young and out to create trouble for the authorities. What he did not know at that time was that a little later he would have to take charge of four small children. One of our friends, Shakuntala Chawla, had left three small children behind and another friend one child. Once they heard of their wives' arrest, the husbands brought these children to be with their mothers.

At last the formalities were complete and we were ushered into the jail. What celebrations there were then! We were treated as heroines coming home. Everyone rejoiced that there had been so many arrests in one day, although we did not yet know that thirty-five young men had been arrested. That sixteen women had been arrested from sleepy Lahore was a great thing! The movement would certainly continue. Since the magistrate had forgotten to classify us in A, B, or C categories, we all stayed together. The jail authorities immediately provided us with dry rations because it would be evening before we could get food from our respective homes. This became a picnic lunch, with everyone helping with the cooking and talking excitedly. The trial magistrate, Mr. C.H. Disney, came in the afternoon and informed us that our trial would begin the next morning on the jail premises. He classified us as A and B prisoners and left. Whether he left instructions with the jailor or the latter thought of it himself, I do not know, but soon after he left, the jailor said he was separating A and B prisoners. B prisoners were to be taken to another barracks in a separate compound where they would be locked up at night. We did not personally know all the women who had come with us, and we were afraid that a few of them might be persuaded to apologize in court the next day and be released. That would be a great setback to the movement.

We protested that this classification should take effect after the trial was over. Until then, we were all pretrial prisoners entitled to the same privileges, that is, wearing our own clothes and receiving food from home. The jailor was adamant. He said he had to obey the orders of the magistrate. We were equally determined to demand our rights. The jailor tried persuasion first and then threatened to have the B group forcibly removed. He left us, saying that he would round up his wardresses who would not hesitate to drag the B group off. At that time, we had no idea of the geography of the prison. We later on discovered that the class B barracks was in a separate compound, part of a much larger compound that housed other buildings used for class C prisoners and long-term prisoners. It also housed the hospital block and solitary cells. It was quite a distance from our barracks. Had the jailor carried out his threat we would have been badly hurt, but we squatted in a circle, with our arms linked, on the hard earthen floor outside the A barracks, determined to resist all efforts to break up our group. Mother threatened to deal with the wardresses should they so much as lay a finger on any of her daughters.

We sat like this until it became pitch dark. The jail compound was quiet and peaceful. No sinister figures came out of the office. Some friends had sent us dinner, but we returned it as we were in no mood to eat. The other women were so upset at these developments that they had not cooked for themselves either. Finally, at about 9:00 P.M., Satyavati went to the office and asked the jailor what he intended to do, as the women were still squatting. Was he going to carry out his threat of dragging them off? Was he prepared to face public censure if any of the women were manhandled and hurt? He laughed and said to tell the women not to be silly but to go to bed as it was quite late. As we had eaten no dinner we went to sleep hungry, but we were triumphant after our long and eventful day. [. . .]

⋏

Algerian Women Fighters

Guerilla fighters and independence activists were not just men. Women also fought for independence using a variety of strategies, as the Sahgal excerpt demonstrates. Sahgal was not a militant, but some independence movements did make use of trained female combatants. Such was the case in Algeria, as is well documented in the 1966 film The Battle of Algiers. *This photograph shows a women's section of the Algerian independence movement, the FLN (National Liberation Front) participating in a rally in support of Algerian independence.*

⋏

QUESTIONS

1. In what ways do these women appear to be participating in the Algerian independence movement?

2. Does this image challenge your assumptions about women in the Arab world? If so, how?

3. What tools for liberation do you see in this image?

Source: Getty Images Inc.— Hulton Archive Photos.

⋏

A Viet Cong Memoir

TRUONG NHU TANG

Whereas some anticolonial activists chose to use nonviolent strategies to gain independence, in other cases colonial peoples felt it necessary to use violence and employ military strategies to liberate themselves. Independence activists in Algeria and Vietnam, in particular, fought fierce battles against the French empire. In the Vietnamese case, the battle for independence against the French, fought from the end of World War Two until 1954, was quickly replaced by a second battle for independence from the United States, which had largely stepped into the shoes of the French after 1954. The immediate solution to the Vietnamese quest for independence was the partitioning of Vietnam into two countries, North Vietnam, controlled by Ho Chi Minh and the Viet Minh who had fought against French domination, and South Vietnam, controlled by the pro-French president Bao Dai. In the years following 1955, Soviet support for the government in the north and United States support for the government in the south ultimately turned Vietnam into a cold-war battleground.

The following excerpt is from a memoir written by former Minister of Justice for the North Vietnamese Viet Cong, Truong Nhu Tang. Truong discovered his Vietnamese nationalism while studying in France and returned to his homeland to dedicate himself first to ousting the French and later to ousting the United States from Vietnam. This selection describes his first encounter with the Maquis, guerilla warriors combating the French in the early 1950s, and offers the reader an opportunity to consider the relationship between nationalism, independence movements, and military action.

⋏

QUESTIONS

1. What kinds of strategies did Vietnamese activists try to employ in their quest for independence?

2. Who were the guerillas fighting?

3. What kind of military service was Truong drafted for, and why was it problematic for him?

[. . .] By 1951 I had completed my studies, earning a master's degree in political science and going on to take a licentiate in law at the University in Paris. Meanwhile, the war in Vietnam had become a protracted, vicious affair, with Ho Chi Minh's resistance forces operating with increasing effectiveness in both North and South against the modern French army. In 1948 the Soviet Union had begun to take an active interest in the Vietminh's efforts, and the 1949 Chinese Communist

Source: Truong Nhu Tang. *A Viet Cong Memoir*. New York: Vintage Books, 1985. Pp. 25–29.

victory over Chiang Kai-shek opened up a direct pipeline for arms and equipment to the guerrilla army.

Recognizing the power of Ho's appeal to Vietnamese nationalism, the French had attempted to establish credence for their own version of a native government under the hereditary emperor Bao Dai. They had also managed to obtain support from the United States. As the conflict became internationalized, the level of internal violence steadily heightened. In Paris I began to consider seriously whether I shouldn't enlist in the resistance.

But though to me it seemed that the time had come for this move, my friends in the Vietnamese Association counseled against it. They argued that I had no experience with combat or any taste for it. They couldn't imagine how I might fare as a guerilla. Without question, they maintained, I would be more a burden than a help as a jungle fighter. On the other hand, I had already demonstrated a talent for organizing. My place was clearly on the political front in France, helping to arouse overt public resistance to the war.

After mulling over this candid advice, I reluctantly decided that my friends were probably right. I would continue with the work of political agitation in Paris, helping to plan conferences and demonstrations, writing open letters, distributing literature, propagandizing in every way I could for French withdrawal. I cannot say that I altogether regretted the decision to remain in Paris. The city had been the scene of my rebirth. I recognized that my political activities over the last five years, together with my studies, had decisively changed the person I had been. I had arrived in France a superb product of the French colonial system and its *mission civilisatrice.* Paradoxically, life in the French capital had imbued me with an understanding and a love for my own country far deeper than I had previously known. After five years I was at one with my Vietnamese identity, with the history, the national culture, the Asian soul of my country. I felt Vietnam's humiliation, its misery, and its backwardness as my own.

The words Ho had spoken to us in 1946 were my constant companions: "We must fight a war against foreign domination, a war against hunger, a war against ignorance. To gain 'victory, victory, great victory,' we must have 'unity, unity, great national unity.'"

Perhaps I should not have been surprised that my plans to stay in France would fall victim to circumstance. Toward the end of 1951, I received an unexpected letter from my father. In it he told me that the businesses were not going well. The fighting in Thu Dan Mot had badly damaged the rubber plantation, and the printing house was struggling for life in Saigon's harsh economic climate. It had become a great financial effort for him to support my five brothers (all of whom were now studying in European universities). He was unable to be as active as he once was, and he was deathly afraid that my brothers would be forced to terminate their studies. He asked me—with dignity but also with a hint of desperation—to return home to help him.

At this point my older brother, Quynh, was in his last year of medical school at the University of Paris. Bich, the third, was a year away from his degree at the London School of Economics. Like my father, I simply could not stand the idea that they and the others might have to quit. Since I was the only one who had completed his studies, it was my duty to return. I no more questioned that than my father had questioned his own responsibilities, or than my brothers would have questioned theirs if they had been in my position. This time there was no choice to be made. At the end of 1951 I embarked for Saigon.

I had not been back more than several days before I received my draft orders from the Bao Dai government. The playboy king's army was badly in need of recruits, and I had now put myself within reach. Faced with the need to contribute to the family and at the same time to avoid enlistment in the French puppet army, I took the only available path—an alternative service job in one of the distant provinces. I enrolled as a teacher available for work anywhere there was a need.

It so happened that just then the government was opening a secondary school in the province of Chau Doc on the Cambodian frontier, about two hundred miles west of Saigon. The bad roads and worse communications meant that this job would be a real exile. But with no other options available, off I went to become a teacher. Not just a teacher, as it turned out, but the senior teacher. Just as during the August Revolution my high school diploma (along with my gun) had automatically made me the leader, here my Paris degrees qualified me as the senior teacher, entitled to be addressed as "professor." But the reverence accorded to teachers in the South Vietnam countryside, as I quickly discovered, in no way lessened the demands made on them by a people starved for education. Before long I was bearing up under a teaching load that included courses in French, mathematics, history, chemistry, physics, even English.

Each week my salary went directly to my family, and whenever I had three days or more off, I would return to Saigon to help my father with the businesses. In addition to the financial and organizational assistance I could give, I knew I was also becoming increasingly important to my parents emotionally, with all the other children away and beset as they were by unfamiliar money worries and anxieties about the war.

Still, as I got to know my colleagues and people in the town where I was teaching, I became aware of how truly national the war against the French was. Almost everyone sympathized with the Vietminh and either had relatives who were fighting or were themselves supporting the struggle in some practical way. As I adjusted to the new job and new people, I began to fall into my old habits of agitating and organizing support, as well as lending a hand in sending badly needed medicines to the guerrillas. Yet, I was keenly aware that my contribution was meager. I wanted to do something more.

With this thought in mind, during the Easter holidays I made contact with a Maquis [guerrilla] unit operating in the Cai Lay region southeast of the capital and arranged to join them on a temporary basis. I was anxious to see how the guerrillas lived—to understand their motivations. I wanted to know how they survived the hardships and how their aspirations enabled them to persevere against the French, year in and year out. For the first time I would see what combat was like.

Despite a severe hemorrhoid problem complete with hemorrhaging and considerable pain, I managed to get to my contact point at the given time. In a good deal of physical discomfort but with a light heart, I began to share the dangers of guerrilla life.

During the week I was with the unit, its chief mission was an ambush they had planned for a French detachment that would be moving down the Chau Van Tiep Canal, a minor branch of the Mekong. Just beyond a bend in the river, the guerrillas set obstacles made of logs and branches bound together and camouflaged with thick bunches of aquatic plants. A good distance before the bend they prepared other obstacles, and poised them on the banks ready to slide into the water behind the French riverboats, to prevent them from escaping. At the expected time, the French appeared—maybe a dozen boats all together—carrying nearly four hundred soldiers. As they reached the barrier, the guerrillas, hiding on either side of the river, opened fire. Downstream, others pushed the escape barriers into place, trapping the flotilla. Caught in a deadly cross fire and unable to move, many of the French were simply mowed down. Even their machine guns and heavier firepower were ineffective against the guerrillas, who moved unseen behind the high reeds that choked the banks. One boat began to sink, then another. By the time the French planes arrived to drive the guerrillas off, a number of the riverboats lay half submerged in the water; others had disappeared below its surface.

I watched all this from relative safety, hunched in the reeds next to the Maquis chief. I realized, not without some surprise, that I could stomach the sight of death. I was full of admiration for the guerrillas, for the skill and bravery with which they carried out their attack, though they were facing greater numbers and superior weapons. After we had retreated and regrouped, I found I wanted to stay with them, but I knew that in my condition (not to mention my family responsibilities) it would be impossible. I understood instinctively that I would never make a soldier myself. Nevertheless, I was equally sure that I could play a role in the propaganda and psychological war which, as I was already beginning to understand, was as important as the actual fighting. At the end of the week, I was still quite sick, and the guerrilla commander advised me to go back and get my condition taken care of before I made any decisions. [. . .]

⟡

Che Guevara: Guerilla Warfare

Brian Loveman and Thomas M. Davies, Jr., Editors

Ernesto "Che" Guevara was the most controversial figure in Latin America in the second half of the twentieth century. He was born into a middle-class family in Argentina in 1928 and became a revolutionary activist and theorist. He was involved in a number of political and military conflicts in the 1950s and 1960s, including Fidel Castro's successful revolution in Cuba. After his death in Bolivia in 1967, Guevara became the symbol of guerilla-based resistance to generations of revolutionaries. Not everyone who followed in Guevara's tradition adopted his version of guerilla warfare, but virtually all of them laid claim to his legacy. Of course, Latin American dictators, conservative elites, and their international allies loathed Guevara and the tradition he came to symbolize.

In this selection, Brian Loveman and Thomas M. Davies, Jr., editors of Guevara's writings, review his influence upon a wide variety of revolutionary groups in Latin America, Central America, and the Caribbean from the 1960s to the 1990s. The piece shows not only how guerilla warfare itself could be used as a tool of liberation but also how the legend and legacy of Che Guevara came to represent revolutionary armed struggle.

⟡

Questions

1. According to Guevara and those who followed him, what were the conditions in Latin America, Central America, and the Caribbean that made guerilla activity likely if not necessary?

2. What modifications or adaptations in guerilla techniques or strategy did later revolutionaries make to Guevara's original theories?

3. In your estimation, how potent are political symbols themselves, such as "Che the revolutionary," as tools of liberation?

Since the end of World War II, U.S. foreign policy toward Latin America has been dominated by global cold war concerns. Reagan administration policymakers justified economic and military assistance to Latin American nations as responses to the threat of Soviet imperialism, perceived of as a deadly menace to the very existence of the United States. From the first CIA covert military operation in 1954 through the 1980s, U.S. officials regularly justified their Latin America policy in terms of superpower confrontations.

Even as U.S. concerns for Latin America focused on Soviet-inspired Communist influence, the peoples of Latin America underwent profound

Source: Che Guevara. *Guerilla Warfare* (with revised and updated introduction and case studies by Brian Loveman and Thomas M. Davies, Jr.). Wilmington, DE: Scholarly Resources, 1997. Pp. 421–25. Reprinted with permission of Scholarly Resources, an imprint of Rowman & Littlefield Publishers, Inc.

socioeconomic change that intensified the already extreme inequities in the distribution of wealth, income, and opportunities throughout the region. The modernization of export agriculture, increased industrialization, and massive urbanization altered the demographic and occupational structure of the hemisphere. These changes placed even more pressure on the fragile yet often repressive governments of the region.

The old order in Latin America offered little hope for the vast majority of the people. Without land to till, adequate nutrition or jobs, housing, health care, or educational opportunities, the majority of Latin Americans cared little about superpower cold war conflicts. The shibboleth of "Communism versus capitalism" and the notion of Soviet threats to hemispheric security meant nothing to the poor and malnourished as they toiled to provide for their daily subsistence. Yet as the region's rulers routinely and cynically labeled political opponents of all sorts as "Communists," U.S. policymakers, with few exceptions, identified with the old order against "subversion." The "logic" of cold war tended to blind these policymakers to the internal conditions that demanded reform or necessitated revolution.

After 1959 the Cuban revolutionaries' ideological and political confrontation with the United States, as well as their proclaimed intent to stimulate and support "anti-imperialist" (anti-U.S.) revolutions, exacerbated the United States' opposition to autonomous political change in the region. Cuban, Soviet, and U.S. international machinations overshadowed the underlying polarization of social, ethnic, race, and class struggle that characterized the period of 1959–90. The drama of Latin America, the immense tragedy of repression and despair, appeared to Americans as a minor subplot to the center-stage theater of world politics.

In this context, Che Guevara's *Guerrilla Warfare* represented a dramatic challenge. His initial call for a handful of "brave and dedicated men" in each nation to spark the struggle that would oust the Caribbean-style dictatorships quickly

evolved into a call for continental and international struggle against imperialism. Guevara's inspiration, combined with the ideological underpinnings of the revolutionary struggles he promoted, contaminated, in the eyes of U.S. policymakers, the battle for social, economic, and political justice in Latin America. The cycles of insurgency and counterinsurgency that followed tore apart the fabric of the region.

In much of Latin America, this struggle replaced the old oligarchs and Caribbean-style dictatorships with "modernizing" military regimes. Increasingly, the progressive elements in Latin America, whether Christian, Marxist, or social democratic, viewed U.S. policy as a principal obstacle to the creation of a more humane, egalitarian society in the region. More and more, the anti-imperialist vision promoted by Che Guevara, if not the method of guerrilla warfare, became the dominant view of large sectors of non-Marxist Latin Americans.

Ironically, Che Guevara's original formulations in *Guerrilla Warfare* offered authentic reformers and U.S. foreign policymakers hope for the future. His insistence that the guerrilla struggle could not be germinated successfully where "the possibilities of peaceful struggle have not yet been exhausted" proved highly accurate. Only where local elites, bolstered by U.S. policy, destroyed beliefs in a democratic alternative did guerrilla and revolutionary politico-military movements achieve notable success. In Nicaragua, El Salvador, and Guatemala, farcical elections and repressive dictatorships made "peaceful struggle" a dangerous, often fatal charade. In contrast, in Venezuela, and even in Colombia and Peru, the appearance of alternatives to armed struggle and the existence of real—if not profound—reformist programs offered precisely the obstacles to widespread popular support of guerrilla movements that Guevara predicted.

Che Guevara's modification, in "Guerrilla Warfare: A Method," of his original thesis urged that the guerrilla method—armed struggle led by the *foco*—be used against the formal democracies ("oligarchical dictatorships") of the region. To the obvious targets, such as Somoza, were added the reformers and moderates such as Betancourt in Venezuela or Belaúnde in Peru. The mistaken broadening of the original thesis alienated nationalists, reformists, and democratic forces and legitimized increased U.S. military assistance programs in Latin America. Defending the reforms of Acción Demócrátia in Venezuela or even the fragile efforts of President Belaúnde in Peru could not be equated in the U.S. Congress or in U.S. public opinion with support for Somoza in Nicaragua or for the Guatemalan military dictators.

But as Guevara failed to limit the applicability of the guerrilla method to the targets indicated in *Guerrilla Warfare,* so, too, did the United States fail to limit its military assistance and political support to the formal democratic regimes most able to resist guerrilla warfare and least likely to engage in institutionalized torture and terrorism. Neither Che Guevara, nor his Latin American disciples, nor the policymakers of the United States recognized the legitimacy of truly *national* reformist or revolutionary movements that refused to identify with international socialism or the Western bloc. The overwhelming influence of cold war ideological and security concerns in U.S.–Latin American relations, and in Guevara's modifications of *Guerrilla Warfare,* contributed to over a quarter century of political polarization, tragedy, and death in the region.

Then the Berlin Wall came down, the cold war ended, and the Soviet Union imploded. In the post–cold war global disorder, Latin America again largely disappeared from the forefront of U.S. foreign policymaking. But the debt crisis of the 1980s as well as the dramatic economic readjustments and restructuring that accompanied the "end of history" and the "victory of democracy" (the replacement of authoritarian regimes with elected governments) made millions of Latin Americans poorer and more desperate. The "lost decade" of the 1980s and armed conflicts in Central America, Colombia, and Peru brought economic deterioration and personal tragedy despite

the Bush administration's optimistic pronouncements as the 1990s began.

Many Latin Americans, voting with their feet, migrated north to escape the wars and lack of economic opportunity. Others intensified the flight to cities from the countryside, exacerbating the stress on inadequate infrastructure and government services in national capitals and major urban areas. The terrible socioeconomic conditions identified by Che Guevara as the sources of discontent that had created the objective conditions for guerrilla warfare in the late 1950s had not been overcome. Indeed, in much of the hemisphere they had become worse. Counterinsurgency had defeated most guerilla movements and stalemated others, but it had not created the conditions necessary for decent lives and improved opportunities heralded by the Alliance for Progress.

And political violence, including guerrilla movements, had not been eliminated. In much of the hemisphere, daily violence and ongoing insurgency bloodied civilian populations and combatants alike some thirty years after Che Guevara's assassination in Bolivia at the hands of his captors. In Colombia the guerrilla war, complicated by the depredations of drug-lord armies and violence as business (kidnapping, extortion, sabotage, murder for hire), persisted despite more than a quarter century of "peace negotiations" and "pacification" campaigns. Much the same was true in Guatemala, El Salvador, and Peru. And in Mexico, new guerrilla movements—the Emiliano Zapata Liberation Front (EZLN), the Revolutionary Peoples Army (ERP), and others—joined political party opposition to the long-dominant Institutional Revolutionary Party's (PRI) authoritarian rule.

Che Guevara was a romantic—a romantic who believed that human volition and small bands of armed guerrillas could be instruments for overturning tyranny and creating more just and humane societies. If his utopian vision of socialism proved illusory, then it remains true that no new political order has ever been born without violence as a midwife. The entrenched institutions, the embedded values and customs, and the "proper" notions of law and civility give way reluctantly, whether through reform or revolution. The spectacular operations of Mexico's EZLN and Peru's Túpac Amaru guerrillas from 1994 to 1997, and the endemic guerrilla operations in Colombia and elsewhere, had no hope of real military success or of ousting governments, but they did make clear that the plight of millions of Latin Americans was not improving, and often getting worse, in the 1990s.

As Che Guevara (and John F. Kennedy) had predicted, those who make reform impossible make political violence more likely. Ironically, when government policymakers learn this lesson, the guerrillas become effective arguments for reform but also even more unlikely victors in the sort of national liberation wars imagined by Guevara. The United States and the Soviet Union thus could declare an end to the cold war, of which the Latin American guerrillas became a part, but not to the social and economic misery in the Western Hemisphere. As long as such misery exists and humans can imagine political alternatives—by whatever name the utopian alternatives are known—guerrilla fighters and political fronts backed by the threat of violence remain a part of Guevara's living legacy to Latin America.

Although the guerrilla struggles in Venezuela, El Salvador, Guatemala, Bolivia, Peru, and elsewhere hardly ended as he would have preferred, governments deigned to negotiate with adversaries whom they would rather have eliminated. They not only negotiated but also changed policies and government institutions because eliminating the guerrillas proved impossible, even with massive military assistance from abroad and the waging of horrific "dirty wars." Of course, the story is not over, nor can the final judgment on Che Guevara's legacy yet be written. That he is not forgotten—by those who continue the guerrilla struggle and by those who combat the guerrillas—is certain.

⋀

Cuban Protest

PHOTOGRAPHER: MIGUEL VINAS, PRENSA LATINA

Because he died young and was still a committed revolutionary, Che Guevara remains a pow-
erful symbol in Latin America and around the world. His image continues even today to be linked
to anti-imperialist protest in Cuba and Latin America. Here we see a Cuban protest against
the United States' invasion of Grenada in the mid-1980s. Protestors hold signs reading "I Hate
to Death Imperialism," with a large image of Che in the background.

⋀

QUESTIONS

1. Why might Cubans or other Latin Americans have perceived American intervention in the Caribbean or Latin America as imperialist or neo-imperialist?

2. How might icons be used as tools for liberation?

Source: Miguel Vinas, Prensa Latina /Getty Images Inc.— Hulton Archive Photos.

▲

Hawaii's Story

LILIUOKALANI

Born in 1838 into the Hawaiian royal family, Queen Liliuokalani was Hawaii's last monarch. She was a remarkable woman, well educated in Western as well as Hawaiian languages and traditions, well traveled, a composer of music, a writer, and an advocate for improving the health, education, and welfare of her people. She was also a devout Christian. Hawaii was brought into the Western orbit in 1778 after the arrival of Captain Cook, who named the islands after Britain's Earl of Sandwich (hence Liliuokalani's references in the text to the Sandwich Islands). King Kamehameha later took two Westerners to be his advisors, and it was under their influence that an increasing number of Hawaiian chiefs converted to Christianity. Throughout the nineteenth century, Christian missionaries continued to serve as advisors to the Hawaiian royalty and to introduce ideas that led to transformations of the Hawaiian political and social system.

Named heir apparent in 1877 and made Queen in 1891, Liliuokalani reigned against the backdrop of increasing American and Western expansion in the Pacific. Almost immediately upon her accession to the throne, Liliuokalani was faced with the problem of American efforts to annex Hawaii, and she spent the early years of her reign attempting to implement a new Hawaiian constitution that would empower the native Hawaiians. By 1893, however, her rights as a monarch to proclaim a new constitution were being called into question by a group of elite businessmen and plantation owners led by Sanford Dole, who overthrew her in 1894. She was placed under house arrest for some time and then forced to abdicate in 1897 and lived in retirement until her death in 1917. The following selection is her formal response to the annexation treaty of 1897. It constitutes a final plea for Hawaiian autonomy in the face of American encroachment.

▲

QUESTIONS

1. How does Liliuokalani use Western concepts to argue against the annexation of Hawaii?
2. How does Liliuokalani view the United States?
3. How does she view Hawaii?

My Official Protest to the Treaty

"I, LILIUOKALANI of Hawaii, by the will of God named heir apparent on the tenth day of April, A.D. 1877, and by the grace of God Queen of the Hawaiian Islands on the seventeenth day of January, A.D. 1893, do hereby protest against the ratification of a certain treaty, which, so I am informed, has been signed at Washington by Messrs. Hatch, Thurston, and Kinney, purporting to cede those

---

Source: Liliuokalani. *Hawaii's Story*. Boston: Lee and Shepard, 1898. Pp. 354–57.

Islands to the territory and dominion of the United States. I declare such a treaty to be an act of wrong toward the native and part-native people of Hawaii, an invasion of the rights of the ruling chiefs, in violation of international rights both toward my people and toward friendly nations with whom they have made treaties, the perpetuation of the fraud whereby the constitutional government was overthrown, and finally, an act of gross injustice to me.

"Because the official protests made by me on the seventeenth day of January, 1893, to the so-called Provisional Government was signed by me, and received by said government with the assurance that the case was referred to the United States of America for arbitration.

Yielded to Avoid Bloodshed

"Because that protest and my communications to the United States Government immediately thereafter expressly declare that I yielded my authority to the forces of the United States in order to avoid bloodshed, and because I recognized the futility of a conflict with so formidable a power.

"Because the President of the United States, the Secretary of State, and an envoy commissioned by them reported in official documents that my government was unlawfully coerced by the forces, diplomatic and naval, of the United States; that I was at the date of their investigations the constitutional ruler of my people.

"Because such decision of the recognized magistrates of the United States was officially communicated to me and to Sanford B. Dole, and said Dole's resignation requested by Albert S. Willis, the recognized agent and minister of the Government of the United States.

"Because neither the above-named commission nor the government which sends it has ever received any such authority from the registered voters of Hawaii, but derives its assumed powers from the so-called committee of public safety, organized on or about the seventeenth day of January, 1893,

said committee being composed largely of persons claiming American citizenship, and not one single Hawaiian was a member thereof, or in any way participated in the demonstration leading to its existence.

"Because my people, about forty thousand in number, have in no way been consulted by those, three thousand in number, who claim the right to destroy the independence of Hawaii. My people constitute four-fifths of the legally qualified voters of Hawaii, and excluding those imported for the demands of labor, about the same proportion of the inhabitants.

Civic and Hereditary Rights

"Because said treaty ignores, not only the civic rights of my people, but, further, the hereditary property of their chiefs. Of the 4,000,000 acres composing the territory said treaty offers to annex, 1,000,000 or 915,000 acres has in no way been heretofore recognized as other than the private property of the constitutional monarch, subject to a control in no way differing from other items of a private estate.

"Because it is proposed by said treaty to confiscate said property, technically called the crown lands, those legally entitled thereto, either now or in succession, receiving no consideration whatever for estates, their title to which has been always undisputed, and which is legitimately in my name at this date.

"Because said treaty ignores, not only all professions of perpetual amity and good faith made by the United States in former treaties with the sovereigns representing the Hawaiian people, but all treaties made by those sovereigns with other and friendly powers, and it is thereby in violation of international law.

"Because, by treating with the parties claiming at this time the right to cede said territory of Hawaii, the Government of the United States receives such territory from the hands of those whom its own magistrates (legally elected by the people of the United States, and in office in 1893) pronounced fraudulently in power and unconstitutionally ruling Hawaii.

Appeals to President and Senate

"Therefore I, Liliuokalani of Hawaii, do hereby call upon the President of that nation, to whom alone I yielded my property and my authority, to withdraw said treaty (ceding said Islands) from further consideration. I ask the honorable Senate of the United States to decline to ratify said treaty, and I implore the people of this great and good nation, from whom my ancestors learned the Christian religion, to sustain their representatives in such acts of justice and equity as may be in accord with the principles of their fathers, and to the Almighty Ruler of the universe, to him who judgeth righteously, I commit my cause.

"Done at Washington, District of Colombia, United States of America, this seventeenth day of June, in the year eighteen hundred and ninety-seven.

LILIUOKALANI

‸

Speech at the Opening of the Asian-African Conference

INDONESIAN PRESIDENT SOEKARNO

By 1955, when Asia had achieved its independence and Africa was at its most militant in the quest for its own, representatives from numerous Asian and African countries met in Bandung, Indonesia to discuss ways in which they might support each other and work together to achieve common goals. As it drew to an end, the conference issued a communiqué (The Final Communiqué of the Conference), which underlined the need for developing countries to establish patterns of economic and technical cooperation that would enable them to secure their place in global politics and economics. The communiqué suggested that they provide technical assistance to one another through the exchange of experts, cooperate to establish research and training projects, and supply each other with equipment. Further, it recommended collective action to stabilize international prices and the demand for primary commodities and to diversify the export trade through the processing of raw materials before export. It also encouraged the establishment of national and regional banks and insurance companies. The Bandung Conference thus sought to rework the patterns of economic interaction between newly independent states and not-yet independent colonies in ways that would help them to help themselves. The selection that follows is from the opening remarks by Indonesian President Soekarno (Sukarno) in which he discusses the underlying principles of the Asian-African Conference. He sees the great potential for collective action and thus emphasizes brotherhood and harmony among the non-aligned nations.

‸

QUESTIONS

1. What are some of Soekarno's aspirations for Asian-African cooperation?

2. What does Soekarno say about the religious and cultural diversity of Africa and Asia?

[. . .] Nor am I disinterested when I speak of the battle for peace. How can any of us be disinterested about peace?

Not so very long ago we argued that peace was necessary for us because an outbreak of fighting in our part of the world would imperil our precious independence, so recently won at such great cost.

Today, the picture is more black. War would not only mean a threat to our independence, it may mean the end of civilisation and even of human life. There is a force loose in the world

---

Source: "Speech by President Soekarno at the Opening of the Asian-African Conference, April 18, 1955." In George McTurnan Kahin, *The Asian-African Conference: Bandung, Indonesia, April 1955.* Ithaca, NY: Cornell University Press, 1956. Pp. 45–51.Reprinted from George McTurnan Kahin, *The Asian-African Conference.* Copyright © 1956 by Cornell University. Used by permission of the publisher, Cornell University Press.

whose potentiality for evil no man truly knows. Even in practice and rehearsal for war the effects may well be building up into something of unknown horror.

Not so long ago it was possible to take some little comfort from the idea that the clash, if it came, could perhaps be settled by what were called "conventional weapons"—bombs, tanks, cannon and men. Today that little grain of comfort is denied us, for it has been made clear that the weapons of ultimate horror will certainly be used, and the military planning of nations is on that basis. The unconventional has become the conventional, and who knows what other examples of misguided and diabolical scientific skill have been discovered as a plague on humanity.

And do not think that the oceans and the seas will protect us. The food that we eat, the water that we drink, yes, even the very air that we breathe can be contaminated by poisons originating from thousands of miles away. And it could be that, even if we ourselves escaped lightly, the unborn generations of our children would bear on their distorted bodies the marks of our failure to control the forces which have been released on the world.

No task is more urgent than that of preserving peace. Without peace our independence means little. The rehabilitation and upbuilding of our countries will have little meaning. Our revolutions will not be allowed to run their course.

What can we do? The peoples of Asia and Africa wield little physical power. Even their economic strength is dispersed and slight. We cannot indulge in power politics. Diplomacy for us is not a matter of the big stick. Our statesmen, by and large, are not backed up with serried ranks of jet bombers.

What can we do? We can do much! We can inject the voice of reason into world affairs. We can mobilize all the spiritual, all the moral, all the political strength of Asia and Africa on the side of peace. Yes, we! We, the peoples of Asia and Africa, 1,400,000,000 strong, far more than half the human population of the world, we can mobilise

what I have called the *Moral Violence of Nations* in favour of peace. We can demonstrate to the minority of the world which lives on the other continents that we, the majority, are for peace, not for war, and that whatever strength we have will always be thrown on to the side of peace.

In this struggle, some success has already been scored. I think it is generally recognised that the activity of the Prime Ministers of the Sponsoring Countries which invited you here had a not unimportant role to play in ending the fighting in Indo-China.

Look, the peoples of Asia raised their voices, and the world listened. It was no small victory and no negligible precedent! The five Prime Ministers did not make threats. They issued no ultimatum, they mobilized no troops. Instead they consulted together, discussed the issues, pooled their ideas, added together their individual political skills and came forward with sound and reasoned suggestions which formed the basis for a settlement of the long struggle in Indo-China.

I have often since then asked myself why these five were successful when others, with long records of diplomacy, were unsuccessful, and in fact, had allowed a bad situation to get worse, so that there was a danger of the conflict spreading. Was it because they were Asians? Maybe that is part of the answer, for the conflagration was on their doorstep, and any extension of it would have presented an immediate threat to their own houses. But I think that the answer really lies in the fact that those five Prime Ministers brought a *fresh approach* to bear on the problem. They were not seeking advantage for their own countries. They had no axe of power-politics to grind. They had but one interest—how to end the fighting in such a way that the chances of continuing peace and stability were enhanced.

That, my Sisters and Brothers, was an historic occasion. Some countries of free Asia spoke, and the world listened. They spoke on a subject of immediate concern to Asia, and in doing so made it quite clear that the affairs of Asia are the concern of the Asian peoples themselves. The days are now long past when the future of Asia can be settled by other and distant peoples.

However, we cannot, we dare not, confine our interests to the affairs of our own continents. The States of the world today depend one upon the other and no nation can be an island unto itself. Splendid isolation may once have been possible; it is so no longer. The affairs of all the world are our affairs, and our future depends upon the solutions found to all international problems, however far or distant they may seem.

As I survey this hall, my thoughts go back to another Conference of Asian peoples. In the beginning of 1949—historically speaking only a moment ago—my country was for the second time since our Proclamation of Independence engaged in a life and death struggle. Our nation was besieged and beleaguered, much of our territory occupied, a great part of our leaders imprisoned or exiled, our existence as a State threatened.

Issues were being decided, not in the conference chamber, but on the battlefield. Our envoys then were rifles, and cannon, and bombs, and grenades, and bamboo-spears. We were blockaded, physically and intellectually.

It was at that sad but glorious moment in our national history that our good neighbor India convened a Conference of Asian and African Nations in New Delhi, to protest against the injustice committed against Indonesia and to give support to our struggle. The intellectual blockade was broken! Our Delegates flew to New Delhi and learned at first hand of the massive support which was being given to our struggle for national existence. Never before in the history of mankind has such a solidarity of Asian and African peoples been shown for the rescue of a fellow Asian Nation in danger. The diplomats and statesmen, the Press and the common men of our Asian and African neighbours were all supporting us. We were given fresh courage to press our struggle onwards to its final successful conclusion. We again realised to the full the truth of Desmoulin's statement: "Have no doubt of the omnipotence of a free people."

Perhaps in some ways the Conference which has assembled here today has some roots in that manifestation of Asian-African solidarity six years ago.

However that may be, the fact remains that everyone of you bears a heavy responsibility, and I pray to God that the responsibility will be discharged with courage and wisdom.

I pray to God that this Asian-African Conference succeeds in doing its job.

Ah, Sisters and Brothers, let this Conference be a great success! In spite of diversity that exists among its participants,—let this Conference be a great success!

Yes, there is diversity among us. Who denies it? Small and great nations are represented here, with people professing almost every religion under the sun,—Buddhism, Islam, Christianity, Confucianism, Hinduism, Jainism, Sikhism, Zoroasthrianism, Shintoism, and others. Almost every political faith we encounter here—Democracy, Monarchism, Theocracy, with innumerable variants. And practically every economic doctrine has its representative in this hall—Marhaenism, Socialism, Capitalism, Communism, in all their manifold variations and combinations.

But what harm is in diversity, when there is unity in desire? This Conference is not to oppose each other, it is a conference of brotherhood. It is not an Islam-Conference, nor a Christian Conference, nor a Buddhist Conference. It is not a meeting of Malayans, nor one of Arabs, nor one of Indo-Aryan stock. It is not an exclusive club either, nor a bloc which seeks to oppose any other bloc. Rather it is a body of enlightened, tolerant opinion which seeks to impress on the world that all men and all countries have their place under the sun—to impress on the world that it is possible to live together, meet together, speak to each other, without losing one's individual identity; and yet to contribute to the general understanding of matters of common concern, and to develop a true consciousness of the interdependence of men and nations for their wellbeing and survival on earth.

I know that in Asia and Africa there is greater diversity of religions, faiths, and beliefs, than in the other continents of the world. But that is only natural! Asia and Africa are the classic birthplaces of faiths and ideas, which have spread all over the world. Therefore, it behooves us to take particular care to ensure that the principle which is usually called the "Live and let live" principle—mark, I do not say the principle of "Laissez faire, laissez passer" of Liberalism which is obsolete—is first of all applied by us most completely within our own Asian and African frontiers. Then only can it be fully extended to our relations with our neighbouring countries, and to others more distant.

Religion is of dominating importance particularly in this part of the world. There are perhaps more religions here than in other regions of this globe. But, again, our countries were the birthplaces of religions. Must we be divided by the multiformity of our religious life? It is true, each religion has its own history, its own individuality, its own "raison d'être," its special pride in its own beliefs, its own mission, its special truths which it desires to propagate. But unless we realise that all great religions are one in their message of tolerance and in their insistence on the observance of the principle of "Live and let live," unless the followers of each religion are prepared to give the same consideration to the rights of others everywhere, unless every State does its duty to ensure that the same rights are given to the followers of all faiths—unless these things are done, religion is debased, and its true purpose perverted. Unless Asian-African countries realise their responsibilities in this matter and take steps jointly to fulfill them, the very strength of religious beliefs, which should be a source of unity and a bulwark against foreign interference, will cause its disruption, and may result in destroying the hard-won freedom which large parts of Asia and Africa have achieved by acting together.

Sisters and Brothers, Indonesia is Asia-Africa in small. It is a country with many religions and many faiths. We have in Indonesia Muslims, we have Christians, we have Civa-Buddhists, we have

peoples with other creeds. Moreover, we have many ethnic units, such as Achenese, Bataks, Central-Sumatrans, Sundanese, Central-Javenese, Madurese, Toradjas, Balinese, etc. But thank God, we have our will to unity. We have our Pancha Sila. We practise the "Live and let live" principle, we are tolerant to each other. *Bhinneka Tunggal Ika—Unity in Diversity*—is the motto of the Indonesian State. We are one nation.

So, let this Asian-African Conference be a great success! Make the "Live and let live" principle and the "Unity in Diversity" motto the unifying force which brings us all together—to seek in friendly, uninhibited discussion, ways and means by which each of us can live his own life, and let others live their own lives, in their own way, in harmony, and in peace.

If we succeed in doing so, the effect of it for the freedom, independence and the welfare of man will be great on the world at large. The Light of Understanding has again been lit, the Pillar of Cooperation again erected. The likelihood of success of this Conference is proved already by the very presence of you all here today. It is for us to give it strength, to give it the power of inspiration—to spread its message all over the World.

Failure will mean that the Light of Understanding which seemed to have dawned in the East—the Light towards which looked all the great religions born here in the past—has again been obscured by an unfriendly cloud before man could benefit from its warm radiance.

But let us be full of hope and full of confidence. We have so much in common.

Relatively speaking, all of us gathered here today are neighbours. Almost all of us have ties of common experience, the experience of colonialism. Many of us have a common religion. Many of us have common cultural roots. Many of us, the so-called "underdeveloped" nations, have more or less similar economic problems, so that each can profit from the others' experience and help. And I think I may say that we all hold dear the ideals of national independence and freedom. Yes, we have so much in common. And yet we know so little of each other.

If this Conference succeeds in making the peoples of the East whose representatives are gathered here understand each other a little more, appreciate each other a little more, sympathise with each other's problems a little more—if those things happen, then this Conference, of course, will have been worthwhile, whatever else it may achieve. But I hope that this Conference will give *more* than understanding only and goodwill only—I hope that it will falsify and give the lie to the saying of one diplomat from far abroad: "We will turn this Asian-African Conference into an afternoon-tea meeting." I hope that it will give evidence of the fact that we Asian and African leaders understand that Asia and Africa can prosper only when they are united, and that even the safety of the World at large can not be safeguarded without a united Asia-Africa. I hope that this Conference will give *guidance* to mankind, will point out to mankind the way which it must take to attain safety and peace. I hope that it will give evidence that Asia and Africa have been reborn, nay, that a *New Asia* and a *New Africa* have been born!

Our task is first to seek an understanding of each other, and out of that understanding will come a greater appreciation of each other, and out of that appreciation will come collective action. Bear in mind the words of one of Asia's greatest sons: "To speak is easy. To act is hard. To understand is hardest. Once one understands, action is easy."

I have come to the end. Under God, may your deliberations be fruitful, and may your wisdom strike sparks of light from the hard flints of today's circumstances.

Let us not be bitter about the past, but let us keep our eyes firmly on the future. Let us remember that no blessing of God is so sweet as life and liberty. Let us remember that the stature of all mankind is diminished so long as nations or parts of nations are still unfree. Let us remember that the highest purpose of man is the liberation of man from his bonds of fear, his bonds of human degradation, his bonds of poverty—the liberation of man from the physical, spiritual and intellectual bonds which have for too long stunted the development of humanity's majority.

And let us remember, Sisters and Brothers, that for the sake of all that, we Asians and Africans must be united.

As president of the Republic of Indonesia, and on behalf of the eighty million people of Indonesia, I bid you welcome to this country. I declare the Asian-African Conference opened, and I pray that the Blessing of God will be upon it, and that its discussions will be profitable to the peoples of Asia and Africa, and to the peoples of all nations!

Bismillah!

God speed!

FURTHER RESOURCES

Anderson, Benedict. *Imagined Communities. Reflections on the Origin and Spread of Nationalism.* London: Verso, 1991.

Bhana, Surendra and Bridglal Pachai, eds. *A Documentary History of Indian South Africans.* Stanford: Hoover Institution Press, 1984.

Harlow, Barbara. *Resistance Literature.* New York: Methuen, 1987.

Lajpat Rai, Lala. *The Political Future of India.* New York: B. W. Huebsch, 1919.

Mandela, Nelson. *The Long Walk to Freedom: The Autobiography of Nelson Mandela.* New York: Little, Brown, 1994.

Mayo, Katherine. *Mother India.* New York: Blue Ribbon Books, 1927.

Morris, Bernard S. *Imperialism and Revolution: An Essay for Radicals.* Bloomington: Indiana University Press, 1985.

Pieterse, Jan P. Nederveen. *Empire and Emancipation: Power and Liberation on a World Scale.* London: Pluto, 1990.

Sachs, Wulf. *Black Anger: The Mind of an African Negro.* Boston: Little, Brown, 1947.

Singh, Hari. *Gandhi, Rowlatt Satyagraha, and British Imperialism: Emergence of Mass Movements in Punjab and Delhi.* Delhi: Indian Bibliographies Bureau, 1990.

Sithole, Ndabaningi. *African Nationalism.* Cape Town: Oxford University Press, 1959.

Taylor, Robert H. *The Idea of Freedom in Asia and Africa.* Stanford, CA: Stanford University Press, 2002.

Tran, Van Dinh. *Independence, Liberation, Revolution: An Approach to the Understanding of the Third World.* Norwood, NJ: Ablex, 1987.

Wilson, Keith M. *Imperialism and Nationalism in the Middle East: The Anglo-Egyptian Experience, 1882–1982.* New York: H. W. Wilson, 1983.

Films

Gandhi. VHS (2 videocassettes). Directed by Richard Attenborough. Burbank, CA: RCA/Columbia Pictures Home Video, 1983.

Motorcycle Diaries. DVD. Directed by Walter Salles. United States: Universal, 2005.

The Battle of Algiers. VHS. Directed by Gillo Pontecorvo. Rome, Italy: Igor Films, 1967.

The Longest Hatred: The History of Anti-Semitism. VHS (2 videocassettes). Directed by Rex Bloomstein. Princeton, NJ: Films for the Humanities and Sciences, 1991.

TIMELINE FOR PART VI

1945	Korea Partitioned
1945	United Nations Established
1945	**Ho Chi Minh, "Declaration of Independence of the Democratic Republic of Vietnam"**
1947	**Partition of India and Pakistan (Singh)**
1945–49	Indonesia Acquires Independence
1950–53	Korean War
1955	**South African Freedom Charter**
1955–1980s	Non-Aligned Movement
1957	Republic of Ghana Formed
1958	**Nasser, "The Arab Revolution"**
1960s	Civil Rights Movement in the United States
1962	**Algeria Votes for Independence (Women Voting)**
1963	Kenya Achieves Independence
1970	**Cabral, "National Liberation and Culture"**
1970s	Sandinista Liberation Front Fights the Somoza Regime in Nicaragua
1971	**Gutiérrez, *A Theology of Liberation***
1973	**American Indian Movement Occupies Wounded Knee (AIM)**
1974	**Kim Il-sung, "The Newly Emerging Forces Should Unite"**
1975	Angola Achieves Independence
1980	Rhodesia Becomes Republic of Zimbabwe
1988	**Dangarembga, *Nervous Conditions***
1990	**Namibia Achieves Independence (Mural)**
1990s	**Huaorani in Ecuador Struggle Against Oil Companies (Kane)**

Entries in bold indicate sources.

Part VI

Decolonization

INTRODUCTION

The end of the Second World War saw the beginnings of a decolonization process that has continued to this day, although its period of greatest intensity was between 1947 and 1970. This chapter considers both decolonization movements around the globe and the construction of new nations in the former colonies. It further considers anti-imperialist movements and activities in the era of decolonization that were shaped by continuing perceptions of imperialist control even in the absence of formal empire.

With the end of the Second World War, the Axis powers were stripped of their remaining colonies and, especially in Asia, new neocolonial structures sprung up in areas such as Korea and Taiwan, while territories that had been colonized by Allied powers before the war reverted to their control. The war had given colonial peoples in South and Southeast Asia, in particular, the opportunity to form anti-Japanese independence movements that they now redirected toward the French, Dutch, and British. We see an example of this in Ho Chi Minh's "Declaration of Independence." India, which had been on the path to self-government well before the outbreak of the Second World War, was the first to gain its independence, but as we see in the excerpt from Kushwant Singh's *Train to Pakistan*, independence came at a price, as colonial India divided itself into two nations built on religious foundations, and thousands were killed in the violent process of partition.

The formation of new states required the new leadership of each state to make a wide range of decisions. Just what shape should the new nations take? Should they be modeled on European nation-states? If so, how? To what extent should they draw upon indigenous political, cultural, and religious traditions? The need to construct new national cultures is discussed in the piece by Amílcar Cabral, who identified the African masses as the source of African culture. The construction of new national cultures is also represented by the excerpt from Zimbabwean novelist Tsitsi Dangarembga's *Nervous Conditions*, which explores the theme of independence through the metaphor of a young girl's coming of age. Even while participating in the creation of a modern, indigenous culture, writers such as Dangarembga often chose to write in the languages of their former colonial rulers.

With the construction of new states came the formation of new alliances, only some of which were based on the old imperial structures. Most of Britain's former colonies joined the Commonwealth of Nations, which continues to exist to this day, and most of France's former colonies joined the French Community, which, though short-lived, formed a basis for continuing close but informal relationships between France and its former empire. The Commonwealth of Nations, which was originally made up of Britain, Ireland, Canada, Australia, New Zealand, Newfoundland, and South Africa in the early twentieth century, expanded to include India, Pakistan, and Burma in 1947. Eventually, most of the newly independent nations in territories that had been controlled by Britain elsewhere in Asia, Africa, and the Caribbean joined the Commonwealth as well. Commonwealth members accept the British monarch as the head of the Commonwealth and benefit from membership in terms of favorable trade and immigration policies.

As the new states sought their own ways in a postcolonial world, however, they found global politics increasingly defined by cold war divisions. Many emerging nations thus realized that without clear-cut ties to either the United States or the Union of Soviet Socialist Republics, they needed to forge their own alliances in order to defend their economic and political interests. The Non-Aligned Movement, discussed in selections by Gamal Abdul Nasser and Kim Il-sung, was intended to provide a voice for these new states that would be loud enough and sufficiently unified to enable them to compete in a polarized world dominated by two superpowers. These nations hoped to avoid any sort of neocolonial paternalism or international domination. Even so, we can see in the differences between these two pieces that not all members of the Non-Aligned Movement were in complete accord on all matters.

Even though for most colonies the formal decolonization process had occurred by the 1970s, many indigenous residents of places not generally thought of as colonies have continued to fight for autonomy in ways that are similar to the earlier struggles for independence from colonial control. In South Africa, for example, non-whites continued to struggle against a system of apartheid—institutionalized racism—that severely limited their political, economic, and social freedoms. Nelson Mandela's "South African Freedom Charter" called for a South Africa with equal rights and opportunities for all of its citizens. In the Americas, indigenous peoples continue to struggle to regain control of land and resources their ancestors once controlled and to protect their native cultures and ways of life. Examples of such movements can be seen in the reading about the American Indian Movement and the story of Ecuador's Huaorani Indians. Liberation theology was also an ideology that aimed to defend the interests of the world's poor, many of whom are indigenous peoples, in the face of oppressive social, economic, and political policies and institutions that protect the interests of social and political oligarchies.

The age of high imperialism, though quite different than it was in the early part of the twentieth century, is not entirely over. Not all colonies have chosen to become independent, and some (mostly small colonies) have found it economically and politically beneficial to retain their positions within the now shrunken empires. Holland, Britain, France, and the United States all still have possessions with varying degrees of autonomy in the Caribbean, for example. Thus, the contemporary global landscape is complicated. With the collapse of the Soviet Union in the early 1990s, many countries have realigned themselves yet again. Former colonial empires and colonies find themselves confronted by an increasingly interconnected and complex political, economic, and environmental world.

▲

Declaration of Independence of the Democratic Republic of Viet-Nam

HO CHI MINH

On September 2, 1945, immediately following Japan's surrender in World War II, Ho Chi Minh (see Part II for biographical information) authored the Vietnamese Declaration of Independence that follows. French Indochina, like many parts of Southeast and East Asia, had been conquered by the Japanese in 1940 and became a Japanese colony until the end of the war in the late summer of 1945. Although the Vietnamese, Indonesians, Filipinos, and Malaysians were as eager to oust the Japanese as they had been their Western colonial masters, the Japanese defeat, albeit temporary, of the French, British, Dutch, and U.S. colonial powers in the region inspired Southeast Asian nationalists to believe that European and American colonialism could be overturned and that this task could be accomplished by Asian peoples. With the end of the war, Southeast Asian nationalists hoped to convince their colonial masters not to resume the colonial enterprise but instead to offer them independence.

The following piece demonstrates how colonial nationalists sought to draw upon the political rhetoric of the West and use it for their own purposes. It also offers insight into the conflicted impressions of both the French and the Japanese that some Vietnamese might have had in the wake of the Second World War.

▲

QUESTIONS

1. Why do you think Ho makes such explicit reference to the American "Declaration of Independence" and the French "Declaration on the Rights of Man and Citizen"?

2. Compare this piece to "Equality!" (Part II) written 23 years earlier. What common themes do the two pieces have?

3. Do you think a declaration of independence of this sort would be an effective method of achieving decolonization? For what audience was the declaration intended?

4. Based on this document, what sorts of perspectives on the French and the Japanese do you think the Vietnamese people might have had at the end of the Second World War?

Source: Ho Chi Minh. "Declaration of Independence of the Democratic Republic of Viet-Nam" (September 2, 1945). In Bernard Fall (Ed.), *Ho Chi Minh On Revolution: Selected Writings, 1920–1969*. New York: Frederick A. Praeger, 1967. Pp. 143–145. Copyright 2000 by University of the Pacific. Reproduced with permission of University Press of the Pacific in the format Textbook via Copyright Clearance Center.

Declaration of Independence of the Democratic Republic of Viet-Nam

(September 2, 1945)

All men are created equal; they are endowed by their Creator with certain unalienable Rights; among these are Life, Liberty, and the pursuit of Happiness.

This immortal statement was made in the Declaration of Independence of the United States of America in 1776. In a broader sense, this means: All the peoples on the earth are equal from birth, all the peoples have a right to live, to be happy and free.

The Declaration of the French Revolution made in 1791 on the Rights of Man and the Citizen also states: "All men are born free and with equal rights, and must always remain free and have equal rights."

Those are undeniable truths.

Nevertheless, for more than eighty years, the French imperialists, abusing the standard of Liberty, Equality, and Fraternity, have violated our Fatherland and oppressed our fellow citizens. They have acted contrary to the ideals of humanity and justice.

In the field of politics, they have deprived our people of every democratic liberty.

They have enforced inhuman laws; they have set up three distinct political regimes in the North, the Center, and the South of Viet-Nam in order to wreck our national unity and prevent our people from being united.

They have built more prisons than schools. They have mercilessly slain our patriots; they have drowned our uprisings in rivers of blood.

They have fettered public opinion; they have practiced obscurantism against our people.

To weaken our race they have forced us to use opium and alcohol.

In the field of economics, they have fleeced us to the backbone, impoverished our people and devastated our land.

They have robbed us of our rice fields, our mines, our forests, and our raw materials. They have monopolized the issuing of bank notes and the export trade.

They have invented numerous unjustifiable taxes and reduced our people, especially our peasantry, to a state of extreme poverty.

They have hampered the prospering of our national bourgeoisie; they have mercilessly exploited our workers.

In the autumn of 1940, when the Japanese fascists violated Indochina's territory to establish new bases in their fight against the Allies, the French imperialists went down on their bended knees and handed over our country to them.

Thus, from that date, our people were subjected to the double yoke of the French and the Japanese. Their sufferings and miseries increased. The result was that, from the end of last year to the beginning of this year, from Quang Tri Province to the North of Viet-Nam, more than two million of our fellow citizens died from starvation. On March 9 [1945], the French troops were disarmed by the Japanese. The French colonialists either fled or surrendered, showing that not only were they incapable of "protecting" us, but that, in the span of five years, they had twice sold our country to the Japanese.

On several occasions before March 9, the Viet Minh League urged the French to ally themselves with it against the Japanese. Instead of agreeing to this proposal, the French colonialists so intensified their terrorist activities against the Viet Minh members that before fleeing they massacred a great number of our political prisoners detained at Yen Bay and Cao Bang.

Notwithstanding all this, our fellow citizens have always manifested toward the French a tolerant and humane attitude. Even after the Japanese *Putsch* of March, 1945, the Viet Minh League helped many Frenchmen to cross the frontier, rescued some of them from Japanese jails, and protected French lives and property.

From the autumn of 1940, our country had in fact ceased to be a French colony and had become a Japanese possession.

After the Japanese had surrendered to the Allies, our whole people rose to regain our national sovereignty and to found the Democratic Republic of Viet-Nam.

The truth is that we have wrested our independence from the Japanese and not from the French.

The French have fled, the Japanese have capitulated, Emperor Bao Dai has abdicated. Our people have broken the chains which for nearly a century have fettered them and have won independence for the Fatherland. Our people at the same time have overthrown the monarchic regime that has reigned supreme for dozens of centuries. In its place has been established the present Democratic Republic.

For these reasons, we, members of the Provisional Government, representing the whole Vietnamese people, declare that from now on we break off all relations of a colonial character with France; we repeal all the international obligation that France has so far subscribed to on behalf of Viet-Nam, and we abolish all the special rights the French have unlawfully acquired in our Fatherland.

The whole Vietnamese people, animated by a common purpose, are determined to fight to the bitter end against any attempt by the French colonialists to reconquer their country.

We are convinced that the Allied nations, which at Teheran and San Francisco have acknowledged the principles of self-determination and equality of nations, will not refuse to acknowledge the independence of Viet-Nam.

A people who have courageously opposed French domination for more than eighty years, a people who have fought side by side with the Allies against the fascists during these last years, such a people must be free and independent.

For these reasons, we, members of the Provisional Government of the Democratic Republic of Viet-Nam, solemnly declare to the world that Viet-Nam has the right to be a free and independent country—and in fact it is so already. The entire Vietnamese people are determined to mobilize all their physical and mental strength, to sacrifice their lives and property in order to safeguard their independence and liberty.

⋏

Algerian Women Voting

On July 1, 1962, after more than seven years of fighting against French rule, the Algerian people went to the polls to vote in a referendum on independence. Of the total electorate of roughly 6.5 million people, nearly 6 million voted, and the voters included women. The outcome of the vote was an almost unanimous preference for independence. Two days later, on July 3, 1962, France's President de Gaulle declared Algeria independent.

⋏

QUESTIONS

1. What do you notice about the women who are voting in the photograph?

2. What does it tell you about Algeria that both women and men were voting on this matter?

Source: AP Wide World Photos.

▲

Train to Pakistan

KHUSHWANT SINGH

As the decolonization process got underway, the fragility of the colonies was exposed. In many cases, colonies had unified people and land in ways that overlooked important, pre-existing political, geographical, economic, social, and cultural differences. The British Raj provides an excellent example of this, and tensions that have their roots in the colonial experience are still being played out between India and Pakistan in places like Kashmir. India was a multicultural colony that united people with varied religious beliefs under a single political system. As calls for Indian independence took place over the course of the first four decades of the twentieth century, it became clear that India's Muslim population, in particular, was concerned about its future in a Hindu-controlled independent India. In the early 1940s, partition of India into Hindu and Muslim states was proposed as the solution to India's religious situation, and in 1947 votes on partition were held in the legislative assemblies of India's provinces. Several representative bodies voted in favor of the move. As a result, East and West Pakistan (now Bangladesh and Pakistan) were formed as a geographically-split Muslim state. In the last weeks before independence, roughly eight million refugees migrated between India and Pakistan, fearing religious reprisals if they remained in their traditional homes. As it was, roughly 200,000 refugees died in the migration.

Train to Pakistan, by Khushwant Singh, himself a Sikh, offers a fictional representation of the partition. It tells the tale of a village on the newly-formed border between India and Pakistan. The arrival of a ghost train filled with the corpses of murdered refugees brings religious war to this village, where Sikhs and Muslims had earlier lived in harmony. The following passage describes the moment at which the villagers begin to identify themselves with their larger religious groups more than with the village.

▲

QUESTIONS

1. What appears to be more important to the characters in this story, religious identity or village identity? How do they reconcile the two?

2. How might identity issues such as the ones portrayed in this story affect independence movements?

[. . .] The head constable's visit had divided Mano Majra into two halves as neatly as a knife cuts through a pat of butter.

Muslims sat and moped in their houses. Rumors of atrocities committed by Sikhs on Muslims in Patiala, Ambala and Kapurthala, which they had heard and dismissed, came back to their minds. They had heard of gentlewomen having their veils taken off, being stripped and marched down crowded streets to be raped in the market place. Many had eluded their would-be ravishers by killing themselves. They had heard of mosques being desecrated by the slaughter of pigs on the premises, and of copies of the holy Koran being torn up by infidels. Quite suddenly every Sikh in Mano Majra became a stranger with an evil intent. His long hair and beard appeared barbarous, his kirpan menacingly anti-Muslim. For the first time, the name Pakistan came to mean something to them—a haven of refuge where there were no Sikhs.

The Sikhs were sullen and angry. "Never trust a Mussulman," they said. The last Guru had warned them that Muslims had no loyalties. He was right. All through the Muslim period of Indian history, sons had imprisoned or killed their own fathers and brothers had blinded brothers to get the throne. And what had they done to the Sikhs? Executed two of their Gurus, assassinated another and butchered his infant children; hundreds of thousands had been put to the sword for no other offense than refusing to accept Islam; their temples had been desecrated by the slaughter of kine; the holy Granth had been torn to bits. And Muslims were never ones to respect women. Sikh refugees had told of women jumping into wells and burning themselves rather than fall into the hands of Muslims. Those who did not commit suicide were paraded naked in the streets, raped in public, and then murdered. Now a trainload of Sikhs massacred by Muslims had been cremated in Mano Majra. Hindus and Sikhs were fleeing from their homes in Pakistan and having to find shelter in Mano Majra. Then there was the murder of Ram Lal. No one knew who had killed him, but everyone knew Ram Lal was a Hindu; Sultana and his gang were Muslims and had fled to Pakistan. An unknown character—without turban or beard—had been loitering about the village. These were reasons enough to be angry with someone. So they decided to be angry with the Muslims; Muslims were basely ungrateful. Logic was never a strong point with Sikhs; when they were roused, logic did not matter at all.

It was a gloomy night. The breeze that had swept away the clouds blew them back again. At first they came in fleecy strands of white. The moon wiped them off its face. Then they came in large billows, blotted out the moonlight and turned the sky a dull gray. The moon fought its way through and occasionally patches of the plain sparkled like silver. Later, clouds came in monstrous black formations and spread across the sky. Then without any lightning or thunder it began to rain.

A group of Sikh peasants gathered together in the house of the lambardar. They sat in a circle around a hurricane lantern—some on a charpoy, others on the floor. Meet Singh was amongst them.

For a long time nobody said anything apart from repeating, "God is punishing us for our sins."

"Yes, God is punishing us for our sins."

"There is a lot of *zulum* in Pakistan."

"That is because He wants to punish us for our sins. Bad acts yield a bitter harvest."

Then one of the younger men spoke. "What have we done to deserve this? We have looked upon the Muslims as our brothers and sisters. Why should they send somebody to spy on us?"

"You mean Iqbal?" Meet Singh said. "I had quite a long conversation with him. He had an iron bangle on his wrist like all of us Sikhs and told me that his mother had wanted him to wear it, so he wore it. He is a shaven Sikh. He does not smoke. And he came the day after the moneylender's murder."

"Bhai, you get taken in easily," replied the same youth. "Does it hurt a Mussulman to wear an iron bangle or not smoke for a day—particularly if he has some important work to do?"

"I may be a simple bhai," protested Meet Singh warmly, "but I do know as well as you that the babu had nothing to do with the murder; he would not have been in the village afterwards if he had. That any fathead would understand."

The youth felt a little abashed.

"Besides that," continued Meet Singh more confidently, "they had already arrested Malli for the dacoity . . ."

"How do you know what they had arrested Malli for?" interrupted the youth triumphantly.

"Yes, how do you know what the police know? They have released Malli. Have you ever known them to release murderers without a trial and acquittal?" asked some others.

"Bhai, you always talk without reason."

"Accha, if you are the ones with all the reason, tell me who threw the packet of bangles into Jugga's house."

"How should we know?" answered a chorus.

"I will tell you. It was Jugga's enemy Malli. You all know they had fallen out. Who else would dare insult Jugga except he?"

No one answered the question. Meet Singh went on aggressively to drive his point home. "And all this about Sultana, Sultana! What has that to do with the dacoity?"

"Yes, Bhaiji, you may be right," said another youth. "But Lala is dead: why bother about him? The police will do that. Let Jugga, Malli and Sultana settle their quarrels. As for the babu, for all we care he can sleep with his mother. Our problem is: what are we to do with all these pigs we have with us? They have been eating our salt for generations and see what they have done! We have treated them like our own brothers. They have behaved like snakes."

The temperature of the meeting went up suddenly. Meet Singh spoke angrily.

"What have they done to you? Have they ousted you from your lands or occupied your houses? Have they seduced your womenfolk? Tell me, what have they done?"

"Ask the refugees what they have done to them," answered the truculent youth who had started the argument. "You mean to tell us that they are lying when they say that gurdwaras have been burned and people massacred?"

"I was only talking of Mano Majra. What have our tenants done?"

"They are Muslims."

Meet Singh shrugged his shoulders.

The lambardar felt it was up to him to settle the argument.

"What had to happen has happened," he said wisely. "We have to decide what we are to do now. These refugees who have turned up at the temple may do something which will bring a bad name on the village."

The reference to "something" changed the mood of the meeting. How could outsiders dare to do "something" to their fellow villagers? Here was another stumbling block to logic. Group loyalty was above reason. The youth who had referred to Muslims as pigs spoke haughtily: "We would like to see somebody raise his little finger against our tenants while we live!"

The lambardar snubbed him. "You are a hotheaded one. Sometimes you want to kill Muslims. Sometimes you want to kill refugees. We say something and you drag the talk to something else."

"All right, all right, Lambardara," retorted the young man, "if you are all that clever, you say something."

"Listen, brothers," said the lambardar lowering his voice. "This is no time to lose tempers. Nobody here wants to kill anyone. But who knows the intentions of other people? Today we have forty or fifty refugees, who by the grace of the Guru are a peaceful lot and they only talk. Tomorrow we may get others who may have lost their mothers or sisters. Are we going to tell them: 'do not come to this village'? And if they do come, will we let them wreak vengeance on our tenants?"

"You have said something worth a hundred thousand rupees," said an old man. "We should think about it."

The peasants thought about their problem. They could not refuse shelter to refugees: hospitality was not a pastime but a sacred duty when those who sought it were homeless. Could they ask their Muslims to go? Quite emphatically not! Loyalty to a fellow villager was above all other considerations. Despite the words they had used, no one had the nerve to suggest throwing them out, even in a purely Sikh gathering. The mood of the assembly changed from anger to bewilderment.

After some time the lambardar spoke.

"All Muslims of the neighboring villages have been evacuated and taken to the refugee camp near Chundunnugger. Some have already gone away to Pakistan. Others have been sent to the bigger camp at Jullundur."

"Yes," added another. "Kapoora and Gujjoo Matta were evacuated last week. Mano Majra is the only place left where there are Muslims. What I would like to know is how these people asked their fellow villagers to leave. We could never say anything like that to our tenants, any more than we could tell our sons to get out of our homes. Is there anyone here who could say to the Muslims, 'Brothers, you should go away from Mano Majra'?"

Before anyone could answer another villager came in and stood on the threshold. Everyone turned round to see, but they could not recognize him in the dim lamplight.

"Who is it?" asked the lambardar, shading his eyes from the lamp. "Come in."

Imam Baksh came in. Two others followed him. They also were Muslims.

"Salaam, Chacha Imam Baksh. Salaam Khair Dina. Salaam, salaam."

"Sat Sri Akal, Lambardara. Sat Sri Akal," answered the Muslims.

People made room for them and waited for Imam Baksh to begin.

Imam Baksh combed his beard with his fingers.

"Well, brothers, what is your decision about us?" he asked quietly.

There was an awkward silence. Everyone looked at the lambardar.

"Why ask us?" answered the lambardar. "This is your village as much as ours."

"You have heard what is being said! All the neighboring villages have been evacuated. Only we are left. If you want us to go too, we will go."

Meet Singh began to sniff. He felt it was not for him to speak. He had said his bit. Besides, he was only a priest who lived on what the villagers gave him. One of the younger men spoke.

"It is like this, Uncle Imam Baksh. As long as we are here nobody will dare to touch you. We die first and then you can look after yourselves."

"Yes," added another warmly, "we first, then you. If anyone raises his eyebrows at you we will rape his mother."

"Mother, sister, and daughter," added the others.

Imam Baksh wiped a tear from his eyes and blew his nose in the hem of his shirt.

"What have we to do with Pakistan? We were born here. So were our ancestors. We have lived amongst you as brothers." Imam Baksh broke down. Meet Singh clasped him in his arms and began to sob. Several of the people started crying quietly and blowing their noses.

The lambardar spoke: "Yes, you are our brothers. As far as we are concerned, you and your children and your grandchildren can live here as long as you like. If anyone speaks rudely to you, your wives or your children, it will be us first and our wives and children before a single hair of your heads is touched. But Chacha, we are so few and the strangers coming from Pakistan are coming in thousands. Who will be responsible for what they do?"

"Yes," agreed the others, "as far as we are concerned you are all right, but what about these refugees?"

"I have heard that some villages were surrounded by mobs many thousands strong, all armed with guns and spears. There was no question of resistance."

"We are not afraid of mobs," replied another quickly. "Let them come! We will give them such a beating they will not dare to look at Mano Majra again."

Nobody took notice of the challenger; the boast sounded too hollow to be taken seriously. Imam Baksh blew his nose again. "What do you advise us to do then, brothers?" he asked, choking with emotion.

"Uncle," said the lambardar in a heavy voice, "it is very hard for me to say, but seeing the sort of time we live in, I would advise you to go to the refugee camp while this trouble is on. You lock your houses with your belongings. We will look after your cattle till you come back."

The lambardar's advice created a tense stillness. Villagers held their breath for fear of being heard. The lambardar himself felt that he ought to say something quickly to dispel the effect of his words.

"Until yesterday," he began again loudly, "in case of trouble we could have helped you to cross the river by the ford. Now it has been raining for two days; the river has risen. The only crossings are by trains and road bridges—you know what is happening there! It is for your own safety that I advise you to take shelter in the camp for a few days, and then you can come back. As far as we are concerned," he repeated warmly, "if you decide to stay on, you are most welcome to do so. We will defend you with our lives."

No one had any doubts about the import of the lambardar's words. They sat with their heads bowed till Imam Baksh stood up.

"All right," he said solemnly, "if we have to go, we better pack up our bedding and belongings. It will take us more than one night to clear out of homes it has taken our fathers and grandfathers hundreds of years to make."

The lambardar felt a strong sense of guilt and was overcome with emotion. He got up and embraced Imam Baksh and started to cry loudly. Sikh and Muslim villagers fell into each other's arms and wept like children. Imam Baksh gently got out of the lambardar's embrace. "There is no need to cry," he said between sobs. "This is the way of the world . . . ."

⋀

The Newly-Emerging Forces Should Unite Under the Banner of Independence Against Imperialism

Kim Il-sung

The fight against imperialism continued to motivate political leaders around the world even after formal decolonization had taken place, and alliances were formed on the basis of common colonial and anticolonial experiences. Korea was formally decolonized at the end of the Second World War, in the autumn of 1945, when a defeated Japan was stripped of its colonies. However, it was rapidly inserted into a neocolonial structure when it was divided at the 38th parallel and the Soviet Union (USSR) took control of the North and the United States began to control the South. In spite of a bloody war in the early 1950s launched by North Korea in a bid to reunite the entire nation, Korea remains divided, and anti-imperialist rhetoric continues to be employed by North Korean leaders who still blame Western imperialist interests as the major obstacle to the reunification of Korea under their leadership.

Kim Il-sung, North Korea's "Great Leader," was installed by the USSR soon after the end of the Second World War on the basis of communist sympathies and his leadership of an anti-Japanese guerilla resistance movement before and during the war. Although closely allied with the USSR, he nonetheless sought an active role in the Non-Aligned Movement of third world countries in the 1970s (see Speech at the Opening of the Asian-African Conference, Bandung, Indonesia in Part V). The speech that follows was delivered at a mass rally by Kim to welcome Zaire's President Mobutu to Pyongyang on December 15, 1974. It is similar to many other speeches and essays that he delivered and published around the world, especially in Latin America and Africa, as North Korea sought to develop solidarity with nonaligned countries. In this speech, Kim explores the themes of decolonization and independence and discusses ways in which both Zaire and North Korea were fighting to overcome imperialism and its residual effects.

⋀

QUESTIONS

1. Why was opposition to imperialism so important to Kim Il-sung even after Korea became independent from Japan in 1945?

2. Why might countries like Zaire and North Korea have chosen to become allies in the 1970s?

3. What type of language does Kim use in this speech?

Source: Kim Il-sung. "The Newly-Emerging Forces Should Unite Under the Banner of Independence Against Imperialism." *The Non-Alignment Movement is a Mighty Anti-Imperialist Revolutionary Force of our Times*. Pyongyang: Foreign Languages Publishing House, 1976. Pp. 233–36.

[. . .] The visit of His Excellency Mr. President to our country demonstrates that friendly relations between the Korean and Zairese peoples have entered a new stage of development; it clearly shows that solidarity between the peoples of Korea and Africa and the unity of the newly-emerging forces are growing in strength day by day.

This mass rally is an expression of our people's high respect for Your Excellency Mr. President and a manifestation of the unbreakable friendship and solidarity between the two peoples.

The peoples of Korea and Zaire have formed a firm bond of friendship on the basis of their common stand of opposing imperialism, colonialism and racism and maintaining independence.

The Korean people are very happy to have such a close friend as the Zairese people in the heart of Africa.

Zaire today is a dignified, sovereign and independent state which is vigorously advancing along the road of a new life under the correct leadership of His Excellency President Mobutu Sese Seko, upholding the banner of independence.

Through our meeting with His Excellency Mr. President this time, we have acquainted ourselves better with the grim history of Zaire, its brilliant successes in the struggle to build a new society after the victory of the revolution and the greater prospects of its future development.

Even after its liberation in 1960 Zaire suffered from temporary division and confusion for five years. This was due entirely to the uninterrupted criminal machinations of modern colonialism.

His Excellency President Mobutu Sese Seko opened up a new era of dynamic advance in the history of the Zairese people by overcoming the difficulties in their way and achieving the stability and unification of the whole country.

Today the Zairese Government is developing the national economy and national culture at a fast rate to suit the national peculiarities by "Zairi-anizing" everything through various progressive social and political reforms.

The Zairese people have become the owner of the resources of their country thanks to the "Zairianization" measure taken by the Zairese Government in November 1973.

Newly independent nations which have freed themselves from colonial rule must adhere to political independence, build an independent national economy and arm and unite the entire people with the ideas of their leader, if they are to defend and consolidate their independence already won.

The people of Zaire are now equipped with the "authenticite" idea of their valiant leader His Excellency President Mobutu Sese Seko and are firmly rallied around the People's Movement of the Revolution.

We fully support the struggle of the Zairese people who are advancing towards independence and self-support.

On the international scene, too, the prestige of the Republic of Zaire is growing as the days go by because of the unique line and policies it pursues.

Following a policy of non-alignment in its external relations, the Republic of Zaire is actively struggling against imperialism, colonialism, old and new, and racism and striving to eliminate all forms of aggression and interference, subjugation and inequality and is making a great contribution to realizing the complete liberation and unity of Africa and cementing the unity of the newly-emerging forces.

The reality of Zaire vividly shows that a people who have an excellent leader and party and rise to build a new life in firm unity, can display great force.

The Korean people warmly congratulate the friendly Zairese people on the achievements they have made in the struggle to defend the revolutionary gains and increase the might of the country as a whole under the correct guidance of their esteemed leader His Excellency President Mobutu Sese Seko and sincerely wish them greater successes in their future struggle to build a new, prosperous Zaire.

The process of revolutionary change now taking place in the land of Zaire, a striking example of the process of great regeneration of Africa, clearly reflects the main trend of development in our time whereby many countries of the world are advancing along the path of independence.

We have experienced through our own actual life that in order to defend national independence and develop rapidly, the newly independent nations must cling hard to an independent spirit and, in particular, most important of all is to emancipate the people from the shackles of obsolete ideas.

Our people had to build a new life, removing the evil aftermath of colonial rule and healing the severe wounds caused by the three-year war, under the difficult conditions in which our country remained artificially divided owing to the occupation of South Korea by US imperialism, and they stood directly opposed to imperialism.

In a short space of time our Party has been able to turn our once backward country into an advanced socialist state, independent in politics, self-supporting in the economy and self-defensive in national defence, by firmly arming the popular masses with the Juche [self-reliance] idea and vigorously pushing ahead with the revolution and construction on the principle of self-reliance.

In our struggle to establish Juche, we have rooted out flunkeyism, national nihilism and dogmatism from the minds of the people and further heightened their national pride and consciousness of independence and registered great successes in the revolution and construction.

Although the world is swept by a very serious economic upheaval, our people are now developing the whole national economy at a high rate without interruption, immune to the impact of that upheaval, because they have laid the solid foundations of an independent national economy.

This year, too, we have not only ensured a high rate of industrial growth but also reaped an unprecedentedly bumper crop in agriculture.

All this is a victory for our Party's independent line, and signifies that the blockade policy of the imperialists to isolate and suffocate our country has gone totally bankrupt both politically and economically.

The practical experience in Korea, Zaire and many other newly independent states shows that the time has come when the formerly oppressed and humiliated peoples are fully able to create a new life and build prosperous, sovereign and independent states with their own efforts. [. . .]

⋏

The Arab Revolution

GAMAL ABDUL NASSER

Gamal Abdul Nasser was born in Alexandria, Egypt, in 1918. He was brought up and edu-cated in Cairo. He joined the army, which eventually propelled him into politics. Later, he became president of Egypt and a strong advocate for African and Asian independence movements.

By the end of the Second World War, the process of decolonization of Asian and African countries had begun. This produced a number of new, independent national states. In Egypt, the British had installed King Fuad in the hope of maintaining control over the Suez Canal. In 1952, a group of disaffected army officers (the "free officers"), led by the at that time Lieutenant Colonel Nasser, overthrew Fuad. Nasser evolved into a charismatic leader not only of Egypt but of the Arab world, promoting and implementing an "Arab Revolution," a theme that he empha-sized throughout his political career and the subject of this speech.

Nasser also helped to establish the Non-Aligned Movement of developing countries in September 1961 and continued to be a leading force in that movement until his death in 1970.

⋏

QUESTIONS

1. Why does Nasser identify himself with the Arab world?
2. According to Nasser, how has Arab solidarity expressed itself in political conflicts?

[. . .] The revolution in Egypt was launched in 1952 and we all proclaimed as I said in "The Phi-losophy of the Revolution" that it had a vital scope that included the whole Arab area. We felt with you in your struggle—you the people of this part of the Arab land, despite imperialistic pressure and domination, and despite the forced seclusion enforced on us and their attempts to make us deny our Arabism through establishing in Egypt a coun-try fastly attached to its Pharaonic origins. When you struggled for your freedom, the whole of Egypt was moved to the core by your slogans and your sentiments. When Syria rose to fight French imperialism and demanded its freedom and inde-pendence, Egypt was swept with demonstrations

in support of the uprising in Syria. Each individ-ual here felt he had brethren elsewhere from whom he was severed, brethren who fought and strug-gled for freedom. Egyptian poets and singers wrote and sang in support of Syria's struggle. When Lebanon rose to fight France and bring French occupation to an end, Egypt was roughly shaken for the bond between us is a thing of the heart. However hard the imperialist powers—with their agents and stooges—might try to divide us and raise obstacles between us, they will never succeed in destroying our unity, solidarity and brotherli-ness which God established and firmly engraved in your hearts. This, my dear brethren, is the true Arab revolution which depends solely on the Arab

Source: Gamal Abdul Nasser. "The Arab Revolution." *President Gamal Abdul Nasser's Speeches and Press-Interviews* (March 9, 1958). Cairo: United Arab Republic Information Department, 1958. Pp. 96–98.

peoples in every Arab country. This is the revolution which believed in you—you the Arab peoples in every Arab country as well as elsewhere. This is the revolution which refused to join any foreign or imperialist alliances to achieve its freedom, for freedom stands in open contradiction to imperialism which can only imply slavery. This is the revolution which depended first on God and then on the Arab peoples everywhere. It rose to fight Zionism, to fight imperialism and its agents.

This is the revolution we can pride ourselves on and say that it grew up in our soil, from our blood and from our hearts, the revolution that expressed Arab feelings and aspirations. This is the revolution which has suffered no contamination because it firmly believed in God and in the Arab people everywhere. These beliefs it considered were the power which could defeat the navies and land forces of the Big Powers. You remember, my brethren, how at Port-Said, when we were besieged by the Big Powers, you rose from Syria, Lebanon and practically every Arab country to support your brethren in Egypt. Our unity of hearts succeeded in defeating their naval forces, in destroying the Big Powers and causing them to slide down to rank among second class powers. God willing our unity will never suffer any weakness. No power in the world can drive us apart. They may succeed in raising artificial partitions or boundaries, they may succeed in winning over some agents in the area, but they cannot reach those hearts who firmly believed in their right to freedom and independence, those hearts that believed that their unity was the only way to strength. They may succeed in having agents in the Arab fatherland but they will never succeed in suppressing the feelings of the Arab peoples.

Voices from Wounded Knee, 1973

An AIM Leader

The American Indian Movement (AIM) was founded in 1968 in Minneapolis, Minnesota, as a group dedicated to protecting the rights of urban Native Americans, but it soon grew into a movement to promote the rights of all Native Americans. AIM was involved in a number of high-profile protest actions in the late 1960s and early 1970s, including the occupation of Alcatraz Island from 1967 to 1971, the 1972 takeover of the headquarters of the Bureau of Indian Affairs (BIA), and the 1973 occupation of Wounded Knee. The general intention of all of these acts was to draw attention to the impoverishment and ill treatment of Native Americans by the federal government and to demand the return of lands and resources to Native Americans.

The following statement comes from a collection of interviews and documents about the occupation of Wounded Knee. It was made by one of AIM's leaders not long after the siege ended.

QUESTIONS

1. In what ways is the opposition to the United States government described in this statement similar to the opposition to colonial powers that we see in other readings in this part?

2. In what ways does this AIM leader suggest that Native Americans have been oppressed by the American government?

3. Where did AIM find its largest bases of support? Why?

Our people are sovereign, each tribe unto itself, and have been like that for thousands of years. We fought against white people and were conquered. And we've had to try a system of government that's foreign to us. We've tried this government and it's failed. It's degraded our people and caused the ills that have fallen upon us. So we can see that the only way to regain what we've lost, regain our relationship with the Mother Earth, is to go back to the system of government that's done so well for us for so long.

Sovereignty means the ability to guide our own lives, the ability to even make mistakes if that's what it takes. We know the way we want to live, and how we want to survive. We know how to live with the world, instead of on it, or off it, or against it. What it all boils down to is how we can make things better for our people.

Standard of living and economic conditions are a problem for Indian people only in so far as we are related to the white economic system. Once we're divorced from that, our problem won't be to upgrade our standard of living. We want to have, of course, enough food to eat, and we want our tribes to be able to live without starving.

We're concerned with having our people free to live on their land and not have a constant pressure from the U.S. Government to move them off

Source: Robert Anderson, Joanna Brown, Jonny Lerner, and Barbara Lou Shafer. Akwesasne Notes. *Voices From Wounded Knee, 1973: In the Words of the Participants.* Akwesasne Notes: Mohawk Nation, 1974. Pp. 246–47. Reprinted by permission of Indian Time/Akwesasne Notes.

it. We see this as the Government's main aim in Indian relations—to finally take all our land and have Indian people become homogenized into American society and not have any identity of our own. That is our greatest danger, and that is the real genocide against our people. They kill off the dissident ones—what they used to call "hostile" ones, now the "militant" ones—get rid of them physically. And then they get rid of the rest of our people by trying to get them to become brown white people.

The U.S. Government has pretty well kept us as a race of paupers by making us dependent on their economic system. The BIA [Bureau of Indian Affairs] has complete control of the economy of the reservation, and the monies generated by the reservation go into white hands. The Government in return gives Indian people welfare, and commodities—surplus food—to keep them alive.

That's *their* plan. *Our* plan is to take the white ranchers and leasers off of all our land and then tell the Government we don't need their welfare and we don't need any of their services.

At first, when we close a reservation, we're going to have to live like we lived at Wounded Knee. We're going to have to be killing them cattle to eat, and live on beans and stuff for a while. And we're just going to have to toughen up until we can get all our shit straight. We drive the white ranchers out, and our people no longer get those lease payments that they depend on. But those lease payments are the very things that's held them in bondage for so damned long. Now they might get $1000 a year for a family of 20 people. That's not enough to live on, but it's been enough to subsist on if they also get those rations from the Government. They'll just have to do without that $1000 and those rations. But eventually, we'll have control of our economy. On Pine Ridge Reservation, the white ranchers generate over $12 million a year. If that money were controlled by Indian people, it would far exceed the welfare roll for this reservation.

We also have to make it where no person owns the land any more. We don't believe in ownership of land because the land is part of us—you can't own each other and you can't own land. Once we have control of a reservation and its borders, you can live anywhere you want. The land that isn't lived on will belong to all the people and the benefits derived from that will be given to all the people on the reservation.

. . . You know, our people believe very much in the paths of life, that there are different paths to follow. We talk about the path of peace—and how sometimes you have to go the path of war because there's nowhere else to go and still remain as an Indian. Our people have wanted to do that for a long time.

Our revolution never ended. A lot of the old people on the reservations remember the time when they bore arms against white people. This has been passed right down to their children and now their grandchildren. Wherever the American Indian Movement has gone we've found our widest support amongst the old people and people who live traditional lives on the reservations. Where we don't have support is among those who got over-educated in white schools, living in the cities, working for the BIA—but that's a minority of Indian people. So I don't have to make revolution. The revolution is going on in the minds of the people.

Our people have to get organized, particularly our young people—and then they have to be taught exactly how it is. Because many of them are growing up in a white society, white education, and you know, their outlook is a white outlook. They have to be taught by our traditional people and our medicine men what it is to be Indian, and then all Indian people have to gather in that kind of unity and that kind of force before we can have other people with us. [. . .]

⬣

National Liberation and Culture

AMÍLCAR CABRAL

Amílcar Cabral (1924–73) was an architect and undisputed leader of the African Party for the Independence of Cape Verde and Guinea (PAIGC) and the national liberation movement in Guinea Bissau (formerly Portuguese Guinea). Born in 1924, Cabral studied agronomy and in the 1950s was employed in that capacity in rural areas of Portuguese Guinea for the Portuguese Civil Service. His position as an agronomist enabled him to keep in touch with the local people; he traveled to virtually every village in the country. With other civil servants, Cabral founded the PAIGC in 1956, and in 1963 he started a full-blown military campaign to overthrow Portuguese colonial rule.

The following document, "National Liberation and Culture," is a speech Cabral delivered at Syracuse University in the United States in 1970. It provides an insight into the importance of national culture in the liberation struggle. Cabral stressed the importance of contemporary relations within indigenous Guinean society for the purposes of transformation and its mechanics. Having focused its activities among the minuscule urban working class, the PAIGC realized the limited scope of its organizational membership and influence. Despite the limited impression that Portuguese colonialism had made upon Guinean culture and society, the colonial authorities maintained enough ideological and physical control in the cities to nearly destroy the PAIGC. It was outside the urban centers and in the countryside of Guinea that Cabral found more support and a people less influenced by colonial culture and ideology. For Cabral, this "African culture" was the people's genuine collective identity, which could serve as a base of resistance in an anticolonial struggle.

⬣

QUESTIONS

1. What value does Cabral see in culture as a factor of resistance to foreign domination?
2. What does Cabral say about assimilation versus resistance in Africa?

A Cruel Dilemma for Colonialism: Elimination or Assimilation?

When Goebbels, the brain behind Nazi propaganda, heard the word 'culture', he reached for his pistol. This shows that the Nazis—who were and are the most tragic expression of imperialism and of its thirst for domination—even if they were all degenerates like Hitler, had a clear idea of the value of culture as a factor of resistance to foreign domination.

History teaches us that, in certain circumstances, it is very easy for the foreigner to impose

Source: Amílcar Cabral, "National Liberation and Culture." In *Unity and Struggle.* New York and London: Monthly Review Press, 1979. Pp. 139–43. Copyright © 1979. Reprinted by permission of Monthly Review Press.

his domination on a people. But it likewise teaches us that, whatever the material aspects of this domination, it can be maintained only by the permanent and organized repression of the cultural life of the people concerned. Implantation of domination can be ensured definitively only by physical elimination of a significant part of the dominated population.

In fact, to take up arms to dominate a people is, above all, to take up arms to destroy, or at least to neutralize and to paralyse their cultural life. For as long as part of that people can have a cultural life, foreign domination cannot be sure of its perpetuation. At a given moment, depending on internal and external factors determining the evolution of the society in question, cultural resistance (indestructible) may take on new (political, economic and armed) forms, in order fully to contest foreign domination.

The ideal for foreign domination, whether imperialist or not, lies in this alternative: either to eliminate practically all the population of the dominated country, thereby excluding the possibilities of a cultural resistance; or to succeed in imposing itself without damage to the culture of the dominated people, that is, to harmonize economic and political domination of these people with their cultural personality.

The first hypothesis implies genocide of the indigenous population and creates a void which empties foreign domination of its content and its object: the dominated people. The second hypothesis has not, until now, been confirmed by history. The broad experience of mankind enables us to postulate that it has no practical viability: it is not possible to harmonize the economic and political domination of a people, whatever the degree of their social development, with the preservation of their cultural personality.

In order to escape this alternative—which might be called the *dilemma of cultural resistance*—imperialist colonial domination has tried to create theories which, in fact, are only crude formulations of racism, and which, in practice, are translated into a permanent state of siege for the aboriginal populations, on the basis of racist dictatorship (or democracy).

This, for example, is the case with the supposed theory of progressive *assimilation* of native populations, which is no more than a more or less violent attempt to deny the culture of people in question. The unmistakable failure of this 'theory', put into practice by several colonial powers, including Portugal, is the most evident proof of its non-viability, if not of its inhuman character. It reaches the highest degree of absurdity in the Portuguese case, where Salazar [Portuguese leader] asserts that *Africa does not exist*.

This is likewise the case with the supposed theory of *apartheid*, created, applied and developed on the basis of economic and political domination of the people of southern Africa by a racist minority, with all the crimes against humanity that this entails. The practice of *apartheid* takes the form of unrestrained exploitation of the labour force of the African masses, incarcerated and cynically repressed in the largest concentration camp mankind has ever known.

National Liberation, an Act of Culture

These examples give a measure to the drama of foreign domination in the face of the cultural reality of the dominated people. They also show the close, dependent and reciprocal connexion existing between the *cultural factor* and the *economic* (and political) *factor* in the behaviour of human societies. In fact, at every moment of the life of a society (open or closed), culture is the result, with more or less awakened consciousness, of economic and political activities, the more or less dynamic expression of the type of relations prevailing within that society, on the one hand between man (considered individually or collectively) and nature, and, on the other hand, among individuals, groups of individuals, social strata or classes.

The value of culture as an element of resistance to foreign domination lies in the fact that culture is the vigorous manifestation, on the ideological or idealist level, of the material and historical reality of the society that is dominated or to be dominated. Culture is simultaneously the fruit of a people's history and a determinant of history, by the positive or negative influence it exerts on the evolution of relations between man and his environment and among men or human groups within a society, as well as between different societies. Ignorance of this fact might explain the failure of several attempts at foreign domination as well as the failure of some national liberation movements.

Let us examine what *national liberation* is. We shall consider this phenomenon of history in its contemporary context, that is national liberation in the face of imperialist domination. The latter is, as we know, distinct both in form and content from preceding types of foreign domination (tribal, military-aristocratic, feudal and capitalist domination in the age of free competition).

The principal characteristic, common to every kind of imperialist domination, is the denial of the historical process of the dominated people by means of violent usurpation of the freedom of the process of development of the productive forces. Now, in a given society, the level of development of the productive forces and the system of social utilization of these forces (system of ownership) determine the *mode of production.* In our view, the mode of production, whose contradictions are manifested with more or less intensity through class struggle, is the principal factor in the history of any human whole, and the level of productive forces is the true and permanent motive force of history.

For every society, for every human group considered as a dynamic whole, the level of the productive forces indicates the status reached by the society and each of its components in the face of nature, its capacity to act or react consciously in relation to nature. It indicates and conditions the type of material relations (expressed objectively or subjectively) existing between man and his environment.

The mode of production, which at every stage of history represents the result of the ceaseless search for a dynamic equilibrium between the level of productive forces and the system of social utilization of these forces, indicates the status reached by a given society and each of its components before itself and before history. In addition, it indicates and conditions the type of material relations (expressed objectively or subjectively) existing between the various elements or groups which constitute the society in question: relations and types of relations between man and nature, between man and his environment; relations and types of relations between the individual or collective components of a society. To speak about this is to speak of history but it is likewise to speak of culture.

Culture, whatever the ideological or idealist characteristics of its expression, is thus an essential element of the history of a people. Culture is, perhaps, the resultant of this history just as the flower is the resultant of a plant. Like history, or because it is history, culture has as its material base the level of the productive forces and the mode of production. Culture plunges its roots into the humus of the material reality of the environment in which it develops, and it reflects the organic nature of the society, which may be more or less influenced by external factors. History enables us to know the nature and extent of the imbalances and the conflicts (economic, political and social) that characterize the evolution of a society. Culture enables us to know what dynamic syntheses have been formed and set by social awareness in order to resolve these conflicts at each stage of evolution of that society, in the search for survival and progress.

Just as occurs with the flower in a plant, the capacity (or responsibility) for forming and fertilizing the germ which ensures the continuity of history lies in culture, and the germ simultaneously ensures the prospects for evolution and progress of the society in question. Thus it is understood that imperialist domination, denying to the dominated people their own historical process, necessarily denies their cultural process. It is further understood why the exercise of imperialist domination, like all other foreign domination, for its own security requires cultural oppression and the attempt at direct or indirect destruction of the essential elements of the culture of the dominated people.

Study of the history of liberation struggles shows that they have generally been preceded by an upsurge of cultural manifestations, which progressively harden into an attempt, successful or not, to assert the cultural personality of the dominated people by an act of denial of the culture of the oppressor. Whatever the conditions of subjection of a people to foreign domination and the influence of economic, political and social factors in the exercise of this domination, it is generally within the cultural factor that we find the germ of challenge which leads to the structuring and development of the liberation movement.

In our view, the foundation of national liberation lies in the inalienable right of every people to have their own history, whatever the formulations adopted in international law. The aim of national liberation is therefore to regain this right, usurped by imperialist domination, namely: the liberation of the process of development of the national productive forces. So national liberation exists when, and only when the national productive forces have been completely freed from all kinds of foreign domination. The liberation of productive forces and consequently of the ability freely to determine the mode of production most appropriate to the evolution of the liberated people, necessarily opens up new prospects for the cultural process of the society in question, by returning to it all its capacity to create progress.

A people who free themselves from foreign domination will not be culturally free unless, without underestimating the importance of positive contributions from the oppressor's culture and other cultures, they return to the upwards paths of their own culture. The latter is nourished by the living reality of the environment and rejects harmful influences as much as any kind of subjection to foreign cultures. We see therefore that, if imperialist domination has the vital need to practise cultural oppression, national liberation is necessarily an *act of culture*. [. . .]

▲

The South African Freedom Charter

NELSON MANDELA

Nelson Rolihlahla Mandela was born in Transkei, South Africa, on July 18, 1918. He was educated at University College of Fort Hare and the University of Witwatersrand and qualified in law in 1942. He joined the African National Congress (ANC) in 1942 and by the late 1940s was engaged in resistance against the ruling National Party's apartheid policies. Throughout the 1950s Mandela and the ANC were persecuted by South African authorities. In 1962 Mandela was sentenced to five years imprisonment, though his sentence was later changed to a life sentence. He was finally released in 1990. After the fall of white minority rule and the apartheid system, Mandela became head of state of the new democratic South Africa. Mandela played a significant role in popularizing the Freedom Charter, which was adopted by the Congress of the People in 1955. The document was not well received by the state, which accused its framers of being pro-communist. The Charter became a powerful force in uniting all the anti-apartheid forces and became the basis for the establishment of a nonracial democratic state.

▲

QUESTIONS

1. What contribution do you think the Freedom Charter made to the liberation struggle in South Africa?

2. Why might the apartheid state have viewed the Freedom Charter as a document that was influenced by socialist or communist ideology?

3. What declarations or charters do you think the framers of the Freedom Charter drew upon in constructing their document?

Freedom Charter

Drafted by a sub-committee of the National Action Council from contributions submitted by groups, individuals and meetings all over South Africa, approved by the ANC National Executive and adopted at the Congress of the People, Kliptown, Johannesburg, 25–26 June 1955.

Each section of the Charter was adopted by the three thousand delegates by acclamation with a show of hands and shouts of 'Afrika! Mayibuye!'

Preamble

We, the people of South Africa, declare for all our country and the world to know:

That South Africa belongs to all who live in it, black and white, and that no government can justly claim authority unless it is based on the will of the people;

That our people have been robbed of their birthright to land, liberty and peace by a form of government founded on injustice and inequality;

Source: Nelson Mandela. "The South African Freedom Charter." In Nelson Mandela, *The Struggle Is My Life*. New York: Pathfinder Press, 1986. Pp. 50–54. Copyright © 1978, 1986, 1990 by The International Defence and Aid Fund. This edition copyright © by Pathfinder Press. Reprinted by permission.

That our country will never be prosperous or free until all our people live in brotherhood, enjoying equal rights and opportunities;

That only a democratic state, based on the will of all the people, can secure to all their birthright without distinction of colour, race, sex or belief;

And therefore, we, the people of South Africa, black and white, together—equals, countrymen and brothers—adopt this FREEDOM CHARTER. And we pledge ourselves to strive together, sparing nothing of our strength and courage, until the democratic changes here set out have been won.

The People Shall Govern!

Every man and woman shall have the right to vote for and stand as a candidate for all bodies which make laws.

All the people shall be entitled to take part in the administration of the country.

The rights of the people shall be the same regardless of race, colour or sex.

All bodies of minority rule, advisory boards, councils and authorities shall be replaced by democratic organs of self-government.

All National Groups Shall Have Equal Rights!

There shall be equal status in the bodies of state, in the courts, and in the schools for all national groups and races;

All people shall have equal rights to use their own languages and to develop their own folk culture and customs;

All national groups shall be protected by law against insults to their race and national pride;

The preaching and practice of national, race or colour discrimination and contempt shall be a punishable crime;

All apartheid laws and practices shall be set aside.

The People Shall Share in the Country's Wealth!

The national wealth of our country, the heritage of all South Africans, shall be restored to the people;

The mineral wealth beneath the soil, the banks and monopoly industry shall be transferred to the ownership of the people as a whole;

All other industries and trade shall be controlled to assist the well-being of the people;

All people shall have equal rights to trade where they choose, to manufacture and to enter all trades, crafts and professions.

The Land Shall Be Shared Among Those Who Work It!

Restriction of land ownership on a racial basis shall be ended, and all the land re-divided amongst those who work it, to banish famine and land hunger;

The state shall help the peasants with implements, seed, tractors and dams to save the soil and assist the tillers;

Freedom of movement shall be guaranteed to all who work on the land;

All shall have the right to occupy land wherever they choose;

People shall not be robbed of their cattle, and forced labour and farm prisons shall be abolished.

All Shall Be Equal Before the Law!

No one shall be imprisoned, deported or restricted without a fair trial;

No one shall be condemned by the order of any Government official;

The courts shall be representative of all the people;

Imprisonment shall be only for serious crimes against the people, and shall aim at re-education, not vengeance;

The police force and army shall be open to all on an equal basis and shall be the helpers and protectors of the people;

All laws which discriminate on grounds of race, colour or belief shall be repealed.

All Shall Enjoy Equal Human Rights!

The law shall guarantee to all their right to speak, to organise, to meet together, to publish, to preach, to worship and to educate their children;

The privacy of the house from police raids shall be protected by law;

All shall be free to travel without restriction from countryside to town, from province to province, and from South Africa abroad;

Pass laws, permits and all other laws restricting these freedoms shall be abolished.

There Shall Be Work and Security!

All who work shall be free to form trade unions, to elect their officers and to make wage agreements with their employers;

The state shall recognise the right and duty of all to work; and to draw full unemployment benefits;

Men and women of all races shall receive equal pay for equal work;

There shall be a forty-hour working week, a national minimum wage, paid annual leave, and sick leave for all workers, and maternity leave on full pay for all working mothers;

Miners, domestic workers, farm workers and civil servants shall have the same rights as all others who work;

Child labour, compound labour, the tot system [payment in kind] and contract labour shall be abolished.

The Doors of Learning and of Culture Shall be Opened!

The government shall discover, develop and encourage national talent for the enhancement of our cultural life;

All the cultural treasures of mankind shall be open to all, by free exchange of books, ideas and contact with other lands;

The aim of education shall be to teach the youth to love their people and their culture, to honour human brotherhood, liberty and peace;

Education shall be free, compulsory, universal and equal for all children;

Higher education and technical training shall be opened to all by means of state allowances and scholarships awarded on basis of merit;

Adult illiteracy shall be ended by a mass state education plan;

Teachers shall have all the rights of other citizens;

The colour bar in cultural life, in sport and in education shall be abolished.

There Shall be Houses, Security and Comfort!

All people shall have the right to live where they choose, to be decently housed, and to bring up their families in comfort and security;

Unused housing space to be made available to the people;

Rent and prices shall be lowered, food plentiful and no one shall go hungry;

A preventative health scheme shall be run by the state;

Free medical care and hospitalisation shall be provided for all, with special care for mothers and young children;

Slums shall be demolished, and new suburbs built where all have transport, roads, lighting, playing fields, crèches and social centres;

The aged, the orphans, the disabled and the sick shall be cared for by the state;

Rest, leisure and recreation shall be the right of all;

Fenced locations and ghettos shall be abolished, and laws which break up families shall be repealed.

There Shall be Peace and Friendship!

South Africa shall be a fully independent state, which respects the rights and sovereignty of all nations;

South Africa shall strive to maintain world peace and the settlement of all international disputes by negotiation—not war;

Peace and friendship amongst all our people shall be secured by upholding the equal rights, opportunities and status of all;

The people of the protectorates—Basutoland, Bechuanaland and Swaziland [now Lesotho, Botswana, and Swaziland]—shall be free to decide for themselves their own future;

The right of all the peoples in Africa to independence and self-government shall be recognised, and shall be on the basis of close co-operation.

Let all who love their people and their country now say, as we say here: 'THESE FREEDOMS WE WILL FIGHT FOR, SIDE BY SIDE, THROUGHTOUT OUR LIVES, UNTIL WE HAVE WON OUR LIBERTY.'

▲

Namibian Mural

PHOTOGRAPHER: RALEIGH INTERNATIONAL

Namibia's struggle for independence was protracted and involved many players. In 1966, the United Nations declared Southwest Africa, also known as Namibia, independent from South Africa, but the white-controlled South African government refused to yield. Black independence activists quickly organized a guerilla group to fight against white elites for Namibian independence, and in the late 1970s, this group was offered training and assistance by newly independent Angola as well as by Cuban soldiers who were fighting in Angola. The dispute continued until Namibia finally gained its independence in 1990.

▲

QUESTION

1. What values are portrayed in this mural?

Source: Raleigh International/Robert Harding World Imagery.

⅄

Savages

Joe Kane

Decolonization is a concept that can be broadly applied. Its use is not limited to the formal process through which former colonies gained independence in the mid-twentieth century and beyond. Decolonization can also be interpreted as the insistence by a people on their right to political, economic, or even cultural self-determination. Moreover, as earlier selections from Latin America have shown, not all imperialism is political or carried out by states. In fact, many Latin Americans believe that much of their continent has been subject to an informal, economic colonization that has been facilitated by international political relationships. Such is the case for the Huaorani, a semi-nomadic indigenous group in Ecuador, who experienced several waves of imperialist expansion into their territory, some of which are described in the following reading.

The Huaorani's most recent struggle has been against oil companies, which, with the support of the Ecuadorian government, have sought to drill into a massive oil field under Huaorani land. The Huaorani would not receive any economic benefit from this drilling; they collectively own rights to the land, but they do not have rights to what lies beneath it. Moreover, the environmental impact of the drilling would be devastating to their traditional hunter-gatherer lifestyle, which depends on a well-balanced ecosystem. The passage that follows comes from a book about the Huaorani and their fight against the oil companies, written by Joe Kane, an environmental activist and writer. It briefly describes a series of recent incursions into Huaorani territory that might be considered imperialistic and that have had a substantial impact on the Huaorani.

⅄

QUESTIONS

1. What varieties of imperialist activity do the Huaorani appear to be encountering?

2. In what ways do the Huaorani seek to liberate themselves? To what extent do you think their struggle is actually a struggle of decolonization?

3. On page 75 of *Savages*, Kane quotes one of his interviewees as saying, "Change is inevitable. The Huaorani cannot avoid change. The real question is, on what terms will change occur? The right the Huaorani have—a basic moral right that all people have—is to be allowed to evolve their own cultural tools for dealing with change, rather than having that change imposed upon them." Are you persuaded by this argument?

Source: Joe Kane, *Savages.* New York: Alfred A. Knopf, 1995. Pp. 15–23. Copyright © 1995 by Joe Kane. Used by permission of Alfred A. Knopf, a division of Random House, Inc.

The port of Coca sits on the north bank of the broad, brown Napo River, in the very heart of the Oriente, which may well be the richest biotic zone on the planet. But as I entered town for the first time, bouncing on the back of a flatbed pickup, what I smelled most strongly was raw petroleum. Coca is ringed by oil wells, and every few days its dirt streets are hosed down with waste crude. Oily mud splashed across my clothes and pack. Down along the roadside, oil had spattered chickens, mules, pigs, barefoot schoolchildren, and peasants slip-sliding along on rickety bicycles. It even slopped up onto the spanking-new four-wheel-drive trucks that now and then came blasting down the road at breakneck speed.

Some of these trucks bore the insignia of the state oil company, Petroecuador, but most of them did the work of American companies: Texaco, Occidental Petroleum, ARCO, Unocal, Conoco, Maxus Energy, Mobil, Oryx Energy, all of which have, or had, oil developments in the otherwise sylvan wilderness that surrounds Coca for hundreds of square miles. Indeed, though Coca was small, with a permanent population of less than five thousand, there were always Americans around. The truck dropped me outside a restaurant called El Buho. The menu featured such jungle fare as tapir, capybara, paca, venison, caiman, and peccary, but you could also get a cheeseburger and fries, which is what the four white men sitting across the room ordered, in English, in accents unmistakably southern. The Mission, Coca's only hot-water hotel, was booked solid with Occidental Petroleum executives in from the States, and at dawn the next day, when a squad of Ecuadorian soldiers jogged down the main street in earnest formation, what caught my attention in the sea of brown Latin skin were the blond hair and blue eyes of the man leading them: His uniform identified him as an officer in the U.S. Army.

If oil was the first thing you noticed in Coca, the second was the suggestion of Aucas, the people indigenous to the vast and mostly uncharted stretch of the Oriente that begins across the Napo and extends over a hundred miles south and east, to the Peruvian border. Trinket shops sold Auca blowguns and spears, tour guides promoted river trips to the Auca homeland to see "naked savages," and on the walls of the Hotel Auca, in the center of town, hung black-and-white photographs of Aucas dressed in, at most, bellybands and earrings, their short, powerfully muscled torsos painted and tattooed, their earlobes perforated and hugely distended. If you happened to mention that you were heading into Auca territory, you were likely to be told that the Aucas regularly killed travelers, other Indians, and their own people, and that they would not only kill you but eat your flesh. Without a doubt you would hear the story of a Capuchin missionary named Alejandro Labaca.

In the late 1970s, Labaca, then the bishop of Coca, crossed the Napo and made the first sustained contact with several Auca bands living deep in the forest. The Aucas robbed him blind. (They survive mainly by hunting and by gathering forest crops, and they regarded his belongings much as they would ripe coconuts.) But Labaca kept returning, and over the years he came to feel comfortable with his new friends. Then, in 1984, an oil crew succeeded in killing Taga, the notoriously fierce leader of the Tagaeri, the most reclusive of the Auca clans. The other Tagaeri managed to escape deeper into the forest, but in 1987 an oil-exploration team investigating the Auca territory by air spotted a clearing they believed to be the clan's new home. Labaca was worried that the company would track the Tagaeri down and kill them, and he asked permission to attempt friendly contact first. A helicopter crew dropped him in the clearing. It returned a few days later to find him pinned to the ground, spread-eagled, by seventeen palm-wood spears, each of them about ten feet long, which jutted like porcupine quills from his throat, chest, arms, and thighs. His corpse was punctured in eighty-nine places.

I heard the Labaca story one steamy night at the Hotel Auca, on a thatch-roofed patio where half a dozen Australian and Israeli students, young and long haired, had gathered to drink beer. The patio was lit by a single candle, and by its dim light you couldn't really tell that four dark-skinned young men who happened to be sitting on the grass a few yards away weren't of Latin blood. The tourists ignored them—not that these men would ever identify themselves as Aucas. They would call themselves Huaorani: the People. In the language of their traditional enemies, the Quichua Indians, *auca* means "savage," and the Huaorani consider it a gross insult.

The four Huaorani hardly resembled the hotel's lurid photographs. They wore spotless denim jeans, brightly shined plastic loafers, and bleached white cotton shirts. The man nearest me sometimes went by the name Eugenio, because he found it convenient to use a Latin name when he was visiting a foreign country, which is what he considered Ecuador to be. But if you looked closely when he smiled, you could catch the candlelight glinting off his left front tooth, which had been inlaid with gold in the shape of an *A*. This was for Amo, his Huaorani name.

The man next to him, Enqueri, had hardly any teeth at all, and he was wearing a pair of headphones that appeared to be plugged into his right hip pocket. When I asked him what he was listening to, he replied in a tone so solemn I was sure I'd committed a horrible breach of Huaorani etiquette. "I am listening," he said, "to my pants." He let that hang for a moment, and then he and Amo collapsed with laughter, rolling on the ground and cackling wildly.

"To your pants!" Amo gasped. "What do they say?"

"They say, 'Wash me, you moron!'"

The other two men, whose names were Nanto and Moi, sat with their arms around each other's shoulders. Nanto told me that to reach Coca they had traveled by foot, canoe, and truck for three days. They had been in town five days, and had not eaten since they arrived. They had come to Coca to find the Company. The Company was going to drill oil wells inside the Huaorani territory, and build new roads, and the Huaorani did not want this. Nanto was going to tell the Company to stay out.

He had the authority to do so, he said, because he was president of the Huaorani federation, which was called—here he rolled his eyes up into his head, searching for the name.

"The Organization of the Huaorani Nation of the Ecuadorian Amazon," Moi said. (The acronym, ONHAE, is also the Huaorani word for "flower.") Like the others, he spoke fair Spanish. Unlike the others, he wore a crown of toucan feathers, and he didn't smile. Moi, Amo, and Enqueri were ONHAE's vice president, secretary, and treasurer, respectively. All were in their midtwenties, though there was some disagreement on just where in his midtwenties Enqueri was, and they had been elected by their people to speak to the *cowode*—the cannibals, who included the missionaries, the Company, me, and everyone else on earth.

This reaching out was an extraordinary step for the Huaorani, who until the middle of this century were almost completely isolated from the world beyond their territory. These, however, were extraordinary times. In the heart of the Huaorani homeland, the Company had found oil reserves it estimated at 216 million barrels. It was about to begin constructing a 90-mile access road, 150 miles of service roads, and a pipeline, and drilling 120 wells. None of the Company's projected $2 billion in revenues would be shared with the Huaorani, because the Ecuadorian state retains all subsurface mineral rights. But from the Huaorani point of view, money wasn't the issue. The issue was survival. Ecuador had a crippling international debt (of more then $12 billion, or about its annual gross national product), and it depended on oil production for nearly half its revenues. The government had outlawed any attempt by the Huaorani to impede the Company. In any case, from what I gathered, ONHAE had no office, no phone, and no money.

What, I asked, did the Huaorani propose to do?

It was Moi who answered, softly but without hesitation. "We will find the Company and talk to them," he said. "If they do not listen, we will attack with spears from all sides."

The Huaorani were not hard to spot in Coca, once you knew what to look for. They hate to travel alone—it's dangerous and boring—so they were usually in groups of two or three or more, often with their arms around one another. They are shy but keenly observant. They would stand for hours in front of the Kamikaze Disco or the Hotel Auca or a greasy spoon called Rosita's, studying the action as intently as if they were scanning the forest canopy for monkeys. If they were Huaorani making one of their first trips to town, you might see them on a street corner, mesmerized by the spectacle of cars and electric lights, or, if someone had given them shoes, by their own feet. A barefoot Huao from the far backcountry, a real tree climber, was particularly easy to spot: His big toes took off at right angles, like opposable thumbs. Sometimes you'd see a Huao walking through town innocently carrying a blowgun the length of a bazooka, while passersby froze in terror. Now and then a young Huao would come into some cash, by selling a blowgun or spear, or a harpy eagle, or a jaguar cub, or by earning slave wages as a boatman for a tour guide or a laborer for the Company, and he would bring an entourage of other Huaorani with him to Rosita's and spend everything he had buying his friends fried chicken and soft drinks. This was not profligacy: The Huaorani ideal is to be independent and self-reliant, and every effort is made to give the appearance, at least, of being so clearly in tune with the abundance of the forest that one is without fear of need. (By the time he is ten a Huao is expected to be able to survive on his own.) There is no higher manifestation of this ideal state than unqualified generosity, and no act more generous than to give away food.

You could often find Huaorani out toward the east end of Coca, at the Huaorani Hotel, as it's known—a cinder-block shack that the Capuchin mission let them use as a bunkhouse, and to which the Capuchins directed me shortly after I arrived in Coca and rang the bell at the mission gate. One morning a dozen Huaorani were sprawled across the shack's four bunk beds,

draped one over another, wrestling and laughing. T-shirts, a couple of pairs of pants, and a blanket were hanging on a line outside—to dry, the Huaorani told me, although it was raining so hard you couldn't see ten feet.

"Moi, what time it is?" Enqueri yelled from beneath a pile of brown bodies.

Moi, sitting in a corner, looked at his wrist. "In Japan it is nine o'clock," he said. "In Europe it is ten. In Ecuador it is eleven. In America it is twelve."

"Twelve o'clock!" Enqueri said. "Time for the *cowode* to be hungry!"

Enqueri was the first Huao I came to know well. At five feet seven he was tall for a Huao. He had the meaty, forest walker's quadriceps that give the Huaorani an almost bowlegged lope on a city street, but his shoulders were uncharacteristically narrow, and when he laughed they shook up and down furiously, nearly touching his ears. When he laughed around *cowode*, he tried to keep his mouth closed, because he had learned to be ashamed of his bad teeth, but this was like holding a cat in a sack. Inevitably, he exploded in a steady cadence that went quite literally, "ha-ha-ha-ha-ha." The other Huaorani called him Condorito, after a popular South American comic-book character—an avian, frenetically absentminded cross between Woody Woodpecker and Elmer Fudd. "Enqueri is like Condorito because his head has too many ideas," Amo told me. "One day he wants to be a school teacher, and the next day he wants to devote his life to the People, and the next day he is working for the Company, and the next day he wants to kill the Company, and the next day he is going to be a nurse, and the next day he wants to go to the sky and be with God."

Enqueri might well have been confused, but a man forced to leap from Stone Age to Petroleum Age is going to have a few things on his mind. He was perhaps the most literate of the Huaorani, able to read and write basic Spanish. These skills owed directly to the day in 1956 when his father helped kill five American evangelical missionaries who had plunged into the Huaorani territory bent on saving the "Aucas" from their heathen existence. They were a "hazard to explorers, an embarrassment to the republic of Ecuador, and a challenge to missionaries of the Gospel," one of the men, Nate Saint, wrote in his journal—a journal in which he recorded sharing dinner with the naked brown savage he called George, and which he kept right up until the moment George's friends ran him through with a spear. Nate had an older sister, Rachel, who'd raised him like a son, and when she got word of the massacre, she went after the savages. She applied herself with a holy vengeance. Within a few years, through sheer stubbornness, the intimidating magic of airplanes and bullhorns, and the seductive luxury of salt, white rice, and aluminum pots, she'd managed to establish a Christian beachhead inside the Huaorani territory, a few miles from the very spot where her brother Nate had eaten his last hamburger.

Supported by the Ecuadorian government and by legions of believers back home, Rachel built a chapel and an elementary school and set about sculpting a new model of Huao: one who spoke Spanish, saluted the flag, honored God, understood the value of the dollar (or, at least, an Ecuadorian sucre), and rejected such heathen practices as shamanism, nomadism, nudity, and "free love." The Condorito excelled in his studies and won the privilege of attending an evangelical secondary school outside the territory. Once on the outside, however, he fell under the influence of more worldly and sophisticated Indians who had begun to organize their people into federations of a decidedly leftist bent. He went home with some new ideas. When he got together with Nanto and Moi to found ONHAE, he said, Rachel branded him a Communist and his family ostracized him—and such ostracism in a clan society can be tantamount to a death sentence.

I asked Enqueri to define *Communist.* He thought about it for a moment, and said, "Someone from Cuba."

"Where is Cuba?"

"In France," he said, and added that when a Communist dies he cannot go to the sky.

I asked the Huaorani about the letter that had come to the Rainforest Action Network. Nanto said yes, it was from ONHAE. Why would anyone claim it wasn't? It was an official communication: It had been signed by the president, the vice president, and the secretary. What did I think of the ONHAE seal? He reached into a plastic bag, rummaged among shirts and pants, and produced a shiny black-plastic briefcase, the sole contents of which were an ink pad and a rubber stamp. He inked up the stamp and banged out a harpy eagle ringed by the name of the organization. "Isn't that beautiful?" he asked.

How had the letter reached the United States?

Nanto shrugged and said, "We gave it to a *cowode* we met here in Coca."

I asked the Huaorani what they thought of the various proposals being put forth in their name, or for their land, by environmental and human-rights groups in the United States and Europe. As it turned out, the one thing all the groups had in common was that the Huaorani didn't recognize any of them.

"How can these people speak for us," Nanto asked me, "if we have never met them?"

DuPont's Edgar Woolard had made it known that he would not give Conoco the go-ahead for its Oriente project unless the oil company came up with some sort of "green" blessing—some stamp of approval from the nonprofit community. In secret negotiations that inadvertently had been made public two weeks before I left the United States, the Natural Resources Defense Council, an environmental group based in New York City, had indicated to Conoco that it was willing to confer such a blessing if Conoco would fund a foundation to benefit the Oriente's Indian groups. No one knew how much money that would be, though the numbers being used in the negotiations ran from $10 million to more than $200 million.

I tried to explain to the Huaorani what such numbers meant, but these were men who on the rare occasions when they worked for wages earned about a dollar a day, and whose fathers counted "one, two, one and two." Still, Moi dismissed the foundation idea outright. "You cannot put a price on our land," he said.

I asked if it was true, as I'd been told by Conoco and by the NRDC, that only ten Huaorani lived in Block Sixteen, the concession that was first in line for development.

When Moi heard this he almost exploded. "No!" he said. "That is what the Company wants people to believe, but it is not true at all. There are at least five clans in there."

"Are you sure?" I asked.

"Yes," he said. "Some live inside and some live outside, but all hunt and travel in that place."

"Can I see this?" I asked.

"Why do you want to see this?"

"I would like to see the Huaorani you have spoken about and write about what I see."

"You will write a letter to the United States of North America?"

"I will write something like a letter."

He thought this over. After a while he said, "Many people talk about the Huaorani. But they do not come to see."

Nanto proposed a deal: If I would cover the costs of the trip and a fee for Enqueri's time, Enqueri would take me to Block Sixteen. He would make a census of the area, and I would be a witness. Our optimal route would be roughly circular. In Coca, we—I—would hire a small truck to haul us sixty miles south down an oil-exploration road called the Vía Auca, until we reached the Shiripuno River, which could be followed east by canoe to the Cononaco River. There Amo's grandfather, Quemperi, lived with his clan. From the Cononaco we would walk seventy-five miles north, to the Yasuní River, crossing Block Sixteen. With luck, one of the Huaorani clans on that river would take us by canoe down the Yasuní and back up the Napo, west to Coca.

Advised of this plan, Enqueri said, "The trip will take two weeks or four weeks or six weeks."

"It might even take a month," Amo said. [. . .]

⋏

Nervous Conditions

Tsitsi Dangarembga

Tsitsi Dangarembga was born in 1959 in colonial Rhodesia (Zimbabwe). At age 2, she moved to England with her parents. In 1965, she moved back to her homeland and found herself to be very much a person between cultures. She has said that English is her first language, but she has not lost contact with her native Shona. As a young adult, Dangarembga also moved back and forth between Rhodesia and England; she spent three years at Cambridge studying medicine and pursued psychology at the University of Zimbabwe. She has written plays, short stories, and worked in film. Her greatest success, however, has come as a novelist with the appearance of Nervous Conditions, *a partially autobiographical tale. The book was the first novel to be published in English by a black Zimbabwean woman.*

Nervous Conditions *is the story of Tambu, a young, poor girl who has to negotiate traditional African culture and confront ideas about what is proper for girls and women. Tambu desperately wants to educate herself and goes to great lengths in the novel to do so. The book is simultaneously a coming of age story about a young woman in Africa and an allegory about decolonization and the emergence of Zimbabwe, and by extension other African nations, from colonial rule.*

⋏

QUESTIONS

1. What educational opportunities are described in this selection from *Nervous Conditions?*
2. What do we learn about work conditions in this part of Africa?
3. What do we learn about family relations?

Nhamo [narrator's brother] began school in the year that he turned seven. This was the age at which the Government had declared that African children were sufficiently developed cognitively to be able to understand the abstractions of numbers and letters: 1 + 1 = 2; k-i-t-s-i = kitsi. Nhamo was one of the youngest pupils in his class. Perhaps other parents, believing that we really were a retarded lot, thought it best to let their children's abilities mature a little before exposing them to the rigours of formal education. And, of course, there was the question of fees. Whatever the reason, many of us did not begin school until we were eight or even nine years old, but the precedent of early entry had been set for our family by Babamukuru [narrator's uncle], who had obtained a Bachelor's Degree in South Africa and consequently knew a lot about education. 'They should go early,' Babamukuru told my father, 'while their minds are still malleable.' Inevitably, therefore, Nhamo began school in the year he turned seven and I followed the next since I was a year younger than him.

Now, for some reason that I do not ever remember understanding since we had fair rains that year, our crops were poor in the year that I began school. Although we harvested enough maize to keep us from starving, there was nothing left over to sell. This meant there was no money in the house. No money meant no school fees. No school fees meant no school. Nor was there any hope of procuring money since Babamukuru had left the mission to go to England to study more about education.

I was only five when Babamukuru went to England. Consequently, all I can remember about the circumstances surrounding his going is that everybody was very excited and very impressed by the event. Since then, in order to find out what really happened at that time so that I can understand what followed, I have asked many people—Maiguru and Babamukuru, my father, my mother, Nyasha, and Chido—to tell me what they recollect. I have discovered, as is not surprising, that there were debates and conflicts and tensions surrounding the departure that as a young child I could not have been aware of.

Babamukuru did not want to leave the mission. He did not want to go far from home again because he had already left his mother once, to go to South Africa, and had not been back long enough to see that she was settled and comfortable in her old age. In addition to this, he now had a family of his own. Although the missionaries who had offered him the scholarship to study in England had offered Maiguru a scholarship as well (so anxious were they that this intelligent, disciplined young couple be trained to become useful to their people), there was the question of the children. The debate and the tensions surrounding Babamukuru's departure centred not so much on the question of his going as on what to do with the children. Babamukuru was appreciative of the opportunity that had been offered; and further, to decline would have been a form of suicide. The missionaries would have been annoyed by his ingratitude. He would have fallen from grace with them and they would have taken under their wings another promising young African in his place. Unable to obtain the necessary qualifications at home, he had no alternative but to uproot himself for a period of five years in order to retain the position that would enable him, in due course, to remove himself and both his families from the mercy of nature and charitable missionaries. My grandmother thought the children would be better off at home, where our ways were familiar and they would be at ease in the family environment. But Babamukuru, remembering how difficult life was on the homestead, did not want his children to experience the want and hardship that he had experienced as a young child. In addition, he preferred to have his children with him so he could supervise essential things such as their education and their development. Therefore Chido and Nyasha were taken to England. My father, of course, thinking that five years without his brother to provide for him was a long time in which to be obliged to provide for himself, consoled himself with the knowledge that on Babamukuru's return with his high qualifications, he would be provided for more abundantly than before. My mother was hopeful. She thought my father would at last grow responsible.

I remember discussing the phenomenon of Babamukuru's education with Nhamo. Nhamo was very impressed by the sheer amount of education that was possible. He told me that the kind of education Babamukuru had gone to get must have been of a very important sort to make him go all that way for it. 'England,' he told me with weighty authority, 'is very far away. It is much further away than South Africa.' How did he know?

Nhamo knew a lot of things in those days. He knew more then than he did when he died. For instance, he knew that when he grew up he was going to study for many degrees like Babamukuru and become a headmaster like Babamukuru. He knew that it would be up to him to make sure that his younger sisters were educated, or look after us if we were not, just as Babamukuru had done and was doing for his own brothers and sister. He knew that he had to help in the fields and with the cattle and be pleasant to people. Above all, he knew that he had to work hard at school and keep coming top of the class. This latter he did diligently in Sub A and Sub B. He was particularly pleased with his Sub B result because he had beaten the next boy by only two marks. Then, having done so well, he was told he could not go to school any longer because there was no money for the fees. He cried.

Fortunately, my mother was determined in that year. She began to boil eggs, which she carried to the bus terminus and sold to passengers passing through. (This meant that we could not eat them.) She also took vegetables—rape, onions, and tomatoes—extending her garden so that there was more to sell. Business was fair, and good during public holidays, when visitors from as far as Salisbury, Fort Victoria, Mount Darwin and Wankie would be tempted to buy a little extra to take home with them. In this way she scraped together enough money to keep my brother in school. I understood that selling vegetables was not a lucrative business. I understood that there was not enough money for my fees. Yes, I did understand why I could not go back to school, but I loved going to school and I was good at it. Therefore, my circumstances affected me badly.

My father thought I should not mind. 'Is that anything to worry about? Ha-a-a, it's nothing,' he reassured me, with his usual ability to jump whichever way was easiest. 'Can you cook books and feed them to your husband? Stay at home with your mother. Learn to cook and clean. Grow vegetables.'

His intention was to soothe me with comforting, sensible words, but I could not see the sense. This was often the case when my father spoke, but there had not before been such concrete cause to question his theories. This time, though, I had evidence. Maiguru was educated, and did she serve Babamukuru books for dinner? I discovered to my unhappy relief that my father was not sensible.

I complained to my mother. 'Baba says I do not need to be educated,' I told her scornfully. 'He says I must learn to be a good wife. Look at Maiguru,' I

continued, unaware how viciously. 'She is a better wife than you!'

My mother was too old to be disturbed by my childish nonsense. She tried to diffuse some of it by telling me many things, by explaining that my father was right because even Maiguru knew how to cook and clean and grow vegetables. 'This business of womanhood is a heavy burden,' she said. 'How could it not be? Aren't we the ones who bear children? When it is like that you can't just decide today I want to do this, tomorrow I want to do that, the next day I want to be educated! When there are sacrifices to be made, you are the one who has to make them. And these things are not easy; you have to start learning them early, from a very early age. The earlier the better so that it is easy later on. Easy! As if it is ever easy. And these days it is worse, with the poverty of blackness on one side and the weight of womanhood on the other. Aiwa! What will help you, my child, is to learn to carry your burdens with strength.'

I thought about this for several days, during which I began to fear that I was not as intelligent as my Sub A performance had led me to believe, because, as with my father, I could not follow the sense of my mother's words. My mother said being black was a burden because it made you poor, but Babamukuru was not poor. My mother said being a woman was a burden because you had to bear children and look after them and the husband. But I did not think this was true. Maiguru was well looked after by Babamukuru, in a big house on the mission which I had not seen but of which I had heard rumours concerning its vastness and elegance. Maiguru was driven about in a car, looked well-kempt and fresh, clean all the time. She was altogether a different kind of woman from my mother. I decided it was better to be like Maiguru, who was not poor and had not been crushed by the weight of womanhood.

'I shall go to school again,' I announced to my parents.

My father was sharp with me, thinking that I expected him to obtain the money somehow, perhaps by working. 'Your nonsense, you are about to begin it! I can tell. You know your Babamukuru will not be home for a while yet!'

'I will earn the fees,' I reassured him, laying out my plan for him as I had laid it out in my own mind. 'If you will give me some seed, I will clear my own field and grow my own maize. Not much. Just enough for the fees.'

My father was greatly tickled by this. He annoyed me tremendously by laughing and laughing in an unpleasantly adult way. 'Just enough for the fees! Can you see her there?' he chuckled to my mother. 'Such a little shrub, but already making ripe plans! Can you tell your daughter, Ma'Shingayi, that there is no money. There is no money. That's all.'

My mother, of course, knew me better. 'And did she ask for money?' she enquired. 'Listen to your child. She is asking for seed. That we can give. Let her try. Let her see for herself that some things cannot be done.'

My father agreed. A little seed was not a large price to pay to keep me quiet. I began my project the next day, a day in December 1962. The next January my brother entered Standard One. I worked on the homestead, in the family fields and on my own plot. How I mumbled adoring, reverent prayers to my grandmother in those early days of my market gardening. My grandmother, who had been an inexorable cultivator of land, sower of seeds and reaper of rich harvests until, literally until, her very last moment. When I was too small to be anything more than a hindrance in the family fields, I used to spend many productive hours working with my grandmother on the plot of land she called her garden. We hoed side by side strips of land defined by the row of maize plants each carried, I obstinately insisting I could keep pace with her, she weeding three strips to my one so that I could. Praising my predisposition towards working, she consolidated it in me as a desirable habit.

She gave me history lessons as well. History that could not be found in the textbooks; a stint in the field and a rest, the beginning of the story,

a pause. 'What happened after, Mbuya, what happened?' 'More work, my child, before you hear more story.' Slowly, methodically, throughout the day the field would be cultivated, the episodes of my grandmother's own portion of history strung together from beginning to end.

'Your family did not always live here, did not move to this place until after the time that I was married to your grandfather. We lived up in Chipinge, where the soil is ripe and your great-grandfather was a rich man in the currency of those days, having many fat herd of cattle, large fields and four wives who worked hard to produce bountiful harvests. All this he could exchange for cloth and beads and axes and a gun, even a gun, from the traders. They did not come to stay in those days; they passed through and left. Your great-grandfather had sons enough to fill a kraal, all big, strong, hardworking men. And me, I was beautiful in those days,' her eyes twinkling at me so that I was ashamed of examining her so closely to find the woman she described. Why did she tell me this? She was not beautiful now, but I loved her, so I was ashamed that she saw me search for the lost beauty. 'I wasn't always this old, with wrinkles and grey hair, without teeth. At one time I was as small and pretty and plump as you, and when I grew into a woman I was a fine woman with hair so long you could plait it into a single row down the middle of my head. I had heavy, strong hips.' This is where she usually ended the first episode. I was on tenterhooks. The princess and the prince. What happened? What happened?

Wizards well versed in treachery and black magic came from the south and forced the people from the land. On donkey, on foot, on horse, on ox-cart, the people looked for a place to live. But the wizards were avaricious and grasping; there was less and less land for the people. At last the people came upon the grey, sandy soil of the homestead, so stony and barren that the wizards would not use it. There they built a home. But the third-born son, my grandfather, lured by the wizards' whispers of riches and luxury and driven by the harshness of the homestead, took himself and his family to one of their wizards' farms. Yuwi! Only to find that they had been enticed into slavery. But one day my grandfather managed to escape to glittering gold mines in the south, where good men were said to be quickly made rich. The white wizard had no use for women and children. He threw my grandmother and her children off his farm. Destitute, they travelled back to the homestead, where my great-grandfather, although he had not regained his former standard of living, had managed to keep the family together. And then my great-grandfather died and the family broke up, and it turned out that my grandfather had not been a good man, for he was killed in the mines, and my grandmother was left with six children to support. And then she heard that beings similar in appearance to the wizards but not of them, for these were holy, had set up a mission not too far from the homestead. She walked, with my uncle, with Babamukuru, who was nine years old and wearing a loin cloth, to the mission, where the holy wizards took him in. They set him to work in their farm by day. By night he was educated in their wizardry. For my grandmother, being sagacious and having foresight, had begged them to prepare him for life in their world.

It was truly a romantic story to my ears, a fairytale of reward and punishment, of cause and effect. It had a moral too, a tantalising moral that increased your aspirations, but not beyond a manageable level.

My uncle was not afraid of hard work, having grown used to it from an early age on the farm and on the homestead. He surprised the missionaries by performing exceptionally well at school, in spite of putting in a full day's work on the farm. He was diligent, he was industrious, he was respectful. They thought he was a good boy, cultivatable, in the way that land is, to yield harvests that sustain the cultivator. When he completed his Standards on the mission, they arranged for him to go to secondary school. This only became possible when a secondary school for people like my uncle had been built, which meant that he had to wait for some years in between. During

this time and during his secondary-school years they gave him odd jobs at the mission so that he could pay his fees and help his family. Then the Government took over with a scholarship to South Africa. My uncle became prosperous and respected, well enough salaried to reduce a little the meagreness of his family's existence. This indicated that life could be lived with a modicum of dignity in any circumstances if you worked hard enough and obeyed the rules. Yes, it was a romantic story, the way my grandmother told it. The suffering was not minimised but the message was clear: endure and obey, for there is no other way. She was so proud of her eldest son, who had done exactly this.

When she died, which she did peacefully as she took a rest from her work on a day that I was not with her, my mother took over the plot and made it her vegetable garden. It was a big plot. My mother did not need the whole of it, so that half an acre or so lay fallow. This was the plot I chose for my field.

That year I grew older, stronger and sturdier than any eight year old can usefully grow. More often that not I woke up before dawn, the first lifting of the darkness occurring while I was sweeping the yard. Before it was fully light I would be on my way to the river and then returning along the footpath through the trees and past other homesteads, where the women were just waking, my water-drum balanced on my head-pad of leaves and green twigs, and the drum not quite full because when it was full it was too heavy for me to lift on to my head without help. While the cocks were crowing and the hens were shaking the sleep out of their feathers, I made the fire, swept the kitchen and boiled water for washing and for tea. By the time the sun rose I was in my field, in the first days hoeing and clearing; then digging holes thirty inches apart, with a single swing of the hoe, as we had been taught in our garden periods at school; then dropping the seeds into them, two or three at a time, and covering them with one or two sweeps of my foot; then waiting for the seeds to germinate and cultivating and waiting for the weeds to grow and cultivating again. At about ten o'clock, which I judged by the height and heat of the sun, I would go to the family fields to work with my mother, sometimes my father and, in the afternoons after school, my brother.

I think my mother admired my tenacity, and also felt sorry for me because of it. She began to prepare me for disappointment long before I would have been forced to face up to it. To prepare me she began to discourage me. 'And do you think you are so different, so much better than the rest of us? Accept your lot and enjoy what you can of it. There is nothing else to be done.' I wanted support, I wanted encouragement; warnings if necessary, but constructive ones. On the day that she discouraged me once too often I decided she had been listening too devoutly to my father. Ceasing to pay attention to her, I sought solidarity with Nhamo instead, but he could not help because he was going to school.

'Why do you bother?' he asked, his eyes twinkling maliciously. 'Don't you know I am the one who has to go to school?'

'You said you would take care of me. Help me in my field.'

'How can you ask when you see I am so busy?'

This was true. With the herd staying in the kraal until he came home from school in the afternoon to take them out to graze and to water before joining us in the fields; with milking before school and after when a cow was in milk; with his books; with my father in the busy times insisting that he help us all day, so that sometimes he missed as much as a week of school at a time; with all these tasks and odd jobs here and there he was very busy. I opened my mouth to say I would take over the milking and the grazing, but self-preservation was stronger than compassion. I closed my mouth without saying the words. Still, I had to do something about my brother's plight.

'Will he concentrate if he is so busy?' I asked my father.

'Why not, if he wants to?'

My mother was right. Some things could not be done.

Nhamo laughed when I related my story. 'So what! I don't care what he says,' he shrugged, shocking me with this disrespectful language that I had not heard before. 'I'm at school, aren't I? It doesn't worry me what he says about me. So what's your problem? It doesn't even affect you.'

'But you can't study.'

'Who says? I should know. I go to school. You go nowhere.'

'But I want to go to school.'

'Wanting won't help.'

'Why not?'

He hesitated, then shrugged. 'It's the same everywhere. Because you are a girl.' It was out. 'That's what Baba said, remember?' I was no longer listening. My concern for my older brother died an unobtrusive death.

By February my maize was dark green, taller than me and still growing. I strutted about as I inspected my crop as though I owned a hundred-hectare farm. Nor was I over-tired these days, because the fields no longer needed much attention. It was a fine feeling. A fine crop. All that remained was to wait for the harvest—cultivate once or twice, but really, wait for the harvest to harvest my fine little crop. Fine little crop. I had to be careful in thinking about the harvest in case I was discouraged. I had to push away the knowledge that I could not earn much from my crop.

A few weeks later, when the cobs were ripe for eating, they began to disappear.

'What did you expect?' Nhamo said. 'Did you really think you could send yourself to school?' [Nhamo is stealing her corn.] [. . .]

⋏

Indonesian Coin

PHOTOGRAPHER: RICHARD WATSON

This image shows a 100-rupiah coin from Indonesia from after independence. Many newly independent states chose to use indigenous symbols and images of independence activists on their new coins. In independent Indonesia, politicians reverted to conventional Indonesian clothing styles, and Indonesia's various indigenous cultural features were widely celebrated.

⋏

QUESTION

1. How can nationalism and national identity be expressed through items like coins?

Source: Richard Watson © Dorling Kindersley.

A

A Theology of Liberation: History, Politics, and Salvation

Gustavo Gutiérrez

Gustavo Gutiérrez was born in Peru in 1928. He studied medicine and literature there and went on to study psychology and philosophy at Louvain, Belgium. He completed a doctorate at the Institut Catholique in Lyons, France, after which he returned to Peru as a theologian and Catholic priest and worked mostly among the poor. In 2001, he became Professor of Theology at the University of Notre Dame.

In July 1968, Gutiérrez coined the term "liberation theology," and through the 1970s, a liberation theology movement emerged throughout Latin America. The most essential idea of the movement was that theology could not be separated from day-to-day life but should instead be responsive to this-worldly social issues. Theology, and by extension the Catholic church, needed to understand the real oppression that the masses experienced on a daily basis in order to be able to respond to them and communicate with them appropriately. The role of the church, according to Gutiérrez and other liberation theologians, should be to work to change oppressive economic and political systems. By the early 1980s, liberation theology and its practitioners were under attack by the Vatican as well as by Western political leaders for their subversive qualities. Its critics saw liberation theology's challenge to the sociopolitical establishment as being marxist and therefore threatening to the regional political and economic status quo.

The following excerpt comes from Gutiérrez's best-known work, A Theology of Liberation, *originally published in 1971. It considers the causes of poverty in Latin America and outlines approaches that the church might employ to help impoverished Latin Americans.*

A

QUESTIONS

1. What kinds of injustice in Latin America does Gutiérrez describe, and what does he consider the causes of the injustice to be?

2. What does Gutiérrez suggest might be the role of the church in overcoming social and economic injustice?

3. What do socialism, liberation, and the Catholic Church have to do with each other in Gutiérrez's view?

4. Compare Gutiérrez's views to those of Mariátegui in Part IV.

Towards a Transformation of the Latin American Reality

One unifying theme which is present throughout these documents and which reflects a general attitude of the Church is the acknowledgment of the *solidarity of the Church* with the Latin American reality. The Church avoids placing itself above this reality, but rather attempts to assume its responsibility for the injustice which it has supported both

---

Source: Gustavo Gutiérrez. *A Theology of Liberation: History, Politics, and Salvation.* Translated and edited by Sister Caridad Inda and John Eagleson. Maryknoll: Orbis Books, 1988. Pp.63–68. Used with permission.

by its links with the established order as well as by its silence regarding the evils this order implies. "We recognize that we Christians for want of fidelity to the Gospel have contributed to the present unjust situation through our words and attitudes, our silence and inaction," claim the Peruvian bishops. More than two hundred lay persons, priests, and bishops of El Salvador assert that "our Church has not been effective in liberating and bettering the Salvadoran. This failure is due in part to the above-mentioned incomplete concept of human salvation and the mission of the Church and in part to the fear of losing privileges or suffering persecution."

As for the bishops' vision of reality, they describe the misery and the exploitation in Latin America as "a situation of injustice that can be called institutionalized violence"; it is responsible for the death of thousands of innocent victims. This view allows for a study of the complex problems of counterviolence without falling into the pitfalls of a double standard which assumes that violence is acceptable when the oppressor uses it to maintain "order" and is bad when the oppressed invoke it to change this "order." Institutionalized violence violates fundamental rights so patently that the Latin American bishops warn that "one should not abuse the patience of a people that for years has borne a situation that would not be acceptable to anyone with any degree of awareness of human rights." An important part of the Latin American clergy request, moreover, that "in considering the problem of violence in Latin America, let us by all means avoid equating the *unjust violence* of the oppressors (who maintain this despicable system) with the *just violence* of the oppressed (who feel obliged to use it to achieve their liberation)." Theologically, this situation of injustice and oppression is characterized as a "sinful situation" because "where this social peace does not exist, there we will find social, political, economic, and cultural inequalities, there we will find the rejection of the peace of the Lord, and a rejection of the Lord Himself." With this in mind, an important group of priests declared, "We feel we have a right and a duty to condemn unfair wages, exploitation, and starvation tactics as clear indications of sin and evil."

The reality so described is perceived ever more clearly as resulting from a situation of dependence, in which the centers of decision-making are to be found outside the continent; it follows that the Latin American countries are being kept in a condition of neocolonialism. It has been asserted that underdevelopment "can be understood only in terms of the *dependency relationship* with the developed world that it results from. In large measure the underdevelopment of Latin America is a *byproduct* of capitalist development in the West." The interpretation of Latin American reality in terms of dependency is adopted and considered valid "insofar as it allows us to seek a causal explanation, to denounce domination, and to struggle to overcome it with a commitment to liberation which will produce a new society." This perspective is also clearly adopted by a seminar on the problems of youth sponsored by the Education Department of the Latin American Episcopal Council. It stresses that "Latin American dependency is not only economic and political but also cultural."

Indeed, in texts of the Latin American Church of varying origins and degrees of authority, in the last few years there has been a significant although perhaps not completely coherent replacement of the theme of *development* by the theme of *liberation.* Both the term and the idea express the aspirations to be free from a situation of dependence; the "Message of the Bishops of the Third World" states that "an irresistible impulse drives these people on to better themselves and to free themselves from the forces of oppression." In the words of 120 Bolivian priests: "We observe in our people a desire for liberation and a movement of struggle for justice, not only to obtain a better standard of living, but also to be able to participate in the socio-economic resources and the decision-making process of the country." The deeper meaning of these expressions is the insistence on the need for the oppressed peoples of Latin America to control their own destiny. Quoting *Populorum progressio,* Medellín advocates therefore a "liberating education." The bishops see this as "the key instrument for liberating the masses from all servitude and for causing them to ascend 'from less human to more human conditions,' bearing in mind that humanity is responsible for and 'the principal author of its success or failure.'" Moreover, liberation from this servitude is considered in an important passage of Medellín as a manifestation of liberation from sin made possible by Christ: "It is the same God who, in the fullness of time, sends his Son in the flesh so that he might come to liberate all persons from the slavery to which sin has subjected them: hunger, misery, oppression and ignorance—in a word, that injustice and hatred which have their origin in human selfishness."

The Church wishes to share in this aspiration of the Latin American peoples; the bishops at Medellín think of themselves as belonging to a people who are "beginning to discover their proper self-awareness and their task in the consort of nations." "We are vitally aware of the social revolution now in progress. We identify with it." Argentinian priests and lay persons also declare their total commitment to the process of liberation: "We wish to express our total commitment to the liberation of the oppressed and the working class and to the search for a social order radically different from the present one, an order seeking to achieve justice and evangelical solidarity more adequately."

Faced with the urgency of the Latin American situation, the Church denounces as insufficient those partial and limited measures which amount only to palliatives and in the long run actually consolidate an exploitive system. Therefore superficial projects that create mirages and cause setbacks are criticized. At a deeper level, considering that the problems are rooted in the structures of capitalist society which produce a situation of dependency, it is stated that "it is necessary to change the very bases of the system," for "a true solution to these problems can come about only within the context of a far-reaching transformation of existent structures." Hence the criticism of "developmentalism," which advocates the capitalist model as a solution, and the calls for radicalization of reforms which would otherwise "in the long term run . . . serve to consolidate new forms of the capitalist system, bringing with them a new dependence less evident but no less real." Hence also the term *social revolution* appears more frequently and opposition to it less.

For some, participation in this process of liberation means not allowing themselves to be intimidated by the accusation of being "communist." On the positive side it can even mean taking the path of *socialism*. A group of Colombian priests affirmed, "We forthrightly denounce neocolonial capitalism, since it is incapable of solving the acute problems that confront our people. We are led to direct our efforts and actions toward the building of a Socialist type of society that would allow us to eliminate all forms of man's exploitations of his fellow man, and that fits in with the historical tendencies of our time and the distinctive character of Colombians." According to the Argentinian Priests for the Third World, this socialism will be a "Latin American socialism that will promote the advent of the New Humanity."

In a speech which has been bitterly debated and attacked, one of the most influential figures of the Mexican Church, Don Sergio Méndez Arceo, asserted: "Only socialism can enable Latin America to achieve true development. . . . I believe that a socialist system is more in accord with the Christian principles of true fellowship, justice, and peace. . . . I do not know what kind of socialism, but this is the direction Latin America should go. For myself, I believe it should be a democratic socialism." Old prejudices, inevitable ideological elements, and also the ambivalence of the term *socialism* require the use of cautious language and careful distinctions. There is always the risk that statements in this regard may be interpreted differently by different readers. It is therefore important to link this subject to another which enables us at least under one aspect to clarify what we mean. We refer to the progressive radicalization of the debate concerning private property. The subordination of private property to the social good has been stressed often. But difficulties in reconciling justice and private ownership have led many to the conviction that "private ownership of capital leads to the dichotomy of capital and labor, to the superiority of the capitalist over the laborer, to the exploitation of man by man. . . . The history of the private ownership of the means of production makes evident the necessity of its reduction or suppression for the welfare of society. We must hence *opt for social ownership of the means of production.*"

The case of Chile is particularly interesting. The electoral victory of a socialist government poses a decisive and potentially very fruitful challenge to Chilean Christians. The first reactions are already being felt, but it is well to remember that they come out of a long tradition of participation by various groups in the struggle for liberation of the oppressed sectors. A group of priests attached to the university parish in Santiago writes: "The capitalist system exhibits a number of elements which are antihuman . . . Socialism, although it does not deliver humanity from injustices caused by personal attitudes or from the ambiguity inherent in all systems, does offer a fundamental equality of opportunity. Through a change in the relationships of production, it dignifies labor so that the worker, while humanizing nature, becomes more of a person. It offers a possibility for the even development of the country for the benefit of all, especially the most neglected. It asserts that the motivation of morality and social solidarity is of higher value than that of individual interest, and so forth." Human transformation emerges as a simultaneous task: "All this can be implemented if together with the transformation of the economic structure, the transformation of humanity is undertaken with equal enthusiasm. We do not believe persons will automatically become less selfish, but we do maintain that where a socio-economic foundation for equality has been established, it is more possible to work realistically toward human solidarity than it is in a society torn asunder by inequity." The attitude of Christians is based on the understanding that the coming of the Kingdom implies the building of a just society. "If our country engages in an all-out struggle against misery, the Christian, who should participate fully in it, will interpret whatever progress is achieved as a first implementation of the Kingdom proclaimed by Jesus. In other words, today the gospel of Christ implies (and is incarnated in) multiple efforts to obtain justice." The MOAC (Workers' Catholic Action Movement) has this to say regarding the victory of the new Chilean regime:

"This fact embodies a great hope and a great responsibility for *all* workers and their organizations: active and watchful collaboration to bring about a more just society which will permit the integral liberation of those oppressed by an inhuman and anti-Christian system such as capitalism."

More recently, a large group of priests has taken a clear stand in favor of the socialist process occurring in Chile. "Socialism, characterized by the social appropriation of the means of production, opens the path to a new economy. This economy makes possible an autonomous and more rapid development as well as an overcoming of the division of a society into antagonistic classes. Nevertheless socialism is not only a new economy. It should also generate new values which make possible the emergence of a society of greater solidarity and fellowship in which workers assume with dignity the role which is theirs. We feel committed to this process already underway and wish to contribute to its success." Further they state, "The profound reason for this commitment is our faith in Jesus Christ, which is deepened, renewed, and takes on flesh according to historical circumstances. To be a Christian is to be in solidarity. To be in solidarity at this time in Chile is to participate in the historical task which the people has set for itself." In a document directed to the bishops' synod in Rome, the Peruvian bishops stated: "When governments arise which are trying to implant more just and human societies in their countries, we propose that the Church commit itself to giving them its backing; contributing to the elimination of prejudice; recognizing the aspirations they hold; and encouraging the search for their own road toward a socialist society."

Finally, the process of liberation requires the *active participation of the oppressed*; this certainly is one of the most important themes running through the writings of the Latin American Church. Based on the evidence of the usually frustrated aspirations of the popular classes to participate in decisions which affect all of society, the realization emerges that it is the poor who must be the protagonists of their own liberation. "It is primarily up to the poor nations and the poor of the other nations to effect their own betterment." Rejecting every kind of paternalism, the ONIS priests say, "We believe that social transformation is not simply a revolution for the people, but that the people themselves, especially farmers and working men, exploited and unjustly kept in the background, must take part in their own liberation." The participation of the oppressed presupposes an awareness on their part of their unjust situation. "Justice, and therefore peace," say the Latin American bishops, "conquer by means of a dynamic action of awakening (*concientización*) and organization of the popular sectors which are capable of pressing public officials who are often impotent in their social projects without popular support."

However, existing structures block popular participation and marginate the great majorities, depriving them of channels for expression of their demands. Consequently, the Church feels compelled to address itself directly to the oppressed—instead of appealing to the oppressors—calling on them to assume control of their own destiny, committing itself to support their demands, giving them an opportunity to express these demands, and even articulating them itself. At Medellín a pastoral approach was approved which encourages and favors "the efforts of the people to create and develop their own grass-roots organizations for the redress and consolidation of their rights and the search for true justice." [. . .]

FURTHER RESOURCES

Achebe, Chinua. *No Longer at Ease.* London: Heinemann, 1960.

Adas, Michael. *Prophets of Rebellion: Millenarian Protest Movements against the European Colonial Order.* New York: Cambridge University Press, 1987.

Camus, Albert. *The Stranger.* New York: Alfred A. Knopf, 1946.

Chabal, Patrick. *Amílcar Cabral: Revolutionary Leadership and People's War.* New York: Cambridge University Press, 1983.

Enwezor, Okwui, and Chinua Achebe. *The Short Century: Independence and Liberation Movements in Africa, 1945–1994.* New York: Prestel, 2001.

Mao, Zedong. *On Guerilla Warfare.* Mineola, Ny: Dover, 2005.

Meer, Fatima. *Higher than Hope: The Authorized Biography of Nelson Mandela.* New York: Harper and Row, 1988.

Phillips, John Frederick Vicars. *Kwame Nkrumah and the Future of Africa.* New York: Praeger, 1961.

Rushdie, Salman. *Midnight's Children.* New York: Alfred A. Knopf, 1981.

Ward, Stuart. *British Culture and the End of Empire.* New York: Palgrave, 2001.

Films

Apocalypse Now. DVD. Directed by Francis Ford Coppola. Hollywood, CA: Paramount, 1999.

Arguing the World. DVD. Directed by Joseph Dorman, New York, NY: First Run Features, 1998.

Cry Freedom. DVD. Directed by Richard Attenborough, Universal City, CA: Universal, 1999.

Lumumba. VHS. Directed by Jacques Bidou. New York, NY: Zeitgeist Films, 2001.

Michael Collins. DVD. Directed by Neil Jordan, Burbank, CA: Warner Home Video, 1997.

Platoon. DVD. Directed by Oliver Stone. Santa Monica, CA: MGM Home Entertainment, 2001.

Radio Bikini. DVD. Directed by Robert Stone, USA: New Video Group, 2003.

The Quiet American. DVD. Directed by Phillip Noyce. Burbank, CA: Beuna Vista Home Entertainment, 2001.

The Year of Living Dangerously. DVD. Directed by Peter Weir, Burbank, CA: Warner Home Video, 2000.

TIMELINE FOR PART VII

1886	*Hobson-Jobson* **First Published**
1940s–Present	**Migration of Former Colonial Subjects to Britain (McAuley)**
1940s–1980s	**Economic Decolonization in Africa (Fieldhouse)**
1947	Commonwealth of Nations Replaces the old British Commonwealth
1948	World Health Organization Founded
1949	NATO Formed
1955	Bandung Conference
1967	ASEAN Formed
1972	**Idi Amin Expels Asians from Uganda (Kramer)**
1979	**Iranian Revolution (Manny)**
1980s–1990s	Democratization Movements in Latin America
1983	**Charef, *Tea in the Harem***
1984	AIDS Virus First Identified
1986	**Emecheta, "The Miracle"**
1989	Fall of the Berlin Wall
1990s	**Nuclear Issues Between India and Pakistan (Greenpeace Image)**
1994	**Chege, "What's Right With Africa"**
1997	**Kyoto Conference on Climate Control ("Understanding Climate Change")**
1999	**Protests Against the WTO in Seattle**
2001	September 11 Terrorist Attack
2001	**Said, "The Clash of Ignorance"**
2004	**France Bans Headscarves in Schools**
Today	**Masai and Other Peoples Continue to Use Traditional Agricultural Methods**

Entries in bold indicate sources.

Part VII

Further Reconfigurations:
The Post-Colonial World

INTRODUCTION

Although the formal imperialism described in the earlier portions of this volume has largely
ended, the world was indelibly transformed by imperialism. Part VII explores ways in which
the world has been reshaped by the experience of imperialism. The readings in this part particularly emphasize the impact that the colonies (and the colonized) have had on the metropoles (and the colonizers) in the postcolonial world. They also consider ways in which imperialism
continues to affect the world.

Not only were the cultures of the colonies transformed by the colonial experience, the
cultures of the metropoles were as well. These transformations are perhaps most obviously evident in language. As English and French (as well as other European languages) were used to
govern empires, for example, they absorbed new vocabulary from other languages, and new
words were created to describe new phenomena, as we see in the case of the three words defined
in the reading from *Hobson-Jobson*. These languages have been indelibly transformed by the colonial experience and continue to change as increasing numbers of people from the former colonies
move to Europe.

The readings by Kramer, Charef, Emecheta, and McAuley, in addition to the map of Muslims in Europe, all show ways in which the human geography of Europe has been transformed
by empire in the postcolonial era. In part because commonwealth structures facilitate movement of former colonial peoples to the metropole, and in part because European economies and
political systems have offered better opportunities for some residents of former colonies, immigration from recently independent states has continued in the postcolonial era as in the era of
empire. Economic opportunity appears to have drawn Majid's father to France in the excerpt
from Charef's *Tea in the Harem*. As we see in the example of Rabia, a Ugandan Asian immigrant
to the United Kingdom in the 1970s, described by Jane Kramer, political oppression in some
former colonies has also driven immigration to Europe.

Although Europe's doors have been relatively open to its former colonial subjects, it has
not always been an easy thing for these people to assimilate to their new homes or for Europeans to embrace the new people with different foods, habits, religions, and social practices.
Buchi Emecheta describes England as "indifferent" in "The Miracle," and in Rabia's story we

The Modern World

ARCTIC OCEAN

SWEDEN
FINLAND
ESTONIA
LATVIA
LITHUANIA
POLAND   BELARUS
GERMANY
1   UKRAINE
2   MOLDOVA
3   5
6 7   ROMANIA
8   9   GEORGIA
ITALY   BULGARIA
     11 10   ARMENIA
GREECE   CYPRUS   TURKEY
LEBANON   SYRIA   AZERBAIJAN
ISRAEL   IRAQ   IRAN   AFGHANISTAN
JORDAN   KUWAIT
LIBYA   BAHRAIN   PAKISTAN
EGYPT   QATAR
SAUDI   U.A.E.
ARABIA
NIGER   OMAN
CHAD   SUDAN   ERITREA   YEMEN
CAMEROON   DJIBOUTI
CENTRAL   ETHIOPIA
AFRICAN
REP.   SOMALIA
GABON   RWANDA   UGANDA   KENYA
DEM. REP.
OF CONGO   BURUNDI
TANZANIA
ANGOLA   MALAWI
ZAMBIA
NAMIBIA   ZIMBABWE   MADAGASCAR
BOTSWANA   MAURITIUS
MOZAMBIQUE
SOUTH   SWAZILAND
AFRICA   LESOTHO

RUSSIA

KAZAKHSTAN

UZBEKISTAN
TURKMENISTAN

MONGOLIA

KYRGYZSTAN
TAJIKISTAN

CHINA

N. KOREA
S. KOREA

JAPAN

NEPAL   BHUTAN

INDIA

BANGLADESH   MYANMAR

TAIWAN
HONG KONG

PACIFIC
OCEAN

Midway

Okinawa
Iwo Jima

NORTHERN
MARIANA
ISLANDS
Saipan

Wake Island

THAILAND   LAOS
VIETNAM   PHILIPPINES

Guam

CAMBODIA

SRI   BRUNEI
LANKA   MALAYSIA

SINGAPORE

INDONESIA

INDIAN
OCEAN

Palau

Truk

CAROLINE ISLANDS

MARSHALL
ISLANDS

Makin
GILBERT
ISLANDS
Kiribati
Tarawa   Tuvalu

Samoa
Islands

PAPUA
NEW
EAST TIMOR   GUINEA

SOLOMON
ISLANDS

VANUATU

Fiji

Coral
Sea Islands

NEW
CALEDONIA

AUSTRALIA

NEW
ZEALAND

1. CZECH REPUBLIC
2. SLOVAKIA
3. AUSTRIA
4. SWITZERLAND
5. HUNGARY
6. SLOVENIA
7. CROATIA
8. BOSNIA & HERZEGOVINA
9. SERBIA & MONTENEGRO
10. MACEDONIA
11. ALBANIA

0   1000   2000 Miles

0   1000   2000 Kilometers

see how difficult it can be for newly arrived immigrants to find friends and build communities. As Mehdi Charef shows us, it is not uncommon for these immigrants to find themselves caught between two worlds and to experience this feeling all the more deeply because they already have cultural and linguistic ties to the imperial center. At the same time, not all of these immigrants wish to assimilate fully and choose instead to retain traditional practices even when, on occasion, to do so means to flaunt the law. An example of this is the controversy over the Muslim head scarves that became quite heated in France in the early twenty-first century.

Over time the populations of Britain, France, and parts of Europe have been transformed by these new groups, as we see in the map of Muslims in Europe. According to the 2001 census of England and Wales, about 4.5 percent of the total population was of colonial origins, most of whom were concentrated around London and some other northern cities. As is the case in cities around Europe, certain London neighborhoods have become enclaves for particular immigrant communities from former colonies. Southall, for example, has a very high percentage of residents of South Asian origins, and Brixton has had a large number of residents of Caribbean origin for several decades. As we see in the excerpt from McAuley's *Guide to Ethnic London,* many of the stores, restaurants, and cultural spots in Brixton reflect its links to the Caribbean.

The newly-independent states, too, have experienced further reconfigurations in the postcolonial era. The new states had high expectations for their futures as they gained their independence, but although many of them have experienced considerable success, things have not always proceeded as planned for all the new states. David Fieldhouse discusses some of the causes of these failures in Africa. Michael Chege, on the other hand, writes about some of the many ways in which African states have succeeded. Manny, of the London Iranian Women's Liberation Group, offers insight into the sorts of sociocultural tensions between tradition and modernity that have arisen as postcolonial societies have sought to construct their identities, in this case, the tension felt by women between modern social practices and Islam.

As indigenous religions and cultural traditions have become increasingly celebrated by nationalist movements in the former colonies and elsewhere, questions of difference rather than similarities between newly independent states and their old colonial parent states have often been highlighted by political leaders. Ideas about difference have tended to shape the discourse of the Arab-Israeli conflict and the post–September 11 conflict between parts of the Islamic world and the West, for example. The selection by Edward Said argues that there is far more that is similar than different between these various warring groups and that hope for the future rests in finding a middle ground rather than continuing to focus on difference.

Although the world would surely have shrunk into a global village in the twentieth century even in the absence of imperialism, there is little question but that the imperialism of the late nineteenth and early twentieth centuries facilitated a globalization of economy, culture, and political and social practice. To help manage the global village, nongovernment institutions such as the United Nations and grassroots organizations such as Greenpeace have been created, but such institutions are always constrained by shifting power relations and the imperatives of nationalism. In the selection on climate change, a document produced by the United Nations, we see just how challenging it is to find solutions to global problems when dealing with self-interested governments and economic actors. One of the greatest challenges is to negotiate the relationship between rich and poor states, especially when they have had colonial relationships in the past, and the controversial role of institutions such as the World Trade Organization highlights this problem.

Even as the world appears in so many ways to have become increasingly homogenized over the course of the twentieth century, a process that was surely accelerated by the age of high imperialism, not all traditional cultural, economic, social, and political practices have been abandoned. The part ends with a contemporary image of some Masai herdsmen who both wear traditional dress and continue to engage in agricultural practices that are substantially similar to those they participated in prior to the imperialist era.

⋏

Tea in the Harem

Mehdi Charef

Mehdi Charef was born in Algeria in 1954. He remained there, living in the midst of the war for independence, with his mother and brother while his father immigrated to France in search of work, returning to Algeria only occasionally to see his family. In 1962, Charef and the rest of his family moved to Paris to join his father. There, he learned to be a mechanic and worked from 1970 until the 1980s in a factory, writing in his spare time. After the publication of his novel Tea in the Harem *in 1983, Charef directed a film based on the novel, which won a prize for best first film at the Cannes Film Festival, and he has since directed a number of other films.*

Tea in the Harem *is about a young Algerian immigrant, Majid, who is growing up in a housing estate in suburban Paris. Majid, who moves back and forth between his mother's Algerian world at home and a French and largely anti-Arab world at school, feels caught in the middle and out of place in both worlds. This novel was the first to be written by and to describe the life of a* beur, *that is, a second-generation Algerian or Morrocan living in France.*

⋏

Questions

1. What seem to be the cultural differences and tensions between Majid and his mother?

2. How has Majid been shaped by his environment?

Majid takes off his shoes and heads straight down the corridor to his room. His is a large family, and his brothers and sisters are round the front-room table arguing over their homework. His mother—Malika—is a solidly-built Algerian woman. As she stands in the kitchen, she sees her son sneaking down the corridor.

'Majid!'

Without turning round he goes straight into his room. 'Yeah?'

'Go and get your father.'

'In a minute!'

Malika bangs her pan down on the draining board and shouts:

'Straight away!'

He puts the Sex Pistols on the record player and plays *God Save the Queen* at full blast. Punk rock. That way he doesn't have to listen to his mother. He lies back on the bed, hands behind his head, and shuts his eyes to listen to the music. But his mum isn't giving up so easily:

'Did you hear what I said?'

She speaks lousy French, with a weird accent, and gesticulates like an Italian. Majid raises his eyes to the ceiling, with the air of a man just returned from a hard day's work, and in a voice of tired irritation he replies:

'Lay off, ma, I'm whacked!'

Since she only half understands what he's saying, she goes off the deep end. She loses her temper, and her African origins get the upper hand. She starts ranting at him in Arabic.

She comes up to the end of the bed and shakes him, but he doesn't budge. She dries her hands on the apron which is forever about her waist, switches off the stereo, tucks back the tuft of greying hair that hangs across her forehead, and begins abusing her son with all the French insults she can muster—'Layabout . . . Hooligan . . . Oaf . . .' and suchlike, all in her weird pronunciation. Majid pretends he doesn't understand. He answers coolly, just to irritate her:

'What'd you say? I didn't understand a word.'

By now his mother is beside herself. 'Didn't understand, didn't understand . . . Oh God . . .!' and she slaps her thighs.

She tries to grab him by the ear, but he ducks out of range. Finally he admits defeat and gets off the bed, scratching his head.

His mother follows him:

'Yes. Layabout! Hooligan!'

While she continues ranting at him and calling him every name under the sun, he puts the Sex Pistols back in their sleeve and gives a long-suffering sigh.

Then Malika informs her son, in Arabic, that she's going to see the Algerian consul. 'They'll come and get you, and you'll have to do your military service. *That* way you'll learn about your country . . . *and* you'll learn the language . . . *that'll* make a man of you. You say you won't do your military service like all your friends have to, but if you don't you'll never get your papers, and me neither. You'll lose your citizenship, and you'll never be able to go to Algeria because you'll end up in prison. *That's* where you'll end up. No country, no roots, no nothing. You'll be finished.'

Majid understands the occasional phrase here and there, and his reply is subdued, because whatever he says is bound to hurt her.

'I never asked to come here. If you hadn't decided to come to France, I wouldn't be "finished", would I, eh? So leave me alone, will you?'

She continues haranguing him, unleashing all the bitterness that is locked in her heart. It's not unusual for her to end up crying.

Someone knocks at the front door.

'Who is it?' she shouts, still furious.

She leaves the room and Majid flops down on the bed, reflecting that for a long time he's been neither French nor Arab. He's the son of immigrants—caught between two cultures, two histories, two languages, and two colours of skin. He's neither black nor white. He has to invent his own roots, create his own reference points. For the moment, he's waiting . . . waiting . . . He doesn't want to have to think about it . . .

[. . .]

Lessons and homework took second place.

At the time, Majid and his parents were living in Nanterre bidonville—the rue de la Folie—the largest and the cruellest of any in the Paris suburbs. Shantytowns that could equal anything in Brazil, but without the sun and the music. When Majid's dad had sent for his wife and son to come from Algeria, he'd not told them in his letter that they'd be coming to live in a cold, smoky barracks. When she first saw the place, Malika burst into tears, and Majid wondered if it was some kind of practical joke, because back home there was never enough to eat, but at least you had your little stone-built house; at least you had a home. You can always hide an empty stomach, but a hovel is there for all to see. Whatever happened to dignity? Malika used to clutch her little boy in her arms and wish she'd never made the voyage. His father used to say:

'They're going to rehouse us somewhere decent . . . I've been down to see them at the Town Hall . . .'

Months, years, spent living on their nerves—and always on the alert for fires, because in the shanty town the fires were a weekly event. Sometimes they were huge and lasted for hours. People would finally go back to bed in the early hours of the morning, with the flames dying down and the firemen exhausted.

Majid was seven years old when he and his mother found themselves waiting, one November morning, on the platform of a Paris station. His father was supposed to be meeting them, but he wasn't there. They waited for him, wandering around the station as the early editions hit the news stands and commuters stood drinking their morning coffees. Malika was still wearing her veil—as if caught between two civilizations. The suburban commuters on their way to clock in at the office eyed her curiously. This was the first time she'd left her village in Eastern Algeria, and here she was, all of a sudden, catapulted to the other side of the Mediterranean. Everything seemed so very huge here. 'This must be progress,' she told herself behind her veil. She had bought a new *haik* specially for the trip. It was her best outfit, and she wore it only to discover that women don't wear them here. Finally Majid's dad arrived, dressed in his fez. Majid didn't recognize him—when his father had emigrated, he had been too young to know him. He let himself be kissed by the man, because Malika told him that this was his father.

Then came the taxi, and then the shanty town. Young Majid went out looking for kids, and there were kids everywhere. 'Don't go getting lost,' Malika would tell him when he went out.

He was surprised by the Arab children—they all spoke French! And the kids weren't worried by this slum city, with its mud and its piles of rotting garbage. They spent their time—the Arab kids, with the Portuguese and the French—playing among the wrecked cars. [. . .]

The Revolution That Failed Women

MANNY

The following piece comes from a book of interviews and articles by women from all over the third world that explores the topics of feminism and women's organizations. This essay was written by Manny, a member of the London Iranian Women's Liberation Group, in 1981. The group was established in 1979, just after the Iranian Revolution and the replacement of the highly Westernized Persian government with an Islamic republic led by the Ayatollah Khomeini. The group sought to raise consciousness about women's rights in Iran and supported women's groups located in Iran. It also published newsletters in Persian, books in English, and sponsored at least one photographic exhibit on Muslim women.

Though never formally a colony, Iran was subject to first Russian and later British influence in the early twentieth century. In spite of strong anti-British sentiment among the Iranian population, Iran's post–Second World War leader, the Shah, oversaw a secularization and Westernization of Iranian politics and society. One facet of this process was the emancipation of women in 1963. With the Iranian Revolution of 1979, however, women were expected to give up their Westernized ways and live instead according to Islamic traditions. In the following essay, we see the tension between Westernization and a revival of social and religious traditions being played out in an anti-Western Iran of the early 1980s.

QUESTIONS

1. How might indigenous traditions and Western influences be reconciled in the postcolonial world?

2. Why does this author think some women supported Khomeini's Revolution?

In 1953, the Shah was restored by a CIA engineered coup. To the ally of America and gendarme of the Gulf, as was intended, Iran's economy had to be totally 'modernized.' Because of the international need of capitalism and its dependency on Gulf oil, the Shah created a dependent capitalism in Iran. Along with this came wealth for the middle classes, wealth but no democratic rights. The working class got jobs but very little else. Women

too received a share of the boom, but only as tools to suit the State's needs.

The Shah gave women the right to vote in 1964. The industries' demand for cheap labour had opened the job market to women. Skilled labour was needed, so education was encouraged, and women were accepted in technical colleges and universities. In later years, some factories, hospitals, and government offices got their own

Source: Manny of the London Iranian Women's Liberation Group, "The Revolution that Failed Women." In Miranda Davies (Ed.), *Third World—Second Sex: Women's Struggles and National Liberation, Third World Women Speak Out.* London: Zed Books, 1983. Pp.150, 152–158. Reprinted by permission of Zed Books Ltd.

nurseries. Powdered milk was given free to children in the countryside, and children at school were given breakfast. Family planning was introduced, with free contraceptives, and abortion became legal.

Consumer goods like washing machines, televisions, dishwashers, Japanese electric rice cookers, poured into the country. The most banal aspects of Western life and imperialistic culture, with all its consumerism, were injected into women's lives. Most of the cinemas began showing semi-pornographic films, and advertisements on the television used women more and more as sex objects. Violence against women rose to an incredible extent. Women were attacked in the streets, were raped in their cars, on their way to work or shopping, and everybody was advising women to be home by nine p.m.

Iranian social life was topsy-turvy, and Tehran had become a sick and diseased society. Ironically, working-class boys and girls enjoyed the growing relaxation in their social life, frequenting the café and cinema, and discarding the veil, although most of them later joined Khomeini and supported him against these middle-class values. Women too, working outside or at home, benefited in some ways from these reforms, but they too did not ultimately defend them. They helped to bring Khomeini to power.

Women under Khomeini's Regime

When Khomeini created his Islamic Republic in 1979, he relied on the institution of the family, on support from the women, the merchants, and the private system of land ownership. The new Islamic constitution declared women's primary position as mothers. The black veil, symbol of the position of women under Islam, was made compulsory. Guards were posted outside government offices to enforce it, and women were sacked from their jobs without compensation for refusing to wear the veil. The chairman of the Employment

Office, in an interview with the government's women's magazine (*Zan Rooz* No. 777) said, 'We can account for 100,000 women government employees being sacked as they resisted the order of the revolutionary government when it was demanded of them to put the veil on.'

Schools were segregated, which meant that women were barred from some technical schools, even from some religious schools, and young girls' education in the villages was halted. Lowering the marriage age for girls to 13, reinstating polygamy and *Sighen* (temporary wives), the two major pillars of Islam, meant that women did not need education and jobs, they only needed to find husbands.

The Ayatollahs in their numerous public prayers, which grew to be the only possible national activity, continuously gave sermons on the advantages of marriage, family, and children being brought up on their mother's lap. They preached that society would be pure, trouble free, criminal-less, (look at the youth problem in the West) if everybody married young, and if men married as many times as possible (to save the unprotected women who might otherwise become prostitutes). The government created a marriage bank at a time when half the working population was unemployed, whereby men were given huge sums—around £3,500—to get married. Another *masterpiece* of the revolutionary Islamic government was to create a system of arranged marriages in prisons, between men and women prisoners, to 'protect' women after they leave prison.

Because abortion and contraception are now unobtainable, marriage means frequent pregnancy. If you are 13 when you get married, it is likely that you will have six children by the time you are 20. This, in a country where half the total population are already under 16, is a tragedy for future generations.

Women prostitutes were executed under Khomeini, who said that the cause of prostitution is woman's lust for sex. Any woman, however, who disobeys her father or brother, doesn't wear the veil, demands education and a job, is called a prostitute anyway. When 15,000 women demonstrated in

Tehran against the compulsory wearing of the veil on International Women's Day 8 March 1979, Muslim men harassed the women, shouting 'You want to come out unveiled, you want to be prostitutes! If you want my prick, come on, I'll fuck you,' and holding out their pricks.

Khomeini's representatives at the United Nations conference in Copenhagen last year [1980] defended the execution of prostitutes and homosexuals by saying that 'We only shoot a few of them.' They also said in an interview, 'If we were going to execute all the women prostitutes, we would have to shoot a million women.' An Iranian woman from the group told us, 'They mean us too.'

Religious morality demands that all pleasures and entertainments be banned. Wine, music, dancing, chess, women's parts in theatre, cinema and television—you name it, Khomeini banned it. He even segregated the mountains and the seas, for male and female climbers and swimmers.

But compulsory morality, compulsory marriage, and the compulsory wearing of the veil did not create the Holy Society that Khomeini was after; but public lashings, stonings, chopping of hands and daily group executions sank Iran into the age of Barbarism.

Why Women Did It

Why do women, workers and unemployed, support this regime which has done everything in its power to attack their rights and interests? The power of Islam in our culture and tradition has been seriously underestimated by the Marxist Left, and it was through this ideology that Khomeini directed his revolutionary government. The clergy dealt with everyday problems and spoke out on human relationships, sexuality, security and protection of the family and the spiritual needs of human beings. It was easy for people to identify with these issues and support the clergy, although nobody knew what they were later to do. When Khomeini asked for sacrifices—'we haven't made the Revolution in order to eat chicken or dress better'—women

(so great in the art of sacrifice) and workers accepted these anti-materialist ideas. (Numerous workers' strikes were ended at his call, and their attention redirected towards the siege of the American Embassy and the main enemy, American imperialism.)

Women's attraction to Khomeini's ideas was not based simply on his Islamic politics, but also on the way he criticized the treatment of women—as secretaries and media sex objects—under the Shah's regime. Women were genuinely unsatisfied and looking for change. Some educated Iranian women went back to Iran from America and Europe to aid the clergy with the same messages, and became the government's spokeswomen. They put on the veil willingly, defended Islamic virtues and spiritual values, while drawing from their own experiences in the West. They said it was cold and lonely, Western women were only in pursuit of careers and self-sufficiency, and that their polygamous sexual relationships had not brought them liberation, but confusion and exploitation. These women joined ranks with an already growing force of Muslim women, to retrieve the tradition of true/happy Muslim women—in defence of patriarchy.

The most oppressive aspect of the role of these Muslim women intellectuals can be seen for instance in the case of Safar Zadeh, a leading poet and also a strong opponent of the Shah. She wrote poems that praised Khomeini as 'The Leader', 'God's representative on Earth', 'The Leader of the Oppressed', 'Our Saver'. These poems were published in the daily press in large thick black letters with a photo of her, returned to wearing the veil. A new literature was in the process of being made, a literature of women's oppression and how women should adore it. Z. Rahnavardi is a leading woman theoretician. She points to Marx and Engels and rejects their materialist view, saying that they ignore all the spiritual values of Islam, and also ignore women's vital role as producers of human life and labour. She defends the Qusas Law of retribution—a law which legitimizes the execution of homosexuals and lesbians, women adulteresses and thieves, and degrades and humiliates women publicly (women are put in a sack for public lashing). Rahnavardi says: 'There is no doubt that the laws should contain violence . . . [as] steps for reaching the purified Islamic society'.

Women and the Clergy

The clergy's contact with people in the cities and countryside has always been with women. The clergy's most important role is as administrator of the religious laws and also the economic role of collecting religious dues. Most of them were largely landowners themselves, and as a class they have been reactionary and corrupt.

The economic network created through the clergy's collection of dues plays an important social welfare base of women who are widowed or are ill, handicapped, have husbands away in jail, or are responsible for their elderly relations. (These are the common duties of women in a Third World country, where there is no social security system.) This charity function supports the indoctrination that women are helpless, and must rely on 'God the mighty, the gracious and his Imams'. It is also another reason why the religious hierarchy successfully fights against women becoming wage workers.

The clergy is also intellectually a dominant class. Many women are illiterate and they go to the clergy for help in writing letters or dealing with legal documents. For centuries, women have depended on the clergy in this way.

The mosque is not just a place of prayer, it is also a social club for women. It provides a warm, safe room for women to meet, chat or listen to a sermon, and there are traditional women-only parties and picnics in gardens or holy places. Take away these traditional and religious customs for women as the Shah—with his capitalist and imperialist reforms, irrelevant to women's needs—tried to do and a huge vacuum is left. Khomeini stepped in to fill that vacuum. The reason why Khomeini won was that the Shah's social-economic programme for women was dictatorial, bureaucratic, inadequate (especially in terms of health education) and therefore irrelevant to women's needs.

What little the Shah's reform brought to women was just a token gesture. Women dissatisfied with the Shah's reform felt that they had benefited little from him and would not miss it if it was taken away.

The Veil

Perhaps nowhere else in the world have women been murdered for walking in the street open-faced. The question of the veil is the most important issue of women's liberation in Muslim countries. The veil, a long engulfing black robe, is the extension of the four walls of the home, where women belong. The veil is the historical symbol of woman's oppression, seclusion, denial of her social participation and equal rights with men. It is a cover which defaces and objectifies women. To wear or not to wear the veil, for Muslim women is the 'right to choose'.

However, this question has always been raised in conjunction with women's rights to education, health, work, divorce and custody of their children. Male leaders have dictated to women for too long, what to do. Reza Shah enforced the veil, his son banned it, and his successor had enforced it. Mujahidin (the Marxist movement in Iran) men, say women should love it and wear it. But I believe the slogan of the Iranian Women's Movement, chanted in their demonstration before they were banned, 'With veil and without veil, we opposed the Shah, with veil and without veil, we will march to uphold freedom, till the day of our liberation'.

The Future?

Iranian women's struggles since the end of the nineteenth century have been harassed, slandered, stifled and banned. Khomeini was the last man who crushed women's strikes in the factory for the right to work, their sit-ins in the universities for women's rights to education, women's press meetings, demonstrations and the new Independent Women's Movement in Iran. But the movements are not remembered for victories or defeats, but for their mass participation and the messages they transmit to the future. The experience and memories of the Iranian Revolution will still linger on into the future.

The position of Left-wing parties in Iran is pretty much the same as here (small, in conflict with each other, and with very little mass support). Out of the numerous small socialist groups that exist even the revolutionary Left supported the war with Iraq and the American hostage taking as anti-imperialist struggles against the 'main enemy': American imperialism. The Communist Party of Iran has put all of its weight behind Khomeini with one hand, and blind submission to the Soviet Union with the other.

After Khomeini made the veil compulsory in March 1979 one month after the Revolution, there was little doubt in the Iranian woman's mind that the Revolution was being betrayed. But the Left continued calling it a revolutionary government and supported it. In August last year, *Liberation,* the French radical newspaper carried a feature entitled 'Women's Groups are the only opponents of Khomeini'. And so it was. It is only since Khomeini began persecuting the Muslim socialists, the Mujahidin, that they have come out to oppose him openly. (1,800 of their members, among them many women, have been executed during the last few months.)

The Mujahidin is growing in Iran. They have socialist views on class struggle and the planned economy, but on the women's question they uphold Quranic principles. Their leader in Paris has created together with ex-president Bani-Sadr, a government in exile. Mujahidin could become a mass movement to overthrow Khomeini. Although their guerrilla activities could go against them they could use the contradiction inherent in Islamic theology to push for social reforms. But we will not be fools, 'Once bitten, twice shy'. However, their strong identification with Islam seems to be working against them, and a takeover by the army and the Shah's supporters is more possible.

When Khomeini came back to Iran, four million people demonstrated in his support. Today, at most 30,000 demonstrate for him when he calls them to the street. He has been losing his supporters faster than the Shah. A mother of a friend in Paris phoned from Tehran and said, 'My dear girl the situation is grim, really bad . . . well . . . praying and the religious duties are not solving our country's problems, nor feeding our bellies'. She was astounded to hear this from her old, pious mother. This is our best hope, the doubts that Khomeini's government is creating in women's minds. Perhaps for the first time women are questioning the usefulness of Islam.

Sisterhood is Strong—Is It International?

I don't know. Britain is an island anyway. But I have come across numerous historical documents where women have expressed such desires on both sides. Today, most important of all the tasks is the creation of *links* and *dialogue* between the individual feminists, feminist groups, and the Women's Liberation Movement in the West with the struggling women in the east. After the revolution Iranian women asked us to send them any materials on women's struggles from here. We posted them any leaflets and papers we could get hold of. The anti-pornography campaign, the *depo-provera* campaign and the ideas of Women Against Violence Against Women are most relevant to the struggles of women in Muslim countries. Why not make the link? An equal link, based on what we have in common. As women struggling for rights—the right to walk in the streets—our struggles have no boundaries wherever we may be.

In one of the Iranian women's demonstrations, the Muslim women were chanting against other women. 'Neither the East, nor the West. Islam is the best'. Iranian women chanted back, 'Liberation is neither Eastern, nor Western, but International'. [. . .]

▲

French Muslim Girl

PHOTOGRAPHER: JEAN-PAUL PELISSIER

In September of 2004 the French government, in an effort to enforce the separation of church and state, enacted a law that forbade students to wear religious symbols in public schools. Although the law was not exclusively directed at Muslims, it nonetheless had the broadest impact on female Muslim students, many of whom wear headscarves as a symbol of piety. The law generated a great deal of protest both in France and around the world because it was widely interpreted as being anti-Muslim.

▲

QUESTION

1. How do this image and the issues that it represents display the further reconfigurations that have occurred in France as a result of the French experience with imperialism?

───────────

Black Africa 1945–80: Economic Decolonization and Arrested Development

D. K. FIELDHOUSE

Since the end of the Second World War, the political map of Africa has been transformed by decolonization. Prior to the mid-1950s, almost all of Africa was under some form of colonial control. Since then, the empires and settler states have vanished and have been replaced by more than fifty sovereign African states.

From the colonial standpoint, decolonization implied a planned elimination of Europe's African empires. In nation after nation, indigenous people witnessed the ceremonial lowering of the imperial flags that signified the successful culmination of colonial policies controlled from European capitals. But what did this mean for the economies of the new nations?

In this selection, D. K. Fieldhouse examines the economic history of Africa from the 1940s to the mid-1980s. He asks why political independence did not lead to the economic autonomy and sustained development that had been predicted on the eve of independence by Western powers and African nationalists alike. Fieldhouse presents an argument that what Africans achieved may be characterized as "false decolonization" in view of the continued dependence by many of the former colonies on their former colonial masters.

QUESTIONS

1. How true is the suggestion that colonial regimes in Africa functioned for purposes of extracting production and cheap labor needed in Europe?

2. In what ways might former colonies have achieved both political independence and economic autonomy?

Performance, Expectations and the 'Policy' Approach

Historians must always be aware of the dangers of a *post hoc ergo propter hoc* argument. To describe the dominant patterns of economic development in Black Africa from about 1960 in terms of 'the economic consequences of decolonization' is not to suggest that what happened was necessarily the direct consequence of the transfer of political power. There were both continuities and discontinuities and it is in most cases impossible to draw a hard line between them. On the one hand, successor states and development economists may point to dramatic increases in national incomes or to rapid industrialization, and claim that these were only possible because of the beneficent forces liberated by decolonization. On the other hand, the critics of Third World regimes may suggest that in fact the best years for Africa were

Source: D. K. Fieldhouse. *Black Africa 1945–80: Economic Decolonization and Arrested Development*. London: Allen and Unwin, 1986. Pp. 69–71, 85–90. Used with permission.

just before independence, perhaps in the booming 1950s, and that the almost universal economic disasters of the 1970s and 1980s demonstrate the unwisdom of adopting the types of economic management common in most post-colonial African states. There is no way of adjudicating between these standpoints. The basic question is rather whether it is possible to pinpoint specific factors which were characteristic of the economic development of these states after they became independent and which may, at least partially, explain their fluctuating fortunes since about 1960.

Surveying the literature, two distinct general approaches can be seen. First there is what can broadly be described as a 'policy' interpretation: whether things went well or badly, they must be seen as primarily the outcome of policies adopted by the successor states of Africa. Success may be attributed to their greater devotion to economic development and the wisdom of the means they employed, failure to their incompetence or misguided strategies. Secondly, there is what can equally loosely be described as a 'non-policy' approach, which reduces or even eliminates the responsibility of African governments, particularly for disasters. One strand of this approach [suggests] . . . that the colonial inheritance circumscribed but did not dictate the options open to the new states. Other explanations include the influence of the international environment (terms of trade, changing interest rates, etc.) and adverse endogenous factors, such as geology, climate and African attitudes to development. All such explanations of what happened after independence have their supporters; all, in some degree, are clearly relevant. [. . .]

There is, however, an underlying assumption which must be made explicit. This is that economic performance is most likely to be influenced by one or both of two major factors. The first is strictly economic and will largely be determined in any one country by the interaction of domestic and international movements in supply and demand, reflected in prices, terms of trade and ultimately an increase or decrease in real incomes. The second is broadly political—the actions of

governments which attempt to regulate domestic economic activity in pursuit of whatever objectives they may adopt. In terms of decolonization, the economic effects of the transfer of power are potentially minimal; the act of pulling down the imperial flag changes neither the facts of the domestic economy nor its relations with the international economy. If the successor regime made no changes in its approach to production, exchange, taxation or investment, the economic development of the ex-colony would barely be affected. Conversely, an interventionist government can radically affect the character of the domestic economy, even if it cannot significantly control the impact on it of external forces.

It is precisely because most post-colonial governments have attempted, or at least claimed to attempt, to develop the domestic economy in ways different from those of the imperialists that one can usefully consider the economic implications of decolonization. Putting it bluntly, have these political interventions made much difference? If there has been growth (taken here to imply an increase in the real national income) and development (the restructuring of the economy to increase the rate of growth and to enable it to be sustained indefinitely), was this because governments were active and successful? Or was it because, in the decades after the mid-1950s, international conditions became generally very favourable to these African economies? Conversely, if growth and development were less than one might reasonably have expected, or if they lost momentum at some point, given international comparisons, was this because governments adopted ill-advised (even if well-intentioned) policies, or because expectations had been pitched too high, or because there were factors beyond governmental control obstructing further progress? These are the fundamental problems to be considered, even if the available evidence is too limited and the statistics too unreliable to provide final answers. [. . .]

False Expectations and Their Origins

Disappointment may result from unreasonable expectations. It is, therefore, prudent to begin by considering on what grounds it was widely supposed around 1960 that political freedom would lead to rapid and sustained economic and social growth and development.

In retrospect it is one of the most astonishing features of post-1950 African history that there should have been so general an expectation that independence would lead to very rapid economic growth and affluence. There was, after all, no historical precedent. The wealth of Western Europe and North America had been accumulated over a long period: even if we accept the hypothesis that income levels in Europe were no higher than those in Africa and Asia in the earlier eighteenth century, it took a century or more of relatively slow growth before these countries achieved comparative affluence; and it was at least possible that this achievement was special, a unique product of congruent conditions not present elsewhere. Moreover, the record of those non-European states which had never been colonies, or (apart from the United States) which had been liberated by the early nineteenth century, did not suggest that political freedom by itself was guaranteed to result in rapid and sustained growth: indeed, Latin America provided a depressing case study in post-colonial poverty. Why, then, the almost universal optimism that accompanied decolonization in Africa?

The main reason appears to be that decolonization coincided with the birth and, as it turned out, short life-span, of a brand of applied economics which claimed to have solved the problem of the origins and nature of poverty and to be able to provide formulas which could ensure its eradication. The fundamental idea was that poverty, rather than affluence, was the abnormal human condition; so that, if one could isolate its causes, affluence should follow naturally. In the 1950s a broad consensus emerged, based on the new economic analysis of the nature of growth that emerged in the 1930s. Poverty resulted from a pathological condition from which any economy could suffer and whose main cause or symptom was an inadequate rate of capital accumulation.

For this various causes were assigned. [What follows are summaries of the interpretations of various economists.] Ragnor Nurkse attributed it either to limitation of the division of labour, resulting from the extent of the market, which in turn inhibited capital accumulation by preventing a rise in national income; or, adopting a Keynesian consumption function, to low productivity and incomes keeping per capita incomes low and thus creating a vicious circle of poverty. Leibenstein further defined this 'low level equilibrium trap', in which low initial levels of income growth stimulated population increases which would overtake the growth of national income and force down per capita incomes. Thus only a substantial increase in per capita incomes could break the circle. Many others also emphasized the inhibiting effects of low initial incomes in less developed countries; for example, Gunnar Myrdal, W. W. Rostow, and S. Kuznets. Clearly the only way out of the poverty trap was in some way to raise national and per capita incomes to the point at which savings and capital accumulation were possible on a sufficient scale; and, in analysing how this might be achieved, all these theorists assumed that the social value of an act of investment exceeded its private value because it expanded the size of the market and so tended to attract further investments. Tibor Scitovsky in particular emphasized the importance of externalities resulting from initial acts of investment, particularly in 'import-competing' industries for domestic consumption rather than for export, since in these a larger proportion of the profit was retained locally instead of being shared with the exporting firms and the country to which exports were sent.

Growth, then, depended on investment levels which were above the capacity of most unimproved less developed countries. What was the way out of this dead end? It is important that most economists of the 1950s and 1960s rejected the two standard remedies of previous thought: export-led growth and foreign direct investment. Exports and, by extension, concentration on export commodities on the principle of comparative advantage, could no longer perform the functions defined by classical economics—that is, by widening the market and providing a surplus for investment. Nurkse explained this primarily in terms of declining demand for tropical raw materials as the wealthy countries evolved synthetic substitutes and of markets in more developed countries blocked by protectionism. H. W. Singer, a pioneer of the structuralist school of development economics, using United Nations statistics, held that there had been an adverse trend in the terms of trade of less developed countries since the 1870s (thus providing an argument that was widely used by the left during the next decades), so that exporting commodities provided declining returns. Moreover, the economies of less developed countries were too inflexible for them to be able to respond to market signals of this type. Such arguments, heavily reinforced by evidence drawn from the depressed 1930s, were widely accepted and expanded into a broad denunciation of 'lop-sided' or 'skewed' economies that were over-dependent on a limited range of commodities. Clearly comparative advantage was no longer theoretically respectable.

Nor was foreign direct investment the panacea of colonial development schemes. Although the main attack on multinationals did not develop until the later 1960s, dependency theory was evolving in the early 1950s and with it criticism of foreign direct investment, based mainly on Latin American experience. The central argument, initiated by Singer and Paul Prebisch and taken up by a wide range of theorists who included the Latin American dependency school, Myrdal, Hla Myint and others, was that foreign direct investment was normally concentrated in 'enclaves', insulated from the rest of the host economy. These foreign firms paid low wages to indigenous workers, employed few local managers or technicians (so contributing little to the local stock of skills), bought little from the host economy, exported most of their products (so providing few downstream stimuli) and, above all, transferred their profits rather than reinvesting them locally. Foreign enterprises did not, therefore, contribute significantly to the process of domestic capital accumulation or the creation of local skills and know-how: if anything, they caused a drain of real resources. Clearly, such investment could not help less developed countries to break out of the poverty trap.

If these two well-established escape routes were now blocked, other gradualist solutions based on conventional capitalist assumptions were also discarded. Small markets in the new states led to scale problems, monopoly, imperfect factor markets and dualistic economies; all of which, coupled with poor information flows, resulted in low elasticities of supply. Entrepreneurs also seemed to be in very short supply. In primitive economies the price mechanism had little value. In short, if left to the operation of conventional market forces within a capitalist environment, these countries would almost certainly continue to stagnate. Organic evolution was blocked by structural problems.

This pessimism was the starting-point of the new approach to economic development of the 1950s. The broad consensus was now that a special prescription was necessary for the less developed countries of the modern world: hence the concept of development economics as a specific branch of applied economics. Killick has defined five basic assumptions common to all, or most, of those who pioneered this field.

1. Economic development in the tropics was a discontinuous process, involving structural transformation; it was not a natural growth.
2. This transformation consisted primarily of increasing the level of capital accumulation; once a critical threshold had been reached, the process should be self-sustaining.
3. An initial 'big push' was needed to break the mould of poverty and to make this possible.
4. This push involved a massive increase in the capital investment/national income ratio. It was assumed that the rate of growth of the economy would be roughly in line with the increase of the invested share of the GDP; and it seemed generally agreed (though without any evidential base) that a minimum level

of 10 per cent was essential for what Rostow emotively called 'the take-off'.

5. Finally, industrialization was essential to growth and development; and the arguments for this are important. Industry was more likely to be 'modernizing' than agriculture. Productivity should be higher. Industry would provide a market for increased agricultural production and its products would provide an incentive for farmers to earn the money to buy consumer goods. Import-substituting industry was best, because this would provide both backward and forward linkages into the economy and capture all the benefits. Some, notably (Sir) Arthur Lewis, did not accept this last point entirely, but most swallowed the import-substitution argument whole.

This, then, became the grand strategy of the 1950s and early 1960s. There remained the question of tactics: how best to get the 'big push' going. One almost universal assumption was that colonialism must end before anything serious could be done. Despite their deathbed repentance and the extensive projects carried out by the metropolitan states after about 1950, it was regarded as axiomatic that a colonial state could not wish to carry out the structural changes that were necessary because these would be inconsistent with its own economic interest. Moreover, the colonial state lacked the legitimacy, and therefore the self-confidence, to undertake fundamental social engineering. The onus, therefore, must be on the first successor states just beginning to be visible in Africa, with Ghana moving towards independence and the rest assumed to be following not far behind. On these states and their character the economists—like the eighteenth-century *philosophes,* with whom they had much in common, before them—placed great faith. Their rulers were assumed to be both enlightened and efficient, and so fit to be the main instruments of change and development. The reason was that the economists put great emphasis on economic management and planning as the alternative to the market. The main case for this preference, as expounded [by] Scitovsky in 1954, was that the price mechanism could not give true signals about the future, especially where factor and product markets were as imperfect and entrepreneurs and resources as scarce as they were deemed to be in less developed countries. Moreover, new econometric techniques made indicative planning possible for the first time, and also, of course, exciting for economists. Development, therefore, must be planned and executed by the post-colonial state.

In expounding this doctrine of planning the economists showed several biases that were to have significant consequences. They preferred to deal in national aggregates (saving and investment ratios) and showed little interest in the detail of micro-economic implementation. They postulated closed rather than open economies. They adopted long time-horizons, which implied state rather than private provision of capital. This the state would do through taxation (on the assumption that the state's propensity to consume was lower than that of private individuals), by the creation of new credit institutions and probably by deficit financing. Inflation was not regarded as a serious problem. W. A. Lewis, for example, thought that it would be self-correcting. The main area of disagreement was over whether the state should take a direct role in economic life, as owner of factories, farms, banks, etc., in addition to providing infrastructure and social services. But this was only on the margins of the new consensus. Those who disagreed in principle were few and, for the time being, regarded as old-fashioned and obscurantist [. . . .]

Why, then, was the battle won so easily? One answer is that, since conventional prescriptions for economic development appeared to have failed in the past—with the disastrous 1930s still taken as the most relevant example rather than what proved to be the booming 1950s—there was a general desire for new courses. Intellectually the new economics found ready allies on the left, where Marxist economists such as Maurice Dobb and Paul Baran were able to fit them readily into the Marxist-Leninist schemata and, indeed, added influential ideas concerning the possibility of extracting savings from the indigenous wealthy and from foreign enterprises. But by far the most important fact was that these arguments for 'economic independence' and state control of the economy were extremely attractive to the leaders of nationalist movements in the colonies, the future rulers of the new states. In the so-called struggle for independence, the assertion that colonialism and its associated collection of economic practices and institutions were a bar to progress provided excellent propaganda, both in Africa and Europe. Nkrumah, for example, as early as 1949, made the famous prophecy that 'If we get self-government, we'll transform the Gold Coast into a paradise in ten years'.

Once independence was achieved the economists' prescription had even more to offer. Their emphasis on state power was a useful rhetorical weapon against liberals and political opponents. Economic nationalism was a multipurpose tool which could be used against all foreign interests and justified a wide range of potentially unpopular devices, such as control over imports, credit, productive capacity and prices. The primary role allotted to industry could be used to justify penal taxation of primary producers whose surplus was urgently needed to support the new state apparatus. The need for huge quantities of investment capital, accepted by the West, made it possible to borrow very extensively. The near-promise that,

if the 'push' was big enough, the structural obstacles to growth would be removed suggested that the new states could achieve affluence and self-sufficiency in accumulation in a very short time-span. But, above all, it was probably the nationalist element—the rejection of internationalism and dependence on overseas markets and investors—that was the most attractive feature of the new development economics for the African countries. In short, one way or another, the new development economics was almost universally accepted, with gratitude, by the new states and their leaders. It would have been amazing had it been otherwise.

Thirty years later most of the optimism seems to have been misplaced. No Black African state has 'taken off'. Despite considerable growth of real incomes in some states and often impressive performance in the provision of welfare and infrastructural services and in the relative importance of industry, there has been very limited development in the structural sense. Clearly there were many false expectations. But were the strategies themselves misguided or were they incorrectly executed? The argument of this book is that both factors must be held responsible for relative failure—relative because in fact there were very substantial real achievements in most new states. On the one hand, few of the theorists had any deep understanding of the realities of African life and the problems of overcoming obstacles to growth. On the other, none of the new states proved capable of carrying out the complex requirements of the new development codes. [. . .]

⋏

Unsettling Europe

JANE KRAMER

⋏

Over the course of the 1970s, Jane Kramer researched and wrote Unsettling Europe *as a series of essays for* The New Yorker *magazine. The book chronicled demographic shifts in Europe that resulted from external and internal migration, some of which were related to colonialism. The following selection comes from a chapter on Ugandan Asian refugees in the United Kingdom, a large group of migrants who have helped transform the face of postcolonial Britain.*

Although there had been a long history of South Asian migration to Africa prior to British colonization of the Indian subcontinent and large parts of Africa, the British had encouraged further immigration, often recruiting Asians to move to their African colonies to assist them in the colonial enterprise by building railroads, roads, and plantations, for example. Such a process had taken place in Uganda. In 1971, the military leader Idi Amin used a coup to take control of Uganda, which had been granted independence in 1966. In the fall of 1972, Amin nationalized the properties of Uganda's Asian population and gave them three months to leave the country, prompting an exodus of more than 27,000 people, who, as citizens of the British Commonwealth, sought asylum in the United Kingdom. The Ugandan Asians joined the roughly 1.5 million immigrants from the Commonwealth that already lived in Britain in the early 1970s. Britain, France, and other former European colonial powers have therefore been racially and culturally transformed by the postcolonial influx of people from their former colonies. This excerpt describes the experience of one of the Ugandan Asians, Rabia, whom Kramer interviewed.

⋏

QUESTIONS

1. In what ways might we consider Rabia to be a true citizen of the empire?
2. What expectations did Rabia have of England, and what do you think shaped those expectations? Did England live up to her expectations?

[. . .] Rabia Hassan thought of Southall when her plane landed, because it was only three miles from Heathrow, and she knew that an old Koranic scholar from Masaka had moved there in 1970 to open a travel agency specializing in tours to Mecca and excursion holidays on the Devon coast. Rabia did not think she had the money to get much farther, anyway. She had tried to leave Uganda with £200 sewn into the hem of a length of sari cloth, but the guards at Entebbe Airport found the money when they went through her suitcase. All she had managed to save was a £10 note, which was hidden in her chignon—and which the guards had overlooked because her daughter, Zhora, fainted when they were both stripped forcibly and searched. *That* money went to a London

---

Source: Jane Kramer. *Unsettling Europe*. New York: Random House, 1980. Pp. 140–45. Copyright © 1972, 1974, 1976, 1979, 1980 by Jane Kramer. Used by permission of Random House, Inc.

taxi driver who intercepted Rabia and the children at Heathrow and demanded £10 in advance to take them to the scholar's house.

Rabia still cannot believe that an Englishman would charge £10 for a trip that ordinarily costs less that £1. She is a timid woman, with wide brown eyes that always seem to be asking her why her life has been so disappointing, but she refuses to be disappointed by the British. When she learned from her friend the scholar that she had been swindled, she told him that the taxi was new and beautiful and that the driver must have needed the extra money to meet his payments on it at the bank. When her next-door neighbors—the Hassans now live on the fringe of Southall that is still mainly a neighborhood of white families—did not invite her in on the night she rang their doorbell with a gift of her special mincemeat curry, she asked Akbar if something about her manner could have offended them. When the manager of a local bank, whom she saw secretly about a part-time job that was advertised in the bank window, told her to get out and not come back, she decided that the man must have been exhausted by his important work. It was only after eight months, when Akbar allowed her to take a half-day trip to central London, that Rabia finally complained about the British. She had been looking forward to her day in London. She had imagined London as something like Salisbury, Rhodesia, where she was born and brought up, only bigger, shinier, and even more splendid, but now, on her first free day in a year, she saw nothing but old houses. It was shameful, she said afterward, that the British cared so little for their capital that they did not bother to tear down those drab old houses and put up some modern buildings "in the Rhodesian style."

Rabia still misses Rhodesia, although she left it at sixteen, when she was married, and returned there only once, for her first confinement. She says that sometimes, when Akbar complains that life ended for him at the Mercedes-Benz garage in London, she will think of how her own life ended the day she left Salisbury, as a bride, in a truck

caravan of her husband's relatives, for the fifteen-hundred-mile journey to the Uganda bush. Rabia says she was brought up "free" in Salisbury, by which she means that she went to school, joined the Girl Guides, played field hockey, took walks through town, wore a short, fitted tunic over her serwal, spent Saturday afternoons at the movies, and had her hair washed every other Thursday by a hairdresser. Her father was an eccentric Kutchi merchant who outlived three wives and sired fifteen children—among them nine daughters, whom he decided to "free" while he was under the influence of a white wholesaler with whom he hoped to do a lively business. Like most Rhodesia Asians, he considered the Uganda Asians backward. But he had a strong feeling for his own people, and he worried a lot about finding the proper husbands for his daughters, since there was a shortage of Kutchi Muslims in Rhodesia, and an even greater shortage of Kutchi Muslims with unmarried sons. When Hamid appeared one day at his door, with letters of introduction, a bank statement of the Hassan assets, and a lineage chart drawn up by his friend the Koranic scholar and proving conclusively that they were paternal fifth cousins, Rabia's father saw at once the answer to his problem.

Over the years, starting with Rabia, he married five of his girls to sons of his newly discovered Uganda relatives. Rabia was told that day that she was going to have a husband. She had just started training at a local nursing school, but when she asked permission to postpone the wedding until the term was over, Hamid said that life was very difficult in his village and that his wife had waited long enough for a daughter-in-law to work for her around the house. Three months later, Rabia was in purdah in the village. She says that at first she tried to make friends with the women in her new family. She told them stories about the Rhodes Centenary Exhibition in the town of Bulawayo, where for only five shillings she had ridden in a rickshaw through five square miles of pavilions. She taught them the words to "Old MacDonald," taking the parts of all the animals herself. She even offered to teach them how to read and write. But the women said that she was being snobbish and only wanted to shame her husband, who had never been to school. Besides, Akbar's mother never forgave her for wearing a white European gown at her wedding ceremony instead of a proper Asian costume. She complained to Akbar that the daughter of a fifth cousin was not much of a relative, all things considered, and she resolved to marry her second son to her older brother's daughter, even though the girl was stupid. Akbar, as was proper, took his mother's part. He did not know what to do with an educated, discontented wife, who thought it was hard that there was no cinema in the village, who expected to sit down with him at dinner, who was always trying to keep him at home making conversation when she should have known that his place was with the men. He warned Rabia, who tried her best to please him. She threw away her English handbag and put her English novels in a suitcase. She lengthened her tunics. She kept to the women's path, behind the houses, and stopped asking why she was not permitted to walk on the village roads. But she was lonely in Uganda, and became cranky. When she went to her parents, in Rhodesia, to have Zhora, Akbar did not send money for their passage home. Her father had to drive them back to Uganda, and Rabia did not leave Akbar again until the day he put her on the plane for London.

"When I had the boys, Akbar would tell me, 'Go to England, educate my sons,'" Rabia said one day last spring in her clear, sad Salisbury voice. It was Good Friday. Just to the east, in the borough of Hammersmith, the local Catholics were dragging a great wooden cross along their end of the road to Uxbridge, but in Southhall people were starting to congregate for prayers in honor of the Prophet's birthday. Rabia was in her kitchen arranging biscuits on a 1967 Princess Anne commemorative birthday plate that Abdullah had picked up for a few pence at one of the weekly Southall auctions. She expected the women of the family to come at four for prayers and a long

reading from the Koran. "Akbar would tell me, 'Go to England,'" Rabia said again. "He would promise to come two times a year to visit, but I did not trust him. I knew that if I left, I would never see him. I would be without a husband. So I would say, 'No, thank you. It is too cold for us in England.' And he would get angry and say that it was only the servants I cared about—that I stayed in Africa against his wishes because in Africa I had servants. But I would not go, and then, when Amin said that we *had* to go, all of us, Akbar beat me. 'You see,' he said. 'If you had gone when I asked you, we would have got some of our money out, at least. Now we are losing everything, and it is your fault.'" Rabia says that she settled down in Southall suspecting that Akbar would find a way to stay in Africa. It was Rabia who went out and rented the house where the rest of his family is still living. And it was Rabia who memorized the bus routes through Ealing Borough and then maneuvered her way through the maze of British social-service offices to get money for the family, schools for the children, work for Akbar's brothers, and information about council housing. Every week she wrote to Akbar about her progress, but he never answered her letters, and for over two months the only word she had of him was through the relatives who came. At times, she says, she was certain she had been abandoned. But she had learned by then—from a television set she rented with most of her first week's allowance from social services—that English husbands were devoted and adoring and could not function without their wives' company, and so she was also certain that if Akbar did come, their life would change. "I am so ignorant," she says now. "I had not been to English films in Uganda, and I did not know that English husbands and wives love each other so. But then I saw on the telly that they never fight. No, they are always hugging and kissing. And I thought, Well, life will be just like this for me with Akbar if he comes to London. But then he did come, and it is just like in Uganda. I am not allowed to walk, to talk. We never go to the cinema or eat together at the table. And now I think, Can this be true? Is it only we Asians who have so much trouble?"

Rabia still rents the television set, but now it is her four little boys who like to watch it. She is not altogether happy with her little boys, she says. She is proud of Abdullah because he is her oldest son, and she feels for Zhora because Zhora is her only daughter, but she is bedeviled by Habib, Hanif, Yusuf, and Ayub, who take advantage of her. They used to tell their father whenever she left the house without them, and now she has to bribe them with sweets and by letting them take their lunch at home rather than at school, where it is free and nourishing. Habib, who is eleven, is ruining his teeth with all the candy, but Rabia, despite her month at the Salisbury nursing school, does not believe that the cheap candy has anything to do with rotting teeth. She does not believe that colds are caught, either. She believes that bad teeth and runny noses come from weak character, and she suspects her little boys of weak character, both because they carry tales to their father and because they readily accept her bribes. Rabia spends at least a pound and a half of the food money every week on sweets for the children, purchasing her time to walk. The walks are important to her. She never heads toward the center of the village, for fear of running into relatives, but plots a course around the block, hoping to meet a neighbor who could become her friend. One Uganda Asian family was already living in the neighborhood when Rabia moved there. Their name is Ramachandra, and they are Hindu and would prefer to mingle with other Hindus. But the Ramachandra women are as lonely in London as Rabia, and Rabia has struck up a wary friendship with Romila Ramachandra, who is just her age and has six children of her own. Rabia sometimes translates movie magazines for Romila, who does not speak English. Romila, in return, lets Rabia use her telephone, for tenpence a call. Apart, they insult each other. Rabia sometimes says that Hindus like the Ramachandras were responsible for Amin's order. She accuses the Ramachandra brothers, who are jewelers, of having smuggled a fortune in gold out of Uganda on business trips to London—whereas Akbar, who was honorable, kept his money in the country and consequently lost it all. The Ramachandras did salvage some of their money, as it happens, by buying an around-the-world plane ticket for every member of the family and, at their first stop, turning all the tickets in for a flight to London. But most of that money went for the lease on a shop in Fulham, and whatever jewelry they left with—spread under the false bottom of a special suitcase—is still in the shop-window, waiting to be sold. The Ramachandras are actually not much better off than the Hassans. In fact, they suspect that the Hassans brought some gold out, now that a Mercedes is parked in front of the Hassan house. Romila watches ladies from Citizens Aid and social services drive up to Rabia's house with bundles of old clothes and curtains, and she always stops by for tea afterward, trying to discover if they have given Rabia money, too. [. . .]

Definitions from *Hobson-Jobson*

HENRY YULE AND A. C. BURNELL, EDITORS

Empires brought into sustained and intense contact peoples with different cultural and linguistic backgrounds, and this contact yielded change in both the colonies, as discussed extensively in Part IV of this reader, and the metropoles. As imperialists imposed their own languages on empire, these languages were also transformed through the process of governing and interacting with colonial peoples.

Because of the length of the colonial relationship between Britain and India, Indian languages and the experience of governing India had a greater impact on English than the languages and experiences of other British colonies in Africa, the Caribbean, and elsewhere in Asia. Various English language dictionaries were compiled in the nineteenth century that included Anglo-Indian words and slang, but the best known is Hobson-Jobson, *the title of which is an Anglo-Indian word commonly used among British soldiers in the nineteenth century to describe native festivals. The following excerpts are examples of different sorts of change that occurred in the English language as a result of sustained colonial contact between Britain and India. English and other languages absorbed many new words from indigenous languages of the colonies, but it was also the case that entirely new words came into being to express aspects of the very process of colonial government. Although language exchange is very old, it is an ongoing process and still has an effect upon our contemporary world and is an important element of global reconfigurations.*

QUESTIONS

1. What are the origins of the word *civilian?* How was this word the result of British-Indian contact? What does the word mean today?

2. What are the origins of the word *pundit?* How does this word represent a reconfiguration of the English language? What does the word mean today?

3. Consider the ways in which new words enter the English language today.

CIVILIAN, s. A term which came into use about 1750–1770, as a designation of the covenanted European servants of the E. I. [East India] Company, not in military employ. It is not used by Grose, c. 1760, who was himself of such service at Bombay. [. . .] In Anglo-Indian parlance it is still appropriated to members of the covenanted Civil Service [. . .] . The *Civil* Service is mentioned in *Carraccioli's L. of Clive,* (c. 1785), iii. 164. From an early date in the Company's history up to 1833, the members of the Civil Service were classified during the first five years as **Writers** (q.v.), then to the 8th year as **Factors** (q.v.); in the 9th and 11th as *Junior Merchants*; and thenceforward as *Senior Merchants.*

Source: Henry Yule and A. C. Burnell, Eds. *Hobson-Jobson: A Glossary of Colloquial Anglo-Indian Words and Phrases, and of Kindred Terms, Etymological, Historical, Geographical and Discursive.* London: John Murray, 1903. Pp. 222–23, 419, 740.

These names were relics of the original commercial character of the E. I. Company's transactions, and had long ceased to have any practical meaning at the time of their abolition in 1833, when the Charter Act (3 & 4 Will. IV. c. 85), removed the last traces of the Company's commercial existence. [. . .]

HOBSON-JOBSON, s. A native vocal excitement; a *tamāsha* [. . .]; but especially the **Moharram** ceremonies. This phrase may be taken as a typical one of the most highly assimilated class of Anglo-Indian *argot*, and we have ventured to borrow it from a concise alternative title for this Glossary. It is peculiar to the British soldier and his surroundings, with whom it probably originated, and with whom it is by no means obsolete, as we once supposed. My friend Major John Trotter tells me that he has repeatedly heard it used by British soldiers in the Punjab; and has heard it also from a regimental Moonshee. It is in fact an Anglo-Saxon version of the wailings of the Mahommedans as they beat their breasts in procession of the *Moharram*— **"Yā Hasan! Yā Hosain!"** It is to be remembered that these observances are *in India* by no means confined to Shī'as. Except at Lucknow and Murshīdābād, the great majority of the Mahommedans in that country are professed Sunnis. [. . .]

PUNDIT, s. Skt. *pandita,* 'a learned man.' Properly a man learned in Sanskrit lore. The Pundit of the Supreme Court was a Hindu **Law-Officer,** whose duty it was to advise the English Judges when needful on questions of Hindu Law. The office became extinct on the constitution of the 'High Court,' superseding the Supreme Court and Sudder Court, under the Queen's Letters Patent of May 14, 1862.

In the Mahratta and Telegu countries, the word *Pandit* is usually pronounced *Pant* (in English colloquial *Punt*); but in this form it has, as with many other Indian words in like case, lost its original significance, and become a mere personal title, familiar in Mahratta history, *e.g.* the Nânâ Dhundo*pant* of evil fame.

Within the last 30 or 35 years the term has acquired in India a peculiar application to the natives trained in the use of instruments, who have been employed beyond the British Indian frontier in surveying regions inaccessible to Europeans. This application originated in the fact that two of the earliest men to be so employed, the explorations by one of whom acquired great celebrity, were masters of village schools in our Himālayan provinces. And the title *Pundit* is popularly employed there much as *Dominie* used to be in Scotland. The *Pundit* who brought so much fame on the title was the late Nain Singh, C.S.I. [. . .]

▲

Guide to Ethnic London

IAN MCAULEY

In the postcolonial era, London has become one of the most cosmopolitan cities on earth, a "world city," as London Mayor Ken Livingstone said in the wake of the 2005 London bombings. Although its multiculturalism is evident in virtually all parts of the city, there are some parts that have historically been magnets for Britain's colonial subjects from different parts of the Empire. Southall, a suburb just to the west of London, for example, is predominantly South Asian, and Brixton, the subject of the following piece, has historically been home to many of London's Caribbean immigrants. The following excerpt comes from an unconventional guidebook to ethnic London that provides historical and contemporary information on many of the parts of London that have substantial ethnic populations. The book was intended as a guidebook as much for residents of Britain as for foreign tourists; it offers recommendations on shopping and restaurants and provides cultural information.

▲

QUESTIONS

1. How was Brixton reconfigured by British imperialism?
2. What sorts of evidence of Britain's colonial past can be found in Brixton?

[. . .] Following the establishment of new shipping links with the Caribbean and West Africa in the 1880s, small black communities soon developed in the dock areas of many British ports, notably in Liverpool, Cardiff and London's Canning Town. Boosted by the arrival of black merchant seamen in the First World War, they have survived as Britain's oldest black communities.

Nevertheless, the forerunners of the modern era of black settlement were the Caribbeans, and to a lesser extent, the West Africans, who came to Britain during the Second World War. Here they worked in munitions factories, as merchant seamen, and in the armed forces (principally as flight mechanics in the RAF [Royal Air Force]). Their numbers were fairly small, but through sending back knowledge of the opportunities in Britain to their home countries they paved the way for the mass immigration of the 1950s and early 1960s.

Immigrants came from all over the English-speaking Caribbean, with the Jamaicans forming the largest single group. Some were recruited directly from their home countries by the National Health Service, London Transport and British Railways. Immigrants also came, though in lesser numbers, from West Africa, principally from Nigeria and Ghana.

There has been little immigration from the Caribbean since the 1960s, but immigration from Africa picked up again in the late 1980s, as Somalians and Ethiopians fled from civil war in East Africa, and as West African immigration increased again. Today there are about 700,000 black people in Britain, of whom about 425,000 live in London, concentrated in South London in Lambeth and Lewisham and in North-East London in Hackney and Harringay. Africans now make up about one third of London's black population and are becoming an increasingly important and influential part of the black community. [. . .]

Brixton

Britain's first group of post-war Caribbean immigrants arrived in London from Jamaica in 1948 on the liner *Empire Windrush.* Many of this pioneering group settled in Brixton, a once prosperous suburb that was then rapidly decaying into one of the city's poorest districts. Jamaicans were predominant amongst the many black people who settled in Brixton in the 1950s and 1960s, and this is reflected in the area's association with reggae and Rastafarianism [. . .], which are both of Jamaican origin.

Until the late 1980s, Brixton was London's most prominent black district and a symbol of black cultural and political self-assertion, acquiring national attention as a result of the anti-police riots by black youths in 1981 and 1985. Brixton today is less of a focus than it once was, and other areas of London have increased in importance for the black community. However, there is still quite a lot to see of interest in Brixton, and many black institutions and organisations are still based here. [. . .]

Brixton: Shopping

In its heyday in the late 19th C. Brixton was the premier shopping centre in the whole of South London. When Electric Avenue was opened in 1888, it was one of the first shopping streets in London to be lit by electricity. Many people in their 20s and 30s will have heard of Electric Avenue through the lyrics of a chart single by the black singer Eddie Grant: 'We're going to rock down to/Electric Avenue'.

There has been a market in the tangle of narrow streets and arcades of Brixton town centre ever since the end of the 19th C. It is a general market, selling everything from second-hand clothes to fruit and vegetables. Stalls are located in Brixton Station Road, Pope's Road, Electric Avenue, Reliance Arcade, Station Arcade, Market Row and Granville Arcade. The market is closed on Sundays and Wednesday afternoons.

Shops and stalls which stock goods specifically for the black community are found in the greatest density in Granville Arcade. Look out for the following goods:

At the butchers: Caribbean specialties include goat's meat, cow's feet, salted pig's tails.

Fishmongers: Snappers, jackfish, flying fish, shark.

Greengrocers: Breadfruit, limes, mangoes, yams, green bananas, coconuts, plantains.

Grocers: Tins of ackee, breadfruit, and callaloo, bags of black-eyed beans and pounded yam, bottles of West Indian hot pepper sauce, loaves of the heavy Caribbean types of bread.

Record shops: Reggae/soul music

Newsagents: The black British weekly newspapers *Caribbean Times*, *African Times* and *The Voice*. *The Voice* is orientated towards the younger British-born black population; the others have a stronger slant towards news from their readers' countries of origin.

Granville Arcade

Access from Atlantic Road and Coldharbour Lane.

Jackie and Katie Fashion Wear, Second Avenue, 47 Granville Arcade, SW9 (no telephone). Open from 10am to 5pm Monday to Saturday (except to 1pm Wednesday). African-style clothes made to measure. Small selection of ready-to-wear skirts, blouses and trousers.

The Wig Bazaar, Third Avenue, 57 Granville Arcade (071-733-3589). Open from 9am to 5pm Monday to Saturday (except to 1pm Wednesday). Black cosmetics, wigs, and 'tie-ins' (additions to natural hair).

Nasseri Fabrics, Second Avenue, 35-36 Granville Arcade (071-274-5627). Open from 9:30am to 5:30pm Monday to Saturday (except 1pm Wednesday). African fabrics sold by the yard or roll.

Robinsons, Third Avenue, 50/51 Granville Arcade (071-733 2405). Open from 9:30am to 5:30pm Monday to Saturday (except to 1pm Wednesday). Grocers and greengrocers which specialises in West African food. Spices, dried fish, bread, palm oil. A speciality is frozen Nigerian snails. Also stocks traditional West African teeth-cleaning sticks and Nigerian magazines and newspapers.

One Stop, Fourth Avenue, 72 Granville Arcade. Open from 9am to 5:30pm Monday to Saturday (except to 1pm Wednesday). Record shop. Reggae, soul, soca.

Arcade Bakeries, 2nd Avenue, 1 Granville Arcade (071-733 3105). Open from 9am to 5:30pm Monday to Saturday (except to 1pm Wednesday). Caribbean breads, buns and patties.

Back Home Foods, 3rd Avenue, 56 Granville Arcade (no telephone). Open from 8am to 5pm Monday to Saturday (except to 1pm Wednesday). Grocers and greengrocers. Specialities from Ghana and Sierra Leone.

Dagons Ltd., 1st Avenue, 16 Granville Arcade (071-274 1665). Open from 7:30am to 5:30pm Monday to Saturday (except to 1pm Wednesday). Tropical fish including many Caribbean varieties.

Tina's Tropical Foods, 6th Avenue, 90-91 Granville Arcade (no telephone). Open from 7:30am to 5:30pm Monday to Saturday (except to 1pm Wednesday). Greengrocers. African and Caribbean vegetables and fruits.

Elsewhere in Brixton

Red Records, 500 Brixton Road, SW9 (071-274 4476). Open from 9:30am to 8:30pm to Saturday, Sunday noon to 6pm. Record shop. Reggae, soul, jazz, African, dance and rave.

A-Z Connections, 21 Brixton Station Road, SW9 (071-738 6457). Open from 9:30am to 6:30pm Monday to Saturday. Imported clothing from Africa. Also African videos, music cassettes and handicrafts.

Afro Food Centre, 31 Electric Avenue, SW9 (071-274 4466). Open from 9am to 6pm Monday to Saturday. Grocers. Imported produce comes mainly from West Africa.

Franks, 33 Electric Avenue, SW9 (071-737 5073). Open from 9am to 6pm Monday to Saturday. Black cosmetics plus wigs and hair pieces.

Temple Gallery, 23 Brixton Station Road, SW9 (071-737 5332). Open from 9am to 6:30pm Monday to Friday (except closes at 4:30pm Wednesday, 6pm Saturday). Prints by black artists. Some exhibitions of original work by black artists.

Arts Crafts and Culture Shop, 54 Atlantic Road, SW9 (071- 737 0970). Open from 9am to 6pm Monday to Saturday. Arts and crafts of Rastafarian interest.

Timbuktu Books, 378 Coldharbour Lane, SW9 (071-737 2770). Open from 10am to 6pm Monday to Saturday. Books of black interest. Some arts and crafts.

Index books, 10-12 Atlantic Road, SW9 (071-274 8342). Open from 10am to 6pm Monday to Saturday. General book shop, which specialises in politics. Good selection of literature of black interest.

Brixton: Eating Out

Brixtonian Restaurant, 11 Dorrell Place SW9.
Dan Delights, 449 Coldharbour, SW9. [. . .]

Brixton: Places to Visit

Black Cultural Archives Museum, 378 Coldharbour Lane, SW9 (071-738 4591). Open from 10am to 6pm Monday to Saturday. Admission free.

Exhibitions on various aspects of black history. Archives may be inspected by appointment.

The Jamaican reggae musician *Bob Marley* (1945–81) never lived in Brixton but made frequent visits, giving live performances at local venues. A *plaque in Dexter Square*, off Railton Road, SW24, commemorates this 'national hero, poet and composer'. It was unveiled in 1987 by poet and reggae musician Linton Kwesi Johnson. [. . .]

A *plaque in the public gardens facing Brixton Library* commemorates the South African massacre of black people at *Sharpeville*. It reads: 'Sharpeville 21st March, 1960. They died so others may live'.

▲

Greenpeace Protest at the Taj Mahal

Photographer: John McConnico

The advent of nuclear weapons at the end of the Second World War and the acquisition of those weapons by increasing numbers of states in the postwar era has represented a substantial reconfiguration of the world. In an atmosphere in which possessing nuclear weapons puts a nation in an elite and powerful group, many developing nations have sought to acquire them. China and India were among the first non-Western powers to acquire nuclear weapons. In the late 1990s, Pakistan also became a nuclear power, heightening and reviving political tensions that have existed between India and Pakistan since partition in 1947. In this image, we see a 1998 protest mounted by Greenpeace against nuclear escalation in the Indian subcontinent.

▲

QUESTIONS

1. How have nuclear weapons shaped political and perhaps even economic power relations between states in the postwar world?

2. In what ways does the existence of international groups like Greenpeace suggest that the postwar world has been reconfigured?

Source: John McConnico/AP Wide World Photos.

▲

The Clash of Ignorance

EDWARD W. SAID

Edward Said was born in 1935 in Jerusalem, which was then part of Palestine. In 1947, as Palestine was being partitioned and the state of Israel was being formed, his family moved to Cairo as refugees. His parents later sent him to attend high school in the United States, where he went on to study at Princeton University. He eventually received his doctorate from Harvard University, where he wrote his dissertation on Joseph Conrad. As professor of comparative literature at Columbia University, he published numerous influential works on postcolonial literary theory as well as journalistic pieces on Palestinian politics and music. He became one of the best-known advocates of the Palestinian people and was a highly controversial figure. He died in 2003.

In the following piece, Said is responding to two phenomena: first, the September 11, 2001, attacks on the World Trade Center in New York and the Pentagon in Washington, and second, the continuing influence of the ideas of Samuel Huntington, a Harvard professor of international affairs. In the wake of the September 11 attacks, Said was clearly troubled by the polarization in the public discourse about Islam and the West ("us versus them"). He blamed this intellectual and cultural divide, at least in part, on Huntington's ideas as expressed in his 1993 article and 1996 book, both of which addressed what Huntington called "the clash of civilizations." Instead of seeing the world as a polarized and divided place, Said argued that to solve the world's problems one must look for a middle ground. This idea has been taken up by many moderate Muslims in the west. In fact, most of Said's work, including his best-known book Orientalism, *explores the relationship between East and West, and especially the construction by the West of ideas about the "Orient" (by which Said meant primarily the Middle East) and the role of imperialism in this process.*

▲

QUESTIONS

1. Why does Said suggest that labels like "Islam" and "the West" are problematic?
2. What does Said mean when he says that "Islam is no longer on the fringes of the West but at its center"?
3. Why is Said troubled by the idea of a "clash of civilizations"?

[. . .] This is the problem with unedifying labels like Islam and the West: They mislead and confuse the mind, which is trying to make sense of a disorderly reality that won't be pigeonholed or strapped down as easily as all that. I remember interrupting a man who, after a lecture I had given at a West Bank university in 1994, rose from the audience and started to attack my ideas

Source: Edward W. Said, "The Clash of Ignorance (excerpt)," *The Nation* (October 22, 2001). Pp. 12–13. Reprinted with permission from the October 22, 2001 issue of *The Nation*. For subscription information, call 1-800-333-8536. Portions of each week's Nation magazine can be accessed at http://www.thenation.com.

as "Western," as opposed to the strict Islamic ones he espoused. "Why are you wearing a suit and tie?" was the first retort that came to mind. "They're Western too." He sat down with an embarrassed smile on his face, but I recalled the incident when information on the September 11 terrorists started to come in: how they had mastered all the technical details required to inflict their homicidal evil on the World Trade Center, the Pentagon and the aircraft they had commandeered. Where does one draw the line between "Western" technology and, as Berlusconi [former Italian prime minister] declared, "Islam's" inability to be a part of "modernity"?

One cannot easily do so, of course. How finally inadequate are the labels, generalizations and cultural assertions. At some level, for instance, primitive passions and sophisticated know-how converge in ways that give the lie to a fortified boundary not only between "West" and "Islam" but also between the past and present, us and them, to say nothing of the very concepts of identity and nationality about which there is unending disagreement and debate. A unilateral decision made to draw lines in the sand, to undertake crusades, to oppose their evil with our good, to extirpate terrorism and, in Paul Wolfowitz's nihilistic vocabulary, to end nations entirely, doesn't make the supposed entities any easier to see; rather, it speaks to how much simpler it is to make bellicose statements for the purpose of mobilizing collective passions than to reflect, examine, sort out what it is we are dealing with in reality, the interconnectedness of innumerable lives, "ours" as well as "theirs."

In a remarkable series of three articles published between January and March 1999 in *Dawn*, Pakistan's most respected weekly, the late Eqbal Ahmad, writing for a Muslim audience, analyzed what he called the roots of the religious right, coming down very harshly on the mutilations of Islam by absolutists and fanatical tyrants whose obsession with regulating personal behavior promotes "an Islamic order reduced to a penal code, stripped of its humanism, aesthetics, intellectual quests, and spiritual devotion." And this "entails an absolute assertion of one, generally de-contextualized, aspect of religion and a total disregard of another. The phenomenon distorts religion, debases tradition, and twists the political process wherever it unfolds." As a timely instance of this debasement, Ahmad proceeds first to present the rich, complex, pluralist meaning of the word *jihad* and then goes on to show that in the word's current confinement to indiscriminate war against presumed enemies, it is impossible "to recognize the Islamic—religion, society, culture, history or politics—as lived and experienced by Muslims through the ages." The modern Islamists, Ahmad concludes, are "concerned with power, not with the soul; with the mobilization of people for political purposes rather than with sharing and alleviating their sufferings and aspirations. Theirs is a very limited and time-bound political agenda." What has made matters worse is that similar distortions and zealotry occur in the "Jewish" and "Christian" universes of discourse.

It was Joseph Conrad, more powerfully than any of his readers at the end of the nineteenth century could have imagined, who understood that the distinctions between civilized London and "the heart of darkness" quickly collapsed in extreme situations, and that the heights of European civilization could instantaneously fall into the most barbarous practices without preparation or transition. And it was Conrad also, in *The Secret Agent* (1907), who described terrorism's affinity for abstractions like "pure science" (and by extension for "Islam" or "the West"), as well as the terrorist's ultimate moral degradation.

For there are closer ties between apparently warring civilizations than most of us would like to believe; both Freud and Nietzsche showed how the traffic across carefully maintained, even policed boundaries moves with often terrifying ease. But then such fluid ideas, full of ambiguity and skepticism about notions that we hold on to, scarcely furnish us with suitable, practical guidelines for situations such as the one we face now. Hence the altogether more reassuring battle orders (a crusade, good versus evil, freedom against fear, etc.) drawn out of Huntington's alleged opposition between Islam and the West, from which official discourse drew its vocabulary in the first days after the September 11 attacks. There's since been a noticeable de-escalation in that discourse, but to judge from the steady amount of hate speech and actions, plus reports of law enforcement efforts directed against Arabs, Muslims and Indians all over the country, the paradigm stays on.

One further reason for its persistence is the increased presence of Muslims all over Europe and the United States. Think of the populations today of France, Italy, Germany, Spain, Britain, America, even Sweden, and you must concede that Islam is no longer on the fringes of the West but at its center. But what is so threatening about that presence? Buried in the collective culture are memories of the first great Arab-Islamic conquests, which began in the seventh century and which, as the celebrated Belgian historian Henri Pirenne wrote in his landmark book *Mohammed and Charlemagne* (1939), shattered once and for all the ancient unity of the Mediterranean, destroyed the Christian-Roman synthesis and gave rise to a new civilization dominated by northern powers (Germany and Carolingian France) whose mission, he seemed to be saying, is to resume defense of the "West" against its historical-cultural enemies. What Pirenne left out, alas, is that in the creation of this new line of defense the West drew on the humanism, science, philosophy, sociology and historiography of Islam, which had already interposed itself between Charlemagne's world and classical antiquity. Islam is inside from the start, as even Dante, great enemy of Mohammed, had to concede when he placed the Prophet at the very heart of his *Inferno*.

Then there is the persisting legacy of monotheism itself, the Abrahamic religions, as Louis Massignon aptly called them. Beginning with Judaism and Christianity, each is a successor haunted by what came before; for Muslims, Islam fulfills and ends the line of prophecy. There is still no decent history or demystification of the many-sided contest among theses three followers—not one of them by any means a monolithic, unified camp—of the most jealous of all gods, even though the bloody modern convergence on Palestine furnishes a rich secular instance of what has been so tragically irreconcilable about them. Not surprisingly, then, Muslims and Christians speak readily of crusades and *jihads*, both of them eliding the Judaic presence with often sublime insouciance. Such an agenda, says Eqbal Ahmad, is "very reassuring to the men and women who are stranded in the middle of the ford, between the deep waters of tradition and modernity."

But we are all swimming in those waters, Westerners and Muslims and others alike. And since the waters are part of the ocean of history, trying to plow or divide them with barriers is futile. These are tense times, but it is better to think in terms of powerful and powerless communities, the secular politics of reason and ignorance, and universal principles of justice and injustice, than to wander off in search of vast abstractions that may give momentary satisfaction but little self-knowledge or informed analysis. "The Clash of Civilizations" thesis is a gimmick like "The War of the Worlds," better for reinforcing defensive self-pride than for critical understanding of the bewildering interdependence of our time.

The Miracle

BUCHI EMECHETA

Buchi Emecheta is one of the leading African women writers of the last three decades. In fact, her work was among the very first writing by an African woman to receive international attention and acclaim. Born in Nigeria in 1944, she grew up in a traditional African setting and later received a scholarship to attend the Methodist Girls High School in Lagos. In the early 1960s, she moved with her husband to London, England, where she has maintained her primary residence ever since. Her marriage fell apart, and she raised five children as a single mother. All of these life experiences are important for the writing of Buchi Emecheta, in which she frequently describes and analyzes African traditional societies, the condition of people who live between and among cultures (African and British cultures, primarily), and issues of sexuality, marriage, and motherhood. Her writing is an important guide to contemporary cultural exchanges and configurations.

This selection, "The Miracle," is from her autobiography, Head Above Water, *and presents Emecheta's conflicting emotions about and reactions to her mother and family and her adopted country of England. In the piece, she mentions two of her other books,* The Bride Price *and* Second-Class Citizen, *the latter of which is heavily autobiographical. A prolific writer, Buchi Emecheta has received several awards for her work.*

QUESTIONS

1. What type of life had Buchi Emecheta's mother led in Nigeria? What type of woman was she?

2. What type of relationship did Buchi Emecheta have with her mother? How was this relationship affected by Buchi Emecheta's career choices?

3. What types of relationships between men and women are hinted at in this selection?

4. What attitudes toward England are represented in this passage?

Writing can be therapeutic and autobiographical writing even more so, as it affords one a kaleidoscopic view of one's life. For instance, it was only when I started writing these autobiographical episodes that one question that had been nagging me for a very long time seemed to be answered. Why, oh why, do I always trust men, look up to them more than to people of my own sex, even though I was brought up by women? I suddenly realized that all this was due to the relationship I had with my mother.

My mother, Alice Ogbanje Ojebeta Emecheta, that laughing, loud-voiced, six-foot-tall, black glossy slave girl, who as a child suckled the breasts

Source: Buchi Emecheta, *Head Above Water*. Oxford and Portsmouth, NH: Heinemann, 1986. Pp. 3–5. Reprinted by permission of Harcourt Education.

of her dead mother; my mother who lost her parents when the nerve gas was exploded in Europe, a gas that killed thousands of innocent Africans who knew nothing about the Western First World War; my laughing mother, who forgave a brother that sold her to a relative in Onitsha so that he could use the money to buy *ichafo siliki*—silk head ties for his coming-of-age dance. My mother, who probably loved me in her own way, but never expressed it; my mother, that slave girl who had the courage to free herself and return to her people in Ibusa, and still stooped and allowed the culture of her people to re-enslave her, and then permitted Christianity to tighten the knot of enslavement.

She never understood the short, silent, mystery daughter she had. Words said that she died not blessing me. That hurt, it did hurt and for twenty years I carried that hurt. But on going back to Ibusa in 1980, and seeing the people she lived with and the place she was buried, then the image of that tall, lanky, black woman nicknamed 'Blackie the black' seemed to loom over me. Then I felt the warmth of her presence, then I knew right there inside me that my mother did not die cursing me.

Signs showed me that that was said to make me feel guilty, especially now they know that the marriage that caused the rift between mother and daughter did not work out for me. And of course nothing would satisfy our tradition better than to stir up the mud of an ambiguous past. But I have had time to think and that, thanks be to God, has made me stronger both emotionally and spiritually than that girl in *The Bride Price* whose immaturity allowed her to be destroyed by such heavy guilt.

This realization washed over me like an evening balm as I stood there, by the place she was buried. Relatives watching wanted and expected me to break down and cry, thereby devaluing my inner sorrow. Maybe if I had not stayed in cold England for eighteen years—England, a country where people cry in their hearts and not with their eyes—I would have done so. Eighteen years is a long time, and like the people I live with, I cried in my heart.

And as I walked slowly away, wishing Mother had been buried in a more private resting place and not inside our compound, where I could not speak to her privately, it seemed to me in the ears of my mind that I could hear that loud laugh and her voice saying as she used to tell me so many times when I was a little girl, 'You think too much for a woman. This . . . tisha . . . it's nothing, all forgotten.'

I looked back once, and I knew I was right. My mother, although she was very ill before she died, could not have cursed me. Unlike me, her mysterious daughter, she did not possess such inner depth. For, after all, did she not die alone, asleep on her bed in her room?

As if all that was not enough, my mother-in-law, Christy Onwordi, said to me later that evening when we were talking about my mother, 'Your mother went home. The week she died, I saw Nkili Angelina Obiorah (my mother's friend, age-mate and lookalike), I saw her in white singing and she was profoundly happy. She joined a group of happy, white-gowned people. I knew then that your mother was not going to survive that illness.'

Looking back in my mind's eye and remembering the night she died, which I described in *Second-Class Citizen*, I forgave myself and my mother because, you see, I am a woman now in my prime who has suffered and seen so much. If I do not understand the untalked-of agonies of that laughing and doubly culturally-enslaved woman who gave me life, who else is there on this earth who will take the trouble to?

I miss my singing, laughing mother very much and my village, Umuezeokolo Odanta, did not seem the same to me any more without her and my other mothers to hug me when I arrived at Otinkpu.

As for my survival for the past twenty years in England, from when I was a little over twenty, dragging four cold and dripping babies with me and pregnant with a fifth one—that is a miracle. And if for any reason you do not believe in miracles, please start believing, because my keeping my head above water in this indifferent society, which is probably succeeding in making me indifferent and private too, is a miracle.

What's Right with Africa?

Michael Chege

In the last four decades, despite rapid global population growth, a reasonable standard of living has come within reach of many people. The percentage of poor has declined, except in Africa. The percentage of poor in Africa has risen, not fallen. In the following article, Michael Chege suggests that even though Africa is the only continent to lag behind in combating poverty, there are still positive developments going on there. In his view, Africa has made some democratic gains, and despite ethnic conflicts, country after country has experimented with Western-style electoral procedures and the results have been accepted by most people. Food production for export to the world market has increased. Although many things have gone wrong, there are things that are right with Africa.

Michael Chege was born in Kenya, a former British colony. He completed his doctorate in the United States and currently teaches at an American University.

Questions

1. What does Chege think has gone right in Africa in recent decades?
2. Which of Chege's arguments do you find most persuasive? Why?
3. Do you share Chege's guarded optimism about African developments since 1994?

Democratic Gains

[. . .] Beginning in 1990, a new wave of popular demands for democratic rule swept the continent. Yet as shown by events in Zaire, Malawi, Cameroon, Kenya, Guinea, Gabon, Rwanda, Sudan, and Togo, the war against dictatorships has hardly been won. In these and many other countries the heads of government have clung to power through a combination of brute force, manipulation of gullible opposition parties, bribery, crafty exploitation of ethnic loyalties, and cosmetic constitutional reforms to appease Western donors who demand "good governance" as a precondition for further development aid.

Still, there are solid gains that need to be recounted and built on in the quest for fully democratic and accountable government if the momentum is not to be lost. The courage of the independent press in Kenya, as represented by the *Nation* newspaper and the country's new magazines, as well as in Ghana, Nigeria, Malawi, Cameroon, Tanzania, and Ethiopia, marks a new departure. These periodicals run on shoestring budgets and the robust determination of their publishers never to be cowed by hostile authorities. Such spirit is what kept a group of Somali pressmen going—with little more than a mimeograph machine and rolls of paper—at the height of the brutal conflict in Mogadishu. On the whole, the

Source: Michael Chege, "What's Right with Africa?" *Current History*. May 1994, Volume 93, No 583. Pp. 194–196. Reprinted with permission. Copyright © 2005 Current History, Inc.

horizons of freedom of speech have widened beyond all expectations at the start of the agitation for democracy.

Neither can the outcome of competitive multiparty elections since 1990 be dismissed as hopeless. Autocratic governments have given way to democratically elected administrations in Zambia, Cape Verde, São Tomé and Principe, Benin, Madagascar, Lesotho, and Burundi. French-style presidential elections have brought new faces to power in Niger, Mali, Central African Republic, and Congo. Whenever African voters have been given the chance to choose those who will govern them in genuinely free and fair circumstances, they have opted for accountable and more honest leadership than it has been their misfortune to have had in the past. And despite the undeniable attachment to ethnic loyalty, voters recognize leaders who transcend narrow provincial ambitions. Witness the trans-ethnic and cross-cultural backing for Moshood Abiola in the abrogated June 1993 elections in Nigeria, and the broad-based support for Etienne Tshisekedi, the foremost opposition leader in Zaire. That there has subsequently been violent conflict in Burundi, Congo, and Lesotho, and corruption in the government in Zambia, does not discount the progress made. The real test lies in developing the institutional capacity to resolve such political differences by due constitutional process.

Above all, the lesson is now sinking in: actions of rogue military units in countries like Burundi, Guinea, Lesotho, and Congo, no less than in Zaire, Togo, Cameroon, and Nigeria, demonstrate the need to bring the armed forces under civilian democratic control. The difficult process of doing so now needs to be discussed and implemented. A courageous start has been made with the unanimous warning in February 1993 from southern African government leaders, including President F. W. de Klerk of South Africa, to Lesotho's restive army to obey the democratically elected government, and with ongoing efforts by the Organization of African Unity (OAU) to monitor the army's neutrality in the tortured democratic transition in Burundi.

The vast majority of African countries, in fact, are in this sort of indeterminate transition from an authoritarian order rather than being home to the free-for-all violence of Angola, Somalia, and Liberia that the electronic media brings to Western living rooms so frequently. And the picture of a violent region leaves out the African countries that function normally on both the political and social planes.

Over the last 30 years, the southern African state of Botswana, for example, has been a working pluralistic democracy in which regular elections are held and human rights are respected. Though never a media favorite, the country has a grassroots democracy based on village councils (*kgotla*) and no history of large-scale corruption or civil strife. Next door, to the west, the Republic of Namibia, which gained independence in 1990 after a long war against colonial South Africa, has marched on to stability and administrative efficiency under one of the most liberal constitutions anywhere. Pragmatic and realistic, the governing South West African People's Organization (SWAPO) party ditched the doctrinaire socialist program it had espoused as a guerilla organization and is busy courting local and international investors as it looks for sustainable policy alternatives that will bring the black majority into the mainstream of agricultural and industrial life. This February Namibia regained from South Africa the Walvis Bay enclave with its deep-water harbor after several years of conscientious diplomatic efforts. Doomsayers had said Walvis Bay was the powder keg that would set off armed confrontation between South Africa and Namibia.

To the east of Botswana, Zimbabwe, after a difficult political start, has developed a workable formula for ethnic and racial coexistence. All the while the country has maintained a comparatively efficient public service and a nationwide network of roads and telecommunications, water, power, and sanitation systems that stand out against the dereliction of infrastructure not just to the north of Zimbabwe on the continent but also in many richer nations in Europe, South America, and Asia.

Bold constitutional innovations have produced more decent governance and political stability in other parts of Africa. After years of internal warfare and succession of brutally repressive regimes, Uganda has since 1986 settled into tranquility under President Yoweri Museveni. His administration has broken faith with the African mythological belief that ethnic loyalties can be replaced by a single national identity and enduring loyalty to an all-powerful head of state of a monolithic government. Museveni has permitted gradual decentralization that includes acceptance of once-outlawed provincial kingdoms such as Buganda, Toro, Bunyoro, and Ankole. Farther north, the regime of President Meles Zenawi in Ethiopia is pledged to a federalist structure that explicitly recognizes the nation's cultural diversity, but it must reckon with divisive movements that violate the human rights of non-natives in outlying areas, and must instill greater tolerance in its own ranks. The government's boldness is attested to by its own acceptance of the 1993 referendum in favor of Eritrean independence—the first of its kind on the continent—ending 30 years of bloody separatist warfare.

The president of independent Eritrea, Isaias Afewerki, is representative of the new generation of epoch-making African reformers. At last year's OAU summit in Cairo, he broke tradition and criticized to their faces the incumbent gerontocracy of African dictators for violating civil liberties and ignoring the humanitarian plight of Eritreans during the war. His speech drew the spontaneous applause of the African press corps in the adjoining chamber.

Provided they can overcome daunting initial problems, the new liberal constitutional reformers will lead their countries into the small group of democracies in sub-Saharan Africa that include, in addition to Botswana, the Indian Ocean island of Mauritius, and Senegal and Gambia in West Africa. True, these are small states (as critics of political change on the continent are wont to point out), but it is important to note the swelling of their ranks and to see if this has an effect over time on reformist forces in the larger countries. What will happen on that score will most likely be settled by the leadership that emerges in the coming decade.

The catalog of benighted African autocrats leaves out what is right with many of the continent's local and national leaders. Consider Nelson Mandela, released after 27 years of incarceration under apartheid, offering the hand of reconciliation and a fresh partnership to the white community in South Africa, as Robert Mugabe had done in Zimbabwe and Jomo Kenyatta in Kenya years before. And Mandela did this while keeping hope alive in his constituents in the restive black majority and building bridges to the warmongering right-wingers of the Inkatha Freedom party and the Afrikaner Resistance Movement. How many leaders elsewhere in the world can claim to have paid such a high personal price, and to have accomplished so much in such difficult circumstances within such a brief period of time? How many could match the years of patient reconciliation efforts across races and communities carried off with graceful wit by Archbishop Desmond Tutu of Cape Town? And what of dozens of others who have acted as the nagging national conscience in their respective states, among them Wole Soyinka, the winner of the Nobel Prize for Literature, and the Kuti brothers in Nigeria; Archbishop Laurent Monsengwo Pasinya in Zaire; the late Jaramogi Oginga Odinga, the clergy, and the principled legal fraternity in Kenya; and honorably retired heads of government like Julius Nyerere of Tanzania, Leopold Senghor of Senegal, and Kenneth Kaunda of Zambia.

As the lessons of what has gone right with African governance sink in, supreme importance must increasingly be placed on high-quality, principled leadership committed to overhauling the ideas of monolithic rule. In the process, a premium must be placed on coming to constitutional terms with ethnic diversity as an enduring phenomenon—as is now happening in South Africa, Ethiopia, Uganda, and, one hopes, Rwanda and Burundi—without derogating from the principle of territorial integrity and the right to own property and live in peace anywhere in the country. The other challenge lies in regenerating economic growth and raising local incomes so as to give ordinary citizens a stake in the larger system.

Profitable Developments

Although the overall economic development record for Africa during the last 20 years has been discouraging, a different picture emerges when one disaggregates the figures to account for individual country performance. Per capita income in sub-Saharan Africa is said to have declined 1.2 percent annually over the period, but a small number of African countries did as well as if not better than the best in the rest of the world.

The economy in Botswana grew at a faster rate in the last two decades—between 7 percent and 8 percent a year—than the much-vaunted miracles in East Asia. With its emphasis on investment in human resources and sound macroeconomic management, Botswana's economy, centered around diamond production, is now branching out into tourism, manufactured exports, and regional banking services. Over the last 20 years Mauritius has transformed itself from a poor country dependent on the sugarcane crop into a full-employment society based on East Asian–style manufacturing and export of textiles and electronic goods. This was made possible by investment from Asia and Europe. As the country plans a second, deeper phase of economic development, it is moving into offshore banking and new branches of industry.

There are other successes. The region's premier source of development money, the African Development Bank, borrows from African and non-African governments and money markets. It carries a full triple-A rating—the highest possible—from Moody's, Standard and Poor's, and Japan's Credit Rating Agency. Most of its loans have gone into agriculture and public utilities. And in Ethiopia annual profits for the national airline have been good year after year, due to sound management and excellent service. Both the bank and Ethiopian Airlines have enjoyed protection from meddlesome state authorities and employed the skills of local technocrats—a lesson economic reformers must heed.

Despite the portrayal of sub-Saharan Africa as a land of perpetual hunger, some 10 countries—Chad, Cape Verde, Nigeria, Botswana, Guinea-Bissau, Uganda, Benin, Kenya, Tanzania, and Comoros—had what the World Bank termed good to excellent growth rates in agriculture, ranging from 3.5 percent to 20 percent, between 1980 and 1990. Farmers in Burkina Faso have pioneered cost-effective methods of reversing desertification and dispersing of new seeds. A recent study of the Machakos district in Kenya, reported on in the *Economist* last December 11, revealed that, contrary to the conventional wisdom on African development, high population growth rates had not led to overgrazing, soil degradation, and worsening poverty. On the contrary, as the population rose the smallholders of the district had switched from pastoralism to cultivation of neatly terraced farms that halted erosion and produced more for the Nairobi market and for export. To the extent that any outsiders can claim credit, the postindependence government can be cited for its introduction of individual titles for land, high-value cash crops like coffee, and better roads to the capital. In general, a thriving modern economic sector generated jobs, and the savings from those wages went back into agriculture. This has been demonstrated time and again whenever small-scale farming prospers, as in other parts of Kenya and in Ivory Coast and southern Cameroon in the 1950s and 1960s, and as was also the case in cocoa production in Ghana and Nigeria in previous decades.

On the whole, African countries that have a good record in cash crops for markets abroad, such as coffee, tea, and cocoa, have also done well in advancing toward the goal of food production to match the demands of a burgeoning population. And though African economies have been severely buffeted since the 1980s by falling global commodity prices, much has also depended on how they have managed export incomes and sustained farming incentives. Kenya and Malawi, for example, have increased their shares of the world tea market in a relatively short period of time, principally because of an emphasis on high quality and lowering production costs. The private sector in Kenya has pioneered agricultural diversification into horticulture, while African trade diplomats engage in fruitless efforts to negotiate northern funding for it. Food production in Nigeria, which was in distress in the 1970s, has received a boost from exchange rate and price liberalization since the mid-1980s. Similar effects can be observed in Ethiopia even in the brief space of time after the 1991–1993 dismantling of rigid price controls for farm products and the abolition of the disastrous collectivization program undertaken by the Marxist-Leninist government of Mengistu Haile Mariam in the 1970s and 1980s.

As in the political arena, the lessons to be drawn from successful economic enterprises in Africa are the same as those from other rapidly growing areas of the developing world. Political stability and government committed to tangible results on the development transformation front are vital foundations for economic growth. It is in politically tranquil Mauritius and Botswana that decent governance (and macroeconomic stability) has been harnessed to market-based development policies to produce the best results. The same could be said of Kenya and Ivory Coast in their better days of rapid economic growth in the 1960s and 1970s.

What it takes for economic revival and poverty reduction in Africa is becoming clearer all the time. Once stability was restored in Uganda and Ghana in the 1980s and in Ethiopia after 1991, and accompanied by liberal economic policies and fiscal and monetary discipline, growth blossomed in the ruins. The beneficial impact, of course, will not quickly saturate all of society, but a positive beginning has been made. So long as such wisdom is accepted, and the limitations of current reforms are understood, there must be hope for the increasing number of African countries that are allocating markets a greater role in the national economy than ever before. [. . .]

▲

Understanding Climate Control: A Beginner's Guide to the United Nations Framework Convention

UNITED NATIONS ENVIRONMENT PROGRAMME, INFORMATION UNIT FOR CONVENTIONS

As we consider the reconfiguration of the postcolonial world, we might consider the role that industrialization played in imperialism and the subsequent quest for independence. The age of high imperialism originated with Europe's industrial revolutions, and the ideology of industrialization was passed to the colonies so that newly independent nations sought to industrialize themselves in order to become competitive in the modern marketplace. Even as industrialization remains a hallmark of economic success, however, it has increasingly been criticized for having caused numerous ecological problems. Today, the issue that is most often discussed is global warming, or climate change, a problem that affects the entire world, even if the largest producers of greenhouse gases are the old industrialized nations. In recent decades, the United Nations has organized meetings in Rio de Janeiro, Brazil, and Kyoto, Japan, to hammer out solutions to the problem of global warming. Among the greatest challenges has been how to apportion responsibility for reduction of greenhouse gas emissions and how to maintain or create economic productivity while addressing environmental concerns. The document that follows, an excerpt from a U.N. Web site, explains the United Nations Framework Convention on Climate Change in straightforward language and explores some of the global inequities that come up as climate control is discussed.

▲

QUESTIONS

1. Where are most greenhouse gases produced?
2. Why might the problem of apportioning responsibility for reduction of greenhouse gases be difficult?
3. Can you envision ways in which agreements such as the United Nations Framework Convention on Climate Change might exploit old colonial ties?
4. Who might oppose such conventions? Why?

Source: "Understanding Climate Change: A Beginner's Guide to the United Nations Framework Convention." Pp.10–15. United Nations. http://unfccc.int/cop3/beginnerg.htm. Public domain.

Problem No. 4: If the Whole World Starts Consuming More and Living the Good Life, Can the Planet Stand the Strain?

As the human population continues to grow, the demands human beings place on the environment increase. The demands are becoming all the greater because these rapidly increasing numbers of people also want to live better lives. More and better food, more and cleaner water, more electricity, refrigerators, automobiles, houses and apartments, land on which to put houses and apartments . . .

Already there are severe problems supplying enough fresh water to the world's billions. Burgeoning populations are draining the water from rivers and lakes, and vast underground aquifers are steadily being depleted. What will people do when these natural "tanks" are empty? There are also problems growing and distributing enough food—widespread hunger in many parts of the world attests to that. There are other danger signals. The global fish harvest has declined sharply; as large as the oceans are, the most valuable species have been effectively fished out.

Global warming is a particularly ominous example of humanity's insatiable appetite for natural resources. During the last century we have dug up and burned massive stores of coal, oil, and natural gas that took millions of years to accumulate. Our ability to burn up fossil fuels at a rate that is much, much faster than the rate at which they were created has upset the natural balance of the carbon cycle. The threat of climate change arises because one of the only ways the atmosphere—also a natural resource—can respond to the vast quantities of carbon being liberated from beneath the earth's surface is to warm up.

Meanwhile, human expectations are not tapering off. They are increasing. The countries of the industrialised "North" have 20 per cent of the world's people but use about 80 per cent of the world's resources. By global standards, they live extremely well. It's nice living the good life, but if everyone consumed as much as the North

Americans and Western Europeans consume—and billions of people aspire to do just that—there probably would not be enough clean water and other vital natural resources to go around. How will we meet these growing expectations when the world is already under so much stress?

How the Convention Responds

—*It supports the concept of "sustainable development"*. Somehow, mankind must learn how to alleviate poverty for huge and growing numbers of people without destroying the natural environment on which all human life depends. Somehow a way has to be found to develop economically in a fashion that is sustainable over a long period of time. The buzzword for this challenge among environmentalists and international bureaucrats is "sustainable development". The trick will be to find methods for living well while using critical natural resources at a rate no faster than that at which they are replaced. Unfortunately, the international community is a lot farther along in defining the problems posed by sustainable development than it is in figuring out how to solve them.

—*The Convention calls for developing and sharing environmentally sound technologies and know-how.* Technology will clearly play a major role in dealing with climate change. If we can find practical ways to use cleaner sources of energy, such as solar power, we can reduce the consumption of coal and oil. Technology can make industrial processes more efficient, water purification more viable, and agriculture more productive for the same amount of resources invested. Such technology must be made widely available—it must somehow be shared by richer and more scientifically advanced countries with poorer countries that have great need of it.

—*The Convention emphasises the need to educate people about climate change.* Today's children and future generations must learn to look at the world in a different way than it has been looked at by most people during the 20th century. This is both an old and new idea. Many (but not all!) pre-industrial cultures lived in balance with nature. Now scientific research is telling us to do much the same thing. Economic development is no longer a case of "bigger is better"—bigger cars, bigger houses, bigger harvests of fish, bigger doses of oil and coal. We must no longer think of human progress as a matter of imposing ourselves on the natural environment. The world—the climate and all living things—is a closed system; what we do has consequences that eventually come back to affect us. Tomorrow's children—and today's adults, for that matter—will have to learn to think about the effects of their actions on the climate. When they make decisions as members of governments and businesses, and as they go about their private lives, they will have to take the climate into account.

In other words, human behaviour will have to change—probably the sooner the better. But such things are difficult to prescribe and predict. There is, for example, the matter of what sacrifices might have to be made by everyone for the good of the global climate. That leads to . . .

Problem No. 5: Who Has the Energy, Time, or Money Left to Deal With Climate Change, When We Have So Many Other Problems?

A valid point.

How the Convention Responds

—*It starts slowly. It doesn't make too many demands (or requests) for the time being. But stay tuned.* The Framework Convention on Climate Change is

a general treaty with just a few specific requirements. More and bigger requirements will come later, in the form of amendments and protocols. This will happen as scientific understanding of climate change becomes clearer and as the countries of the world, already suffering from a case of "disaster fatigue", adjust to the idea that they have yet another crisis to face and pay for. War, famine, AIDS, the ozone "hole", acid rain, the loss of ecosystems and species . . . Thinking about these problems, people could be forgiven for wondering if they should throw in the towel.

We can't give up, of course. And while the Convention cannot claim to have the issue all sorted out, it does make a start. Things are beginning to happen. Developed countries are making national plans with the aim of returning their greenhouse gas emissions to 1990 levels by the year 2000—thereby reversing the historical trend of ever-increasing emissions. Countries that have ratified the treaty are beginning to gather data on their emissions and on the present climate. More and more, people and governments are talking and thinking about climate change.

What happens next? Step by step, national governments committed to controlling their emissions must begin tightening emissions standards and requiring more replanting of trees; some countries are already working on such standards. Local and urban governments—which often have direct responsibility for transport, housing, waste management, and other greenhouse gas–emitting sectors of the economy—have a role, too. They can start designing and building better public transport systems, for example, and creating incentives for people to use them rather than private automobiles. They should tighten construction codes so that new houses and office buildings can be heated or cooled with less fuel. Meanwhile, industrial companies need to start shifting to new technologies that use fossil fuels and raw materials more efficiently. Wherever possible they should switch to renewable energy sources such as wind and solar power. They should also redesign products such as refrigerators, automobiles, cement mixes, and fertilisers so that they produce lower greenhouse gas emissions. Farmers should look to technologies and methods that reduce the methane emitted by livestock and rice fields. Individual citizens, too, must cut their use of fossil fuels—take public transport more often, switch off the lights in empty rooms—and be less wasteful of all natural resources.

It may seem naive to expect behavioural changes of this magnitude. But the potential for more responsible behaviour on behalf of the climate is nevertheless there. It is possible that as time passes and more is known about the threats posed by climate change, such responses will seem a lot less naive and a lot more vital to humanity's well-being.

—The Convention is based on sharing the burdens of coping with climate change. This is important. The atmosphere is a shared resource, part of the "global commons". The treaty tries to make sure that any sacrifices made in protecting this resource will be shared fairly among countries—in accordance with their "common but differentiated responsibilities and respective capabilities and their social and economic conditions". This means, the participating countries hope, that whatever ultimately has to be done will be done by enough participants to make the benefits worth the sacrifices. It is easier to sacrifice towards the common good when you are sure everyone else is pitching in. [. . .]

⋏

WTO Protest

PHOTOGRAPHER: STEVEN RUBIN

The World Trade Organization has become one of the most important nongovernment organizations in the world. Guided by a group of mostly Western nations that do not necessarily have the world's largest or most vibrant economies, the WTO regulates international trade and its membership rules can have a huge impact on the ways in which the economies of developing nations are shaped. As it pushes for standardization of economic practices and legal frameworks within which trade and industry occur, the WTO is seen by many, including the protestors pictured here, as a neo-imperialist entity that privileges the interests of the West over those of other peoples and states. This image shows part of the protest against the WTO that took place in Seattle in 1999.

⋏

QUESTION

1. Look at the posters that the protestors are carrying: what are some of their concerns? In what ways do they appear to view the WTO as neo-imperialist?

_____

Source: Steve Rubin/The Image Works.

Map: Western Europe, Muslim Population c. 2005

Muslims as Percentage
of National Population

- 6.0 percent and greater
- 3.0 – 5.9 percent
- 1.0 – 2.9 percent

0   250   500 Miles

0   250   500 Kilometers

FINLAND

NORWAY

SWEDEN
3.9%

ESTONIA   RUSSIA

*NORTH
SEA*

BALTIC SEA

LATVIA

LITHUANIA

RUSSIA

BELARUS

UNITED
KINGDOM
2.7%

IRELAND

DENMARK
3.0%

NETHER-
LANDS
5.5%

POLAND

BELGIUM
3.5%

*ATLANTIC
OCEAN*

LUXEMBOURG
1.4%

GERMANY
4.9%

CZECH
REPUBLIC

UKRAINE

SLOVAK
REPUBLIC

FRANCE
8.3%

SWITZ.
4.3%

AUSTRIA
4.2%

HUNGARY

MOLDOVA

SLOVENIA

ROMANIA

CROATIA

BOSNIA-
HERZOGOVINA

PORTUGAL

CORSICA

ITALY
1.8%

ADRIATIC SEA

SERBIA &
MONTENEGRO

BULGARIA

SPAIN
2.4%

SARDINIA

MACEDONIA

ALBANIA

GREECE

*AEGEAN
SEA*

M E D I T E R R A N E A N

SICILY

MOROCCO

ALGERIA

TUNISIA

S E A

Between thirty-five and fifty million Muslims live in Europe. Although most of them live in southeastern Europe, in parts of the long defunct Ottoman Empire, many Muslims also live in western Europe and come from (or are descendants of people who came from) former colonies in Asia and Africa. Islam is not the only religion to flow into Europe from its former colonies; there are also numerous Hindus, Buddhists, Sikhs, and adherents of other non-Western religions throughout Europe as well.

▲

QUESTIONS

1. How might this influx of Muslims from the former colonies be transforming and reconfiguring Europe?
2. Where do you suppose the majority of France's Muslim population has come from?

Source: *Financial Times* at http://news.ft.com/cms

▲

AIDS Pandemic

UNITED NATIONS PROGRAMME ON HIV/AIDS

REGIONAL/GLOBAL HIV/AIDS STATISTICS

Region	Adults and Children Living with HIV/AIDS, End 2005	New HIV Infections Among Adults and Children in 2005	Adult Prevalence (%), end 2005	Adult and Child Deaths Due to AIDS in 2005
Sub-Saharan Africa	25,800,000	3,200,000	7.2%	2,400,000
South/Southeast Asia	7,400,000	990,000	0.4%	480,000
Latin America	1,800,000	200,000	0.6%	66,000
East Asia	870,000	140,000	0.4%	41,000
North America	1,200,000	43,000	0.5%	18,000
Eurasia	1,600,000	270,000	0.9%	62,000
Western/Central Europe	720,000	22,000	0.5%	12,000
Caribbean	300,000	30,000	1.6%	24,000
North Africa/ Middle East	510,000	67,000	0.2%	58,000
Oceania	74,000	8,200	0.5%	3,600
Global	40.3 million	4.9 million	1.3%	3.1 million

Source: United Nations Programme on HIV/AIDS

HIV/AIDS Pandemic from Global Health Reporting, www.globalhealthreporting.org/diseaseinfo.asp?id=23.
Public domain.

The preceding chart from the United Nations Programme on HIV/AIDS shows the spread of HIV/AIDS cases as of the end of 2005. Governments, non-profit organizations, churches, insurance companies, medical professionals, and private citizens have all been concerned about the impact of the disease upon the health of individuals and nations. As the chart makes clear, the greatest threat currently is to sub-saharan Africa. Some commentators believe that HIV/AIDS challenges the basic political and economic stability of this region of the world. Asia, especially south and south-east Asia, has also seen a dramatic rise in HIV/AIDS cases in recent years. The disease is, however, global in nature and has affected every region of the world.

▲

QUESTIONS

1. What conclusions about the spread of HIV/AIDS do you draw from the chart?
2. Why might some regions of the world be affected to a greater extent than others by HIV/AIDs?

Masai Herdsmen

PHOTOGRAPHERS: P. BOURSEILLER AND J. DURIEUX

Although many societies, economies, polities, and landscapes were and continue to be transformed by the experience of imperialism, not all have changed as much as this volume would seem to suggest. This contemporary image of Masai herdsmen wearing traditional garb and watching their cattle graze at the foot of Oldonyo Lengai in Tanzania shows us that the process of globalization that was set in more rapid motion by the age of high imperialism has not eradicated all traditional practices.

Source: P. Bourseiller and J. Durieux/Photo Researchers, Inc.

FURTHER RESOURCES

Ashcroft, Bill. *Post-Colonial Transformation.* London: Routledge, 2001.

Bales, Kevin. *Disposable People: New Slavery in the Global Economy.* Berkeley, CA: University of California Press, 1999.

Bhabha, Homi. "DissemiNation." In Homi Bhabha (Ed.), *Nation and Narration.* London: Routledge, 1990.

Chandhoke, Neera. *Understanding the Post-Colonial World: Theory and Method.* New Delhi: Sterling Publishers, 1994.

Dabydeen, David. *The Intended.* London: Secker and Warburg, 1991.

Harris, Michael T. *Outsiders and Insiders: Perspectives of Third World Culture in British and Post-Colonial Fiction.* New York: Peter Lang, 1992.

Lazarus, Neil. *Nationalism and Cultural Practice in the Post-Colonial World.* Cambridge: Cambridge University Press, 1999.

Naipaul, V. S. *The Enigma of Arrival.* New York: Knopf, 1987.

Prakash, Gyan. *After Colonialism: Imperial Histories and Postcolonial Displacements.* Princeton: Princeton University Press, 1995.

Rushdie, Salman. *Imaginary Homelands. Essays and Criticism. 1981–1991.* London: Granta Books, 1991.

San Juan, Epifanio. *Beyond Postcolonial Theory.* New York: St. Martin's Press, 1998.

Soueif, Ahdaf. *Mezzaterra: Fragments from the Ground.* London: Bloomsbury, 2004.

Williams, Patrick, and Laura Chrisman. *Colonial Discourse and Post-Colonial Theory.* New York: Columbia University Press, 1994.

Films

A Fond Kiss. DVD. Directed by Ken Loach. Santa Monica, CA: Lions Gate Home Entertainment, 2005.

A Place Called Chiapas. DVD. Directed by Nettie Wild. New York, NY: Zeitgeist Films, 1998.

Dirty Pretty Things. DVD. Directed by Stephen Frears. Burbank, CA: Buena Vista Home Video, 2004.

Everyone's Child. VHS. Directed by Tsitsi Dangarembga. Zimbabwe: Media for Development Trust, 1996.

Bend It Like Beckham. DVD. Directed by Gurinder Chadha. Beverly Hills, CA: Twentieth-Century Fox Home Entertainment, 2003.

Mango Yellow. DVD. Directed by Cláudio Assis. New York, NY: First Run Features, 2002.

Mississippi Masala. DVD. Directed by Mira Nair. Burbank, CA: Columbia Tristar Home Video, 2003.

My Beautiful Laundrette. DVD. Directed by Stephen Frears. Santa Monica, CA: MGM Home Entertainment, 2003.

My Son the Fanatic. DVD. Directed by Udayan Prasad. United Kingdom: British Broadcasting Corporation, 1997.

Tea in the Harem. VHS. Directed by Mehdi Charef. Paris, France: KG Production, 1986.

The Gods Must Be Crazy. DVD. Directed by Jamie Uys. Culver City, CA: Columbia Tristar Home Entertainment, 2004.

The Last Wave. DVD. Directed by Peter Weir. Irvington, NY: Criterion Collection, 2001.